ip uct   9⁵⁰

The Hunters and the Hunted

A Non-Linear Solution for American Industry

by James B. Swartz

Publisher's Message by Norman Bodek

Productivity Press
Portland, Oregon

Copyright © 1994 by Productivity Press, Inc.

All rights reserved. No part of this book may be reproduced or utilized in any form or by any means, electronic or mechanical, including photo-copying, recording, or by any information storage and retrieval system, without permission in writing from the publisher. Additional copies of this book are available from the publisher. Address all inquiries to:

Productivity Press
P.O. Box 13390
Portland, OR 97213-0390
United States of America
Telephone: 503-235-0600
Telefax: 503-235-0909

ISBN: 1-56327-043-9

Jacket photograph of a silkscreen reproduction of a prehistoric cave paint-ing in Renigia, Spain, is reproduced with the permission of the copyright holder, Douglas Mazonowicz, director of the Gallery of Prehistoric Art, New York.

Book design by Bill Stanton and Gayle Asmus
Jacket design by Bill Stanton and Gary Ragaglia
Printed and bound by Maple-Vail Book Manufacturing Group
Printed in the United States of America

Library of Congress Cataloging-in-Publication Data

Swartz, James B.
    The hunters and the hunted: a non-linear solution for American industry/by James B. Swartz.
        p.   cm.
    Includes bibliographical references.
    1. Corporate turnarounds—Management—Case studies.   2. Industrial management—Case studies.   I. Title.
HD58.8.S92   1994
658.4'063—dc20   93-41110
                                                          CIP

98 97 96 95 94 10 9 8 7 6 5 4 3 2 1

Dedication

This book is dedicated to all who struggle with the agony of change; who strive to learn, to survive, and to win in the world of business . . . and in life.

Contents

Publisher's Message

*J*im Swartz loves America. He has devoted his life to discovering the reasons for our recent decline and ways to turn the situation entirely around. Jim also loves a challenge. He knows the importance of maufacturing as the foundation for our country's long term financial success. He is a real fighter and nothing will stop his pursuit to help American industry become number one again.

When his senior manager asked Jim to relocate a plant to the Far East, Jim responded with a counterproposal. He stuck his neck out and said that he could deliver the bottomline results desired in Indiana without going to the Far East. "Let me prove it to you," he championed — and he did. He knew that cheap labor was not the answer to America's productivity problems; unions were not the problem; American workers were not the problem; a lack of will was not the problem; and management was not the problem.

He went on a journey to discover the solution for American industry. Jim is a voracious reader. He studied all of the great masters in management: Taylor, Galbraith, Forrester, Deming, Juran, Bhote, Peters, Shingo, and literally hundreds of others. He drew out from each master the key elements from their teachings and then went out to the factory floor to experiment, to apply it. He learned from his mistakes. He tried a million different techniques and slowly built a dynamic methodology that pulled off miracles.

He found that every technique had a value; he started to put them altogether like building a jigsaw puzzle that when finished would result in resounding success throughout American industry. *The Hunters and the Hunted* is the story of his journey as well as the guide to fitting all the pieces together that lead to world class manufacturing.

Jim Swartz was a senior manager at Delco Remy with over 1,000 employees under him; he was an inventor with many patents to his name; he was an engineer; and he was and is a real fighter. Don't dare pick a fight with him. He is a real tiger.

Jim took early retirement with only one thought on his mind — to discover the truths. From his studies of the great masters, he put together a simple training course to demonstrate the new principles he found. He used games and videos and completely enthralled and involved his audiences to learn while having fun. He changed the game and the rules after every single event. His fruitful and creative mind was not going to get stuck. If he was to teach continuous improvement then his techniques must continually improve.

He was like an Olympic athlete, continuously improving his style and continuously polishing his technique. And like Barnum and Bailey he put his show on the road. He wanted to work every single day. He was driven to find the solutions. He taught anyone who would listen. Money was never the object. For the first year when he taught, he charged no fee at all to many companies. When other consultants charged $2,000 per day, Jim would charge $200. He didn't care. He was a true warrior wanting to practice every day, wanting to polish his sword, wanting to perfect his style, wanting to find a way to reach his American audience. His goal was not just to produce simple results; he wanted to create a revolution. He wanted to save a great nation. And he was impatient.

He went into one company and challenged a team of engineers to reduce the time it took to build a die from thirty weeks to nine weeks. He told them that the world benchmark for that process was nine weeks. Of course, not a single engineer in the room believed it could be done. But Jim cajoled them, he challenged them. He fired their American fighting spirit to rise to the occasion.

"Do you want your company to die without a fight? I hesitate to ask you. I don't know if you are ready to rise to the challenge."

And somewhat discouraged he threatened to leave the room and end the meeting.

Always at least one engineer would rise to the bait and say, "Stop, Jim, stop that crap. If someone else can do it then so can we."

"Okay, I will try if you are willing to try. I want you to break up into two groups, go into separate rooms and then figure out how you can build that die in nine weeks. From blueprint to finished product in nine weeks. I give you one hour and fifteen minutes to do it. That's all, one hour and fifteen minutes. And I want you not only to figure out a way to do it but it has to be done in the next ninety days. I want you to build the plan to completely turn this company around, and I want you to do it in the next one hour and fifteen minutes."

And miracles do happen. With their spirit aroused people do find a solution, and they do make a commitment to save their company.

This book is the brilliant story of how American industry started to decline, how we went from the most powerful industrial society in the world, the wealthiest, the highest creditor nation in the world, to a society with almost no productivity growth at all, to the world's largest debtor nation. And it shows the learning path companies can take to lead in the world economy again.

We have lost our markets in television, electronics, cameras, watches, shoes, automobiles, tools, and a thousand other product lines by which we once ruled the world. We were the "ugly

Americans" with factories all over the world. We retrenched. Why? What happened? In 1980 the American dollar was worth close to 300 yen. Today it is close to 100. We have given away our industrial might. Can we regain our power? Jim Swartz believes we can, and he takes us on a journey in his book to destroy every myth about cultural difference, lack of will, low intelligence of the American worker, and all the other nonsense that has held us back from fighting.

He teaches us in a very unique and fun-filled way. His book is a story filled with fiction and facts, with great stories from his fruitful creative imagination and from his real experiences on the factory floor, in engineering bullpens and in the boardrooms of giants in industry.

He was an excellent manager. He has studied well. He writes very well; but the challenge is yours. The book can be quickly read for fun and pleasure, but don't fail to recognize that every chapter is an adventure in learning the tools and techniques to turn your company around. You can easily read and enjoy; and you also can get down to work, understand the principles that Jim makes very clear in this book, and once again become themost powerful industrialists in the world.

The choice is yours. The knowledge is here. Become the hunter or remain the hunted. You pick. Pick right!

I wish to thank all the people who contributed to making this a great book: Diane Asay for developmental editing; Barry Shulak for diction enhancement and consistency and manuscript editing; Mary Junewick for proofreading; Karen Jones as managing editor for a careful pursuit of permissions and thorough preparation of the complex text design for typesetting; Bill Stanton and Gayle Asmus for book design; and Gary Ragaglia and Bill Stanton for cover design; and Douglas Mazonowicz and the Gallery of Prehistoric Art for permission to use their photograph for the cover.

– Norman Bodek, Publisher

Acknowledgments

A special thanks to John Swartz, Debra Jobe, Jim Cameron, Connie Green, John Schlee, John Sheridan, Diane Asay, and Barry Shulak for their valuable suggestions.

Thanks to Elmer Swartz, Ron Gill, Bob Hall, Ken Stork, Lee Sage, Mort Kapitanoff, and Ernie Paskell for being my Mentors in the world of business.

Thanks to Ron Gill, Jim Hall, Gary Robertson, Candace Somers, Tom Endres, Norm Bodek, Al Mataliano, Jeff Grant, Dwight Callaway, Don Carr, Dudley Wass, Jim Brock, Bernie Pierce, Dick Siever, Charlie Mays, Alan Updike, Camilla England, Jim Cameron, Marsha Moses, Mary Lashley, Jovita Vanover, Joan Childers, Dick Campbell, Bob Sargent, John Beaty, Ron Anjard, and the CCHS class of '53 for believing in me.

Thanks to Mona Adams, Jerry Stenklyft, Dick Marshall, Jo Stafford, Don Scalf, Parviz Danesghari, Susan Reed, Eric Pierce, Chuck Christy, Rick Lockridge, Alex Hutchins, Carla Eley, and the editors at Productivity Press for their helpful suggestions.

Thanks to Drs. Adler, Scherschel, and Steele, without whose help, I may not have finished this book.

Thanks to Marguerite and Kay Swartz for believing in me, and to Kay Swartz for the sketches.

Thanks to the Brothers — Hubert, Joe, and Harry.
And thanks to my children, in order of birth

Joe Swartz
Laura Louis
Greg Swartz
Julie Thorpe

for their help and for being the joy of my life.

Fact and Fiction

All persons in this book with last names are actual persons, living or dead. All company names belong to real companies, living or dead. The author has participated in many of the post-1980 turnarounds described in this book.

The turnarounds described in this book are factual. The words of the heroes and heroines are taken from actual conversations with the author, conversations that were recorded in the heat of battle, or quotations taken from their own works and from works written about them.

There are eight fictional characters with no last names.

The Hunters and the Hunted

If you do not know the enemy and do not know yourself, you will always lose.

If you know the enemy and not yourself, you will win half the time.

If you know both the enemy and yourself, you will always win.

– Sun Tzu
The Art of War

You cannot hope to understand the mind and the methods of the Hunter unless you have been one of the Hunted.

Hunted

Bloodletting

*F*irst we bought components, steel, and textiles.[1] They cost us less than those purchased from American companies and the trips to Japan were great. Next we were buying subassemblies, machine tools, motors, integrated circuits, and finished plastic parts. Each new design had more subassemblies made in Japan.

And then one day we were surprised and shocked when the Japanese and Koreans were at our customers' doorsteps offering to sell the entire assembly: automobiles, microwaves, televisions, VCRs, earth movers, and air conditioners. After the shock we were angry; then our anger gave way to negotiation; finally our negotiation gave way to resignation.

We had become one of the Hunted . . .

Sinking Ships

Our labor rate, including fringe benefits, was more than twice that of the Japanese. We reasoned that by moving part of our operations to Singapore or Mexico at $1.00 per hour, we could level our position with the Japanese. Although it hurt, it made sense at the time. In retrospect, however, such an approach seems to make as much sense as when a group of people, seeing that a ship is sinking, decide to throw some people overboard in order to save the rest.

We adopted one of the strategies of the Hunted — chasing low-cost labor . . . to Singapore . . . Mexico . . . Korea . . . China . . . Haiti . . . Nigeria.

For Thirty Pieces of Silver

We licensed the Japanese to build televisions and they took the business. We sold the rights to the VCR and lost the whole $17 billion market. We sold technology licenses for microchips and lost fifty percent of the market. We sold our magnetron technology and production equipment to Samsung, closed our plants, and then bought microwave ovens from them. Now we're jointly developing the F16 fighter aircraft and a new advanced technology commercial aircraft.

Another strategy of the Hunted — selling the future.

They Came in Low

The early attacks were on the low-cost, high-volume units. As each attack took its toll, many argued that the low-priced, low-profit products weren't worth the time and effort to save them. But many were also asking, "Where does it end? At what point do we draw the line?" The answer came to many of us when we started buying some low-priced products from our competitors and reselling them to our customers.

By the mid-seventies, the competitors were offering equal quality and upscale models. The final bastion of our defense — design innovation — was being challenged. We watched, horrified, as U.S. textile and electronics manufacturers, steel makers, and car manufacturers, were destroyed, devoured, or mortally wounded by the new Hunters of the world.

Steve Jobs said it for all of us in an interview with the Wall Street Journal: *"If we aren't able to make what we invent, we might as well start learning to speak Japanese."*

No Safe Ground

Negotiation for coexistence in the competitive business world is at best a temporary refuge for the Hunted. The Hunters thrive on conflict and conquest.

In 1938, Neville Chamberlain, prime minister of England, negotiated for coexistence with Hitler by agreeing to the Munich Pact, which surrendered Czechoslovakia to Hitler. He proclaimed that this agreement assured the British "peace in our time." But Winston Churchill saw this decision for what it was — peace at any price. In his speech to the House of Commons, he stated:

> The people should know they have sustained defeat without war
> . . . and this is only the beginning of the reckoning. This is only the
> first sip, the first foretaste of a bitter cup which will be proffered to
> us year by year.

Churchill's words were prophetic. Hitler was not satisfied with peace offerings. He continued his aggression. Only when the Hunted became Hunters did Hitler's reign of death and destruction end.

To survive we must be the most feared of Hunters, those who attack when and where they choose.

The Hunted Often Mine Their Own Retreat

At first the Hunted ignore and underestimate the young Hunters. As they lose market share they react with cries that they are being victimized. When finally the pain is unbearable, they act. To streamline for reduced volumes and stem negative cash flow, they focus on restructuring and more rapid linear improvement. In restructuring, they reduce layers of management, eliminate losers, retreat from low-margin markets, slash costs and inventories, reduce people and expense, outsource labor and materials, and manipulate finances.

These strategies and defenses are necessary at this point in the life of the company, and they all work to some degree. They all have a common, disturbing theme, however. Regardless of the euphemisms that are used to explain the changes to employees and to Wall Street, these are defensive moves.

I'm not a Monday-morning quarterback. I was a participant in the process, and I was seduced by some of the arguments. I'm not preaching from a safe pulpit. I'm one of the generation that didn't clearly see the handwriting on the wall; one of the generation that squandered our heritage as the Hunters. The strategic decisions we have made to this point are not the issue, but rather the impact these strategies have had on our confidence and will to win. *We have come to believe that American companies with American workers can't compete.*

Is It Our Time to Go?

Prior to 1700, the Hunters did not use productivity as the basis for their growth. The wealthy nations of the past engaged in win-lose means; they plundered, engaged in trade wars and armed conflict. It was not until 300 years ago that growth became based on productivity improvement.

From 1700 to 1785, the Netherlands was the world's economic leader. The Dutch built a worldwide trade network to sell their low-cost textiles and put the textile manufacturers of Genoa, Venice, and Milan out of business. As exporters, international bankers, and shippers, the Dutch became secure with their riches and power. But during the last half of the eighteenth century, the productivity growth in the Netherlands declined, finally reversing itself near the end of their leadership. The Hunter — England — passed the Netherlands in productivity by 1785. The Dutch ignored the decline in productivity and loss in world trade. They quietly and passively slipped into second place. They had become the Hunted.

The nineteenth century belonged to the English. In the latter part of the eighteenth century, English inventors developed machines that dramatically improved productivity in the manufacture of textiles. England's productivity was increasing at a rate of 1.5 percent per year by the mid-nineteenth century. Per capita income rose to the highest in the world as they produced two-thirds of the world's coal and more than half of its steel and cotton cloth. By 1870, England's trade was greater than the combined trade of France, Germany, and Italy, and three times that of the United States. No wonder the British became arrogant and ignored the signs of decline. There were warnings in the British press about the German use of "unfair trade practices." Later, British author E.E. Williams, in a book called *The American Invaders*, expressed concern about the advancing Americans and their "prohibitive tariffs."

While protecting its fledgling industries with high tariffs at home, the United States built its network of trade: cottons to Manchester, England; steel to Sheffield; oatmeal to Scotland; potatoes to Ireland; beef to England. The United States invaded with bed sheets from New England, Yankee safety razors, Boston boots from North Carolina, and wine from California. As England's growth rate fell to .8 percent in the late nineteenth century, the U.S rate rose to 2.1 percent. The Hunter of all Hunters would become number one in the last decade of the nineteenth century.

For almost 100 years the United States has been the dominant economic power in the world. But as new Hunters have challenged U.S. dominance, first they have been ignored, then underestimated, then attacked as unfair.

It has been written that those who do not learn from history are condemned to repeat it. Will the Hunted recognize the symptoms? Will they ignore the lessons of history?

Don't Worry, It's Just a Phase We're Going Through

Some say that we are entering the post-industrial or infor-mation age. Just as we passed from a largely agriculturally based economy to an industrially based economy in the first half of the twentieth century, so have we begun the transition to a ser-vice and information economy. They say that the loss of manu-facturing jobs will be offset by the growth of service and information jobs, just as agricultural jobs were replaced by manufacturing jobs.

This hypothesis that this change is natural has some seri-ous flaws. First, we did not lose the agricultural industry; we improved it until it was the most productive in the world. We didn't phase out of agriculture — we mastered it. And the esti-mates that only four percent of the U.S. population is involved in agriculture does not include jobs in perishable food process-ing, farm machinery, and storage and distribution, to mention only a few.

Manufacturing and manufacturing-dependent jobs account for as many as fifty percent of all jobs in the United States. If we lose the core manufacturing jobs, eventually we'll lose product engineering, process engineering, machine tools, the support-ing suppliers of products and services, and a great deal of the service sector.

And if we lose manufacturing, what's going to ensure our position in the service or information business? Are our service and information businesses any less vulnerable? Or are the problems in manufacturing really inherent in all business?

Can the Hunted Learn to Hunt?

The birth, life, and death of business has been described by many authors. Most agree that the life cycle has three or more stages. Creativity, excitement, rapid growth, financial cliff-hanging, and a can-do attitude characterize the early stages. As the business grows, it begins to institutionalize itself, installing all the trappings of bureaucracy. In its final stages it is attacked by its successors — the spirited, innovative, fast-moving Hunters. For most businesses, this stage is the beginning of the end. Unable to comprehend what is happening to them, unable to respond because of inflexible corporate mind-set, and lacking the passion needed for the fight, they succumb.

Businesses, like countries, survive by design. The Hunters are not only lean and mean, but they respond faster, produce higher quality, and are more innovative than the Hunted. They thrive on the rapid changes in markets, technology, expectations of customers, competitors, environmental concerns, world politics, finance, and the work force.

At one time, U.S.-based companies were the Hunters of the world. By expanding and establishing foreign operations, they dominated the marketplace. After World War II, however, the former military powers of Germany and Japan focused their energies on economic development. With the help of the United States, these once-military Hunters have since become economic Hunters, prowling the globe. The governments of Germany, Japan, Taiwan, Korea, Singapore, Sweden, and France adopted national policies enabling them to compete internationally while we rested on past success. While the rest of the world went on the prowl, many U.S. companies regressed from being Hunters to prey. Unwittingly, they had become the well-fed Hunted.

But Hunters don't forget how to hunt. A cougar can be tamed temporarily by captivity and regular feedings, but once returned hungry to the jungle, a cougar quickly regains its primacy as the dominant Hunter.

Turning the Hunt Around

By the early 1980s, teams at Hewlett-Packard, Hughes Aircraft, Motorola, Steelcase, Cadillac, Simpson Timber, Harley-Davidson, General Electric, Delco Electronics, Cincinnati

Milacron, Buick, Ford, Westinghouse, Allied Signal, Douglas Aircraft, Chrysler, Tektronix, Nucor, and many other companies began to turn the hunt around. These teams should have been decorated for meritorious service in what had clearly become a global war. They believed in a survival philosophy, as stated articulately by Winston Churchill in his famous speech at the Harrow School in the fall of 1941:

"Never give in, never give in, never, never, never, never."

This book is a study of "hunted" businesses that stood their ground and learned to become Hunters once again. It's about the heroes, heroines, teams, and champions who fought back, often against the tide of resignation. In every case of the Hunted turned Hunter there was first a major change in mindset. Second, they learned how to redesign the very structure of their businesses — their delivery systems. Third, they learned how to design structures that produce fast, high-quality learning and improvement in their systems. Finally, and most importantly, they discovered the Non-Linear Solution.

This book is also a study of the Hunters and their arsenal of weapons.

By learning the fundamental principles that drove these turnarounds, you'll learn a process for redesigning manufacturing, engineering, administration, and business systems which can turn your company into a feared Hunter. In the final analysis, to remain the Hunter always, you must discover the Non-Linear Solution . . . But this is getting ahead of the story.

Our story begins in 1970 in a midwestern town . . .

———

CHAPTER ONE

Lou

March, 1970

N umber two's down," a small, barrel-chested man says as he pokes his head into Lou's office.

"Did you call Stan?"

"Yeah, he's headed over already."

"Then let's get out there," Lou barks. He feels a bit dizzy and short of breath as he grabs his hard hat.

Number one furnace is pouring as they enter the melt shop. A red glow bathes the room and the crackling noise from number one is deafening. Lou approaches a foreman standing in front of the number two furnace and shouts, "What's wrong with number two?"

"Don't know for sure, but I think it's in the control panel. I called for an electrician twenty minutes ago."

"Then where the hell is he?" Lou demands. At that instant the electrician saunters in and Lou steps toward him, glowering. "Where've you been? We've got a furnace down!"

"Installing a spare pump in the pump house 'til Stan pulled me," the electrician says just as Stan comes around the corner.

"What's the problem?"

Lou breathes deeply, then says sarcastically, "Oh, no problem . . . I've got an electric furnace down and your electrician is installing a pump!"

"Sorry, Lou, I didn't know it was completely down. I got the call five minutes ago. I'll work with the electrician 'til we get it back up."

"Damn!" Lou winces and puts his hand to his chest.

"Lou, we're pulling all the stops to get it up again. What's wrong?"

"It's nothing . . . Figures that this breakdown had to happen just before those eastern MBAs from Penn-Dixie get here. I'd like to get a few of them down here on the floor. Slick suits and slick slide presentations don't work down here."

Lou shakes his head. "And then there was that guy they sent in a few months back — the one with all those crazy ideas."

Stan smiles. "His ideas really were wild. Nice old guy though.

"What do those guys think they're running here, a bank? Because they sure don't know much about making steel . . . Hell, maybe an old steelmaker's opinions don't matter anymore. MBAs coming at us from one side and young, know-it-all engineers from the other."

"Like your dad says, I guess you have to have that piece of paper."

"In the old days, experience was what mattered. Anyway, get back to me as soon as you find the problem."

Lou turns and walks toward his office, feeling wistful. Times sure have changed. When he and Stan came back from the Pacific after the war and started working in the mill, Europe was rebuilding itself, and the demand for American steel . . . well, they worked. How they worked! If a furnace went down then, an electrician would run to it. Twenty-four hours a day they pumped out steel, and they cared about their work — cared fiercely. But these young fellows . . . it's just a job to them. They have no pride.

If Stan doesn't get number two running soon, Lou is going to have to send some people home. The timing couldn't be worse. Efficiency figures are going to be lousy this week —

Pain suddenly shoots down his left arm; he hears footsteps running toward him and Stan's voice ordering someone to call an ambulance.

It's a struggle to speak, a struggle to breathe. His chest is heaving. "Stan," he says, gasping for breath, "My little girl . . . take care of her . . . please."

Life can only be understood backwards, but it must be lived forwards.

– Søren Kierkegaard

CHAPTER TWO

The Return

Twenty-One Years Later

*L*ou watches as a tall man wearing a blue suit materializes. "You must be Marcus."

The man smiles and shakes Lou's hand. "Have you been waiting long?"

"No problem," Lou laughs. "I only applied for the position five years ago."

Marcus removes a blue portfolio from his briefcase, opens it slowly, and studies Lou's resume. Finally he speaks: "You know, of course, that in Special Forces we help businesses in trouble. My question, Lou, is what makes you think you're the right person for the job?"

Careful, Lou tells himself. He's been waiting over twenty years for a job like this; he's been waiting five years just for an interview.

"Marcus, I know manufacturing. I worked in steel for twenty-four years. Ten of those years I ran the plant — dealt with all kinds of people, solved all types of problems. I know I can do this job."

"You may have been a good manufacturing manager twenty years ago, Lou, but the business world has changed a lot since you left Earth. You're going to have to re-learn a lot."

"Does that mean I've got the job?"

"Slow down, Lou. First, you'll have to go through basic training in the great principles to become an Apprentice Guardian. You will then receive an assignment which, if you complete it successfully, will qualify you as a Journeyman Guardian. Then finally, to become a full-fledged Master Guardian, you'll have to discover for yourself the Non-Linear Solution."

"Hey, I might not have one of those fancy degrees, but I'm no ordinary recruit . . . I don't need basic training."

"If you want this job you do." Marcus turns the page of Lou's resume "Let's see here . . . I see that you took some night courses in economics, marketing, and finance at Indiana University, Kokomo Campus."

"Self-defense," Lou says.

"Self-defense?"

"So the people in the front office couldn't put anything over on me."

"Good grades, too" Marcus muses as he holds up Lou's transcript.

"I did all right 'cause those college kids in class were lazy; they didn't study. Turning around troubled businesses . . . sounds right up my alley."

"Okay. Let's get started then. A lot has happened in the twenty-some years since your fatal heart attack. First, we'll visit your old firm, Continental Steel, in Kokomo."[1]

"Continental! Sounds good to me."

Marcus smiles enigmatically. "We have an appointment at thirteen hundred hours eastern standard time with your old friend Stan. Stan won't recognize you, of course, because you'll have a new face, a new body, and a new identity as a business researcher named Lou."

With his gaze fixed intently on Lou, Marcus continues: "A few important words of advice. First, because you will be dealing with the living on a day-to-day basis, you're going to experience a whole range of human emotions that you haven't felt in years. Try to keep things simple. Remember why you're there: to serve people.

"Second — and this is *extremely* important — at no time are you to reveal your past identity. If you do, you'll be immediately discharged from Special Forces. Got that?"

"Got it."

"Now," says Marcus, "we have an appointment." As he says this, both his body and the conference room begin to fade from view. Lou feels a gentle vibration begin deep within the form that he has been given for his meeting with Marcus. He too is being transformed. Soon he sees nothing but deep blue-black space and the glitter of stars. He is aware of the subtle pulsation that is Marcus beside him, and then, he feels a surge of energy and sees a rush of color. Lou is amazed and exhilarated. He is pure energy hurtling toward a distant galaxy. He is also puzzled because he has heard that Guardians move instantly from one place to another.

"We *can* move instantly from one place to another," Marcus says, seeming to anticipate Lou's question. "But sometimes I like the scenic route, and I thought you might too."

Absolutely, he thinks, as they rush toward the bright blue and green sphere that he hasn't seen in over twenty years.

As they descend through a cloud blanket, a huge complex of buildings comes into view.

Good to be back . . . must have both furnaces down . . . no smoke from the stack . . . strange . . . parking lot empty in the middle of the day. Gentle undulations begin again and Lou is aware once more of his physical form, of the pavement beneath the soles of his black wingtips.

"Remember, Lou, you're doing research. Is that Stan?" Marcus asks as they walk toward a locked gate.

"That's him," Lou says as they cross the parking lot. "Sure have let the outside appearance run down. Why is the main gate locked?"

"Stan, I'm Marcus. We talked on the phone. And this is Lou."

"Good to meet you," Lou says, shaking Stan's hand.

"We lock the gate to keep trespassers out," Stan says as he turns the key in a giant padlock.

"Trespassers?" Lou frowns.

"Mostly kids. We'll start at the melt shop." Stan leads them through the gate.

As they approach the melt shop, Lou halts. "Looks like some equipment has been removed out here."

"Used to be transformers."

"What's going on here? Where is everybody?" Lou asks, ignoring Stan's answer.

Stan looks at him as if he's crazy.

"Don't you know, Lou? The company went belly up a few years ago."

"Impossible, there's no way."

"I'm giving it to you straight. We lost it all."

"What the hell happened?" Lou turns to Marcus. "What's this all about?" Lou picks up the pace, walking toward the melt shop.

At the entrance to the melt shop Lou stands silently. *It's like the world has stopped . . . no fire, no sparks, no heat, no smoke, no whining electric furnaces . . . no banging of metal, no motors whirring, no cranes moving . . .* Sunlight streams in through broken skylights. *It was a good smell . . . burnt carbon and firebrick with a touch of iron. Now it smells like a musty junkyard . . .*

"Unbelievable, unbelievable," Lou's words break the silence. He sees again the watchful faces of John, Bill, and Roland gazing out at the molten metal from the furnace control booths. In his memory he sees the crane lift the huge ladle to the mold line where the furnace helper pulls the flapper at the bottom of the ladle, releasing the red-hot liquid into the mold.

Lou walks over and puts his hand on the giant ladle, lying on its side like a fallen dinosaur. *One of the best mills in the country . . . this melt shop was equipped with the latest electric furnaces . . . the best . . . we had so much work we were running six to seven days a week . . . three shifts a day . . . one of the highest profit/sales ratios in the country . . . melt shop was built in '65 with cash . . . ten million dollars . . . we had it all going right then . . . somebody screwed it up . . .*

A rat darts in front of Lou. *God, a rat . . . where did they go . . . John and Bill . . . this factory was a family . . . fathers, sons . . . a job for life . . . three thousand people . . . now it's left to the rats.* Slowly, Lou begins walking towards the rolling mill area. As they enter the connecting passageway, they pass a row of lockers. Lou pauses to look at the pictures on the door of a locker, then he bends over to pick up a hard hat. The name "Tony" is painted in blue.

The interior of the rolling mill is dark and damp, and Stan cautions them to watch their steps. It's eerily quiet as they thread their way among gaping holes in the floor. Steel bolts protrude from the floor where machinery has been removed. Lou stops and looks back toward the gutted furnaces, remembering the many tours he used to lead through the plant.

" . . . *Over here," he motions to the group of customers, "Watch the second helper," he shouts. The second helper takes a ten-foot oxygen tube and burns a hole through the bottom plug of the furnace. It starts as a trickle, then it's a foot-wide diameter river of white hot metal . . . sparks, cracks, small explosions, as the metal flows from furnace to ladle . . .*

Lou walks the customers into the rod mill . . . they watch as the automatic repeaters grab the red hot rod, whip it up and around, and back into the rollers . . . "Hell of a show . . . Hell of a show . . . ."

"What did they do with all of the equipment?" Lou asks.

"Sold it at auction . . . they even sold the steel in the railroad tracks and the copper wiring in the walls."

"Like vultures," Lou mutters in disgust.

"More like cannibals."

Suddenly Lou turns and heads toward his old office, his pace quickening. The door stands ajar and Lou walks in alone, the others far behind.

The office reminds Lou of Japan in 1945. Piles of papers, records are scattered all over the place. They must have just dumped everything when they came for the file cabinets. He walks over and picks up a handful of papers and sits down on the floor. "How could they have allowed this to happen?" he asks himself. He crouches down and sorts through some papers; he blows the dust off a water-stained award certificate . . . *Seven record months in a row . . . we were the best . . . .*

"Lou, are you alright?" Stan asks as they enter the office.

Lou looks up from the floor, "Yeah, I'm fine. Just got some dust in my eye."

He pulls himself up, "I think I've seen enough."

On the way out Stan suggests they hit the Steel Inn for a few beers.

Lou stops, then turns back to glance a final time at the remains of his past. "I think I could use a drink right now . . . maybe two."

At the nearby bar, Stan leads them to a booth at the back near a worn green pool table. "What happened?" Lou asks as he drops into a chair. "Last I heard, Continental was at the top of the heap. You had just bought two new electric furnaces, revamped the rod mill, and had a continuous caster on the drawing boards. There were no problems."

Stan shakes his head. "Lou, the trouble had already started by then. In late 1970, after Penn-Dixie achieved controlling interest in Continental Steel, they shut down the sheet mill. Then in 1971, when the union caught wind of Penn-Dixie's plan to use the pension trust fund for venture capital, they organized a strike and obtained an injunction to protect the funds. The strike was long and bitter, but it was the beginning of the end. Then the fuel crunch hit us in 1973, and foreign steel started coming in. After that it just steadily went to hell. We never got it together again."

Lou clenches his fist. "Hunted down and destroyed . . . that's what happened."

"Yeah, we were hunted all right, hunted by the takeover people, the money manipulators, the oil cartel, other steel companies, and finally by our own lawyers."

"Damn! It's unbelievable . . . It sounds like you couldn't get your act together when it mattered most — when the enemy was attacking," Lou's face reddened.

"We were fighting among ourselves," Stan says.

"Didn't management and labor see the handwriting on the wall?"

"No. A lot of the older guys kept saying that this mill had survived the depression of the thirties and that there was no way it would ever shut down."

"Have all the people found work?"

"A lot of the office people found jobs, but it was tough on the mill workers. They had spent their lives in that mill, and steel was all they knew. A lot of them didn't even have a high school diploma, and they found out the deck is stacked against fifty-year-olds with no education," Stan replies, shaking his head. "The sad thing is that some guys waited for months, expecting the mill to reopen. Every morning they'd gather at the gate and spend hours out there together, talking among themselves, as if they found hope in numbers. The message that it was over just didn't sink in."

"Hey, it hasn't sunk in with me yet . . . Well, they still had their pensions to fall back on, I guess."

"That's the bad part, Lou. They raided the pension fund and when the company went under, the creditors sued for a piece of what was left and we were stuck with nothing."

"Is that legal?

"Of course not, but they did it anyway. After two long

years of fighting, we finally got a small percentage of our pensions. I don't know if we can hope for much more, but we're not giving up the fight."

Stan motions to the waitress. "You haven't touched your beer, Lou. Drink up; I'm buying." He seems lost in thought for a long while. "You know, I had a friend named Lou once. He was my best friend, in fact. We started at Continental together, joined the marines together . . . even spent eight months together in a Japanese prison camp."

"What was he like?" Marcus asks.

We called him 'the Bear,'" Stan says with a faraway look in his eyes. "He was big and thick and steel was in his blood. We grew up together. As long as I can remember we wanted to be one of them — steelmen. To us they were strong and brave, and they did important work. Lou's dad talked about the mill a lot, and we listened. One year — it was 1931, I believe — at an open house at the mill, Lou's dad took us up on a high platform so we could see through the door of an open hearth just about to pour. I can still hear Lou today. After we'd have a couple beers, he'd say 'Remember the time Dad took us up on that platform?' . . . I can still see it, that white hot metal . . . it was like looking into hell.

"It was that day that we both decided to quit school. We were only sixteen. Lou's dad was mad but he helped us get jobs at the mill as bucket boys. Carrying that bucket around was big stuff to us. When a furnace operator dipped a drink from our bucket, we felt important. Only a dollar a day, but that was a big help to our families. That was the depression. Then came the war, of course. And when we came home we got right back into it again at the mill. Nobody loved working with steel the way Lou did. He was tough, too; and I'll tell you what: a lot of us feel that it would never have happened if Lou hadn't passed away."

"Why do you say that?" Lou asks.

"I'll tell you why. Lou was a demanding guy and he was tough to work with, but he had something those new people would never understand. He cared about steel and he cared about people. Outside the mill, Lou was easy-going, and fun loving, but when we walked through the gate at 6:20 A.M. he became a bear on the prowl.

"Top management thought Lou was rough around the edges, you know, difficult to manage at times, and overprotective of his people. It was alright for him to bite his own people in the butt, but let anyone else do it — especially someone in the front office, and Lou came charging like a grizzly. I could tell you plenty of stories where Lou went up to the front office and chewed somebody out. But they couldn't argue with the performance of the plants he managed. It was Lou's mill, and he bossed it better than anybody in the business. What can I say? He was the best. He had power. He was the only one who could have stood up to corporate when they started milking the business. But after Lou died, there was no one we could count on. Lou always put everybody else first. His last words to me were to take care of his daughter."

Lou is so overcome with emotion that he can't speak. "Sounds like Lou was a fine man," Marcus says. "And he was lucky indeed, to have a friend like you."

"What about the daughter?" Lou asks.

"Candace graduated from Purdue with a Masters in Engineering. I talked to her last week. She has a big job on the West Coast. Lou would have been proud." Stan sighs. "They broke the mold that made Lou. They don't make 'em like that anymore."

Marcus stands and smoothes his suit. "Ready to go, Lou?"

He stands slowly, finishing the last of his beer, and shakes Stan's hand. "Thanks, Stan . . . thanks."

"You're welcome, Lou. Anytime."

It's dark outside. Lou walks around the corner of the tavern and takes another look at the mill. *Like a huge tomb. The moon is just rising in the west over the number two smokestack . . . no smoke to block it . . . what a price to pay . . .*

Marcus walks over to Lou. "What's on your mind, Lou?"

"Hard to believe — boom to bust so fast. I can't believe that they lost it all. So many people worked their whole life for that company. Why did you show me that? I feel a little like Jimmy Stewart in *It's a Wonderful Life*."

"I wanted to show you the consequences of losing the competitive battle."

"Was this a dream then? Is Continental Steel still going today? Is this my assignment — to put Humpty-Dumpty back together again?"

"No, Lou, Continental is bankrupt, and all your friends have lost their jobs. We can't put it back together again. We can study the past and the present, but we can only influence the future."

"Just when I was beginning to think you could do anything . . . It's still hard for me to understand."

Marcus places his hand on Lou's shoulder. "It will be easier to understand when you see what's happened in the world of business since you left in 1970. In the next few hours we'll take a whirlwind trip around the world of business of today to bring you up to date. Twenty years has made a big difference." Marcus leads Lou into the shadows around the corner of the building, and in a flash, they are rising far above the lights of Kokomo.

"When do I get my assignment?" Lou asks as they cross the Ohio River.

"You're getting ahead of yourself. You first have to qualify as an Apprentice Guardian before you can tackle an assignment."

When they arrive in Memphis, Tennessee, Marcus hands Lou a document that shows each level of the Order of the Guardian.

....

Qualifying Requirements for the Order of the Guardian

To Qualify as an Apprentice, one must:

- *complete training in the fundamentals of continuous improvement systems*
- *complete training in the fundamentals of business Delivery System design*
- *identify and understand the great weapons of the Hunters*

To become a Journeyman Guardian, one must:

- *know how to install a linear improvement process*
- *know how to redesign Delivery Systems*
- *understand all the great principles*
- *know the greatest principle*
- *know how mind changes are achieved*
- *know how the Hunters continually transform themselves*
- *provide significant help to turn a Hunted business into a Hunter*
- *learn the transformation drivers*

To become a Master Guardian, one must:

- *discover the Non-linear Solution*

....

Marcus reassures Lou: "You probably don't understand all of the qualifying requirements right now, but you will, in time. Now we're on our way to Federal Express for a 1:00 A.M. tour."

This guy keeps strange hours! "I don't think I need all this to turn a business around. I'm no ordinary recruit, you know. How long does it take to learn all this?"

"There's an old proverb, Lou: 'When the student is ready, the teacher will appear.' "

"What does that mean?"

"There are plenty of Hunters that can teach you when you're ready, and there are plenty of the Hunted out there who need your help. But your first challenge is to open yourself to the learning process. Later, you will be called upon to guide others as they attempt to do the same.

"Even now, a situation is developing somewhere that will be a worthy assignment for you."

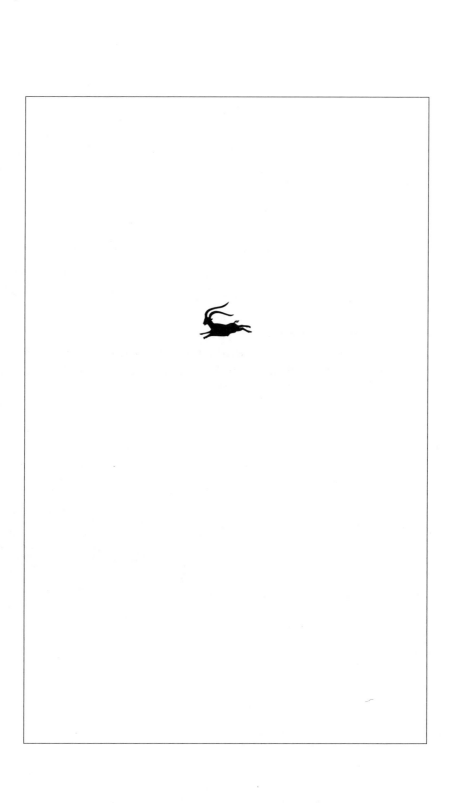

It wasn't until I was at Chrysler a couple of months that I realized how bad it really was. Maybe it's better I didn't know beforehand. I might not have agreed to take the job.

– Lee Iacocca

CHAPTER THREE

Wil

*A*s Lou and Marcus travel to Memphis, Wil Danesi is leaving the corporate offices of Allied Signal on his way to the Los Angeles airport.[1] His mind is reeling from the sudden changes of the last four hours. This morning he was chief of materials engineering for Garrett Engine Division of Allied Signal Corporation in Phoenix; now he's the new general manager of another division of Allied Signal Aerospace Company — Garrett Processing Division in Torrance, California.

Three months earlier Wil participated in a task force which benchmarked the performance of the major U.S. foundries producing castings for turbine engines. The study concluded that Garrett Processing Division, which was losing millions of dollars per year, was non-competitive on both cost and delivery performance. The task force findings doubted that even large capital expenditures could restore the division's competitiveness and Wil knew that Garrett Processing Division was in deep trouble.

But Roy Ekrom, president of Allied Signal Aerospace Company, believed that the in-house casting division still had strategic value, because it guaranteed a supply of certain critical jet engine parts and also provided purchasing leverage for other Allied Signal divisions against suppliers who might be tempted to overcharge for their products. He decided Garrett Processing would get another chance with Wil at the helm. Roy asked his secretary to set up a meeting with Wil.

The following morning, they argued. Wil's biggest concerns were, first, that he had no operations experience, and second, that he lacked a good understanding of the financial aspects of an entire division. But all the arguments ended sharply a half hour later when Roy pounded the table and said, "Dammit, Wil, take the job."

Traffic is heavy, moving at about sixty as he approaches El Segundo. His thoughts run wildly. How will he break the news to his wife Sue? She loves her nursing work at Scottsdale Memorial Hospital, and she's pleased that they have finally managed to stay in one place for over two years — long enough to make some solid friends.

Suddenly Wil realizes he's a mile past the airport exit. As he exits to correct his error, he's amused: *Roy picked me to turn around a division, and I'm having trouble just finding my way back to the airport.* At the rental car return he slides his 195-pound, six-foot-one-inch frame out of the car and walks toward the shuttle bus.

The America West 737 begins its ascent from LAX and banks into a slow roll over the Pacific. From his window seat, Wil can see the sun's golden halo begin to sink into the horizon, and his thoughts return to the charge given him by Roy Ekrom. *Maybe I don't understand the financial complexities of managing a whole division, but I do know one thing for certain — to stop losing money you have to either spend less or take in more.* To bring in more revenue he'll have to recapture lost customers and win new ones, and that'll take major changes in people, equipment, and time. *Time is my biggest worry. Will Roy stick with me long enough for me to show what I can do?* Wil knows he'll have to cut expenses immediately and avoid layoffs as long as possible. He's keenly aware that his decisions will affect many people's careers — even their lives; he also knows the staff needs a transfusion of new blood. *But how can I convince anyone to take a job at a division that may not survive? Nobody wants to sail on a ship with a hole in the hull. Hell, I didn't even want the job myself!* These thoughts consume Wil as he opens his briefcase.

We are in an unprecedented period of accelerated change, perhaps the most breathtaking of which is the swiftness of our rush to all the world becoming a single economy.

– John Naisbitt and Patricia Aburdene
Megatrends 2000

Changes in the nineties will make the eighties look like a picnic — a walk in the park.

– John Welch, Jr., CEO
General Electric

CHAPTER FOUR

The Awakening

One A.M., Memphis.[1] "Federal Express has been going full blast since about 10:00 P.M. when the first planes arrived from the East Coast," says Marcus. "Look down there. The unloading of that 727 will begin immediately as the plane rolls to a stop at its designated parking space. Large containers will go to the main dock to be unpacked. After a small package is taken off the plane it will move through these chutes, conveyors, sorters, and quality checks. It will be in an outgoing bag, ready to be picked up and moved to an outgoing plane, in an hour. The last planes from the West Coast are in before 1:00 A.M., and planes are departing for the East Coast by 3:00 A.M. By 10:30 A.M., all overnight packages will be delivered to their addressees."

"One hundred percent of the time?" Lou asks.

"The Federal Express goal is 100 percent and they're improving all the time. Their bar-code readers log the package at every transaction point along the way, and this information is transmitted by satellite to the computer here in Memphis. They know the location of the package at every step in its journey. If a package is addressed properly, it will reach its target destination 99.9 percent on time."

This place is like the Las Vegas of the shipping world, Lou thinks to himself. It's after midnight and it's going full tilt. "What does it cost to ship a letter cross-country overnight?" he asks.

"Under ten dollars."

"Amazing!"

Later as they leave Marcus explains that when Federal Express first started doing the overnight delivery in 1971, it was considered amazing; today it's taken for granted. "Customers expect fast response, high quality, and high value at a low cost — with no trade-offs. When Federal Express redesigned the process for transporting packages and letters, they dramatically improved the response, quality of delivery, and the value the customer received compared to the cost of the service. Let's look at a few more examples of major change. Let's move to Atlanta."

3:00 A.M., Atlanta: "News from around the world every half hour, this is CNN," the broadcaster announces.

"CNN broadcasts to over eighty-two countries," Marcus says as they walk through a large studio.

"At three in the morning?"

"Twenty-four hours a day, seven days a week. As we talk, reporters are covering breaking stories in hundreds of places around the world. If a story breaks in Munich, the pictures you see on CNN in Munich may have traveled here and back to Munich by satellite just minutes after the news was recorded."

"Sounds like too much news to me."

"Not really, Lou. Knowledge of the outside world is important to people everywhere. In fact, it was so important to the

401 people of the small village of Ocobamba, Peru that they had battery-operated TV sets before they had running water and regular mail service . . . even before electricity.[2]

"I guess it is a different world today."

"Yes . . . and it changes by the second."

4:30 A.M., Buffalo, New York. "Lou, you'll need a set of I.D.s when you're working here on earth. I've had a birth certificate, passport, drivers license, and Visa credit card made up for you. When you need some cash, use this bank card."

"Bank card? But this is from a bank in Jackson, Mississippi."

"That's where the money is deposited."

Lou smirks. "So I have to fly down there every time I run short?"

"Not necessary, Lou. There's an automatic teller machine just around the corner here," Marcus says as they approach the machine. "Take that card and insert it in the slot."

"But it's 3:30 in the morning in Jackson!"

"Trust me, Lou." He does, and he receives a quick training on the convenience of automated teller machines.

"Getting the picture, Lou? Things have changed."

Lou grins. "Always wanted a machine that made money."

"In 1970, when could you withdraw your money from the bank or get your news?"

"When the bank was open or when the broadcaster provided it," Lou says.

"So they were operating in bank time and broadcast network time back then."

"I guess you could say that."

"In whose time are CNN and the banks operating today?"

"My time," Lou says.

"Customer time, Lou! Customer time!" Marcus pauses then asks, "In whose space were the banks of 1970 operating?"

"What do you mean by 'whose space?'"

"I mean where could you withdraw your money?"

"At the bank."

"Right, Lou. Banks in 1970 were operating in bank space, not customer space. At many retail stores today you can present a debit card to the cashier who can use it to withdraw money from your account to pay for your groceries and even give you a cash advance. The Hunters of today operate as much as possible in customer time, customer space, and customer values. They create new expectations in customers that other businesses can't meet. Businesses that can't meet the new expectations become the Hunted."

"Marcus, this is all interesting, don't get me wrong, but you're talking service business. This just doesn't apply to a manufacturing operation like Continental Steel."

"Lou, how long did it take, on the average, from the time you received an order until it was delivered to the customer?"

"We kept about a forty-day order backlog and about thirty days in order entry and engineering . . . then about a month to get through the factory. Total time was about three months."

"So a customer waited two to three months?" Marcus asks.

"They didn't have a problem with that." Lou folds his arms.

"What would happen if a competitor offered delivery a week after an order?"

Lou shrugs, "Not practical, unless you keep a high inventory in your warehouse."

"You were operating in Continental Steel time, Lou, not customer time."

Lou feels his muscles tensing. "We did all right."

"Lou, there's been a revolution in customer expectations. Let's compare what your service expectations are compared to what today's customers expect. How long would you expect it to take in 1970 for someone to lube your car, check and add fluid to the differential, brakes, power steering, and windshield washer; check your air filter, breather element, and PCV valve; inflate your tires, clean your windows, vacuum inside, change the oil and replace the filter?"

"I'd have to leave it for at least four hours at the dealership."

"And how much would you expect it to cost?"

"With the price of a beer I saw yesterday, I would guess thirty to forty dollars."

"Today, you can get all that done in fifteen minutes for around twenty-five dollars at specialized auto service businesses such as Jiffy Lube."

"But how about quality?" Lou asks

"With excellent quality."

"That's hard to imagine."

"The movement of information, materials, services, and people has been revolutionized since you left in 1970. Transatlantic fiber-optic cables carry eighty thousand perfectly clear telephone calls in a single fiber, and the calls travel across the ocean in less than one-eightieth of a second. Low-cost, high-quality FAX machines can transmit a document between continents in fifteen seconds. Video images and computer data can be moved between computers in seconds from one end of the world to another by earth-circling satellites.

"Computers talk to each other?"

"They not only talk to each other, they tell each other when to turn on and off, what to do, and when to do it. Microcomputers are standard equipment at peoples' desks today. In your time, Lou did you use computers?"

"Accounting had a big IBM unit."

"Lou, in a modern steel mill today, almost every operator is using a keyboard connected to a minicomputer. And that's just scratching the surface. There's voice mail, twenty-four-hour telephone interrogation of personal bank accounts, video con-ferencing, cellular car and personal pocket phones, electronic auto maps, and much more.

"In 1970, if you wanted a roll of film developed, how long did it take?"

"Four or five days, maybe," Lou says.

"Today you can drop it off and pick it up an hour later. Computer power speeds calculations, analysis, design, and the storage and recovery of information. High-speed automatic machines place hundreds of parts per minute into electronic circuit boards, fill soup cans, and weld automobile bodies. Today you can get instant breakfast, instant printing, instant instruction by satellite TV, and instant credit checks on credit cards. Customers today expect to have information instantly available and to be able to store it, process it, retrieve it, analyze it, transmit it, and receive it at the touch of a finger on a key-board. High-speed processes provide instant printing, instant health tests, and instant movies."

"Instant movies?"

"Video camcorders, Lou. You can be the producer, director, and camera person all in one. You can record the scene and play it back in the next minute. CNN, bank cards, fast-lube businesses, and computer information systems are all Non-Linear changes because they are dramatic changes in the way in which a business responds, produces quality, and provides more value for the cost."

"Is this Non-Linear jargon necessary? Can't you just call these changes breakthroughs?" Lou says.

"I could, but Non-Linear means much more than that."

"It seems like you're making this too complicated."

"It will clear up, Lou, as you learn more. Be patient and open your mind to some new ideas."

"I'm trying, but you've got some strange ones."

"Let's move on to our next destination — Guardian Command."

En route, Lou breaks a long silence. "I think this computer thing could get out of hand. With computers calculating and talking to each other, and with high-speed robots doing the work, the computers could end up running the show."

"Lou, computers talking to each other is the least of your worries. There's a lot that's happened since you left that's really worth worrying about. When you left, the United States was the world's largest creditor nation. It dominated the industrial and financial world, was a net exporter, had the highest increase in productivity each year, was number one in assets, in steel, in semiconductors, in aircraft. U.S goods were considered the highest quality in the world.

"Today the United States is number one in only two of those areas, aircraft and military power. Of the world's top twenty companies in market value, thirteen are Japanese. Of the top ten banks in the world, all ten are Japanese. When you left earth, the United States had more than ninety percent of the market in color televisions, phonographs, machining centers, semiconductors, and telephone sets. Today this country has less than ten percent of the color TV market, one percent of the phonograph market, thirty percent of the machining center market, forty percent of the semiconductor market and twenty-five percent of the telephone set market. Because U.S. businesses are importing more than they're exporting," Marcus concludes, "the United States's share of world exports has dropped from fourteen percent in 1970 to about eleven percent today."

"Where are the imports coming from?"

"Everywhere — Japan, Europe, Korea, Hong Kong."

"Probably junk from Japan."

"No, Lou. Japan's quality ranks with the best in the world today."

"No way!"

"Lou, quality and cost are the reason for the rise in imports."

"How do they get quality without increasing costs?"

"The old assumption that if you want quality, you have to add cost is no longer valid. Motorola, McDonald's, Toyota, Jiffy Lube, Xerox, Hewlett-Packard, Black and Decker, Federal Express, Apple Computer, American Express, Buick, and Honda have led people to expect high quality at a good price — with fast response. Today, any competitor that wants to be the 'supplier of choice' must supply value with no tradeoff in price, quality, and response. The alternative is that they become one of the Hunted."

Lou laughs.

"What's so funny?" Marcus asks.

"I was just thinking that if you're an expert on fast response, you ought to do something about speeding up the response to applications for Special Forces. It took five years for you guys to respond to mine."

"If you get a response in five years from Heaven, you're on the fast track. They're pretty laid back up there."

"They're definitely not on customer time," Lou says, feeling pleased with himself.

"Yes, they are," Marcus says, "but you're not the customer they have to satisfy," laughs Marcus.

They begin to descend. "You'll be meeting your apprentice partner here at Guardian Command. She's a graduate electrical engineer from MIT, and she has an MBA from Harvard."

"Did you say 'she'?"

"Almost home, Lou. Pyramid Peak just ahead." They descend rapidly toward the side of a mountain and rematerialize inside a large, brightly lit room.

"Welcome to Guardian Command, Lou."

"Guardian Command? Where are we?"

"Pyramid Peak, Colorado, our North American headquarters."

As Lou adjusts to the light, he takes everything in: Beautiful carpets, draperies, marble floors and walls. Electronic equipment and communication systems surround him. Standing at a desk at the far end of the room is a beautiful, dark-haired woman.

Lou follows Marcus as he crosses the room. "Lou, meet Laura, your Special Forces training partner."

My partner? . . . a girl? . . . don't that beat all . . .

"Hi, Lou," Laura smiles and reaches to shake hands. "I'm looking forward to working with you. I've heard that you have some great shop floor experience."

Lou shakes her hand reluctantly. *Good looking girl . . . not built for Special Forces though . . . business suit — not dressed like a girl . . . how did I get stuck with an engineer, and one with a MBA at that . . . it couldn't be worse. Not true, it is worse. She's a girl . . .* "Should be interesting," Lou responds, managing a smile.

She's tall and has an air of self-assurance about her that Lou finds disconcerting. She has an angular face with high cheekbones and her large dark brown eyes are clear and bright. He stares at her. *Sure make 'em tall these days . . . It's not right, a girl that tall . . .*

"Now that I have the two of you together," Marcus says, "we'll head south to Texas to study a modern company that in the late seventies became one of the Hunted. On the way I'll give you some background.

"In the early 1980s Motorola's operations in Seguin, Texas were on top of the world, building a half-million microwave oven touch-pad controls per year. If you had a microwave oven with a touch-pad control at that time, it was probably made in Seguin. Then the bottom fell out of the market. Prices dropped, and they couldn't compete.

"We're meeting a manufacturing manager from Motorola Seguin this morning, and he'll take it from there."

"When do we sleep?" Lou asks.

"We'll get around to that," Marcus says. "There's a lot to learn here and little time to learn it. There's a war going on."

"What war are you talking about?"

"The biggest war in history, Lou. We're on our way to visit one of the warring companies, a modern day Hunter. When we get to San Antonio, you'll have two hours to freshen up before our meeting."

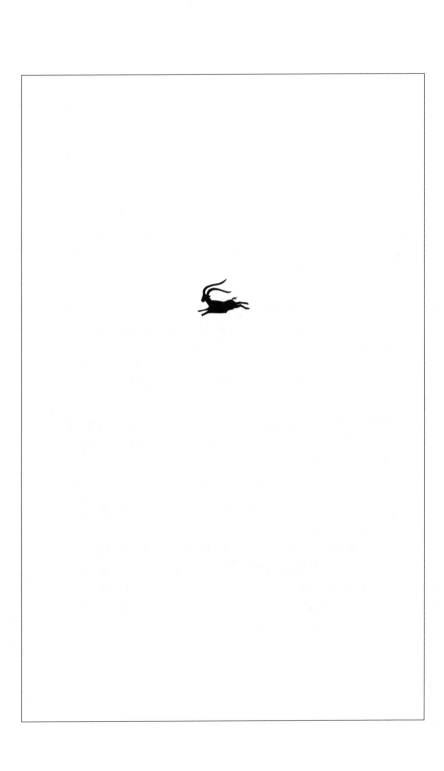

Today we want high quality and a short time to market, so we don't move employment to low-cost countries anymore.

– A. William Wiggenhorn
V.P. Training and Education, Motorola Inc.

Nowadays, I make it a practice to call them into consultation on any new work . . . I observe that they are more willing to set about a piece of work on which their opinions have been asked and their advice followed.

– Columella, Roman Landlord, 100 A.D.

An automobile goes nowhere efficiently unless it has a quick, hot spark to ignite things, to set the cogs in motion. So I try to make every player on my team feel needed — that he's the spark keeping our machine in motion. On him depends our success.

– Knute Rockne, legendary coach of Notre Dame

CHAPTER FIVE

Continuous Improvement

San Antonio, Texas. Marcus and Laura are finishing breakfast at a small table in a coffeehouse overlooking the riverfront. As the sun rises, fingers of light poke their way through the trees and dance on the water below. A gondola works its way against the current as Lou approaches.

"I walked over to the Alamo," Lou says. He takes a seat and wipes a handkerchief over his sweaty brow. "That's quite a story. Davy Crockett and Jim Bowie were part of the 150 defenders who died there. Fought three thousand Mexican soldiers. Did you know that Colonel Travis Williams sent out letters and messengers to try to get help after they were surrounded. Nobody came!"

"Losing the Alamo awakened the country, though," Marcus says, spearing a piece of French toast.

"Motorola lost its television business before it woke up," Laura says.

"I heard that," a cheerful-looking man wearing a blue suit says as he approaches the table.

"Good to see you again, Lee," Marcus says, rising and taking the man's hand. "Lou, Laura, this is Lee Craft, manager of Motorola's Automotive and Industrial Electronics Group."

"Please excuse me," Laura says, "while I extract my foot from my mouth."

"No, you had it right, Laura. We finally woke up and realized we were in a war, a shooting war. And it was the whole electronics business that was at stake," Craft says, settling into a chair. "Our first response was to transfer operations overseas and slash costs here at Seguin. But our customers wanted more than lower costs. They wanted faster response and higher quality. We were losing business because we weren't flexible enough and our manufacturing cycle time — the time from receipt of materials to the shipment of the final product to the customer — was much too long. Because of the long cycle time we had to expedite and prioritize to respond to customers, which led to major inefficiencies that drove costs out of line. Our defect and error rates were too high, and that boosted costs even higher. It's a shame we didn't realize all this a few years earlier, because we almost lost the war while we were figuring it out. Let's head over to the plant so I can introduce you to some of the team leaders. We'll start with our electronic assemblies."

Lou has never been in an electronic manufacturing plant before, and he's impressed by the shiny vinyl floors and the clean, hospital-like environment. Workers line both sides of long tables; conveyors move through the center of the long aisle.

At the front of the electronic assembly line, Craft introduces Marcus, Lou, and Laura to one of the shop floor team leaders, a petite, dark-haired woman named Rita. Lou expects her to be soft-spoken. But she surprises him with a firm handshake, pulling him closer to the easel set up beside her. "You have to take a look at this," she says. "It's a summary of improvements over the last twelve months."

- *manufacturing cycle time reduced from 7 days to 2 days*
- *7:1 decrease in final test defects*
- *30% decrease in required in floor space*

"How did you do it?" Laura asks. This is what Lou would have asked if he hadn't been so taken aback by this little woman's commanding presence.

"Our supervisor told us that we needed to reduce our cycle time. After training us in the methods for doing it, he asked us to set a goal. The goal we set was reducing cycle time from seven days to two.

"The largest lag time, three days, was due to a backlog at final test. We figured out ways to improve the test procedure so we could reduce test time by over 30 percent. In a real short time we were able to cut the backlog ahead of final test to less than an hour. That meant that our test technician was able to spend more time with the assembly operators — to help us identify, correct, and prevent errors before they got to final test. We got big increases in first-time test yields.

"Then we asked Engineering to help us on the cure time, which caused over one day's delay. We experimented until we found that reducing the amount of mask we sprayed on the board decreased the cure time from twenty-four hours to a half hour — without affecting the quality of the soldering. What's even more important than cutting all that time from the

---

Great Weapon of the Hunter

Increase the contributions of the entire workforce.

process, though, is that it allows us in assembly to get feedback within the hour from final test. Final test rejects decreased seven to one. And now that we've got cycle time down to four days, we're going back to chip away at it until we lower it to one day."

"Rita, do you mind if I ask you a personal question?" Laura says.

"Not at all."

"It's clear that you enjoy your work. Have you always felt this way?"

Rita looks at Lee and laughs. "I used to feel like I was working in a sweat shop. But that was before we started quality teams. I was just putting in time, then. Things are a lot different now."

"They sure are," Craft says. "Thanks, Rita." He leads Laura, Marcus, and Lou toward the rear of the building. "It's all about ownership," Craft says. "Operators like Rita, who used to resist taking initiative, now volunteer. We've progressed from a can't-do culture to a can-do culture. Instead of blaming people, we now recognize them for their contributions. What we've learned is that improvement must be a way of life for every person in the business, not just the managers; and the improvement must be self-directed. Quality circles taught us a lot about what not to do."

"Like what?" Marcus asks.

"Like don't leave the objectives and goals open-ended. The goals that teams set must be meaningful, and they must coincide with corporate and site goals. Achievements related to cycle time, quality, and productivity receive the most recognition. All managers are trained in methods to measure and improve in those three areas. They then propose an objective like cycle time reduction for the team and train the team in methods to improve in that area. After the training the team sets their goal. From that point on, management is there to provide support. Hey, this is everybody's war, isn't it?"

Lou has his doubts. He's particularly amused by Laura's questions. Seems to him that she knows too many fancy theories but hasn't had much *real* experience working with people. "If you turn the place over to the workers, how do you keep them from heading off in the wrong direction?"

"If the team sets goals consistent with cycle time reduction and quality improvement, if they have a process to meet the goals, and if they have supportive managers, they won't go in

---

Productivity

The most commonly accepted measure of productivity is total output per employee-hour. For example, an auto maker might measure its productivity in terms of the total number of employee-hours it takes to build a single car; an insurance company would most certainly be interested in the number of forms processed per employee per hour; and a mail-order company such as L.L. Bean probably measures the performance of its customer service representatives in terms of calls responded to per hour.

Cycle time: The time that elapses from the beginning of a process until its completion.

System cycle time or system response time: The time that elapses from the triggering of a system until it delivers a product or service. Here are some examples:

- time that elapses between receipt of an order and delivery to a customer
- time that elapses from the beginning of the development of a new product or service until that new product or service is on the market
- time that elapses from receipt of a complaint until the problem is corrected and the customer is satisfied.

the wrong direction. In the past few years we have trained everybody in a six-step continuous improvement process." Lee points to a chart on the wall.

Six Steps to Six Sigma and Beyond

1. *Define your product or service.*
2. *Identify customers and their needs.*
3. *Determine how to satisfy the customer.*
4. *Identify the process for creating your product.*
5. *Eliminate waste and defects from the process.*
6. *Measure your results for continuous improvement.*

"How do they decide what's waste?" Laura asks.

"Waste is anything that doesn't add value from the customer's perspective," Marcus says. "First the teams chart and map the process to identify all the activities and delays. Second, they examine the process for bottlenecks and delays that can be reduced. Third, they eliminate activities that add no value to the customers. Fourth, because defects produced in the process cause a lot of valueless activity and reduce the value of the product or service in your customer's eyes, an all out effort is used to eliminate defects and errors."

"What's this 'Six Sigma and Beyond' stuff?" Lou says.

"Six Sigma quality to Motorola means that the product or process is 99.9996 percent defect- and variance-free," Marcus says. "These are quality levels unheard of around here in the early eighties."

"Couldn't do that with steel production," Lou scoffs.

Marcus shakes his head. "Not the way you were operating, Lou. Quality means total customer satisfaction — not just quality of the product."

Craft adds: "It includes all administrative and service processes as well. Let me show you an example over in our shipping area."

The group walks to the rear of the building where they are met by a shipping clerk named Susan who explains that although their last customer ratings were extremely high, shipping errors were running at a level of .3 percent. She explains that this quality level would have been outstanding a few years ago, but today less than .004 percent is their goal. To achieve this level, she adds, they've installed a computer that prints a bar-code label corresponding to the order. Information contained on the bar code label includes a part number, a description, destination, and quantity. The packages are scanned at the point of shipment, and the label is scanned to see that the information matches. "Since we've been using this system," Susan says proudly, "errors have been practically nil, and that makes my job a whole lot easier."

"Our customer ratings speak for themselves," Craft says as they leave the shipping area. "We've won a number of awards for quality and we feel that we played a role in Motorola's winning the first Malcolm Baldrige Award. The bottom line in quality is that assemblies from this facility are not reinspected at our customer plants. Our customers can take our parts directly from their dock to the point of use on the assembly lines.

Great Weapon of the Hunter

Satisfy customers.

The Design, Development, and Support
of High Performance Teams

When you study companies that have been very successful in the development of teams and compare them to companies that have foundered, you will find that the successful companies share four characteristics:

- missioning and contracting
- structure
- leadership
- team development

Missioning and Contracting

First and foremost the team must have measurable goals that are relevant to the strategy of the business. For example, in Motorola's case the teams were assigned goals such as reducing cycle time, reducing defects, and reducing costs — goals that are a subset of Motorola's overall mission.

There should be a clear understanding of the responsibilities and authority (what the team will do and what they won't do) on the part of management and the team. As in the case of the team at Cincinnati Milacron, progress should be regularly reviewed.

Structure

The elements of structure are process, organization, and technology.

- Organization: team members should be located as close together as possible, considering the situation. They should have a clear reporting relationship within the business.
- Process: The team should be provided with training in decision making and problem solving.
- Technology: they should have the best tools available for the job.

Task Leadership

Good team leadership requires a broad range of leadership capabilities, including the ability to both direct and facilitate activities. The most effective leaders focus the team on the mission while at the same time developing the team's ability to manage itself.

Team Development

Teams do not start at the self-managed level regardless of the experience of the members. Their development can be compared to the process of parenting. In the early stages both teams and children need structure and direction. As they mature (Hersey and Blanchard define maturity as a combination of willingness and ability, or "will and skill"[1]), teams can manage more and more without external direction. To be effective, leaders must first be able to assess maturity level. Depending on the maturity level of the team, the flexible leader is able to provide direction and coaching in early stages of team development and provide participative and facilitative leadership in later stages. The effective leader empowers a team in proportion to its maturity.

Motorola has defined development levels that establish the level of empowerment a team should have as it graduates through the stages of development.

– Julie Thorpe

"And everything else has improved. Inventories are down plant-wide by seventy-five percent, and manufacturing cycle time has been reduced eighty percent.

"You're going to get in trouble with those low inventories," Lou warns.

Marcus frowns at Lou, then turns to Lee. "Lee, could you tell Laura and Lou how you got started?"

Craft explains how change started from the top down with a commitment to total customer satisfaction. "Nothing short of the customer saying that our products were the very best in the world was acceptable." In more specific terms, he continues, corporate goals were that Motorola was to have the fastest customer response time in the world and that all operations were to be 99.9996 percent defect- and error-free by 1992.

"Bob Galvin, our past CEO," Lee says, "was so confident that improvements in quality and cycle time mean bigger profits, that during our monthly progress reviews, he left the room during the financial report, which comes after the reports on quality and cycle time.

"Come over here," Lee continues, moving toward a large plaque on the wall. "We've posted our goals so everyone in the company can see them easily."

Our Fundamental Objective
(Everyone's Overriding Responsibility)

Total Customer Satisfaction

Key beliefs. How we will always act:

- *constant respect for people*
- *uncompromising integrity*

Key goals. What we must accomplish:

- *best in class*
  - *people*
  - *marketing*
  - *technology*
  - *product: software, hardware, and systems*
  - *manufacturing*
  - *service*

- *increased global market share*
- *superior financial results*

Key initiatives. How we will do it:

- *defects less than 4 parts per million (.0004%)*[2]
- *total cycle time reduction*
- *product, manufacturing, and environmental leadership*
- *profit improvement*
- *empowerment for all in a participative, cooperative, and creative workplace*

"So what's the bottom line? Are you winning the war?" Lou asks.

"In July of last year we successfully transferred a product from Taiwan back to Seguin because of our flexibility to produce a wide variety of models with fast response times and top quality."

"That's winning," Lou says. He likes the idea of setting far-reaching goals. Might have made a difference at Continental. He's not sure about this employee empowerment stuff, though. "You know," he says as they leave the plant, "I'm impressed that Motorola had their people all fired up about company goals."

"I agree they have them fired up, but I wouldn't have the workers making decisions. That's management's work," Laura replies.

"Motorola's philosophy," Marcus responds, "is to get everyone in every area of the business involved in a continuous redesign process. If you believe that people support what they create, then doesn't it follow that people who must implement the changes should come up with the changes?"

"But that's what management is paid to do," Laura says. "Hourly people work for a paycheck. You can't expect them to care about the company."

Lou turns sharply and glares at Laura. "You're dead wrong on that. I was an hourly worker for years and I cared. And so did almost everyone I worked with. Only people with big educations don't have to care."

Laura starts to say something but stops short. She pushes a loose strand of hair behind her ear, shakes her head, and looks to Marcus.

Marcus looks at both of them sternly, but his expression belies his inward satisfaction. This clash of egos was bound to occur. He used to see the same thing between capable commanders, who, with his guidance, had learned from each others' strengths and compensated for each others' weaknesses.

There is a pregnant silence now while Marcus decides what to say. He keeps it simple: "You both have much to learn. Let's just get back to the matter at hand. The change from direct to participative management may not seem to make much sense at first. But once this change in management philosophy takes place, continuous improvement can take place at all levels. Let's recap the process," he says, taking a cylindrical plastic object from his pocket. He holds the object upright, hits a switch, and it emits a lavender beam of light; and as they stand at the periphery of the Seguin plant's parking lot, Marcus begins to write words in the air!

Continuous Improvement Process

- *Define the mission and continually develop the strategies and objectives of the business to accomplish the mission.*
- *Communicate and sell the mission to all.*
- *Provide a process for continuous improvement and train everyone in the process.*
- *Teach managers how to facilitate the process and teach everyone how to implement it.*
- *Set performance improvement goals at the division, department, and team level.*
- *Empower people to apply the process.*
- *Ensure that the people's actions are supported and their interests are taken care of.*

"Marcus," Laura says, "where did you get that nifty toy?"

"It's called a laser-light stylus," he says, laughing.

"Should we be concerned about being seen?" Lou asks, looking around the parking lot.

"Nothing to worry about," Marcus assures him. "Now, where was I? A continuous improvement process is the bedrock of the transformation process."

Marcus writes again with his stylus:

....

Transformation — The process by which a company continually re-conceptualizes and redesigns itself to remain a Hunter.

....

"Continuous improvement is the base level of the transformation process. Let's draw a picture of the base level.

"The objectives of the improvement process are to reduce valueless time, valueless activity, and valueless variance. This improves response to customers, improves quality, and reduces cost. We will be devoting a lot of time toward learning methods for reducing valueless time, activity, and variance."

"The chart has a lot of empty spaces," Lou says.

Driving Transformational Change

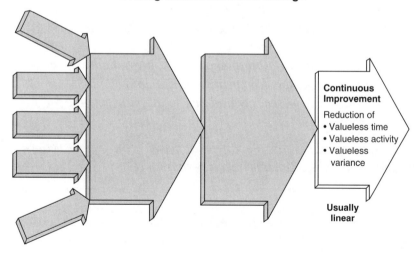

"We'll fill them in as we learn. Right now let's focus on continuous improvement."

"Lee said Motorola's success was due to employee empowerment and continuous improvement, but it seems to me that the most important thing they did was to set ambitious goals — fastest customer response and ultimate quality," Laura says.

"It was both, Laura. They analyzed competition and concluded that their quality performance lagged far behind their competitors. In effect, they realized that they had a performance gap. Let me define performance gap," Marcus says as he writes with the light stylus.

There are four ways to measure performance or performance improvement.[3]

They are:

- *comparing present performance to past performance or standards (past year sales, profit, return on investment, performance to budget)*
- *comparing customers' perceptions versus their expectations or needs (customer complaints, comment cards, surveys, focus groups, etc.)*
- *comparing our performance to the performance of our best competitors (competitive benchmarking)*
- *comparing present performance to ultimate possible performance*

Performance gap is the difference between the present performance and the ultimate possible performance.

"Now you should be beginning to get the big picture," Marcus says. "The Hunters continually measure themselves against the ultimate. They know that if their performance gap is large, either they have to close that gap or risk that a competitor will exploit their weakness. If the performance gap is large, that usually indicates that the company must dramatically increase its rate of learning and improvement. That means that continuous improvement won't be enough; the system must be redesigned. Consequently, a higher level of transformation, Delivery System redesign, is necessary. This higher level will be the focus of my next set of lessons."

"Interesting," Lou says. "At Continental Steel we focused on comparison to past performance."

Marcus nods. He explains that this is the most common approach, because it maintains the status quo; and that the Hunters, although they use all of these performance measures, focus primarily on the last three, because these are the ones that measure competitive position and competitive potential. The first measure compares the company only against its past history and its internal standards.

"People or companies don't usually realize that they have a large performance gap unless they get into deep trouble. A man called Massey calls it a significant emotional event," Laura says. "Wouldn't it be better if companies didn't wait until they were in trouble to start these approaches?"

"A friend of mine, Vaughn Beals, once said that by the time you realize that a competitor is ahead of you, it takes you longer to recover than it takes for the competitor to put you out of business," Marcus explains.

"Vaughn Beals . . . I've heard that name too," Laura says.

"Turned Harley-Davidson around. We'll visit them later."

"Was losing the TV business a significant emotional event for Motorola?" Laura asks.

"You need to get that story directly from a purchasing executive at Motorola. On our way back to Guardian Command we'll take a brief detour and stop by Motorola Headquarters in Chicago and ask Ken Stork that question. Ken is also past president of the Association for Manufacturing Excellence, an organization that promotes improvement and innovation in the field of manufacturing."

"How can we just drop in on people without an appointment?" Laura asks.

"I made an appointment."

"But how did you know ahead of time?" Laura asks.

"I knew you would ask the question."

Less than a hour later they are sitting in Ken Stork's third-floor office. "Ken," Marcus says, "when did Motorola have its significant emotional event?"

"You've always talked to me about non-linear change. Well, in 1980, we had a whale of a non-linear change, but let me give you a little history first. Years ago when friends I knew discovered that I worked at Motorola, they would ask me if I could help them get a deal on a Quasar TV, a product known for its excellence. In 1974 we exited the TV business. It was humbling, but there seemed to be no other way. In 1980, we gave up on the car radio business, a product that Motorola had invented and from which it derived its name. Again we took a jolt. But it was an event that took place in 1979 that dramatically changed us as a company. At an executive meeting, one of our top executives, Art Sundry, shook us all. He simply said 'Our quality stinks.' "

"At some companies those would have been an executive's last words. Every executive knows that you don't tell the emperor that he has no clothes. But his courageous words stirred us. In 1981 our chairman, Bob Galvin, responded decisively. In a series of advertisements he admitted that the Japanese were ahead of us, but he threw down the gauntlet. He called for everyone in Motorola to take the challenge to out-quality the Japanese. It was an unprecedented approach for an American corporate chairman. Simultaneously, he was establishing new corporate goals: we were going to have the fastest response in the world and ten-fold improvement in quality by 1986. As incredible as these goals seemed, we accepted them, and in the next few years we put in place all the structures that it took to get the job done. It was an overhaul from the top to the bottom of the organization. Many new design and manufacturing technologies were developed in this period. By 1986, we had generally achieved a ten-fold quality improvement, and we had some of the fastest responding Delivery Systems in the world.

"In 1986, Galvin reset the goal to continue improving quality ten-to-one every two years. In 1988 we won the first Malcolm Baldrige Award. Today, companies ask us to come and speak to them about how we did it. Nobody was asking us to come and speak to them in the seventies about why we were losing segments of our business. Today, Motorola has its pride back. But we know that what we're doing today isn't good enough for the future."

Leaving Ken's office, Marcus hands Lou and Laura each a drawing.

Motorola's Non-Linear Renaissance

"As you can see from the drawing, Motorola exhibits the classic pattern of the renaissance of a company. After suffering stinging setbacks in the seventies, they underwent a major change around 1980. Top management created a new vision. It's important to realize that they didn't merely improve on their past visions; they created a whole new vision of what they were going to become. I call these large shifts *non-linear* because they make a dramatic break with past thinking. This non-linear change in vision and the commitment to meet the vision resulted in non-linear changes in the minds of the Motorola management and the creation of many radically new Delivery Systems, like the Boynton Beach facility. The Boynton Beach operation produces pagers from order to shipping in two days. It was designed to be the fastest cycle time and highest quality producer of pagers in the world. You can order a color customized pager from a dealer today, and that unit will be produced and delivered to the dealer within two hours. In addition to such quick response, you get the highest quality and value for the price in a product of this kind. My point is this: if you reduce system cycle time and eliminate defects and errors, you also achieve the lowest cost."

"So the Boynton Beach facility didn't result from Continuous Linear Improvement?" Laura asks.

"That's right" Marcus answered. "And most people involved in manufacturing would agree that the radical quality and cycle time goals couldn't have been met in a linear manner, right Lou?"

"Not during my work life," says Lou.

"These non-linear changes dramatically changed the rate and quality of Motorola's learning and improvement. Motorola had discovered part of the Non-Linear Solution," Marcus says. "The Boynton Beach mobile pager line was a non-linear change; We'll be studying other non-linear changes when we meet the Hunters of the past tonight at Guardian Command.

"Businesses that have discovered the Non-Linear Solution are very flexible; they are champions of change. They look beyond past performance; they look beyond what satisfies customers today; they look beyond what the best competitors are doing today. They are guided by ultimate standards for performance. They anticipate and act before they experience trauma." Marcus pauses, then adds, "The Hunters make it happen. It happens to the Hunted."

Lou repeats the words aloud. "I like that. That says it all. But how does all this get to the bottom line?"

"What do you call bottom line?" Marcus asks.

"Productivity improvement, profits, or return on investment."

"Harvard professors Robert H. Hayes and Kim B. Clark and Indiana University professor Roger Schmenner have studied the factors that have improved productivity in hundreds of plants in the U.S., Europe, and Asia. They agree that the most important factors are improved quality, system cycle time reduction, increased work force participation, and process technology advantage." Marcus continues, "These studies indicate that Motorola has a good formula for increasing productivity: reduce system cycle time, improve quality, and increase the participation of the workforce in improvement activities."

"I'm confused," Laura says. "We first talked about Motorola's Continuous Linear Improvement success. Then you say that the big improvements were the result of non-linear change. If the basic design of the Delivery Systems is best for meeting the overall strategy of the business, then linear improvement is sufficient; otherwise, non-linear change is necessary. How do we know if the basic design is sound?"

"That's the subject of our next lessons," Marcus says.

"Are continuous improvement, employee empowerment, and performance gapping all part of the Non-Linear Solution?" Laura asks.

"Yes, they are part of it just as the change in the minds of the Motorola management is part of it. Let's get back to Guardian Command now. I've prepared a history lesson for you."

"History?" Lou says.

"History," Marcus says.

After dinner that evening at Guardian Command, Marcus leads Laura and Lou to a circular flight of steps where they descend to a dimly lit room two floors below. On one wall of the stairway is a large painting of a cheetah in full pursuit of a gazelle. Lou's eyes move to the title at the bottom of the painting, *The Hunter.*

"Real Hunter, the Cheetah," Lou says.

"But, the Cheetah has low lung capacity," Marcus explains, "If she doesn't catch the Gazelle quickly, she runs out of oxygen."

"All right, but in your opinion, which animal is the greatest hunter?"

"Man, Lou, Man!"

At the bottom of the stairway Marcus stops by a portrait of two apelike creatures huddled around a fire. The flames are reflected on the rock walls of a cave.

"Neanderthals," Marcus says softly. "They lived tens of thousands of years ago. Their remains were found along the Neander River in northern Germany. Even while these early people sat at their fire, the seeds of their extinction were already sown. South of here in what will later become France, a more advanced species of man will develop a new machine which throws a spear. With these spear throwers, which increase velocity, distance, and accuracy, the Cro-Magnon man will eventually become the dominant hunter of Europe. The Neanderthals will decrease in numbers, to be eventually replaced with these new hunters and their advanced hunting technology."

As they continue to descend, Marcus continues to explain. "This has always been the way of the Hunter — using advanced methods or tools to dominate and often destroy the Hunted.

> **Great Weapons of the Hunter**
> - Use advanced technology.
> - Use advanced methods.

And often, as in the case of these Neanderthals warming themselves by their fire, the Hunted don't realize their fate until it's too late. It took thousands of years to extinguish the Neanderthals. But to corporations, countries, or armies blind to changes taking place around them, the path to destruction may be measured in a few short years or as in the case of Attila, a few short hours."

"Attila the Hun?" Lou asks.

"At the battle of Chalons in 451 A.D.," Marcus continues, "we killed 250,000 of Attila's army in a matter of a few hours. After the battle Attila wrote in his journal:

> We have held too long to a strategy marked by swift movement, dealing death from horseback with long lances and dragging the enemy to his end by our lariats. Our battle dress and armament have been designed to serve us only under such conditions. They are not suited for infantry warfare against soldiers equipped with shields, helmets and suits of armor. The swords of the enemy have proven superior to our stone axes. Alas, ours was a plan more aligned with past victories. We must not be unprepared for new tactics employed by the enemy. We must watch him closely, using our intelligence, to detect and assess his likely methods.[4]

"You said 'we' killed 250,000? Who's 'we'?" Laura asks.

"The Roman Army — my last battle, Laura," Marcus replies as they reach the bottom of the stairs, where he turns sharply left and leads them down a short corridor to a room with a small bronze doorplate engraved with the words 'Room of the Hunters.' Marcus pushes the door aside and they enter a large circular room. Sunlight is streaming through a huge skylight, giving the whole room an ethereal glow. In the center of the room is a massive oak table with huge upholstered leather chairs. Surrounding them on the walls are dozens of beautiful paintings of people and machines. We're going to have a few short lessons on the history of the Hunters," Marcus says opening his arms and turning in a complete circle. "Meet the Hunters."

Underlying the operations of every company — working like its spine or cerebral cortex — is its value delivery system. A company's performance is the direct result of how effectively the system is structured and managed.

– George Stalk, Jr. & Thomas M. Hout
Competing Against Time

The Hunters: 1400 – 1900

Marcus walks to his left and stands before a large painting of a sea battle. "The Republic of Venice," he begins, "received word in January of 1571 that the Ottomans were planning an attack by sea by early summer. Concerned about being able to repel the attack, the Venetian Senate ordered the republic's arsenal to outfit 100 ships in six weeks."[1]

"Seems like a nearly impossible task," Laura comments.

"For any other shipbuilding operation in the world, yes. But this was no ordinary shipbuilding operation. The Venetians were well attuned to the fact that they had a history of being attacked every fifty to seventy-five years; and since the maintenance of a large navy in peacetime was costly and unnecessary, the Senate devised a creative strategy: the republic's arsenal was designed such that the Venetian war fleet could be increased to over 150 galleys on short notice. But during peacetime, the arsenal would build replacement ships at the moderate rate of twenty per year.

"The galley," Marcus continues, pointing to one of the smaller ships in the painting, "was a fascinating innovation at that time. It was probably the first ship designed solely for war. Having just a single sail, it was propelled largely by rows of oars on each side; and so, because of its superior maneuverability, it was able to flank slower enemy ships and ram them broadside.

Fifteenth-Century Standardization and Process Centers

The arsenal of the Republic of Venice,[2] which covered over sixty acres and employed about fifteen hundred workers, was the largest industrial plant in the world in the fifteenth century. It was organized according to the three stages of a galley's production. First, the carpenters built the frame. Then the planking was fastened into place and the cabins and superstructures were built. Finally, when the galley was called into service, its seams were filled with tar and pitch, the hull was covered with tar or grease, the galley was launched, the deck fixings were fastened in place, the riggings and moorings were provided, and oars and arms given out to the crew.

Components were manufactured in separate buildings. In one building spinners spun the finest Bologna hemp fiber into thread, which was wound into rope by ropemakers. Craftsworkers in other buildings manufactured cannonballs, oars, swords, rudders, spars, and benches. All pieces were numbered and stocked in a designated place close to the loading platforms. This ensured that when outfitting began, the materials could be located, retrieved, and loaded quickly and efficiently.

Uniform materials, methods, and stipulated procedures assured that all bows were made so that arrows would fit any of them; all sternposts were of uniform design so that the rudders would not have to be specially fitted to them; and all rigging and deck furnishing were also uniform. Foremen monitored compliance to standards for all components so that any component could be used for any galley. Standardized components were essential to the galley assembly line. The assembly process's short cycle time impressed a fifteenth-century Spanish traveler named Pero Tafur, who wrote the following entry in his journal:

> And as one enters the gate there is a great street on either hand with the sea in the middle, and on one side are windows opening out to the houses of the Arsenal, and the same on the other side, and out came a galley towed by a boat, and from the windows they handed out to them, from one the cordage, from another the bread, from another the arms, and from another the balistas and mortars, and so from all sides everything which was required, and when the galley had reached the end of the street, all the men required were on board, together with the complement of oars, and she was equipped from end to end. In this manner there came out ten galleys, fully armed, between the hours of three and nine.[3]

The arsenal of the Republic of Venice may very well have been the world's first large-scale assembly line.

— Joe Swartz
JoSoft, Inc.

"They were deadly, to be sure, but if the arsenal hadn't been able to produce enough of them on short notice, the Venetian navy would not have been able to defeat the Ottomans decisively at the battle of Lepanto later that year."

Marcus tells Lou and Laura that due to time constraints, he's not going to discuss the details of the arsenal's shipbuilding facility from an operations perspective. "Perhaps that will be for some other time," he says. "For now, suffice it to say that the arsenal used standardized components for what was probably the world's first large-scale assembly line. In terms of strategy . . . well, as you'll see, there are many lessons we can learn from the Venetian shipbuilders.

Lou walks to the painting and stands beside Marcus. Lou stares at a part of the painting in which a galley is plunging its iron-clad prow through the side of an Ottoman vessel. "I guess it shows that not all good ideas are new," he says.

Marcus glances at Laura, who seems less certain. "Is the lesson that the basic model for manufacturing goes back centuries?"

"That's one lesson, but there are also more important lessons here. Let's begin by defining some powerful concepts that will help us understand these lessons. The first concept is Value Delivery Systems." Marcus reaches into his jacket, removes his laser-light stylus, and turns it on. Rapidly, words begin to appear before them in the air.

A Value Delivery System consists of all the people, processes, procedures, facilities, and machines that provide a group of products, services or information to customers. Value Delivery Systems should be designed to deploy optimally the strategies of the business.

"So the Strategy was to defend Venice against very infrequent sea attacks and the arsenal was the Value Delivery System," Laura says.

"Yes," Marcus says. As Alvin Toffler has noted, the earliest Value Delivery Systems delivered violence as a means of controlling other men, land, trade routes, and resources.[4] My country of birth, the Roman Empire, was a master at designing these types of systems. Those who designed the best Value Delivery Systems became the dominant military powers — the Hunters. Starting in the eighteenth century, however, Value Delivery Systems became more a means of generating wealth through the production of goods and materials than a means of producing coercive power.

"Among the new breed of Hunters was an eighteenth-century watchmaker by the name of Thomas Tompion.[5] He designed a new type of Value Delivery System which would be a cornerstone in the development of industrial technology. This is Tompion's picture," Marcus says as he points to a small painting in a corner niche.

"Since the 1600s, watches had been assembled entirely by individual craftsmen and each was valued highly for the personal touches of its maker. Therefore, although every watch was unique, production was slow. Then, early in 1703, Tompion, a master watchmaker himself, made a breakthrough.

"Trying to increase production, but hampered by a lack of skilled watchmakers, he began experimenting with various ways to increase output before he discovered a method which was instantly successful. He first taught some previously unskilled workers to make certain components of the watch. He had one worker making wheels, one making springs, and another engraving dial-plates. Skilled craftsmen would then inspect the parts and assemble the watches. Tompion expected that the watches would be inferior and the process costly, but because they needed the increased production he took the risk. To his

Great Weapon of the Hunter

Align Process Intent with strategy.

surprise, the watches from the new process were better and the total cost of building a watch went down. Tompion had discovered one of the secrets to mass production — that improved productivity sometimes results from dividing a process into smaller tasks."

"What do you mean by *sometimes* improves productivity?" Lou says. "It's always improved by dividing the work."

"We'll discover cases later where the opposite is true, but let's not argue the point right now. The important lesson here is what Thomas Tompion did to implement a new strategy," Marcus explains.

"He changed his Value Delivery System!" Laura says enthusiastically, "from single craftsman with whole-job responsibility to dividing the work among non-craftsmen. But you implied that the opposite is sometimes true?"

"That's another lesson. There are no ways to organize work that are universally good. When Tompion started receiving more orders than he could produce, he changed his strategy. Once he changed his strategy to become a volume producer, he found that the design of his Value Delivery System couldn't do the job; he needed a new design. My point is that a business must redesign its Value Delivery System if it's to deploy a new strategy."

Lou wrinkles his nose. "You're making this too complicated. He couldn't get enough skilled labor, so he found a way around it."

Without answering, Marcus begins to write with the light stylus again:

....

Process Intent

Simply put, Process Intent is what the process is intended to do. To be competitive a Value Delivery System must be designed for customer response, customer quality, and the customer's perception of a high value-to-cost ratio. The Process Intent of the system is considered in terms of:

- *performance requirements*
- *responsiveness*
- *quality level to be achieved*
- *cost of adding value*

....

"Lou, what was the Process Intent of the arsenal?"

"To be able to build ships at a low level in peacetime, but to be equipped and ready to increase production to twenty times the peacetime rate if needed."

Marcus nods and walks around the table to the opposite side of the room. He points to another large painting. "Our next case begins about eighty years later with this great genius . . . "[6]

"Jefferson," Laura says reverently.

"And ends with *that* great genius," Marcus continues, gesturing toward another painting, "Eli Whitney. When these two brilliant men met in 1799, one could argue that it was the beginning of one of the most significant turning points in the history of manufacturing. The stage for their meeting was set fourteen years earlier, however, when, while in France, Jefferson saw a demonstration of the use of standardized parts in the manufacture of firearms that impressed him greatly.

"Let's watch to see what happened that cold day in December when Jefferson and Whitney met." No sooner has Marcus finished speaking than Lou and Laura both feel momentarily faint, as if they've arisen too quickly after having been lying down. Lou's arms and legs tingle, and he clenches his fists several times, because he's discovered that it sometimes helps the rematerialization process go more smoothly. When he feels whole, he looks up and sees four men in eighteenth-century waistcoats, jackets, and breeches gathered just below the knee. One of the men stands before a window with his hands clasped behind his back. Outside, a light snow is falling.

"That's John Adams," Marcus says, "second president of the United States. We are in his office in Washington. Jefferson is over in the corner. Officially, he still holds the office of vice president, but he'll assume the presidency in another month or so."

"Mr. President," says a man who sits at a large table made of cherry, "permit me to read from a letter written by Captain Decius Wadsworth — a man of impeccable reputation — concerning Eli Whitney's work."

"Who's speaking?" Laura asks.

"Senator James Hillhouse from Connecticut," Marcus says. "To his left is retired Brigadeer General William North."

President Adams turns from the window, approaches the table, and sits across from Hillhouse and North. "Proceed," Adams says.

Hillhouse clears his throat and begins to read aloud.

> I entertain not a doubt that the arms he is making will exceed the best workmanship ever fabricated in any country. His capacity will be larger than the national armory at Springfield, and he will be able to execute the same quantity of work with a much smaller proportion of manual labor. But most importantly, the different parts of the lock are each formed and fashioned successively by a proper machine and by the same hand and they differ so little that they can be mutually substituted.[7]

"In the field?" General North asks incredulously.

"Anywhere, anytime," Hillhouse says.

"It is patently impossible," North snaps. "With filing and fitting, yes. By an armorer perhaps. But even then I doubt it. You must be mistaken."

"He is not mistaken," Jefferson says quietly, "I have seen it."

"You have seen Whitney's work?"

"No, but on a visit to France, I met a gunsmith named Honore LeBlanc who demonstrated the idea to me."

Jefferson is interrupted by a knock on the door. A secretary enters with a note for the President.

"Eli Whitney is downstairs, gentlemen. Shall we invite him up?"

The room breaks into a discord of conversation until the double doors open and Eli Whitney enters with two men bearing a long wooden box. "Where may I put my box?" asks Whitney.

"Over here," the secretary says.

Putting the box down, Whitney fumbles with the key, opens the lid and drops it with a great clatter.

After this embarrassing moment, President Adams says amicably, "I feel I know you, Mr. Whitney. We have been talking about you."

"Mr. Whitney would like to show his work, sir," Hillhouse says.

"By all means."

Whitney pads the table with a thick cloth then begins to remove the contents of the box. He talks while he arranges his display. "General North, if I am correct, in the common way of making a musket each workman bores his barrel on a lathe, then trues it by grinding here and there; he then carves a stock and forges a lockplate. The soft lock parts are then filed and tried until they fit. He then assembles the lock plate and screws the lock plate into the stock. He repeats this process until his filing has all the parts working perfectly. After that he disassembles the parts, hardens each of them, reassembles the musket and starts on the next musket."

"Sounds essentially correct," North answers.

"And the muskets are all different," Whitney suggests.

North flushes red, "Well, of course they're different! What do you expect?"

"On the table, Mr. President, I have arranged the pieces of ten muskets. Would you please choose a barrel, Mr. President. General North, a frizzen, please; President Elect Jefferson, a trigger guard, Senator Hillhouse, a sear; everyone please choose a part from one of the piles."

"Childish exhibition, I'd say," North says.

But when the President reaches for a barrel the others follow.

"Would you place all of your parts on this end of the table, please," Whitney says. "And would General North volunteer to assemble a musket from the pieces. You do know how to do an armorer's work, don't you, General?"

"I was building muskets before you were born, young man. Where's my vise for filing and my tools?"

"No files, no vise; here's a box of screws and a screwdriver," Whitney says, smiling.

Grudgingly, the General begins to assemble the parts. The men in the room crowd in to watch. The tension is thick and North is breathing heavily. In a few minutes he has the musket lock assembled; he pulls back the cock and pulls the trigger.

"By God!" he exclaims. "That's impossible! I swear I've been tricked."

Hillhouse's laughter fills the room.

"North sure was bullheaded," Lou says. He sits at the oak table again, enjoying the warmth of the sun upon his face.

> **Great Weapon of the Hunter**
>
> Designing Process Models that optimally achieve Process Intent.

"Jefferson's meeting with the gunsmith Honore LeBlanc triggered a change in the Process Intent of musket manufacturing," Marcus says. "Wishing to end America's dependence on foreign military equipment, and dissatisfied with the poor quality of small-scale cottage industries of the time, he persuaded George Washington to stipulate interchangeability of parts in a contract for twelve thousand muskets. But only Whitney knew how to do that, and in 1798, he won the contract. He built a factory in New Haven, Connecticut, where he put into practice many significant concepts which advanced production technology. Among these were ordered, integrated work flow through the factory, standardized, interchangeable parts, focused factory areas, dedicated machines, and error-proofing mechanisms to reduce dependence on personal craft. Although Whitney never achieved total interchangeability because of the limitations of machine tools at the time, he laid important foundations for further development. That brings us to another important concept. Whitney developed an entirely new Process Model to meet this new Process Intent." Marcus writes:

....

Process Model

Simply put, the Process Model is the way that work is divided in a Value Delivery System.

....

"What was the Process Model of Whitney's Value Delivery System?" Marcus asks.

> **Process Variance:** The amount by which a process fails to meet the optimum target values that the process is designed to produce for the customer.
>
> **Example:** If a service target is to answer a telephone in three rings or less, then four rings would be a variance of one ring.

Laura responds: "He divided the work up into several process centers and narrowly limited individual job responsibility."

"Good guess. We'll talk more about process variance later in your training. We'll see that Whitney's standardization of components was a fundamental building block in all quality systems of the future. Did Whitney's Process Model and Process Intent fit the strategy that Jefferson pushed?"

"I'd say so," Lou says nodding.

"Whitney's approach fit so well, in fact, that in less than fifty years, standardized interchangeable parts and scientifically divided and controlled work were universally adopted. As steel replaced iron in the last half of the 1800s, machining precision increased. Those failing to adopt these new process models either failed completely or were relegated to small niche markets."

"Are you saying that the design of the Value Delivery System is more important than the strategy?" Laura asks skeptically.

"No. First and foremost, your strategy must be superior to the competitor." But the right strategy is not enough. One must design a superior Value Delivery System to deploy that strategy. If the Value Delivery Systems of a business are not well designed to meet the strategies, the business is vulnerable and will eventually be overcome by a more efficient Hunter. It is important to realize that strategy must dictate the design of a business's Delivery System. If strategy changes, the design must change. But it is equally important to appreciate the effect that delivery design has on strategy, as I show here.

Strategy determines Delivery System design and
Delivery System design determines strategic options

Value Delivery System
(Process Intent and Process Model)

As the delivery system increases its capability to respond quickly to customers, to produce goods or services of high quality, and to produce high value-to-cost ratios, new strategic options become available. These new strategic options become strengths that lead to new strategies."

"So, mathematically speaking, strategy and Delivery System design are functions of each other," Laura says, bringing her hands together in the shape of a tent.

"Well put," Marcus says. "Now let's define the process of transformation. We are now aware of at least two levels of the transformation process. Let me remind you of the meaning of transformation and list the two levels we now know." He writes with the stylus.

Transformation: *The Process by which a company continually reconceptualizes and redesigns itself to remain a Hunter. The two basic levels of the transformation process are:*
- *a systematic approach to Continuous Linear Improvement*
- *a systematic approach to continuous Non-Linear redesign of the Value Delivery System*

"Why do you make it so complicated with these levels?" Lou asks.

"To learn to help businesses transform themselves, you need to understand how transformation takes place. Only then can you make it happen. Let's draw two levels of transformation."

Driving Transformational Change

Delivery Systems Redesign
⇨ New Process Intent
⇨ New Process Model
⇨ New Learning and Improvement System
⇨ New Value-Adding Technology

Continuous Improvement
Reduction of
• Valueless time
• Valueless activity
• Valueless variance

Often non-linear

Usually linear

"What is the Learning and Improvement System you've listed on the chart?" Lou asks.

"We can understand the Learning and Improvement System by re-examining the Motorola story. When Motorola installed their continuous improvement process, they were changing their Learning and Improvement System. As the people became empowered, the rate of learning and improvement increased. And as managers were rewarded for the improvement in response and quality of their systems, learning and improvement toward the goals were increased."

"So the reward system is part of the learning and improvement system," Laura says.

"Very important part," Marcus says.

"What's the difference between learning and improvement?" Laura asks.

"I distinguish between the two for a purpose. You are learning right now as new concepts and new ideas are entering your brain. Improvement is the process by which you use your learning to change what you do, change what others do, or change the system that affects our lives."

"On the chart you show that continuous improvement is usually linear. I understand that. But why is Delivery System redesign often Non-Linear?"

"Delivery System redesign changes are usually Non-Linear in that the changes are often abrupt and substantial. To help understand Non-Linear change, let's review the Non-Linear changes that our pioneers made in their Delivery Systems:

"Thomas Tompion dramatically changed the Process Model for manufacturing watches. Thomas Jefferson pushed for a dramatic change in Process Intent for musket manufacture, and Eli Whitney invented a whole new Process Model to accommodate that Process Intent. Motorola abruptly changed the Process Intent of all its operations when it made radical changes in their cycle time and quality goals. Motorola also changed the design of its Learning and Improvement System by leaps and bounds when it committed itself to ongoing education and training of its work force, thus empowering them to improve continuously. Modern banks and Federal Express have made Non-Linear changes in the Process Model for banking and small package transfer. Does that help, Lou?"

"It does."

Marcus walks further down the row of paintings and stops at a portrait of a bearded man. "Here's another example. In 1841, an enterprising young man approached his boss with the idea of expanding their New York-based express service to the port of Buffalo, because this rapidly growing port was becoming a gateway to the west.[8] His boss scoffed, suggesting that if the young man felt so strongly about express to the Rocky Mountains, that he should do it himself.

"And that's just what Henry Wells did. He quit his job and for the next eighteen months, he took a primitive train from downtown New York to the end of the line at Auburn, a stagecoach from Auburn to Geneva, another train from Geneva to Batavia, and another stage from there to Buffalo. Twice per week he would endure the unheated train cars which jumped the track at least once per trip and survive the violent bucking of the stagecoaches on the rough roads to deliver his carpetbag filled with gold, silver, currency, and commercial paper. Express service had come to Buffalo. In 1850, Henry Wells and his business partner, William Fargo, named their thriving express business American Express, which would in later years innovate many other transfer services such as money orders, traveler's checks, and credit cards."

Laura is puzzled. "Since his Process Intent and Process Model weren't really different from his employer's, his was a linear change, wasn't it?"

"I'd say so. But this case demonstrates another characteristic of an enterprise — flexibility." Marcus writes:

....

Flexibility

- *ability to anticipate the need to change*
- *ability to change or adapt to change*

....

"Where did Henry Wells's employer rank on flexibility?" Marcus asks.

"Low," Lou says.

"Their Value Delivery System was flexible enough. The lack of flexibility was in their heads," Laura says.

"Their heads are part of a larger system that we'll talk about later," Marcus says. "In the 1800s new value-adding technology was invented which had a major impact on the design of Value Delivery Systems. Oliver Evans's high pressure steam engines provided the power that moved trains and steamboats, revolutionizing Value Delivery Systems for transportation. Steam engines also dramatically improved the productivity of grain processing and manufacturing. The development of mechanical reapers improved farm productivity.

"Information systems were transformed first by telegraph machines and later by telephones which magically transmitted messages hundreds of miles in minutes, accelerating the quest to conquer space and time. By the end of the Civil War, 200,000 miles of telegraph line had revolutionized business and personal communication, journalism, and politics. Electric generators were enabling the wide distribution of electric power."

Lou and Laura join Marcus as he stands before a portrait of a young man with a mustache wearing a top hat and long coat. The plate at the bottom of the portrait reads "Herman Hollerith." "Information Value Delivery Systems were revolutionized again in 1890 by an invention so remarkable that it deserves our presence at its inception. It started when this young engineer at the U.S. Census Bureau, Herman Hollerith, took a fancy to the daughter of a co-worker, Dr. John Billings.[9] To pursue his interest, he managed to get himself invited to the Billings' home in the Georgetown section of Washington, D.C. A conversation between Hollerith and Dr. Billings initiated the development of one of the largest corporations on earth. We're going to eavesdrop, unseen, on the momentous dinner conversation between the two men."

Once again, Lou and Laura find themselves unseen entities in a past century. There are four people sitting at a mahogany dining table: Dr. Billings, his wife, his daughter, and Hollerith.

"It takes years to count census data," Billings says. "Tallying with dip pen and ink worked fine in 1790 when there were only four personal questions for four million people. We've barely changed the method, but now we have over fifty million people answering scores of inquiries. Either we come up with a new way or we won't finish counting the 1880 census before we have to begin the 1890 census. It took us years to count the last one in 1870. How about some lemon for your tea, Herman?"

"That would be nice," Herman replies. "What do you think is needed, Dr. Billings?"

"All these new machines are being invented for everything else . . . Someone ought to invent a machine to do the tabulating and counting."

"How could that be done?"

"I was thinking of cards with notches at the corners. For example, a notch on the right edge of the card would mean "male," while one on the left would indicate "female." The machine would quickly feed the card and register on one counter those with right hand notches and those with left hand notches on the other counter."

"It could be powered by electricity," Hollerith says, excitedly.

"Do you know about electricity?" Billings asks as he lights his pipe.

"Of course, sir, from my engineering training at Columbia College."

"Then why don't you invent a machine?"

"What happened then?" Lou asks, irritated at having been pulled back so abruptly to the twentieth century.

Marcus sits upon the edge of the table in the room of the Hunters. "In the following years, Hollerith learned all the details of how census results were tabulated and he built many small wooden models of card readers to test his ideas. But it was during a trip to the American West that he had a significant conceptual breakthrough. In the year or so prior to his trip, there had been a rash of train robberies in that part of the country. Because the robbers typically posed as passengers, the U.S. government asked the railroads to keep detailed records of everyone who rode the rails; and the railroads came up with an ingenious method for doing so. They devised tickets on which, by using a hole punch, conductors could record each passenger's hair color, build, height, and nose size.

"When Hollerith discovered these 'punch-photographs' the railroads were using, he'd found the final piece of the puzzle; and by 1887, he had created a punch-card electric tabulating machine that worked very efficiently. It worked so well, in fact, that the city of Baltimore allowed him to use it to tabulate death records. In just days, he and his battery-operated machine tabulated more data than a dozen clerks could have completed over a period of several weeks.

"Using thirty of Hollerith's machines, the Census Bureau was able to tabulate the results of 1890 census in just six weeks. As you can imagine, the business world was quick to see the potential that lay in such a machine, and by 1910, Hollerith had leased hundreds of his machines to businesses. In 1911 he sold his tabulating machine company to a group who would later take the name International Business Machines — better known to us as IBM.

"The lesson in Herman Hollerith's story is that the new Process Intent of shortening the time to tabulate the U.S. census led to a machine which revolutionized the Process Model for tabulating information."

"So sometimes the Value Delivery System is redesigned by developing a new machine or a new technology," Laura says.

"Yes. Often the elements of time and customer response are the prime Drivers of redesign," Marcus replies. "One last thought: serendipity can bring about a change in Process Intent.

"In 1879, a customer wrote Procter and Gamble with the request that they would like to buy more of 'the soap that floats.' The production people at P&G were bewildered. Somehow they had produced a bad lot, getting too much air in the Ivory soap. The problem was traced to a worker who had left a batch of soap to mix and stir too long in a mechanical stirrer because he was more interested in lunch. Harley Procter saw the soap that floated as not only useful but a competitive advantage. In addition to the selling point that their soap was 99.44 percent pure, P&G could also advertise that it floated. So they changed their Process Intent and Process Model to take advantage of the process that had accidentally been discovered."

Marcus removes his light stylus and writes on the wall. "Let's summarize lessons learned from our first study of the Hunters."

Lessons Learned

- *A Value Delivery System consists of all the people, processes, procedures, facilities, and machines that provide a group of products, services, or information to customers. Value Delivery Systems have three characteristics: Process Intent, Process Model, and the design of the Learning and Improvement System.*
- *Once a strategy is determined, the designer of the Value Delivery System must then determine Process Intent.*
- *Hunters often redesign their Value Delivery Systems abruptly, changing Process Intent and Process Models. We call such changes Non-Linear.*
- *Major changes in technological capability such as the telephone, the Hollerith machine, or accidental discoveries may dramatically change the Process Model.*

- *Flexibility is the ability to anticipate the need for change or the ability to change and adapt to change.*
- *Hunters are flexible and they constantly develop new strategies to win customers.*
- *There are no universally good Process Models. Their suitability is determined by how well they meet the Delivery System's Process Intent.*
- *Delivery System design and capability determine strategic options.*

"Enough for tonight. Get some rest for a trip to Ford tomorrow to learn more about flexibility," Marcus says as he walks from the room.

"I understand you have some big degrees," Lou says a few minutes later.

"Depends on what you call big," Laura says, continuing to write.

"I was told you're an engineer."

Laura nods. "I started as an engineer."

"Marcus says you got an MBA from Harvard. But, you know, I don't think all the degrees in the world can beat good, solid experience," Lou says, his bushy gray brows arching mischievously.

Laura stops writing, straightens her shoulders, and stares intently at Lou. "Good night," she says as she gathers her things and walks from the room.

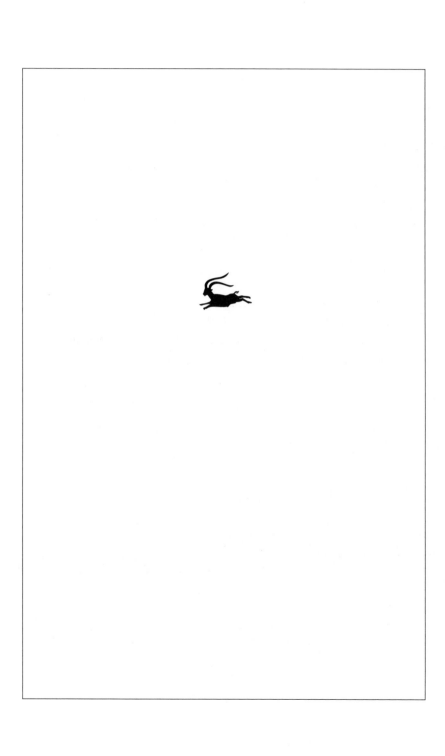

Time waste differs from material waste in that there can be no salvage. The easiest of all wastes, and the hardest to correct, is the waste of time, because wasted time does not litter the floor like wasted material.

– Henry Ford
Today and Tomorrow, 1926

CHAPTER SEVEN

The Hunters: 1900 – 1930

A s they break through the rain clouds, they notice something strange. Marcus said they were headed for Detroit and the Ford Motor Company, but the landscape is wooded with an occasional farm or cluster of homes. As they approach the ground, there appears to be a vintage car exhibition with many older cars and horse-driven carriages on the road. The Ford parking lot is filled with Model Ts. People are dressed in clothing that Lou hasn't seen since he was a small boy. After his rematerialization is complete, he notices that he is now wearing a double-breasted black wool suit.

"What's going on?" he says. He, Laura, and Marcus are sitting inside a Model T.

"It's 1925," Marcus says. "We're about to have a meeting with the father of cycle time management, Henry Ford." Lou is astonished, but his astonishment turns to amazement once they are inside the plant and Ford's secretary is leading them through the large oak door into Ford's inner office.

He's smaller than Lou imagined . . . boyish looking, but with a wrinkled face. His hair is parted perfectly in the middle with little wings to either side. He has deep-set eyes, thin hands, and long fingers.

After introductions, Marcus states the purpose of their visit. "Mr. Ford, we have come a long way to learn about your philosophy of minimizing the cycle time and eliminating waste from your whole manufacturing system." Ford leans forward in his chair and looks directly at Laura. "Are you sure this kind of thing interests you? It would present no problem at all for my secretary to — "

"I'm quite sure I'm interested in what you have to say, Mr. Ford," Laura says pleasantly. "Please, tell us about this . . . this cycle time stuff."

"Well then," Ford says, rubbing his hands together, "let's begin.[1] The time element in manufacturing stretches from the moment the raw material is separated from the earth to the moment the finished product is delivered to the ultimate customer. If we were operating today under the methods of 1921, we should have on hand raw materials valued at about a hundred and twenty million dollars and we should have unnecessarily in transit finished products valued at about fifty million dollars. Instead of that, we have an average investment of only about fifty million dollars, or, to put it another way, our inventory, raw and finished, is less than it was when our production was only half as great.

"The expansion of our business since 1921 has been paid out of cash on hand, which under old methods would have lain idle in piles of iron, steel, coal, or in finished automobiles stored in warehouses. We do not own or use a single warehouse. We take care to limit the amount of inventory on our shop floor to one shift's worth, because having a stock of raw material or finished goods in excess of requirements is waste — which, like every other waste, turns up in high prices and low wages.

"We surround ourselves with reliable suppliers, many on our own property, making our assembly operations close to self-sufficient. I expect that less than three days will elapse between the mining of the iron ore and the exit of the finished automobile from the plant."

"That seems almost impossible," Lou says.

Ford smiles. "Lou, I'm going to personally walk you through the process from the receipt of the ore to the completion of the engine and you can judge for yourself. Ask Marcus, he helped us think it through."

Lou looks at Marcus incredulously as they leave Ford's office and walk to the plant.

At the dock, Ford explains. "After a trip of approximately forty hours from Marquette, the ore boat docks here at the River Rouge plant, let's say at seven in the evening on Monday. These unloaders start removing cargo, which is transformed over here to the high line, and from there to the skip car which charges the blast furnace. By continuous process this takes ten minutes."

When they walk into the foundry, Lou feels at home. He is fascinated and invigorated. This is where it's happening. Ford stops at a cupola and continues. "Seven hours later the ore has been reduced to foundry iron. It is then cast into pig iron and sent to the foundry, where it is remelted with certain proportions of scrap. This takes about four hours in all. The blast furnace metal is also cast direct, which saves four hours."

"Let's move to the mold conveyor," Ford says as he leads them away. "This conveyor brings the molds past the pouring station where the hot metal is cast into cylinder blocks. These then go to the shake-out station and are taken away to cool and be cleaned. The cooling and cleaning process requires several hours.

"At this end of the foundry line the castings go to the machining operations," Ford explains as they walk. "There are fifty-eight operations in all, all of which are done in approximately fifty-five minutes. You will note that all of these operations are performed in the foundry building — a departure from conventional practice, but in line with the Ford method of continuous operation.

"At about 6:00 A.M. the motor block is ready for the assembly line. Ford mechanics have reduced the time required for motor assembly to an average of ninety-seven minutes. This includes everything, even an electrically controlled block test. Except for running in the motor to loosen it up, everything is done on the move.

"When the motor is finished, this conveyor transports it to the loader, which places it on a freight car, and it is shipped to a branch for assembly into a finished car. Allowing twelve hours for transit in the midwest, the engine would arrive at the branch plant by 8:00 A.M. the following morning, where standardized assembly lines will have the engine in a car ready to be driven away four hours later. By noon the dealer will have taken delivery and paid for it," Ford says proudly as they walk past a row of cars ready for shipment. "We have reduced our average total production cycle time from twenty-one days in 1920 to two days today," Ford says. "That's a reduction of ninety percent."

"Mr. Ford," Laura interrupts, "this didn't all happen overnight. When did your first breakthrough ideas develop?"

"Let's head back to the office and I'll answer that one for you."

As Ford leans back in his chair, he remains silent for a long while. "Have to take you back a few years," he says finally. "Continuous, moving disassembly had been practiced for years at the Cincinnati slaughter yards. A carcass moving on an overhead rail was progressively disassembled into smaller and smaller pieces. But continuous progressive assembly was as yet unproven in the auto industry.

"Before the turn of the century Lewis Roebuck had developed a very sophisticated assembly line that each day automatically opened 27,000 mail order letters, sorted them, and distributed the orders to the appropriate stock rooms via pneumatic tube. We had studied both the slaughterhouses and the Sears letter handling system.

"Back in the spring of 1913, in the magneto department at Highland Park, we made a revolutionary discovery. Trying to increase production, workers were lined up side by side, each assigned one or two of the twenty-nine operations that had previously been done by a single worker. The assembly labor time per magnet immediately dropped from fifteen minutes to thirteen minutes. When a motorized conveyor belt was added and further balancing was done, the labor per motor dropped to five minutes. We added a conveyor for engines and transmissions with similar results. The subassembly areas were by then producing at much faster rates than the final assembly team could assemble the motors.

"Similar analysis of the final assembly led to a rope-tow for the chassis. A team of six assemblers moved along with the chassis, picking up parts located along the way, and they assembled as they went. Finally, our engineers moved the final assembly workers to stationary positions along a moving line at just above waist level and supplied all the material at that level. Work was further subdivided again and assembly time fell from nine hours to less than two hours per chassis.

"These discoveries constituted a revolution in approach and were immediately instituted in all operations in the Highland Park plant. Every piece of work in the shop moved on hooks, on overhead chains, on moving platforms, or by gravity; there was no manual moving or lifting of anything. From 1913 to 1914, we doubled our production with no increase in work force. Our engineers believed they had found magic."

"I noticed you had inspectors at the end of each line," Lou says.

"That's another key to our production — inspection. Inspectors make up more than three percent of our entire work force. This is a practice that simplifies management. Every part in every stage of its production is inspected.

"If a machine breaks down, a repair squad will be on hand in a few minutes, but machines do not often break down, for there is continuous cleaning and repair work on every piece of machinery in the place. When new tools are needed, there is no delay. Tool rooms are provided for every department.

"It is impossible to repeat too often that waste is not something which comes after the fact. Picking up and reclaiming the scrap left over after production is a public service, but planning so that there will be no scrap is a higher public service. All of this has greatly contributed to our vision of an affordable, highly reliable car."

Marcus stands. "Mr. Ford, I know that you have another appointment shortly and we need to be running along."

He stands and shakes Marcus's hand. "Marcus, we really appreciate the help you have been to us over the years. Wish we could see more of you, but I know you're busy."

Lou is astonished. This Marcus has had his hands in everything.

After they leave the Ford complex, Marcus takes Lou and Laura for coffee at the Dearborn Inn. "This is still the best coffee I've tasted this century," he says.

"Nice that you can keep coming back for more," Lou jokes.

Marcus smiles. "It's one of the few perks I get." He tucks a heavily starched linen napkin into his collar and watches as the waiter, a thin fellow with brilliantined hair and a pencil-thin mustache, pours steaming black coffee into white porcelain cups. "What are you thinking about, Laura?" Marcus asks.

Throughput

Throughput is the quantity of products or services that flow completely through a Delivery System. The most effective way to increase throughput is to increase the rate of production at the worst bottleneck in the Delivery System.

"It amazes me that all this was done so well at this time. The Ford engineers had those line jobs analyzed down to the second. They knew how to get peak production and through-put out of the workers."

"But I don't think I'd want to be treated like a piece of machinery," Lou says indignantly.

"That's what they're paid for," Laura says.

"Listen to Miss Ironpants," Lou retorts.

"It's just dollars and cents, Lou."

Marcus interrupts quickly. "What was Ford's Process Intent, Laura?"

"To produce a large volume of one model at low cost."

"No doubt that Ford's Process Intent for his factory was revolutionary," Marcus says. "How about his Process Model?"

Laura takes a quick sip from her coffee then says, "Highly divided, standardized jobs."

"Right," Marcus says, "you've got the essence of it."

"But the thing is, there was a weak spot in his design. The plant was designed to produce one model. The machinery and tooling were highly dedicated to that one design and changing them would be costly. If the customer wanted anything differ-ent, he had to have it put on after Ford delivered the car. So Ford wasn't flexible to the demand for variety in the new mar-ketplace; he was sticking with his original Process Intent and Process Model."

Finding Out What Customers Value

In 1985, Cadillac Motor Company's John Grettenberger involved auto dealers in the development of new cars. They found that Cadillac customers wanted roomier, more distinctively styled cars in addition to the high quality and excellent engineering they expected from Cadillac. Presently, Eldorados and Sevilles have dramatically new styling because Cadillac asked its customers what they value. These models have been extremely well received by media and customers alike.

"Big deal," Lou says. "Variety didn't matter back then."

"Of course it did, "Laura says incredulously. "My dad used to say that Ford said you could have any color you wanted so long as it was black; and if it weren't for that kind of inflexibility, General Motors — which introduced a variety of different models as well as yearly model changes — never would have penetrated the market as much as it did. So what I'm saying, Lou, in terms of what we've been learning, is that Ford was for continuous improvement and change as long as the product or Process Model didn't change."

Ford Development to 1928

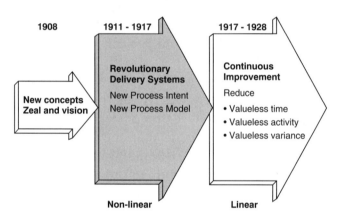

Marcus adds: "It was 1912 when he said that, but you're right. Flexibility *is* an extremely important attribute of a successful business. Ford was very flexible to the increasing volume requirements but inflexible to the desire for variety. He was in a linear improvement mode. He assumed that the Process Intent and the Process Model with which he had achieved so much success would always meet the market demand if he could just continue to refine and improve them. After he invented a revolutionary Value Delivery System, he then stayed in a linear improvement mode until he had no choice but to respond to General Motor's revolutionary Value Delivery System. From 1917 to 1928 Ford was operating with a Continuous Linear Improvement model, where continuous improvement take place but where the Process Intent and the Process Model remain the same.

"So the conclusion is that no company, even Motorola, can afford to stay forever in a linear mode," Lou says.

"You've got it! Motorola doesn't rely on simply the Continuous Linear Improvement approach. They are also constantly transforming their business with revolutionary Value Delivery Systems like the Bandit Pager line in Boynton Beach that I mentioned earlier."

"In the beginning Ford came up with a new Process Intent and some new Process Models, so would you say that his approach was originally Non-Linear?" Laura asks.

"In the beginning he used a Non-Linear approach, but then he went linear," Marcus responds.

Lou taps his finger on the table. "There were sound reasons for Ford's thinking. There's a big tradeoff here; the greater variety a business offers, the greater the overhead costs."

"True, Lou. Normally, as a business offers more models or a greater variety of services, costs tend to go up. When variety is increased by one hundred percent, some costs may increase as much as fifty percent. The Hunters' goal is to have their cake and eat it too. They learn how to increase variety without incurring the increased costs of variety.

"How do they pull that off?" Lou asks.

Great Weapon of the Hunter

Provide variety without incurring the added costs usually associated with it.

"By reducing the time and costs of changeovers, reducing the time and cost of introducing new models, and many other techniques that we're going to study. All of these approaches improve a business's flexibility.

"Can't they charge more for variety?"

"Yes, they charge more for variety, response, higher quality, and higher performance. But they have also learned how to produce this added value at low costs."

"Sounds too good to be true," Lou remarks.

"The big lesson here has to do with flexibility. Let's compare the Ford of 1910 with the Ford of 1925 on the two measures of flexibility — ability to anticipate the need for change, and ability to change or adapt to change. Lou, how would you rank Ford on the first measure, the ability to anticipate the need to change?"

"High in the beginning, but later he lost a lot of his ability to change. It took him a long time to respond, not until 1936 if I remember right."

"Good analysis. Laura, how about the second measure, the ability to change or adapt to change?"

"Their delivery system had dedicated machines. A change from one model to another would have been extremely difficult. So, I'd have to say he'd get a low ranking," she says.

"You're forgetting something," Lou says. "When Ford came along in the business, he succeeded for that very reason. He focused. He saw what the other manufacturers of the day were doing with variety and he rejected it. I can see why he rejected the variety approach."

"True, Lou. And that was a good model for the times. But times changed. When the Hunter invents a very successful Process Intent or Process Model which makes the existing way of doing business obsolete, he seldom can reconsider the old ways, even if those ways might provide the solutions for remaining competitive at the time."

"I've run into that," Laura says. "People say that they've tried that or that's the way they used to do it before they improved. They get set in their ways."

"I can understand Ford's position, but the point I'm trying to make is that although a systematic process for Continuous Linear Improvement is a powerful base from which to improve, it is not enough." Marcus starts to take out his light stylus but looks around and decides against it. "Let's get some exercise and continue our discussion outside," he says, dropping some change onto the table.

Outside, they walk for about an hour in silence along a dirt road until they come to an open, grassy field that slopes down towards a bend in the Rouge River. Marcus leads them to the river's edge, and taking out his light stylus, he writes upon the surface of the dark water.

As the market changes dramatically, there must be a systematic process for achieving Non-Linear redesign of the Value Delivery System.

"What do you think of that statement, Lou?"

"All these trips back in time are interesting," Lou says impatiently, "but when are we going to get on with the job of helping businesses turn themselves around?"

Marcus turns slowly to face Lou. "If you don't know the fundamentals, you won't be much help to anybody, and I know you want to help." Marcus gives him the light stylus, and Lou handles it gingerly. "Go on," Marcus says, "give it a try. Summarize a couple things that you've learned from our visit to Ford today, then give Laura a turn." Sure beats a fountain pen, Lou thinks as he begins to write upon the river's surface.

Lessons Learned

- *Henry Ford developed a new Process Intent for the auto industry — to build reliable, low cost cars which would be affordable enough to attract a wider base of buyers. As volume increased and operations were improved, costs were further reduced. To implement this Process Intent, Ford invented a new Process Model for the auto industry — continuous flow assembly.*
- *Although Ford brought many Non-Linear changes to the auto business, he worked himself into a position of inflexibility.*

Laura takes the stylus from Lou and adds two more points beneath his.

- *Ford mastered the art of Continuous Linear Improvement by eliminating non-value-adding activities from the process. He used inspection and preventive maintenance primarily as a means of controlling variance so that his continuous flow assembly processes would be uninterrupted.*
- *Ford failed, however, to drive Non-Linear redesign of his Value Delivery Systems as the market changed. He rejected the variety model. He waited until he had no other choice but to change.*

"Let's move on and study the application of these concepts to the production and distribution of food. We'll take the scenic route to Pasadena, and I'll tell you a story about the rise of a great food merchandising company."

"Marcus, if you were working with Henry Ford, why didn't you advise him of the consequences of inflexibility?" Lou says.

"I did advise him."

"Too bullheaded, I'll bet."

"He was a strong-willed man," Marcus says.

Takes one to know one, Laura thinks to herself. "Marcus, how long have you been helping businesses?" she asks as they rise above the treetops and begin to travel west.

"About fourteen-hundred years."

"And you're still interested?"

"I learn something new every day."

If Henry Ford were alive today, he would conceive of and implement a system very much like the Toyota production system.

– Taiichi Ohno
Toyota Motor Co.

CHAPTER EIGHT

The Hunters: 1930 – 1950

*I*n 1932," Marcus says as the Mississippi River comes into view, "with the country still in the throes of the Great Depression, the huge Big Bear market opened in the vacated Durant Motor Car plant in Elizabeth, New Jersey.[1] The owner of the market devoted an entire floor of this gigantic warehouse to selling dry grocery items out of opened shipping cartons, priced only slightly above cost.

"Big Bear's advertised low prices, together with a new amenity — plenty of free parking — attracted consumers in carloads from miles around. The total operation generated amazing sales — $100,000 per week — equal to the total weekly volume of all one hundred A&P stores in the surrounding Newark/Elizabeth area.

"A&P had been king of the retail hill for over fifty years but now they were one of the Hunted. As other so-called supermarkets opened, with lower overheads and self-service, George Hartford, the innovative founder of A&P, watched and waited with a mixture of fear and hope; fear that this was the trend of the future and hope that as soon as better times returned and the public could afford the convenience and services of the familiar neighborhood store, they would return."

"Waiting and watching was not what had built A&P. Seventy-three years earlier, Hartford had spotted a weakness in the system that brought tea to the marketplace. He noted that between the Asian tea producer and the customer were many middlemen — exporters, foreign exchange bankers, shippers, importers, brokers, wholesalers, and finally retailers. The retailers sold the tea at one to two dollars per pound, making very large profit margins. George Hartford eliminated most of the middlemen, reduced profit per pound and sold the tea at less than a dollar per pound. From this beginning, A&P added a complete food line and grew at a phenomenal rate.

"John, George's son, knew what had to be done. He felt that the supermarket, in whatever modified form, was clearly the wave of the future and A&P had no choice. If they were to survive, they would have to bite the bullet and convert their operations as quickly as possible. But his father chose to wait. Not until 1936, with the Hunters closing in and the company threatened with extinction, did his father finally relent and agree to an experiment with 100 supermarkets. By the spring of 1937, at John's urging, it was agreed to increase the experiment to include 300 supermarkets. At last the giant had awakened — A&P was again the Hunter.

"While A&P had been agonizingly slow in making the decision to enter the supermarket arena, it was the first major chain store ever to attempt a rapid and total conversion of a previously successful formula. Most of the other grocery chains of that time didn't react and therefore didn't survive. It was this flexibility that kept A&P at the top of the retail food chain for 100 years."

"I remember the first supermarket I ever saw," Lou says. "Our whole family drove fifty miles to get there. It was a big thing in those days. That was a *big* Process Model change."

"The Hunter changed the Process Model for retailing food," Marcus replies. "The self-service concept ran counter to everything the older Hartford believed."

"But the low-price, high-volume idea was the weapon George Hartford used against his competition when he first started," Laura says. "It's ironic that when his own tactic was used against him, he waited so long to respond. So the older Hartford would rank low on our flexibility scale."

"High when he started, low later on. Often works that way with the Hunter. Success can be blinding," Marcus says. "The rise of A&P had a Non-Linear beginning and in its midlife was slow to respond to Non-Linear changes introduced by competitors. In A&P's later life, inflexibility would cause its decline."

Rise of A&P

Mismanagement
Union strife
Staff controls
Malls

Supermarkets

Expansion

Addition of full food line

Building the Delivery Systems

Direct purchase concept

"Next stop, Pasadena, 1941, to meet a couple of guys who changed both the Process Intent and the basic Process Model for the restaurant business."

En route, Laura asks, "Can we go forward in time?"

"Yes," Marcus says.

"Will we?"

"We will after you have become Master Guardians."

"Wouldn't it help us right now to know the future?"

"Probably not. You might lose your ability to influence business people."

"I'd think it'd be just the opposite."

"The people you will help can't see the future, Laura. They will accept lessons from the past and present, but not from the future."

"How do you know they won't?"

"I tried it a few times."

"You mean you looked into the future, saw something they could do, but they wouldn't do it?"

Marcus nods his head. "People must see it for themselves."

1941, Pasadena: "Hey, Marcus, what do you think? Just reopened yesterday," Dick McDonald says, sweeping his arm in a circle to indicate the whole restaurant.[2]

"Impressive, Dick. Could you explain to Laura and Lou why you closed?"

"We closed the store and redesigned it for fast response and low cost. We replaced our three-foot grill with two six-foot grills we designed and built ourselves. We designed this stainless steel lazy susan that holds twenty-four hamburger buns to be dressed by two crewmen. We cut our twenty-five-item menu to nine items, made all hamburgers the same with ketchup, mustard, onion, and two pickles, replaced china and flatware with paper bags, wrappers, and paper cups, and cut the cost of the hamburger to fifteen cents. We've been open about two weeks now."

"What brought this all about?" Laura asks.

"It had been coming for a long time. My brother, Mac and I, opened our first McDonald's drive-in restaurant here in 1937. By 1940 we opened a second drive-in with carhops for faster service. But even that didn't satisfy us. Our whole concept was based on speed, lower prices, and volume. We were going after big volumes by lowering prices and by having the customer serve themselves. My God, the carhops were slow. We'd say to ourselves that there had to be a better way. The cars were jamming the lot. Customers weren't demanding it, but our intuition told us that they would like speed. Everything was moving faster. The supermarkets and dime stores had already converted to self-service and it was obvious the future of drive-ins was self-service! That's when Marcus visited and got us all excited about customer response time."

"And how is it going?" Laura asks.

"Sales are up forty percent, labor costs are down by a third, and profits are up. It worked just the way we thought it would."

"I thought Ray Kroc started McDonald's," Lou says.

"Ray who?" Dick asks.

Marcus glares at Lou. "Just stopped for a minute, Dick. Good to see you again. Say hi to Mac for me," he says abruptly. "Glad you could stop in. I'll tell Mac . . . he'll be sorry he missed you. Here — take a couple for the road," Dick says, handing them a sack full of burgers.

"Thanks, I'll stop by again," Marcus says.

As soon as they pass through the front doors, Marcus turns on Lou. "Can't you get it straight?" His voice is controlled but clearly has an edge to it. "You're not to do anything that will reveal our identity."

"What are you talking about?"

"Ray Kroc! That's what I'm talking about. He didn't come on the scene until 1954 when he came to McDonald's San Bernardino store to find out what in the world they could be doing with eight of the multimixer milkshake machines he was selling. When he saw their delivery system he realized the potential for franchising their idea."

"Ease up," Lou says, "I'm sorry."

Marcus takes a deep breath. "Okay, Lou."

"So that's how the largest restaurant business on earth got started," Laura says in an obvious attempt to cool things down. "I'd give the McDonald brothers an 'A' for flexibility."

"That's how it happened and I'd have to agree that they were very flexible. But, what change did they make in Process Intent?"

"Faster response and lower costs," Lou answers.

"Good. Let's find a park where we can taste the 1941 original McDonald's burger and I'll tell you another story about designing a delivery system for success," Marcus says.

"In 1951, Kemmons Wilson returned to Memphis outraged after a road trip with his wife and their five children.[3] During their travels there had been only two alternatives: cheap fleabags or fancy city hotels. Wilson's disgust gave him an idea.

"Being a builder and developer, Wilson soon erected four ranch-style motels. For six dollars a night, he offered a double room with no extra charge for the children. He also offered his guests free ice, free baby beds, free in-room television, free advance reservations, and self-service baggage handling. Wilson knew what traveling families needed, and also arranged for baby-sitter references, physicians and dentists on call, restaurant service at reasonable prices, swimming pools, and playground equipment. He named his new creation "Holiday Inn."

"These amenities may seem commonplace to us, but in the years after World War II they were nothing short of revolutionary. People were amazed at how well their needs had been anticipated. The Process Intent and the Process Model that Kemmons Wilson developed to meet his strategy were right on target. He invented a whole new Delivery System."

"I remember the first time I stayed at a Holiday Inn," Lou says. "It was in 'fifty-four in El Paso. It was impressive in those days, just like these burgers; sure don't make 'em like this any more."

Marcus nods. "Finish up, and I'll prepare you for another trip back in time. We'll be studying another great success story that was inspired both by the Ford production system and the supermarket.

"In 1949, Kiichiro Toyoda, founder of Toyota, called his grandson Eiji into his office.[4] Kiichiro had arranged with his old friend Henry Ford to have Eiji spend the entire summer at the Rouge plant. But what Eiji was to keep in mind, the grandfather explained, was that Ford's methods were not directly applicable in Japan for many reasons.

"First, he explained that they were operating under different market conditions than Ford. Toyota had to provide small, fuel-efficient cars, because Japanese cities were crowded and gasoline prices were high. Toyota also built large trucks for commercial carriers, small trucks for farmers, and luxury cars for government officials.

"The second reason had to do with differences in labor laws. Japanese labor laws, introduced by American occupation forces after the war, as well as a strike settlement in 1950, strengthened the Toyota work force's position in bargaining for favorable working conditions such as protection from layoff and firing, benefit payments, lifetime employment, and pay graded by seniority.

"The third reason had to do with production quantities and economic feasability. How could Toyota, a small company that had produced less than 3,000 cars in the past twelve years — compared to Ford's 7,000 per day — afford to purchase the technology necessary to copy Ford?"

Marcus continues to tell how, after a detailed three-month study of the Ford Rouge plant, Eiji wrote his grandfather a letter in July of 1950 in which he said he had ideas for improving

> **Great Weapon of the Hunter**
>
> Produce variety with economies of scale.

Toyota's production system. He realized, however, that in order to solve problems posed by the unique demands of the Japanese market while also complying with Japanese labor laws, Toyota would have to take a different approach to improvement than Ford did. The approach that Eiji envisioned would make it possible to produce a relatively low quantity of a variety of different vehicles without incurring the costs normally associated with high-variety, low-volume production. It would also have to compete with the mass producers' economies of scale.

"The result of Eiji's efforts is what is known today simply as the Toyota production system," Marcus says, tossing a piece of hamburger bun toward a group of pigeons that has been watching the three of them eat. "This system has been so successful that its methods presently are the most imitated in the world.

"What we're going to do next," he continues, "is travel to Japan to talk to Taiichi Ohno, Toyota's production manager. He was instrumental in creating and implementing the system. He's agreed to give us a first-hand account of what that experience was like. We'll take the scenic route over the northern Pacific islands."

A short while later Laura looks to her right across the blue-green expanse of ocean. "Those islands on the right are the Aleutians," she says.

"Getting close to your roots, aren't we, Laura?" Marcus says.

"Close."

"You're from up here?" Lou asks.

"Born in Alaska, north of the Arctic circle."

"Really?"

Laura's thoughts drift to her childhood . . . She is in the Alaskan wilderness with her father, and she hears him calling to her above the wild barking of the dogs. "Easy, Kimo!" She tightens her grip on the lead dog's harness, controlling the eight yelping sled dogs. Her other hand feels for the .44 Magnum strapped across her shoulder. Her eyes move from her father standing on the frozen river downstream, then back up along the treeline. It's early afternoon and already dusk . . . something large stirs in the trees . . . probably moose . . .

She unpacks and starts to raise the tent . . . she loves running trap lines for beaver. The dogs are her job . . . harnessing them, unharnessing them . . . separating them at night so they won't fight. Wild dogs, huskies . . . but they fly on top of that snow, barking, jerking, pulling. She smiles. She starts the fire and puts the coffee on.

When it's ready, she takes a cup to her dad. When he sees her, he stops cutting a hole in the ice and claps his mittens together. She laughs hard . . . his beard is frozen so solid that he can't open his mouth to drink. While they both skin and stretch the beaver, she thinks ahead to after supper when she'll be able to read by the lantern. She fills the cast iron kettle with snow to boil the smaller beavers for supper and wonders what they'll talk about later. Probably the usual: life, science, and far-away places. *He'll be tired after running traps all day, but he'll still listen to my questions.* "No clear-cut answers," he'll say . . . "need to figure it out for yourself, Laura." "Time for sleep," he'll finally say. . . . *sleeping by the campfire, nothing like it . . . green, ghostly dancing northern lights . . . they crack and pop in the freezing air . . . and the wolves . . . and the wind . . . howling through the night . . . stars so bright and snow so sparkling and luminescent . . .*

"Where are we headed?" Lou's question snaps Laura out of the past.

"Nagoya, Japan," Marcus says.

"Nagoya? My God! I was in Narumi Subcamp No. 2, just outside Nagoya."

"Subcamp?" Laura says.

"POW camp. I was there when American planes bombed Nagoya. I remember it like it was yesterday. They came right over the camp, no more than 500 feet above us. There were B29s, hundreds of them, engines roaring, bomb bay doors open. Suddenly the whole horizon over there lit up. Incendiaries, fires everywhere . . . Nagoya was in flames."

"Things have changed, Lou. This time you're here to learn," Marcus says.

"Learned all I wanted from them on Bataan."

"Bataan?" Laura says.

"The Death March."

"That war's over, Lou. There's a new war going on today that's for all the marbles. We're coming up on Nagoya. That's Toyota City on your left. Toyota and its surrounding suppliers are as big as a small city. Mr. Ohno's meeting us at his home."

As they are escorted into his garden, Ohno is trimming a beautifully sculptured miniature evergreen. Rocks are strategically placed among creeping ferns, and gold and white carp swim lazily in an immaculate pond.

"Beautiful," Marcus says. "Ohno-San, I would like to introduce you to Laura and Lou."

Ohno bows to them. "Your wife is very beautiful, Lou," Ohno says, looking up at Laura.

Lou frowns, but Laura smiles politely and explains that she and Lou are colleagues, not spouses.

Marcus helps Ohno recover from his embarrassment by asking how it came to pass that Toyota took a different direction than Ford.

Ohno explains that the first difference between the Ford system and the Toyota system lies in the setup process for the die presses.[5] For years, the Ford system used the quantity of sheet metal produced in a given time period as an indicator of productivity. In other words, Ford adopted maximum lot sizes and minimum number of setups as its primary objective. Toyota, on the other hand, strove to reduce lot sizes gradually in order to eventually produce each and every product uniquely.

"We were able to accomplish this by mastering fast, low-cost changeovers," Ohno says.

Lou tries to listen to Ohno, but his thoughts drift back to Bataan, 1942.[6] The commandant stands on a platform. His voice is high and squeaky as he reminds Lou and the other prisoners, in English, that Japan did not sign the Geneva Agreement. "You think you are the lucky ones?" — his voice rises — "Your comrades who died on Bataan are the lucky ones. Americans are dogs, they have always been dogs, and you will be treated like dogs. Caucasians have always been the enemies of the Oriental for 100 years and will always be enemies . . . You are a fourth-class nation . . . "

"The second big difference is in the control of production," Ohno continues. "I visited a supermarket when I was in America in 1956. Customers went around the store with baskets and selected enough goods for a few days to a week. When finished, they checked out, paid at the cash register, and then left. When I saw this shopping flow with my own eyes, I had a great insight. This model, where customers take what they need and the supermarket replenishes what is withdrawn, was the ideal model for our automobile plants.

"We call this model *kanban* in our plants." The most common form of *kanban*, he explains, is a small slip of paper inserted in a rectangular vinyl pouch. This slip of paper indicates the part number, the quantity, when it's needed, and where the part is used next. The subsequent process withdraws from the preceding process exactly what it needs when it needs it. The preceding process supplies exactly that which has been withdrawn using the kanban cards as the replenish order. "This is a major tool in our just-in-time production system."

Lou is looking at Ohno but he sees another face . . . The Japanese soldier moves toward him, takes Lou's canteen out of its cover, takes a drink, fills his own canteen, and drops Lou's on the ground. Lou bends over to pick it up and the soldier rams his rifle butt into the top of Lou's head, sending him face-down onto the cobblestones . . .

"The third key factor was to rearrange the equipment. Instead of arranging lathes with lathes, and milling machines with milling machines to produce a lot of a single item efficiently, the machines were arranged in the order that people work and in the order that value is added. This facilitates low inventories and small lot sizes. These three factors have contributed to Toyota's dominance of the automobile market and their success in the U.S. market," Ohno concludes.

Lou feels a knot in his gut. He thinks: they thought they dominated at Bataan . . . Americans buying Japanese cars. No way!

"Time to move on," Marcus says. "Thanks for taking the time with us, Ohno-San."

"You're very welcome," Ohno replies. "Please visit us again."

Marcus motions Lou and Laura into flight.

Soon Marcus, Lou, and Laura are high above the islands just north of Japan. "Ohno's hung up on making small batches of parts," Lou says. "We used to make big production runs to reduce the number of setups. Every good production manager knows that setups should be minimized. To be efficient you *have* to make large production runs."

"What happened if a customer ordered a small amount of an item that you didn't have in stock?" Marcus asks.

"We'd make up their order the next time we set up to make that item, unless they were willing to pay us enough to justify a special setup for them."

"So if a customer wanted the best cost on a small order, they had to wait," Marcus continues to probe. "What if a competitor offered the customer fast response to a small order with a low cost?"

"Can't win 'em all," says Lou. "We weren't hurting for business."

"At *that* time you weren't hurting. When success blinds the Hunters to changes taking place around them — changes in customers' needs, changes in the market, changes in the technology, changes in the work force, changes in the competitors, or changes in the law — the Hunter can become the Hunted," Marcus says.

Halfway across the Pacific, Lou anguishes. "Is Toyota really dominant in the auto market?"

"It was the rise in oil prices following the oil embargo of 1973 and the recession that followed it in 1976 that brought Toyota's Process Model to prominence. Many Japanese businesses nearly failed during this period while Toyota was profitable and gaining ground. Yanmar, a subcontractor to Toyota facing major losses in their core businesses, turned to Toyota for help.[7] Toyota lent Yanmar a team of engineers that helped them develop a Toyota Process Model for their operations, resulting in a ninety percent improvement in productivity and a fifty percent improvement in quality. Beginning in 1978 an avalanche of Japanese companies followed Toyota's lead, many improving on Toyota's approach. On the average, these companies doubled their productivity in the next five years while increasing product variety.

"This manufacturing Process Model would be later imitated in Product Development, Service Delivery Systems, and Business Management Systems. In the early eighties the concepts would spread to Western companies with similar success. Because of its spectacular results, it was to become one of the leading Process Models of the eighties. If you want to know more details about the Toyota System, I'll give you copies of Shigeo Shingo's *Toyota Production System* and *Single Minute Exchange of Die*, and Robert Hall's *Attaining Manufacturing Excellence*."

"One minute for a die change?" Lou says. "That's impossible for big dies."

"Typical American management — arrogant and stuck in your ways; that's why the Japanese have passed us by," Laura says.

"What experience do you have in business? How the hell do you know so much?" Lou says, his voice rising.

"That's enough," Marcus asserts. "You had both better learn something about teamwork or neither of you will become a Master Guardian.

"Read the SMED book, Lou, before you say it's impossible! And Laura, you need to become familiar with the tremendous achievements that American business has made over the years before you use the word *typical*.

"Let's review the types of Non-Linear change that we have encountered so far," Marcus says. "Look down there." Lou and Laura watch in amazement as white words form upon the surface of the ocean far beneath them.

Types of Non-Linear Change

- *Process Intent and Process Model changes*
- *shifts in assumptions*
- *changes in technology*

- *invention and accidental discoveries*
- *dramatic changes in Learning and Improvement Systems*

"Until 1950, Toyota was continuously improving their Process Model. In the 1950s they dramatically changed it and since then have been in a continuous improvement mode."

"So the belief that Toyota's success is solely due to Continuous Linear Improvement is not true," Laura says.

"That's right," Marcus says. "Toyota's continuous improvement of the past thirty years was preceded by changes in the Process Intent and Process Model of their Delivery System. We can now draw a picture of how the transformation took place at Toyota." A drawing begins to take shape on the ocean's surface.

Toyota Development

After Marcus elaborates on Toyota's transformation, he is silent for a long time. As they cross the Canadian Rockies, Lou sees a river winding its way to the Pacific between snow-capped mountain peaks. A large barge makes its way slowly inland against the current. Lou watches a speedboat make a large wake as it passes the barge. Slow, he thinks, but it gets there with a bigger load.

"New Delivery System designs like the Big Bear or redesigns as made by the McDonald brothers often produce major results in short time periods," Marcus says as they stand on a mountain summit and take in the view. "But in the case of Toyota it took twenty years of continuous improvement before the new Delivery Systems produced big results. This may help you understand the two different types of change. The first type, Continuous Linear Improvement, usually consists of many small, incremental changes, producing gradual improvement over long periods of time. The second type, Non-Linear Delivery System redesign, often produces dramatic improvement in short periods of time because it focuses on changes in the three characteristics of Delivery Systems: Process Intent, Process Models, and design of the Learning and Improvement Systems. Let's consider two levels of transformation," Marcus says, drawing a chart on the snow with his light stylus.

Driving Transformational Change

"In addition to continuous improvement systems, the world's most advanced companies, like Toyota, have a systematically driven process for redesign of their Delivery Systems. Both approaches are based on the same principles that you will learn shortly. Armed with these principles, you'll learn how to help companies build systematic processes for both Continuous Linear Improvement and Delivery System redesign. This is the first step in turning the Hunted into the Hunter."

Lou can no longer contain himself. "From what I've been reading the Japanese pay a lot of lobbyists in Washington to keep our market open to them but they won't open their market!"

"Japan bashing," Laura says.

"It's you academics that are the bashers — American industry bashers. You've been doing it for years."

"U.S. industry deserves bashing," Laura says.

"Damn! Most of you couldn't run a business, but you sure can tear them down."

"Okay, that's enough," Marcus says. "Keep your focus on issues that you can do something about, such as educating yourselves on the basic principles. Lou, you could benefit by studying what Japanese businesses have to teach us; and Laura, you should learn of the tremendous accomplishments American businesses have made in the eighties. So enough. We'll be on our way, and tonight we'll start our education in basic principles."

Toyota's Non-Linear Approach to Lot Sizing

There is a Non-Linear change here that will help you understand the meaning of the term. For years engineers used a simple model called the economic order quantity model to determine the optimum size for both order purchases and production lots. The model looked like this:

Economic Lot Size or Order Quantity

As lot size increases, the costs associated with carrying and managing inventory all increase. On the other hand, as the order or lot size increases, costs decrease due to fewer setups, fewer transactions, fewer moves, and fewer errors. The most economic lot size is obtained when the sum of the setup costs and the carrying costs is the lowest. From a practical point of view, the economic lot size is the quantity that should be made on a particular set-up before it's changed.

Toyota's approach was to reduce the cost of setup and the time to setup, reducing the economic lot size and the cost per part. This Non-Linear thought had entered few minds because it questioned an assumption — that setup costs and time are fixed. Since that assumption was challenged, many companies have dramatically reduced the setup costs and time for setups.

– Gregory J. Swartz
Cygnus Systems, Inc.

New Learning and Improvement Systems Employing
Participation and Empowerment

You can significantly increase the rate of continuous improvement by changing the design of the Delivery System.

Until 1970 in most businesses, engineers, or senior managers initiated most improvement efforts. In addition, many companies had suggestion programs which encouraged employees to come up with ideas for improvement, which were then reviewed by engineering and management. Some of these suggestion programs included monetary rewards. Many companies also had a management proposal system which encouraged managers to submit improvement ideas for review by engineering and senior management.

Continuous improvement systems are essentially different than suggestion or proposal systems. In continuous improvement systems, people and teams are educated on the fundamentals of systems analysis, creative thinking, problem solving, cost analysis, and statistical process control. They are trained in many methods that were formerly the sole domain of engineers or quality managers. They are exposed to the mission and objectives of the business. They are guided to set goals for their improvement effort. Then they are empowered to systematically improve the systems.

These new continuous improvement systems are not just an extension of past suggestion or proposal programs. They are relentless, systematically-driven processes based on knowledge and empowerment and therefore represent essentially new Learning and Improvement Systems.

– Laura Louis
Beacon Light, Inc.

Man is different than other predators. Physically, he is inferior not only to them but to his prey. He cannot run or swim or climb as fast; he cannot pursue winged prey through the air; he has far less stamina than most prey, less strength than some; his hearing is relatively poor; his eyesight is almost nil; and his capacity to withstand cold, heat, hunger, and thirst is unimpressive. Yet he is the most efficient of all predators. His brains and technology are such that he can, if he chooses, devastate all prey.

– George Reiger
The Complete Book of Hunting

CHAPTER NINE

Quicksand

W il Danesi plops his body into a large leather chair in the southeastern corner of the Garrett Processing Division complex in Torrance, California. After three 16-hour days trying to figure out where to begin straightening out this mess, he's overwhelmed. It's much worse than the task force study indicated. The only good news, he thinks, is that maybe it can't get any worse. Maybe.

The first day he met with each member of his staff. He couldn't believe their lack of concern. When asked why they had consistently missed shipping schedules, they blamed worn-out equipment, poor worker attitude, last minute changes from customers, unrealistic test specifications from their customers, and bad drawings. One staff member summed it up:

"We're last on the supply chain, so we're last to get a schedule and design requirements. And when we do get the drawings they want the castings yesterday. We've told them dozens of times that we need three months from the time we get an order to the time we deliver production parts. If we have to make new patterns, it's nine months until we can supply parts. A lot of customers are asking us to speed up their orders, but they aren't willing to pay for it! They think we should expedite at no additional cost. I've told Sales that we'll lose money if we don't get our expediting costs from the customer but Sales always sides with the customer. And one more thing: if you know anything about the casting business, you know it's an art, not a science. We don't know until the end of the process if the castings will be any damn good!"

It seems like a losing battle to Wil. He recognizes the need to improve quality, but as far as he can see, his staff is content with the present level of quality; and he has to find some way to change their attitude.

It's clear to him that his staff agrees on two things, that someone or something else is to blame and that customers are impossible to satisfy. It is also clear to Wil that either they will have to change their attitude or . . . some of them will be replaced.

He couldn't have been clearer about the seriousness of the situation. He explained to everyone that they had less than two years to turn things around or they faced possible closure. A couple of them said outright that they had been threatened with shutdowns before, but in the end they knew that Garrett couldn't do without them.

Today he toured offices and plants, meeting people and asking questions. As he toured the aluminum sand-casting area in the morning, the evidence mounted: the plant was dirty, equipment was old and in various states of disrepair, and quality control amounted to nothing but inspection and rework. As he gazes out the window it begins to sink in — he's stepped into quicksand.

*Companies that learn how to make quick response work,
will be the winners in the 1990s.*

– Roger Milliken, Chairman
Milliken and Company

*"If you knew time as well as I do," said the hatter, "you
wouldn't talk about wasting it."*

– Lewis Carroll
Alice in Wonderland

CHAPTER TEN

Response to Customers

I t's high noon as the trio crosses the Colorado border. They are travelling at about 7000 feet, threading their way northeast through the valleys between the mountains.

Just over Aspen, Marcus tells them some news. "Last week I recommended both of you for Apprentice Guardian status," he says, "and I was just told that the approval came in today."

"That calls for a celebration," Laura says.

"It took only two weeks to get through that Bureaucracy up there? I can't believe it," Lou says jokingly.

"I have my connections, Lou. As for a celebration, we'll have to hold off on that for a while," Marcus says. "This is a turning point in your training and your career as Guardians. Up to this time you've been introduced to the Continuous Linear Improvement foundations that Hunters design into their businesses; and you've had a taste of how Value Delivery Systems have been designed and redesigned in the distant and near past. And you've been spoon-fed.

"That will all change now," Marcus says as they arrive at Guardian Command. "The learning will become more intense and will focus more on how to do it, how to help businesses continually transform themselves into Hunters.

"To begin your mastery of the transformation process, we will focus on the thread that holds it all together — the thread of time. We'll talk about reducing valueless time, because to do so is one of the primary Drivers of the Continuous Linear Improvement process; and we'll also talk a lot about customer response time, because that's the first characteristic that we must consider in determining Process Intent. Also, as we design or redesign Value Delivery Systems, we must recognize that time has a major effect on quality and costs." Marcus begins to draw with the stylus.

Time and the Transformation Process

"I expect you to do a lot of studying on your own. For the next week, you'll stay at Guardian Command and do some independent study to prepare yourselves. When I return a week from today, I expect that you will have finished these assignments." He hands them each a paper and five books: *A Study of the Toyota Production System from an Industrial Engineering Viewpoint* by Shigeo Shingo, *Canon Production System* by Japan Management Association, *Industrial Dynamics* by J.B. Forrester, *The Fifth Discipline* by Peter Senge, *Concurrent Engineering* by John R. Hartley, *Attaining Manufacturing Excellence* by Robert Hall, and *Thriving on Chaos* by Tom Peters.

Assignment 1:

- *Study each of the five books I've given you and be pre-pared to answer the following questions:*
  - *What expectations do customers have of a highly responsive business?*
  - *How are highly responsive Delivery Systems designed?*
- *Use the* Wall Street Journal, Fortune, Forbes, Produc-tivity Newsletter, Target *magazine,* Industry Week, *and any other sources you can find to prepare for or complete the following tasks:*
  - *Research to find either a modern Hunter who prof-ited by adopting a more responsive model or busi-nesses that became Hunted because they failed to respond.*
  - *Write a report on how companies that have restructured recently did so.*

"The library is down the north spiral staircase," Marcus says. "I'm going to dig you a hole and have you learn your way out of it. See you both a week from today," he says, and then he vanishes.

"Marcus's speech sounded like the speech a drill sargeant gave us when we graduated from marine boot camp," Lou says. "He said he'd been our mother and our father for the past sixteen weeks. He said that when we got to the front, we would have just each other; but that would be enough, because each of us was the toughest soldier on earth."

"Where's the north staircase?" Laura asks, ignoring his war story.

Lou shakes his head. "Marcus just takes off. What a way to run a railroad."

"I'm going to look around down there," she says, walking north towards a large door.

"Think I'll take a walk on the mountain," Lou says.

"Suit yourself," Laura says disappearing through the large oak door.

As she passes through the door Laura has the strange feeling that she's being watched. The door leads to a long corridor lined with ancient books and scrolls. At the end of the corridor there is a narrow staircase leading even further down. The staircase is dimly lit and has a rounded ceiling reminding her of scenes from old horror movies. Every twenty steps or so massive doors lead off the main staircase. Above each door inscribed in the stone is a single word. As she descends she pauses at each door and reads the words: Cost, Earth, Humor . . . she smiles . . . Now that's a door that Marcus doesn't open enough, she thinks. She continues to read the inscriptions above the doors: Man, Quality, Time. She pauses in front of the door marked "Time" and pushes the door open slowly. As her eyes become accustomed to the dim light, she is aware that she is in a huge room, extending as far as she can see with row after row of gadgets, drawings, machines, and books on either side.

"May I help you, luv?" The voice startles her. She scans the room for the source of the voice.

"Over here dearie," the voice says in a thick cockney accent, "to your left. Doing a bit of rearranging," an old woman says as she emerges from behind a high shelf of books. "Could I find something for you?"

"No, just looking around. What is all this stuff?" Laura asks, amused.

"Let me introduce myself," The old woman says, "I'm Julia, information resources officer for Guardian Support Group V. We 'ave 'ere a collection of knowledge fit for a king. I'd say you're Laura."

"How did you know that?"

"He told me you'd be coming. A gentleman to work for, that Marcus, that he is. Are you sure there isn't something I can help you with?"

"What information do you have on what customers expect from a highly responsive business?" Laura asks.

"Come along," she says leading Laura down a long aisle. Along the way she sweeps cobwebs and dust away with a large feather duster. "What does Marcus have you doing?"

"I'm training to be a Guardian."

"Bloody good. About time they put some ladies in Special Forces. If I wasn't so old . . . " she trails off . . . "Foolish talk, a commoner like me."

"Julia . . . what a beautiful name." Laura says.

"It's a lady's name. Marcus said I could take it. Always wanted to be a lady like you, and Marcus gave me the chance. I'm doing some research for him," she continues. "Is he with you?"

"No, he's gone."

On the far side of the room Julia pauses and gestures with the feather duster. "Marcus's writings on response are right over here . . . from here to . . . here," she says, running the handle of the duster over the spines of a row of manuscripts.

"Marcus's writings?" Laura scans the shelf. Just as Julia said, every manuscript has been written by Marcus. But one in particular catches her eye. It has no dust and looks newer than the rest: *Designing for Response to Customers*. What a find, she thinks. Right from the horse's mouth! He won't be able to argue with his own words . . . . "Thanks for your help, Julia."

"You're welcome, dearie. Anytime."

As Lou walks down the mountain, the events of the last few days are tumbling through his mind. *Everything has changed . . . gonna take some getting used to . . . letting people in the factory make decisions . . .*

He crosses a small cascading stream and cuts back on a narrow path leading up the side of a high bluff to a lookout point. The climb is steep, but Lou manages it easily. *This new body I got is in good shape . . . better than the huffing, puffing one I had . . .*

At the top of the bluff, he reaches a clearing to the southwest. Snow-capped mountains rise as far as he can see. His thoughts return to the time he spent at the Motorola plant. *I guess I can't argue with the results they're getting . . . and those people were enthusiastic. Amazing how much they knew about their customers, their suppliers, and their competitors. Laura . . . what a hardnose . . . likes to show what she knows . . . she's just trying to impress Marcus . . .*

As he starts his climb back up the mountainside, the sun is setting and snow is beginning to fall. Lou feels grateful to be seeing the simple beauty of a sunset again. *God, the evergreens smell great!* He bends over and picks up some powdery snow and lets it sift through his fingers. The air is brisk, the snow sparkles. *Just the way God would have had it if he had the money.* He smiles.

He's glad Marcus has left. Lou realizes that Marcus isn't too happy with him right now, but then Marcus isn't the type who likes anybody disagreeing with him. *He makes a lot out of this Delivery System design and customer response time thing. Guess he likes to be mysterious . . . works on me, though . . . got me damn curious . . .*

It's time to get back now. His thoughts again drift back to Motorola. It's still hard to believe that they reduced in-process inventory from six weeks to one week and that they have fewer parts shortages than they had before. *Must be a unique situation . . . in the mill the more inventory we had the better it ran . . . and all this linear, Non-Linear stuff Marcus is throwing at us . . . too much theory . . . no wonder the Romans lost it.*

Suddenly Lou senses that he's not alone. Out of the corner of his eye he sees a shape. Slowly he turns to see, less than a hundred yards away, a lone cougar highlighted against the lavender glow of approaching twilight. It's a beautiful, noble-looking animal, and it returns his stare, its amber eyes glowing in the low light. The animal's black-tipped ears are perched wide on a broad head that appears small in comparison to the long, powerfully muscled body. Lou freezes. *Wonder if this Hunter has ever seen a man before . . . beautiful animal.* Minutes pass. Lou doesn't move; the cougar doesn't move. Finally it turns its long, black-tipped tail and moves off down the slope. Lou gazes after it for a while before deciding he'd better get moving.

At the entrance to Guardian Command he stops and looks down the mountain. The cougar is nowhere in sight.

Lou and Laura have only one encounter in the following week. It occurs the night after Marcus's departure. Just as they are finishing dinner, Lou tries to break the ice.

"Do you cook?"

"Sure. Do you?"

"Some, mostly after my wife, Annie, died. Were you married?"

Laura smiles. "You just have to put me in some category, don't you?"

"I just asked a simple question."

Laura frowns. "The answer is no. I was twenty-five when I died and up to that time I was too busy with school and career, and I like men who respect that."

"You don't have to get all bent out of shape about it. I was just asking."

"No problem," Laura says, lifting her napkin to her mouth and standing. "I need to get back to my studies."

"Yeah, Marcus loaded us down pretty heavy with book work."

"Just like some professors I had who tried to grind you down. At Harvard, we worked in study teams and that helped."

Lou coughs. "You do your work and I'll do mine." *She needs to learn the hard way . . . I did.*

"Whatever works, Lou. Catch you later," Laura says as she leaves the table.

Lou sits alone at the huge table . . . *Harvard. It all fits . . .*

A week later, Marcus returns and immediately calls Lou and Laura to the room of the Hunters. After an exchange of pleasantries, Marcus dives in.

"A Value Delivery System must respond to customers in many ways. It must listen to what the customer actually wants, as well as market, advertise, propose, bid, develop, produce, distribute, and service the product or services it offers; and it must perform all of these processes in a highly responsive manner. A complete business Delivery System consists of many subsystems within the major systems of purchasing, product development, production, and many more."

Value Delivery System and Subsystems

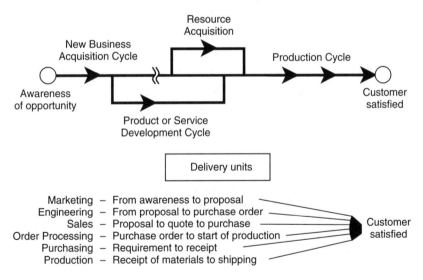

Marcus pulls his shoulders back for a moment, does some other simple stretches, then continues. "And don't lose sight of the importance of measuring everything in customer time. Customer time starts when the customer has a need and it ends when you have fulfilled it and the customer is completely satisfied with the deliverables. But response can't come at the expense of either quality or costs. To be the supplier of choice, a business must have a Delivery System that excels in all three performance categories — response, quality, and value-to-cost ratio — and the system must also be flexible. This no-trade-off approach requires that we design from a systems point of view.

"See the forest instead of the trees," Lou adds as he sits down beside Laura.

"Forest *and* trees, Lou. To see the forest level we'll first have to adjust our perception. It's as if our minds have to learn to function like a zoom lens. First we pull back to a wide-angle setting to get a good look at the whole system. At times we'll have to zoom in to fix the root causes of problems that affect system performance. But when we pull back to a wide-angle view of the system level, it will be to establish the customer requirements of the system. Let's start with customer expectations. What does your research say about what the modern customer expects of a highly responsive business?"

"I have a list of customer expectations," Laura says as she hands a paper to Marcus.

What Customers Expect from a Highly Responsive Business

- *The right service or product is there when needed. Delivery is convenient, on time, and exact in quantity.*
- *Short time to develop new products or services, deliver customized or standard products and services, or change a design to better satisfy customers.*
- *Short time to respond to inquiries, change order quantities, order mix, or delivery time.*

> • *Short time to correct customer complaints, service fail-*
> *ures, defects, or dissatisfactions, so that they never*
> *recur.*
> • *Short time to provide support materials and services.*

"Very impressive list, very impressive," Marcus says.

Laura beams, "Write that down, Lou, a compliment from the old man."

Lou is stone-faced. One-upped again . . .

"Did you come up with this on your own, Laura," Marcus says with a surprised look.

"Got it from your manuscript dated April, 1961."

Marcus smiles. "Thought these looked familiar. I can see you've been talking to Julia. Good! If these are the expectations, then we have to figure out how we can deliver them. In other words, we have to design a Value Delivery System to meet these expectations."

"Why do you use the term *Value Delivery System*?" Lou asks, still irritated. "Sounds like a pizza business."

"Because the system delivers value to a customer. From the time material leaves the mines, oil fields, or farms, or from the time information leaves its source, it's a continuous value-adding process until it gets to the final customer. From the moment a creative idea is generated until the time that idea is a new product or service, the Delivery System is adding value. Let's use your research to gain more insight into the importance of response in customer time and the dependence of customer response on Delivery System design. Do you have an example of a modern Hunter who redesigned its Delivery Systems to provide fast response? You begin, Lou."

"I was reading about this guy, Sam Walton, who revolu-tionized retailing, so I did some research on what he did, and it's impressive."

"Good choice, Lou. What did you find?"

Lou brightens as he opens a folder. "I need to do a Marcus bit here and give you some background. Until the eighties, each segment of the apparel industry operated independently. Textile producers, manufacturers' representatives, wholesalers, and retailers were all focused on what it took to optimize their segment. Because the system was fragmented this way, there was little concern that the industry as a whole had become unresponsive to customers. To help you understand, I drew a picture of the typical Delivery System for the entire industry around 1980." Lou hands a drawing to Marcus. Laura moves closer to view the drawing.

**Apparel Industry
Product Flow vs. Order Feedback**

Lou traces the flow of material on the drawing. "Starting at the yarn maker, the material goes to the textile producer, then to the garment manufacturer, then to a wholesaler, and finally to the retailer. It took many months to go from raw materials to final customer. Orders were routed back along the same path very slowly; the point-of-sale information on what was selling in style, color, and size was fed backwards from retailer to representative to distributor to manufacturer to textile producer, each of them reordering when stocks were low. From raw materials to apparel in the customers' hands was typically a fifteen-month cycle time. With the long manufacturing and distribution cycle time and the long feedback cycle time, as much as sixteen billion dollars, or twenty percent of gross sales, was lost each year at the retail level due to forced markdowns, out-of-stock items, and the cost of carrying excess inventories.

"Then along comes Sam Walton. In 1945, after service as an Army intelligence officer in the big war, Sam bought the franchise of a failing Ben Franklin store in Newport, Arkansas. Sam turned it into the region's top store. He bought other Ben Franklin stores and turned them around, but throughout the fifties an idea nagged at him from time to time. He felt that small towns were ripe for large discount stores, but his parent company, Ben Franklin, disagreed. So Sam started out on his own in 1962 and built his first Wal-Mart discount store. He instilled in his employees the idea that customer service was important even though the customer was getting the best value for the price. His discount store was a success and he began to expand to other small towns. As he expanded, his concept of retailing expanded to include the whole distribution system."

Lou loosens his collar and exhales. "Instead of ordering from wholesalers, Sam located his own distribution centers within a 300-mile radius of each Wal-Mart. These distribution centers received — and still do receive — bulk shipments directly from the factories across the United States. Once the shipment reaches the distribution center, a laser scans the shipment's bar code to determine its routing. Mechanized conveyors move the shipment to a temporary storage location. On the average, stock is replenished at each store twice per week. Information from laser scanning at the check out counters is communicated to the warehouse for type and quantity. By replacing stock every two to three days, instead of the industry average of once every two to three weeks, Wal-Mart can carry more than four times the variety with the same investment in inventory and floor space.

"Also, with this electronic information system, Wal-Mart's buyers can continuously get feedback so that they can alter the mix of products being delivered and shipped to all stores at least once daily. The system also tracks what's selling and what's gathering dust, so that only the inventory that sells is reordered. Wal-Mart also connects its suppliers to this information network. With this feedback system and short-cycle inventory replenishment, Wal-Mart turns net assets much faster than K-Mart, generating fifty percent more sales per dollar invested than K-Mart. How's that for developing a great Process Model?" Lou asks.

"Good example," Marcus says. "You've done some good research, but you seem to have forgotten the bottom line."

"I've got the bottom line. Wal-Mart's profit climbed to $1.6 billion in 1991, and their stock value grew 100 percent from 1980 to 1990. And here's the great part. Before Sam died, he saw the company grow from one store to over 1,700 stores. By 1991, with sales of $43.9 billion, Wal-Mart became the largest retailer in the U.S., passing both Sears and K-Mart. Sam left Wal-Mart with a far-reaching goal: to achieve $100 billion sales by the year 2000. I'd be willing to bet that they'll make it."

"So K-Mart has become the Hunted," Marcus says. "Are they restructuring?"

After a pause, Laura says, "I don't know about K-Mart, but Sears is restructuring itself to cope with the discounters."

"That brings us to a most important lesson we can learn. It is the essential difference between the Hunters and the Hunted.

"When Hunters like Wal-Mart attack or when the market changes dramatically, the Hunted have to restructure. Faced with reduced sales or declining prices, the Hunted must slim down quickly to lower break-even volumes and lower unit costs. So they restructure. Lou, what did you learn about restructuring from your research?"

"When companies restructure," Lou replies, "they typically don't eliminate valueless time or valueless variance. Instead, they reduce layers of management, rid themselves of losers, slash operating costs, withhold investment, cut inventory, reduce people, and begin to purchase material instead of making it."

Marcus nods and walks to the window and stands in the thin stream of light shining down from the large skylight in the center of the room. "Restructuring is an effort by the Hunted to make themselves leaner. But restructuring alone will not turn them into Hunters again. Restructuring will make you lean, but it will not make you mean."

Weyerhaeuser's Restructure and Redesign

From 1989 to 1992 wood pulp prices dropped from $800 to $500 per ton and liner board used in corrugated containers dropped from $410 to $360 per ton.

Weyerhaeuser eliminated 1,500 white collar jobs and cut simple overhead costs for a savings of $100 million per year.

But the real savings have been in continuous improvement and Delivery System redesign. They now cut logs to finished sizes on the first sawing operations instead of rough cutting, then finish cutting.

> ### Brunswick's Consolidation and Divestment
>
> The recession and a 10% luxury tax caused a sales drop of 50% in boat sales. CEO Jack Reichard closed 1/3 of the company's 54 boat and engine plants, consolidating all three engine assembly plants into one.
>
> They sold their transportation components division, industrial filtration division and many others to reduce debt.

Laura can practically hear her own heartbeat it's so quiet now. She walks toward Marcus. "Are you going to tell us what the Hunters do?"

Marcus turns, his gray hair shining in the light. "The Hunters go beyond restructuring, continually transforming themselves to maintain their competitive position."

"Could you be more specific?" she asks.

Marcus flips a switch and a screen on the east wall lights up. The words are in a luminescent red.

Restructuring

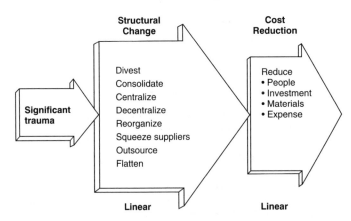

In restructuring, costs are reduced. Quality and response usually are unchanged or deteriorate. The Delivery Systems are unchanged and the mindsets, mental model, and measures are unchanged. The prime driver is trauma.

Union Carbide's Restructure and Redesign

William Joyce, executive vice president at Union Carbide said, "In the past, the cuts followed the business cycles. First we squeezed, then we added the jobs back. This time businesses won't add many of the jobs back because organizations will be redesigned to be efficient at the new levels."

"Restructuring reduces costs but usually does not improve the quality or response of the Delivery Systems of the business.

"Compare that with the transformational approach of the Hunter. At this time, you may not understand everything on this flowchart but eventually you will," Marcus says.

Driving Transformational Change

"The transformation chart is like a drink out of a fire hose," Lou says. "What do you mean by mind-sets, mental models, and measures?"

"The flow chart shows the Non-Linear Solution as an input Driver," Laura says, writing furiously in her notebook.

"We'll get to both of those questions later in your training," Marcus says. "The Hunters choose when and where they wish to compete. They then transform their system to be the dominant competitor. Often, they redefine the very rules under which the competition will take place. The Hunted, faced with a major setback or, as I've called it, significant trauma, must restructure themselves to stay alive. Laura, let's review your report on the fast-responding Hunters."

Laura lifts herself to an erect position in her chair. "Well, after you blasted me a week ago for putting down U.S. industry and told me to learn of some of their accomplishments, I thought I'd better do some research. I looked at the electronics industry for the last seven years since I've been away. It was a big surprise.

"In the 1970s, Japan devastated the American electronics business. First with low-cost copies and later with quality and cost, they took the lion's share of the television, radio, recorder, and office machines business. They made major inroads in the computer and computer printer business in the early eighties and virtually dominated the camcorder and video game systems market by the turn of the decade. In the eighties, they moved upscale to videocassette recorders, televisions, and premium office equipment. By the mid-eighties, the Japanese dominated the DRAM business, had ninety percent of the newly emerging digital signal processing (DSP) business, and were poised to continue their domination of the television business with high definition television (HDTV). The DSP and HDTV business segments were all but conceded to Japan; most experts had written off the U.S. electronics industry."

"What's digital signal processing?" asks Lou.

Laura stands and moves behind her chair. "DSP is the next major revolution in electronic systems, as important as the development of microprocessors and memory chips. DSP converts audio and television images to digital signals that can be processed by microprocessors and stored in integrated circuit memories. That means that the signals can be compressed for transmission, tripling the number of simultaneous transmissions over a phone line, radio line, or television line."

She reaches for a chart from her briefcase. "Would you believe that in the last eight years the U.S. regained technological dominance of DSP, and completely reversed the market share picture? Look at this chart," Laura says as she holds the chart so they can see it.

Worldwide DSP Chip Market Share

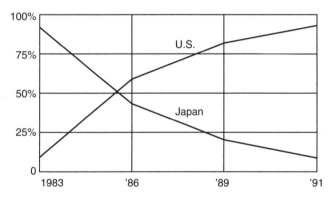

Source: Forward Concepts Co. Reprinted by permission.

"Now you're talking," Lou says. "How did they pull it off?"

"The rapid development of new and improved digital signal processing integrated circuits (DSP ICs) and software was the leading factor. By 1990, DS PICs had been developed that could simultaneously process six functions, such as recording speech, electronically transmitting a copy of a document, and receiving a phone call; these ICs can process the mathematics to do those functions ten times faster than the best microprocessors. Using these new technologies AT&T designed and marketed a tapeless telephone answering machine, the AT&T

1337, and took seventy percent of the U.S market for these machines. Motorola now manufactures the MicroTac Lite Digital Personal Commu-nicator, the world's smallest and lightest cellular phone, using DSP technology.

"AT&T has also introduced a videophone using DSP ICs, and many U.S. computer companies have used the new technology to develop a new breed of computers called multimedia computer systems. These new multimedia systems bring together video processing, speech recognition, fax, electronic mail, and computing into a single system."

"But the Japanese will just copy all those inventions," Lou says.

"Not if U.S. business continues to invent faster than anybody can copy," Laura says. "And that's what U.S. high density television developers have done. The Japanese version of HDTV uses the old analog technology with considerably less capability."

"So the Japanese are simply improving in a linear way what they already have," Lou says.

Laura nods in agreement. "Right, and that may not be good enough in this case. Two American groups, Zenith Corp. and AT&T as one group and General Instrument Corp. and MIT as the second group, have the inside track on the only approved standards for transmission."

Lou laughs and raises his fist. "I like that — invent faster than they can copy."

"There's nothing wrong with copying," Marcus says. "While the Japanese are copying our products, we're copying some of their manufacturing methods. Copying is part of Continuous Linear Improvement. We can all learn from the best in any field. U.S. businesses must not only develop new products and approaches, but improve their manufacturing capability, or we will invent, but not produce, in the future. This is part of the Non-Linear Solution."

Marcus stands and takes his light stylus from his pocket. "Very good report, Laura. The strategic importance of the response of a business Delivery System cannot be overstated."

Laura reaches for a chart. "I've studied the strategic implications and I've listed them on this chart for three companies with wide differences in response capability.

Time Advantage of the Hunter

Hunted

Average system cycle time is 8 weeks
Normal delivery time is 8 weeks
To deliver order, supplier must prioritize, expedite
They must solve many crisis problems
They will usually deliver late
They can't recover if something goes wrong
They must charge more for faster response
Quality is at risk as they push the system to deliver faster

Customer perception: Poor response

Surviving

Average system cycle time is 4 weeks
Average delivery time is 4 weeks
Some prioritizing, expediting
Routine problems
High percentage of on time delivery
Recovery possible
Minimum sacrifice of quality and costs to deliver in 4 weeks

Customer perception: Fair response

Assumption: Customer expectations of the market response is 4 weeks

Hunter

Average system cycle time is 1 week
Average delivery time is 2 weeks
No prioritizing, expediting
Few problems
Offer quick response with no added price or quality compromise
Recovery easy

Customer perception: Fast response

> **Great Weapon of the Hunter**
> Fast Response.

"The strategy of the market leaders is to hunt in a market where the competitors are slow," Laura says.

"That's one of the great weapons of the Hunters," Marcus says. "But how do we design to improve response to a customer and reduce system cycle time in a real business environment?" Marcus asks.

"I found the six major influences from your manuscripts," she says handing a paper to Marcus.

Six Major Influences on Customer Response Time and System Cycle Time

- *Management and work force commitment to fast response*
- *The Process Model*
- *Work-in-process (WIP)*
- *Capacity versus demand*
- *Variance*
- *Valueless activity in the process*

Marcus smiles. "You did your homework well, Laura." He stands and begins to pace back and forth. "We're going to explore these major influences on customer response in the next few lessons. We've already seen the influence that Motorola's workforce commitment had on response time. So, now we'll explore how a change in Process Model dramatically reduced the time it took Cincinnati Milacron to bring a new plastic injection-molding machine to the market. We'll also analyze McDonald's and Wendy's to understand the importance of designing Process Models that meet the Process Intent. Second, we'll look at the dramatic improvement at Harley-Davidson where they learned the importance of the Process Model, work-in-process, and valueless process variance. Third, we'll examine the influence of both Process Model and capacity constraints on Douglas Aircraft's production of commercial aircraft. Fourth, we'll visit Simpson Timber to see how they revitalized an old sawmill by eliminating valueless time and activity in the process. Fifth, we'll examine how Motorola dramatically reduced valueless process variance in their quest for high quality and fast customer response.

"We're meeting another Hunter tonight at eight in Cincinnati, Ohio, and I want you to listen carefully to what he has to say; you can learn a lot from him. But before we go," he adds, "let's summarize the lessons we learned about responding to customers."

....

Lessons Learned

- *The average response time to a customer is a designed-in characteristic of the Delivery System.*
- *Customers' response expectations today are that a supplier will deliver quickly, conveniently, and in the correct quantities. Customers also expect that suppliers will immediately correct any mistakes, deal with complaints, and provide support if needed.*
- *There are six major factors that influence the response of the Delivery System: management and work force commitment to customer response, the Process Model, capacity versus demand, work-in-process (WIP), variance, and valueless activity in the process.*
- *It is strategically critical today that a competitor have a highly responsive Delivery System — not just to increase*

response to customers, but also because systems that are designed with poor response are high-cost, poor-quality systems.

- *The Hunters transform themselves continually to become the suppliers of choice. The Hunted, lacking flexibility, wisdom, or commitment to transformation, lose market share. The loss of market share prompts them to restructure.*

- *Restructuring seldom changes the basic design of the Delivery System or management's mind-set, mental models, and measures. Although costs go down, neither response nor quality improves; and so the restructured competitor is not ready to Hunt. Instead, it often continues to be Hunted and requires further restructuring.*

"Met a Hunter on the side of the mountain a week ago," Lou says as they travel across the plains.

"A Hunter?" Marcus asks.

"A cougar! I've done a lot of hunting in my time, but I've never seen an animal like that before. Beautiful creature. They keep to themselves, I guess. It was sort of a stare-down. I'm not sure whether I won, or whether the cougar had no interest in me."

"Lou, the cougar has no equal in its ability to attack its prey without being seen or heard. If that cougar had been hunting you, it would have had you."

"The wise old scraper's changin' his direction," his father said. "Likely he's headin' for the saw-grass ponds. Iffen that's his notion, we kin mebbe slip around and surprise him."

Some understanding came to Jody of the secret of his father's hunting. The Foresters, he thought, would have plunged after old Slewfoot the moment they had found his kill. They would have shouted and bellowed, their pack of dogs would have bayed until the scrub echoed with it, for they encouraged them in it, and the wary old bear would have had full warning of their coming. His father got game, ten to their one. The little man was famous for it.

Jody said, "You shore kin figger what a creetur'll do."

"You belong to figger," his father said. "A wild cree-tur's quicker'n a man and a heap stronger. What's a man got that a bear ain't got? A mite more sense. He cain't out-run a bear, but he's a sorry hunter if he cain't out-study him."

– Marjorie Kinnan Rawlings
The Yearling

CHAPTER ELEVEN

Response and Process Model

*B*etween 1980 and 1990," Harold Faig says, "the plastic injection-molding machine industry was ravaged by foreign competitors. Of fifteen U.S. companies in 1980, only five were still in business in 1990."[1]

Faig is vice president and head of the Plastic Molding Machine Division of Cincinnati Milacron. They're meeting at Grammers, an authentic German restaurant in downtown Cincinnati.

"We didn't see it coming in 1980. Few foreign machines were being purchased in the U.S. The market was growing at a brisk pace so that when the imports started coming, the U.S. companies were increasing sales. But, by 1985 the foreign plastic molding machine companies had captured fifty percent of the U.S. market, and U.S. companies were feeling it.

"One Sunday early in 1985, I was working at our Batavia, Ohio headquarters when I ran into Bruce Kozak, our regional sales manager from California. Bruce said he was worried. Imported plastic molding machines were about to wipe out our California market. He said our machines were just not competitive with the new imports. I asked what was better about the imported machines. I wasn't prepared for the answer. As he went down the list of performance, quality, and cost factors, I was getting a sick feeling. He was talking about the product that I was responsible for. I bit the bullet by asking Bruce to help me put together a list of requirements that a world-beating machine would have. I took that list and sold our management on building such a machine.

"The task was a formidable one. The other manufacturers were not standing still. To move ourselves into the lead we would have to reduce the cost of the machine by forty percent, increase its performance, and develop it in one year. It was the last requirement, cutting development time, that posed the biggest doubts. Our organization was not designed to do that. With the Process Model we were using we moved the design from one organization in our business to another and then to another. And each organization had its own set of objectives. I have a drawing that shows how it works. Each function is separate and self-contained. The managers of each of the functions report to the president.

Traditional Process Model for Product Development

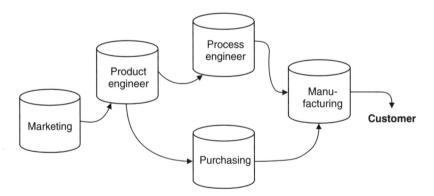

"The value-added Delivery System is traced by the arrows. In other words, because we had to manage the new product development process through many functions to finally deliver it to the customer, the process took two years.

"To cut the development time in half we needed a new Process Model. We had read of the reduction in product development time at Xerox, Motorola, and Toyota through the use of multidisciplined, tightly knit teams. So, we decided to put a team together, locate them all in the same area, and have them report directly to the vice president of plastics machinery, Raymond Ross. Next, we had to find a way to reduce the amount of time needed to design and build the prototype, which meant reducing the time it took to create the design, get the parts from suppliers, make decisions, and solve problems. So how did we do it? I'll tell you.

"**The first thing we had to grapple with was defining what we were going to design.**" He pauses to sip from his coffee. "We visited present customers, past customers, and even competitors' customers. We disassembled the best competitor's machines and analyzed not only how they designed them, but also how they were developing their product strategy; in other words, where they were going in the future. The real target is not what customers want but what they buy. What sold us was a guy in California who told the team he had been a prisoner of war in Japan but still bought the lower-priced Japanese machine because he was now a businessman. The guy had tears in his eyes when he told us that."

"That would get me too," Lou says.

"Because we made a comprehensive product strategy study before we started to design, we knew the target market, and when we designed the new molding machine, we only had to make minimal changes as the project proceeded.

"Also, in any given product or process development project, you've got to decide how radical a departure to take from proven designs or processes. It's absolutely critical that you make such decisions right at the onset of each project. On each development project, we used a form of the Pareto Principle and targeted the most probable eighty percent of what we thought was possible. We established a guideline to use standard, proven, American-made parts wherever possible to avoid unnecessary design time and startup problems. However, when it was necessary for financial reasons, we made big changes, like the use of a die-cast part to replace a multiple-machined forty-five-ton part.

"**Second, to reduce supplier lead time we had to bring our suppliers in as part of the development team.** To get them to provide design help we had to share our design plans with them. To each supplier who provided design help, shorter lead time, reduced cost, and higher quality, we promised all the business for years. Essentially, this gave us access to their knowledge and technology and they accessed our business.

"**Third, the co-location of team members reduced the time to make decisions and solve problems.** Locating all team members in the same place allowed them to interact continuously. By doing this we avoided discovering late in the project that something couldn't be done or that mechanical and

---

The Pareto Principle

The Pareto Principle is sometimes referred to as the 20/80 rule. The general idea is that a great percentage of some effect has its origins in a small number of causes. Recent environmental studies, for example, show that 20% of the motor vehicles on the road today account for 80% of the most noxious exhaust emission released into the air. In a manufacturing setting, perhaps ten percent of all errors account for ninety percent of all defects.

electrical layouts were incompatible. We established a single weekly communications meeting during which no decisions were to be made. We reasoned that if a decision waited for the weekly meeting, it was delayed too long. Decisions and problems were to be resolved daily as they arose. Also, because the team did not need the approval of every middle manager and every staff member, the decision process was much faster. Our decision to use metric measurements might never have been made in the old system, because it would have required the approval of every middle manager.

"Our new Process Model emphasized early involvement and participative decision making from the whole team, including manufacturing, suppliers, and engineering. Here's a drawing that illustrates the time at which each of these groups was involved in the past compared to the time that we got them involved on the Vista project.

Functional Involvement Profile for Product Development and Introduction

"On Pearl Harbor Day, December 7, 1985, nine months later, our top management switched on the big P-279 prototype, designed to leap-frog the competitors. It was fitting that it be Pearl Harbor Day, because Japanese and German competition had already caused the death of ten of the fifteen largest plastic injection-molding machine manufacturers in this country. By late 1986, the new machines, nicknamed Vistas, were beginning to roll off the production line, and we all were holding our breath. Sales of the Vista's predecessor were continuing to fall, and work on the shop floor was thinning out. And then it happened. Suddenly sales took off, over twice as high as our previous best year. We were back in the competition again. We felt good when Toyota chose to purchase three of these new machines for its U.S. plants."

"The Hunter returned," Marcus says.

"We're back," Harold agrees. "Since 1986, we've redesigned twenty-three basic product lines from scratch."

Faig's busy schedule forces him to leave before dinner is over.

Marcus stands to say goodbye. "You've been a big help. I appreciate the time you've given us."

After Marcus takes a bite of bratwurst, he directs the discussion back to Cincinnati Milacron. "When they realized they were being hunted, they used one of the most powerful elements in the arsenal — time. By reducing development time to nine months they recaptured their position in the marketplace. Shortening the time from the idea to the sale is now the basis for preemptive strikes many top companies are making on their competitors. Cincinnati Milacron not only learned to hunt again but they discovered part of the Non-Linear Solution, making them a deadly Hunter . . . at least for a while."

"For a while?" Laura says. "Sounds ominous."

"No solution is permanent. To remain a Hunter, the process of transformation must be a continuous one. Let's discuss the vulnerability of a company that takes a long time getting products to market. In 1983, when I was working with a company in Beaverton, Oregon, the president of the company presented this graph." Marcus hands a paper to each of them.

Major Instrument Manufacturer Response to Market

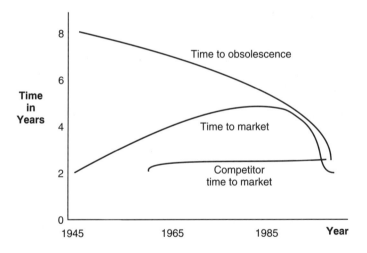

"As the graph shows, when this company started business at the end of World War II, they could develop a new product and bring it to production in less than two years. In 1983, the development time from concept to production had increased to almost four years. Of course, newer products are more complicated, they require custom integrated circuits with long lead times, and they also require a much greater level of manufacturing engineering to be cost effective. But, at the same time, a product's life in the marketplace was dropping from almost seven years or longer in 1945 to less than four years in 1983. If the trend continued, the best competitor would be designing products in less than three years and making their own products obsolete every three years."

"That's like shooting yourself in the foot," Lou says. "To get the best return on investment we ran a product for seven to ten years."

"If you maintain the seven-year cycle and a competitor brings the eclipsing product to the marketplace in three years, what's going to happen to your sales?"

"I understand that, but what I'm saying is why doesn't the competitor plan to maximize return on investment by extending product life cycles as long as they can?" Lou insists.

"Good question," Marcus says, nodding. "The Hunter's thinking beyond short range return on investment, though. They know that being late to market causes loss of sales and loss of profit as shown by this chart."

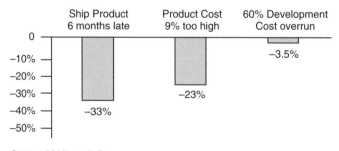

**Profit Loss over Product Life due to
Lateness to Market, Product Cost, or Cost Overruns**

Source: McKinsey & Co.

**Profit versus Time in
New Product Introduction**

"You can see that the longer it takes to bring a product to market, the longer it takes to recover the development costs to reach the breakeven point. If the product becomes obsolete soon after it reaches the marketplace, it will never break even. If the competitor brings the product to the market earlier than you, they make more return on their investment in development of the product. That's the strategy today's Hunters use to maximize their return on investment."

Lou mutters, "Dog eat dog."

"That's the idea, Lou. The second point I want to make regarding your question is that the Hunter's real reason for the rush to market is to put you out of the business. As you saw in the chart I gave you earlier, when the two curves cross — when the time to obsolescence is less than the time from the beginning of product development to the introduction of the product to customers — you're in serious trouble. You can now say even before you begin development that your product will be obsolete by the time you get it to the marketplace."

"Very vulnerable position," Laura says.

Marcus takes a drink of water. Still looking at them over the rim of the glass, he replies: "More than vulnerable — lethal!"

"There's also a third reason the competitor may play the game this way. The competitor can take advantage of a system effect that you may not be aware of — time to detect."

"Time to detect is as treacherous as a stalking cougar in today's competitive world. For example, if a customer is dissatisfied with your product or service, that customer may not purchase from you the next time. But the next time they purchase may be weeks, months, or years in the case of automobiles, refrigerators, or air conditioners. So, by the time you lose customers, it may be too late to recover. Long system-cycle times such as long time to market, long time to acquire materials, long manufacturing times, long distribution times, and long service times all cause long time to detect. These long times between cause and observed effect can dangerously delay decisions and changes that are essential to survival. The following chart shows the long time to detect. The time to detect and correct is at least six to eight years."

"The point I'm trying to make is that the Delivery System design for today's marketplace must be the best in every aspect of the business — from the initial awareness that a customer has a potential need to the time you completely satisfy the customer with the product or service. The consequences of a weak engineering and development process are tragic."

Fast to Market at Hewlett-Packard

Using an integrated team approach, Hewlett-Packard brought the XL95 handheld computer from concept to consumer sale in fifteen months. This innovative device generated $50 million in sales in a little over a year from the time it was introduced to the market.

Time to detect a miscalculation of customer values or a failure to deliver customer expectations

"Did this company you're talking about go under?" Laura asks.

"No, they saw the problem coming and they turned it around in a way similar to Cincinnati Milacron. Is it clear how the Process Model of the Delivery System affects response?" Marcus asks.

"Clear," Lou says. "It's about time someone figured out how to fix engineering." He smiles at Laura.

Honda — Development Time as a Weapon

In the motorcycle wars of the early eighties, Honda not only cut prices but bombarded Yamaha and Harley-Davidson with a flood of new models. In less than two years, Honda made over 100 new model introductions, in many cases making its own models obsolete.

With this massive design turnover, Honda made everyone else's motorcycles look antiquated. Honda had learned to dramatically reduce its new product development time.

Yamaha surrendered. Harley-Davidson almost folded.

Laura shakes her head. She'd better just accept it, she thinks. He's hopeless.

Marcus continues. "Let's study product development at Toyota and at the Japanese companies with the fastest, highest quality, and lowest cost development processes. They excel due to four factors: leadership, teamwork, communications, and simultaneous development.[2] We'll discuss each of these factors briefly. But first . . . " He motions to their waiter to bring him the check.

One moment Lou and Laura are standing in the shadow of a building near the restaurant; the next moment they are back at Guardian Command in the room of the Hunters.

Marcus says, "Let's pick up where we left off — "

"Could we please just wait a minute?" Laura asks, "I always feel a little out of sorts when you just zap us from one place to another like that."

"Of course. *Et tu,* Lou?" he asks, a grin spreading across his face.

Lou nods. He feels out of sorts too, but he never would have admitted it.

Marcus asks them to please sit down. Then he sits down himself and remains quiet while Lou and Laura adjust. After about five minutes, he rises. "Forgive me," he says. "I sometimes forget how difficult the abrupt site changes can be for those who are just starting out." He takes the light stylus out of his pocket and taps it in his palm. "Continue to sit quietly if you like, and I'm going to write some notes on some of the factors of success that the best Japanese product development teams have in common."

Four Factors of Success

Leadership. *On large projects, there is a single, heavy-duty boss called a* shusa. *All the people on the project report directly to the* shusa. *This is in contrast to the project coordinator in western companies who often has very limited authority and power.*

Teamwork. *Team members, although retaining some ties to their functional department, are assigned to the project for its duration. The advancement of each team member's career depends on the* shusa's *favorable evaluation. So the team's mission is taken very seriously.*

Communication. *They determine the product plans and product definition early. They resolve potential conflicts over design tradeoffs early and each team member signs a formal pledge to do exactly what the whole team agrees to.*

Simultaneous development. *All activities are initiated in parallel as soon as information is available.*

"So you're saying that to reduce development time, companies must form teams that work outside the normal functional organization?" Laura asks.

Marcus makes a pyramid with his hands. "Not necessarily, Laura. This method may not work well in very large organizations where the functional groups are powerful, because they may not buy into the plans developed by a separate team. Ford Motor Company has had that experience, and so in 1980, when Ford organized a team to develop the Taurus/Sable product line, they did so with members from each of the functional organizations. These team members served dual roles, as working members of their functional organizations and as members of the Taurus team."

Ford Taurus Team

First, the team's mission was clearly defined and communicated.[3] CEO Philip Caldwell set the guidelines when he said, "Why should anyone walk across the street and buy our car? Finding answers to this question must be a constant concern as we implement this entire program. What are we doing differently to make sure that we come up with a winner and not a loser? Let's set up an organization so that each member of the team keeps these questions in mind." Caldwell's words were later translated into a common goal to produce a truly world-class car, and this goal was shared by every team member.

Second, they chose a strong, experienced, and widely respected manager to captain the project. Lew Veraldi had spent time in both engineering and manufacturing and had a reputation for understanding both points of view. He had just led the highly successful European design team that designed the Fiesta. He had a powerful position as vice president of Advanced Vehicles Development.

Third, they brought the manufacturing, sales and marketing, service, and suppliers into the process in the earliest design phase. Three years in engineering taught Veraldi how designs got on paper, and during three years in manufacturing, he learned what happens to a design after it leaves engineering. People in manufacturing would complain that the car couldn't be made the way it was engineered, and engineers would complain that the design was no good. In many parts of Ford these groups didn't talk to each other. So when Philip Caldwell named Veraldi to head the Fiesta team to design a car for European sale, he had the freedom to try some new team-design concepts.

He got the respect of the manufacturing people right off simply by asking, "Before we put this design on paper, how do you, the manufacturing and assembly people, want us to proceed to make your jobs easier?" Asking this simple question, as it turned out, drastically reduced the number of changes that had to be made later, saved a lot of money, and simply led to the manufacture of a better car.

The rear door of the Fiesta is a case in point. The manufacturing people did the design and the engineers drew it up. The result of this collaborative design was that there wasn't a single rear door leakage problem among the five million Fiestas that were built, even though historically rear doors were notorious for this problem.

In summary, the Fiesta project convinced Veraldi that he must bring downstream people in as part of the design team right from the start. But on the Taurus project, the concept was expanded to include suppliers, line workers, sales and marketing, service, manufacturing, dealers, customers, UAW leaders, independent service people, lawyers, and insurance experts.

Suppliers were chosen over two years prior to production. They were given single-source, long-term, system contracts. For example a single company was given a long-term contract for all interior moldings. Suppliers were asked to contribute ideas and they did.

Fourth, they conducted a competitive analysis of the competition and of consumer wants. They purchased hundreds of foreign and domestic cars in order to identify the world's 400 best-designed and best-engineered automotive features — from sun visors to steering systems. Focus groups around the country were shown designs, then clay models, then prototypes, and finally pre-production units to get their reaction. They incorporated many of the recommendations into the design.

Taurus was named the 1986 Car of the Year by *Motor Trend,* and by 1987, the Taurus was the top-selling car in the United States.

"Isn't that exactly what Harold Faig said wouldn't work?"

"He didn't say it wouldn't work. He said that what they did in his organization was the best way to meet their goals of extremely short development time. If we talked to Lew Veraldi, the leader of the Ford Taurus team, he would tell us that the functional representative team was best for them."

"In all of your examples, the leaders were very powerful," Lou says.

"Yes, but in addition to that," Marcus replies, "in every case the Process Model was designed to meet the Process Intent, although they were organized in very different ways. It is important to recognize the difference between the organizational chart and the Value Delivery Systems of the business."

"But wouldn't it be best to design the Value Delivery Systems of the business first, then design the organization to facilitate the Delivery Systems?" Laura asks.

"Very powerful thought, Laura, very powerful; and that's how it should be done," Marcus says.

"Let's move on. The same relationship between response and Process Model applies to the service sector. Let's visit both Wendy's and McDonald's to learn from two Hunters."

Suddenly the scenery around them changes. They are inside a McDonald's restaurant. "Take a minute or so to adjust, if you need it," Marcus says, "and then let's order some food."

Conventional Approach to Organizational Design

- design pyramidal, functionally structured organization
- provide procedure to move product or services through the functional structure

Transformational Approach

- design the Delivery System to deploy the business strategy
  - determine Process Intent
  - determine Process Model
  - design the Learning and Improvement System

- organize people in such a way as to optimize the performance of the Delivery System

---

"But we just ate," Laura says.

"Yes, but instantaneous molecular transport burns a lot of calories."

"I am hungry, come to think of it," Lou says.

"Be sure to take note of how long it takes from the time you order until the time you're served."

Lou orders a standard Quarter-pounder with fries and coffee. Laura orders a Quarter-pounder with nothing on it and a diet Coke. "Nothing on it?" the server asks. "Nothing," Laura says.

"Under one minute," Marcus says as Lou receives his order.

"Your order will be a few minutes," the server says to Laura. Four minutes later, Laura is served.

"Observe the process for awhile," Marcus says. "How is it that McDonald's can do a standard order so fast?"

After some silent observation, Marcus leads them outside. "So what do you think, Lou?"

"It's obvious. The grillers and sandwich makers in the back are making sandwiches in batches and storing them in chutes that keep them warm until the servers pick them up. Since the sandwiches are ready, the server can take the order and dispense the drinks, pick up the sandwiches and fries, and take payment in less than a minute — less than the time it takes to cook the meat."

"Excellent analysis. How about drawbacks, Laura?"

"Custom orders disrupt the system."

"What if a burger sits under the heat lamp too long and gets all dried out?" Lou asks.

Marcus reaches into Lou's bag and pulls out the burger. "See this mark on the wrapper? When the sandwich makers complete the sandwiches and wrap them, they check off the time when the burger was made. Periodically, the manager checks the front burgers in the heating bin, and if any have been in the heating bin for more than ten minutes, they are thrown away."

"Really thrown away?" Laura says.

"Garbage can, Laura. That is their upper quality limit on freshness. They have to constantly balance burger freshness against delivery time."

"That means they have to control the inventory they make ahead and put in the warming bin. What happens if they get a sudden surge of people?" Laura asks.

"They put a lot of effort into avoiding surprise surges. The manager of the store has a computer printout every morning of what was done last year on that day and whether there are any trends or upcoming events that need to be considered. The manager must schedule the right number of people at all the work stations to maximize people efficiency through the day and week. If there are too few people, service suffers; if there are too many, costs go out of line. It's a world-class balancing act. Here's a flow chart of McDonald's Process Model," Marcus says as he hands each of them a drawing.

McDonald's Process Model

........▸ Customer flow   - - - -▸ Order flow   ⟶ Burger flow

1 Meat unwrapped
2 Meat grilled
3 Move to dressing
4 Dress
5 Move to wrap
6 Store
7 Customer enters
8 Server takes order
9 Server goes to chutes
10 Server delivers burger

dressing table

2 grill

Process Intent
– Fast on standard orders
– Good cost/value
– Quality consistency

heated burger storage

Suddenly, Lou, Laura, and Marcus are standing in a line at Wendy's restaurant. "Now let's refocus. We're here to get a different angle on the relationship between the Process Intent and the Process Model."

After just a few minutes in line, they are at the order counter. Marcus says. "Order the same as you did at McDonald's. Lou, you keep the time."

Lou places his order and pushes a button to activate the stopwatch function on the fancy new digital watch Marcus gave him the day before. Both orders are completed in a little over thirty seconds.

"How much difference in the time required to make a standard or a custom burger?" Marcus asks.

"None," Laura answers. "It doesn't matter because the cheese and all the condiments are added after the customer orders."

"You see? Wendy's customers expect to have it any way they want it and still have it pretty fast. How is the layout and flow of work designed to produce custom orders fast?"

"The grill is in the front by the counter and they keep a moving stock of burgers on the grill. They customize them immediately after the order is taken," Lou explains.

"How do they know how many hamburger patties to keep on the grill at any given time so that every customer gets a just-cooked burger?" Marcus asks.

"I suppose by counting the number of people in line and estimating the number of patties that should be cooking," Laura answers.

"Very good. As you can see, our burgers and fries were cooking as we got in line. By looking at the line and figuring the time of day, the day of the week, and whether any special events are in town, they try to have just the right amount cooking so that customers' burgers are finished just as they order."

"Neat trick. Fast, customized, and just-cooked quality," Laura says. "Even the single line is an important part of the Process Model. So that's what you mean when you say design to produce what customers value."

"Yes. Here's a flow chart with Wendy's Process Intent and Process Model," Marcus says handing them another sheet of paper.

"When the single-order taker calls out the order, what part of the order does the grill person hear?"

"How many hamburger patties?" Lou says.

"And one more thing," Marcus says.

"Cheese or no cheese," Laura says. "And the dresser hears only the condiments on each burger."

Wendy's Process Model

"The manager must have heard the rest of the order: french fries, drinks, chili, and Frosties," Lou says.

"Good, very good," Marcus says. "At Wendy's, how would you reduce the time from the customer entry until the time they receive their order?"

"Seems like that would be tough to do," Laura says.

"Right. I don't think you could speed it up any and still have the burger just finishing as the order is taken," Lou adds.

"Get the idea?" Marcus says to both of them.

"Do you mean the idea that Wendy's is good?" Laura asks.

"I think he means that if they're really good, it's tough to improve them," Lou says.

"Let me see if I have this straight," Laura says. "McDonald's Process Model is not designed to produce custom orders fast, and Wendy's Process Model is not designed to produce a standard burger instantly. To design the best Delivery Systems you must thoroughly define the Process Intent in terms of response required, quality required, and value/cost required, and then you must use a Process Model that is optimum for the Design Intent."

"You have it straight," Marcus says.

"That also means that since McDonald's and Wendy's haven't changed their Process Intent or Process Model in years, they are in a Linear Continuous Improvement mode only," Laura adds.

"But Wendy's has added a salad bar and a food bar, and Mcdonald's has added Mexican food and pizza as standard products in many of their restaurants," Marcus says.

"It's interesting that neither has changed its Process Intent. McDonald's is adding standard products and Wendy's is adding customized products like do-it-yourself salad and food bar," Lou says.

"Brilliant observation, just brilliant," Marcus says as Lou gives Laura a self-satisfied smile. "Let's move on now. Instantaneous or gradual molecular transport?"

"Gradual," Lou and Laura answer in unison.

There's a long silence as they pass over the salt beds near Salt Lake City. Lou can't contain himself. "Even with all that fast, just-cooked quality and personal service at Wendy's, it looked like McDonald's had more customers."

"You're right, Lou. McDonald's has about ten thousand locations and has more customers than Burger King, Wendy's, and Hardee's combined. In 1992, one out of six people who visit a restaurant will go to a McDonald's. The largest restaurant in the world, with fifty thousand customers a day is a

McDonald's in Moscow, and a McDonald's is operating just off of Tiananmen Square in Beijing. But Wendy's started thirty years after McDonald's. And Wendy's is doing well. Net income was up thirty-one percent to $51.3 million in 1991. They have almost four thousand restaurants open now and they are opening two hundred per year. This war isn't over yet. We'll take another look thirty years from now."

"This is interesting but how does this relate to manufacturing?" Lou asks.

"All businesses can be reduced to Delivery Systems that add value, and the basic principles are the same for all of them. Business is a lot more than heavy manufacturing. Fast food is a $50 billion business and we're studying the best in the business. Anytime you study the best in the business you learn something. And one more thing, today the service businesses in the U.S. are the Hunters of the world, expanding their world class operations all over the globe. There's a lot to be learned by studying the best."

As they arrive at Guardian Command, Laura speaks. "Marcus, I can see how the choice of a Process Model is a key factor, but how do you go about choosing a particular Process Model to meet a given Process Intent?"

"Very good question. The ways to divide work are as old as work itself. In the earliest records of humans, there is evidence that work was divided among tribe members. Later, industrialists like Thomas Tompion discovered the increased productivity that was obtained when work was divided. Unfortunately, because of the success of the subdivision of manual work into specialities, the model was universally applied to administrative, service, and engineering work also. But as you learned from Harold Faig, the model didn't work so well in some engineering applications."

"So is there a logical way to determine the ideal Process Model for a certain Process Intent?"

"Yes, there is. First, the Process Model must meet the Process Intent. So if fast customer response is important, you've got to choose a fast Process Model. But in addition, you also have to take into account a number of other important things: the degree of learning that must take place in the execution of the work itself; the degree of interaction with the customer; and the influence that the scope of the work plays in the interest, satisfaction, and productivity of the workers.

"To understand the importance of the role of learning, let's analyze the relative learning that takes place in three different types of work: repetitive, custom, and new.

"Thomas Tompion's watchmaking is an example of repetitive work. Once the watch was designed, a set of processes was repeated by worker specialists to produce the components, such as dial plates and top covers. These parts were then assembled by craftsmen, because adjustment was required in the assembly. Ford's engineers, on the other hand, standardized the component-fabrication processes to the extent that even assembly required very little learning in the execution of the steps of the process itself.

"This method of standardizing the manufacturing process itself was developed into a set of practices by Frederick Taylor and his followers that became known as scientific management. In the early 1900s, scientific management was generally accepted as a universally applicable model, and it was aggressively applied to all forms of work. In addition to manufacturing tasks, administrative work and service work was divided into small specialities, and entire departments were organized along functional specialties.

"In this model, Delivery Systems involved dozens of people each doing their individual specialty. The theory was that if each functional or individual task was optimized, the whole could be optimized. In practice however, dividing tasks increases the number of interfaces, transactions and communications that must take place in order to process a service or order through an entire Delivery System. In addition, in complex Delivery Systems, extensive coordination and shepherding is required to ensure that all these activities take place when they are required. As a consequence, highly subdivided administrative and service systems respond slowly and often unsatisfactorily to customers.

"For the sake of our theory about Process Models, let's call the highly subdivided model the 'many minds-many missions' model and the other extreme the 'one mind-one mission' model. Frederick Taylor and his associates advocated the many minds-many missions model — which I'll call 'many' for short; Harold Faig, on the other end, was advocating a one mind-one mission model for the purpose of product development. I'll this model 'one' for short.

"You still call the Harold Faig approach a 'one,' even though many people were involved?" Laura asks.

"But were they not of a single mind and united on a single mission?" Marcus responds.

"I suppose they were, now that you mention it. Interesting."

"You still haven't answered the question about how one knows which model to choose," says Lou.

"I'm getting there," Marcus says, readying his light stylus. "Let's divide the work into three categories: repetitive, custom, and new, and ask the following questions about each:

....

- *Is learning required in the execution of the work itself?*
- *Is interaction with the customer required from those who do the work?*
- *Does the scope of the work influence the worker's job satisfaction or productivity?*

....

"The answers to these questions will help us choose the best model," Marcus says, pushing a button on the light stylus and calling up a chart.

	Learning required to execute work	Interaction with customer	Influence of scope on work performance
Repetitive	low	low	varies
Custom	medium	high	high
New	high	high	high

"The more highs that we list for a type of work, the more likely that the 'one' model will work best. But first and foremost, the Process Model must meet the design intent."

"So for example, since the development of the new plastic molding machines that Harold was telling us about rates three highs," Laura says, "it leads to the choice of the 'one' model."

"Exactly."

Lou sighs. "You two sure like to play around with the theory, but what's the practical side to all this?"

Marcus gives Lou a disapproving look. "Nothing so practical as a good theory, a wise man once said. Lou, where did Henry Ford's model fit into this theory?"

"It was repetitive work, so I guess his choice of the 'many' model was a good one. Wow, isn't this hilarious, us saying that Ford was okay in his choice. As if he would have given a damn." Lou guffaws.

Marcus doesn't smile. "Lou, do you think that the narrow scope of the jobs in the Ford plant had an influence on the performance of the workers on the assembly lines?"

"A narrow scope is fine for some people, but most of the guys I worked with didn't like being tied down to a narrow, routine job."

"Can you think of an example of custom work that requires a high interaction with the customer?"

"Service work like medical, legal, or cosmetology usually involves direct contact with the customer," Laura says. "And most of it is the 'one' model."

Marcus nods in agreement. "There are many forms of the one mind-one mission model for the division of work. It's the ideal model for entrepreneurial work. A single entrepreneur starting a business is the basic unit of this model. The single individual may design the product and the process, do the marketing and sales, produce and inspect the service or product, and manage the finances. As the business grows, and as the entrepreneur hires people, it will be increasingly difficult to keep everyone focused on the mission of the company. The challenge is to have many people function as if they are of one mind and one mission," Marcus says as he presses a button on the light stylus.

Teams

Manufacturing has traditionally emphasized individual accountability. Every worker was individually measured. Today, teams operating synchronously perform much faster than individuals operating separately.

Customer Focused Model

The following chart illustrates how three groups organized along a customer focused Delivery System can have different objectives, but maintain a common mission to be the supplier of choice and gain by it.

Process Model for Customer-Focused Delivery System

New Product or Service Development

Performance Objectives
• Reduce time to market
• Superior product or service
• Optimum design definition
• Assembly (cost/value ratio)

Performance Objectives
• Reduce cycle time
• Eliminate defects and variation
• Supplier certification and rationalization
• Reduce costs

Supplier Delivery Systems

Performance Objectives
• Satisfy customers
• Reduce cycle time
• Eliminate defects and variation
• Reduce costs

Product or Service Manufacturing

Supply team	Development team	Manufacturing team
Customer	Customer	Operator
Engineer	Product engineer	Operator
Quality	Process engineer	Operator
Supplier	Supplier	Manager
	Marketing	Quality
	Manufacturing	Logistics
	Quality	

"You should also keep in mind," Marcus continues as he writes with the stylus, "that there are many modern forms of the many minds-many missions model. One in particular is the functionally focused version that Harold was talking about."

Functionally Focused Model

Functionally focused organizations group people by the type of work performed, (e.g.: finance, engineering, manufacturing, service, sales, marketing, personnel). The advantages are that the people in a functionally focused group can share expertise and learning in their function. Economies of scale may result if common activities are grouped (centralization).

Each separation of a Delivery System into functions creates an interface. Interfaces between functions create paperwork, handling activity, need for communication and coordination, and higher level arbitration of conflicting purpose. This increases system cycle time and costs.

Process Model for Functionally Focused Delivery System

"I'd like now to show you another chart," Marcus says. "This one shows the two major models for dividing work. It also shows supporting flow models, demand management models, and learning models. The learning models we'll talk more about later."

"But for now, let's get back to the response characteristic of Process Intent." Marcus says handing them some papers. "I've written this material on common fast- and slow-flow models for your reference."

....

Fast Response Flow Models

Some of the faster flow models are parallel/concurrent, pull, synchronous, and continuous.

Parallel/concurrent. *For fast response, activities should be scheduled in parallel as much as possible.*

Pull. *In this model, demand is forecast and scheduled but not executed until orders are received. Individual departments in a sequence do not build anything until the following operation needs components. Toyota, Buick, and General Electric use this model for manufacturing, and the Toyota model is much imitated. Supermarkets have used this model since the thirties. Its disadvantage is that it doesn't respond well to sudden changes in demand.*

Synchronous. *To achieve synchronous flow, all of the activities must occur in precise chronology. In assembly processes, activities are grouped so that the cycle times at each operation are equal. To obtain true synchronous flow, a base beat (takt) must be established much as it is in a symphony orchestra. To contrast synchronous flow with pull flow, imagine how a ballet would be executed if each dancer had to wait for a cue from the previous dancer before moving.*

Continuous. *In continuous flow, the product or service moves through the Delivery System without interruption. In its ultimate form, the product or service doesn't wait at all between value-added operations, and the customer can obtain delivery in little more time than it takes to add the value.*

Slow Response Process Models

Of the flow models, the push model is often the slowest. But it does have its favored applications.

Push model. In the push model, demand is forecast, operations are scheduled, material is ordered, and work begins as soon as possible. This model is essential if changes in demand are sudden but predictable. For instance, consider a hot dog stand at a football stadium. Hot dogs, buns, and syrup for drinks must be ordered in advance and be available hours prior to game time.

Models for Managing Demand

There are at least eight models for managing demand: build to order, forecast and schedule, load leveling, appointment scheduling, flexible capacity, multiplexing, first in-first out, priority expedite, open heart surgery, and stock.

Appointment scheduling. In this model the demand is leveled by requiring appointments. Cadillac Livonia requires component trucks to have appointments for unloading so that they can maintain a thirty-minute maximum time for moving material from the trucks to their assembly lines. Tanning-bed salons and doctors use this model, which allocates capacity in advance. If a resource in an office or factory serves many customers, they must obtain forecasts from, and allocate time for all customers, or it's likely they will likely have to maintain a backlog to be efficient.

Flexible capacity. Von's and Ralph's supermarkets add additional cashiers immediately if more than two people are in a checkout line. Domino's Pizza and Shoneys maintain a slight excess of servers to ensure fast service. Companies with flexible capacity and short system cycle times can respond faster. Poorly designed systems respond slowly to changes in demand. If demand increases faster than a company can respond, customers have to wait. If demand falls more rapidly than output, excess inventories accumulate.

Stock. Many industries maintain some finished goods inventory so they can respond to standard orders. But this inventory must be carefully controlled. During the 1990-91 recession, L.A. Gear did not cut production fast enough to match orders and was encumbered with huge unsold inventories, which caused reductions in their profits.

FIFO or lead job model. In this model a person or team works exclusively on the next job into the process until they cannot work on that job any longer due to lack of information, tools, parts, or approvals. They then work on the next job into the process until they can resume work on the first job. This assures a FIFO job order, provides self-balancing work distribution, and controls the amount of work-in-process.

Load leveled. A machine shop is a good example because it typically has to deal with the following conditions:

- Demand is highly variable.
- The work force is highly skilled and highly paid.
- Workers that are laid off have a probability of not returning, and a skilled machinist is not easy to hire.
- Machine investment is high so equipment utilization must be high to achieve reasonable return on investment.

To optimize their performance with all these conditions, machine shops maintain one to three months of order backlogs and charge a premium to bypass the order backlog and give fast response.

Multiplexed. People often apportion their time to many tasks that are in progress in such a way that they spend a little time on task one, a little time on task two, and so on. There *may be many reasons for this approach such as shifting priorities, interruptions, or tradition, but the most common cause is that work cannot be continued on the current task due to lack of information, unavailability of tools, lack of parts, or waiting for decisions or approval.*

Consequently, a person or team may have many tasks in progress causing large amounts of work-in-process (WIP). As the number of incomplete jobs increases, WIP increases, system cycle time increases, and customer response time gets worse. As more people multiplex more jobs, others must wait and are forced to multiplex more themselves. It's a vicious cycle. The worse it gets, the worse it gets.

Open heart surgery model. *This model can be best understood by imagining that your father is undergoing open heart surgery, and the surgeon has his chest cavity open and is in the process of replacing an artery. What criteria would you establish for the interruption of the surgeon at this critical time? Should the surgeon be interrupted for a call from his broker? Should the surgeon be called to a meeting with the staff director? Should the surgeon suspend surgery for a lunch break? Most of us would be hard pressed to come up with any satisfactory reason for interruption.*

Any activity that will hold up the introduction of a new product in the marketplace should be considered critical because the life of the company is at stake. For example, if an engineer is designing a new product, certain subsequent processes will be delayed until design information is available. If subsequent processes will be delayed, the engineer should focus exclusively on developing that information. There should be no interruptions unless the need for interruption is an unconditional imperative. The engineering development process is as critical to the company's success as surgery is to your father's life.

"When misused," Marcus comments after Lou and Laura have finished reading, "demand management models can be slow to respond to customers, as is true of the load leveled model and the multiplexed model.

"Now, although we've already discussed the customer time, space, and value model, it's important enough to review," he says, writing with the stylus.

Customer Time, Customer Space, and Customer Value Model

Many hotels offer automatic checkout and billing if you specify the day of departure when you check in. Automatic teller machines (ATMs) provide services at any time the customer wishes and are physically close to the customer. When businesses refer to their manufacturing or service lead time they are thinking in their time, not customer time. A couple of points to remember:

- *acceptable quality level (AQL) is a measure in supplier values*
- *total customer satisfaction is a measure in customer values*

"Are there any Process Models that are universally applicable?" Laura asks.

"No," Marcus replies, "the most applicable Process Model is *always* the one that best meets the Process Intent."

"Also keep in mind," Marcus continues, "that in all these models, work-in-process is a very important factor. Tonight we'll have a lesson on the effect of work in process on the response of the Delivery System. Julia made us a fire in the room of the Hunters. I'll be telling a fireside fable after dinner."

Lou looks at Marcus. *He's got to be kidding . . .*

The Parallel Work Flow Model

It's no small feat for a home cook to have hot bacon, eggs, biscuits, and gravy hit the table at the same time.

To do this, the cook fries bacon, bakes biscuits, sets the table, and signals the eaters in a parallel, multiplexed, continuous flow. There is a schedule in the cook's head that directs the work. All of the implements are within easy reach, the materials are less than a few steps away, and the oven is at the center of it all. The activity is charted below.

Operation	Operation Cycle Time	Preparation Time	Preheat Time
1. Make coffee	4 min.	2 min.	
2. Fry bacon	12 min.	2 min.	
3. Bake biscuits	16 min.	2 min.	6 min. (oven)
4. Set table	3 min.	1 min.	
5. Make gravy	5 min.	1.5 min.	
6. Fry eggs	5 min.	0.5 min.	1 min. (pan)
7. Put food on	0.5 min.	1.5 min.	
8. Pour juice	0.5 min.	0.5 min.	

For one cook operating with synchronized parallel work flow, the time that elapses from the start of breakfast preparation until food is placed on the table is about 22 minutes. If the work were performed in a serial sequence, the time to serve would be 61 minutes. Therefore, synchronized parallel work flow is the best way to achieve high performance in on-time delivery, food quality, and efficiency while minimizing the time from preparation to actual food service.

In a commercial kitchen like Denny's, the grill would be preheated and the gravy, biscuits, and coffee would be prepared ahead of time, reducing the time to serve to less than ten minutes. By preparing standard menu items before they are actually ordered, McDonald's has reduced the time to serve to less than a minute.

Managing the Demand Side

Customers order and buy products when they choose and they use services when they are ready, creating a fluctuating demand. If a business (General Unlimited in the figure below) wishes to respond quickly under all conditions, it needs to have enough capacity available to meet peak demand. This requires an investment much higher than that required to meet average demand and in many cases the additional investment is not justified. If attempting to increase capacity at bottleneck operations does not produce additional throughput, then General Unlimited (GU) has available a number of options.

Carrying finished goods inventory. This option provides fast response but increases inventory carrying costs and may result in obsolete inventory.

Buffering demand. In this option, GU creates a backlog of orders prior to the start of their process. They then release the orders into their process at the average demand level on a priority basis.

By establishing this buffer, GU's response to customers is slowed by the time length of the buffer. To use this option and not lose customers they must reduce their Delivery System cycle times such that the total of the external buffer time and the Delivery System cycle time is less than market expectations.

Managing time of purchase. Instead of reducing internal cycle times, they may offer price reductions to those willing to wait longer for delivery or if the market will bear it, they may establish standard delivery lead times and charge additional for faster than standard response. Companies that build industrial machines and tools commonly do this.

Managing load demand. GU may offer discounts for purchases made during certain periods of the year when the expected demand is low, or they may charge more during times of peak demand. If GU is a public utility, it may encourage its customers to reduce power usage during peak demand periods or offer incentives to reduce overall power usage.

CHAPTER TWELVE

His Father's Son

The flames sear the underside of the steaks on the grill. Wil watches as the fat drops attack and the hot charcoal bed fires back. Fat drops don't have a chance. His wife, Sue, pats him on the back.

"This is the first time in my life that I've felt like quitting something," he says as he turns the steaks.

"Anytime you want to go home to Phoenix, just say the word," she says.

"It's worse than I imagined."

She nods as she chops zucchini for the salad.

"For starters," he continues, "at the rate things are going the division will lose millions this year. It's so bad that there's no way it can be turned around without cutting staff and laying off some people in the plant."

"That worries you, doesn't it?"

"That's a biggie, but it's not the only worry."

She quietly continues to set the table for Sunday dinner. She's curious about what is causing her husband to work all night and all day but she knows that if Wil wants to talk about it, he will. "I'm glad you didn't work today," she says. "You need to get away from that place . . . Are the steaks ready?"

"Almost . . . I can hardly believe it. There's no daily internal tracking systems for reporting scrap, production by department, and purchases. There seems to be a total lack of concern by most salary personnel for meeting customer commitments of quality and delivery. There's huge amounts of inventory everywhere but everything has to be expedited to get it out to our customers. The equipment is in poor condition, and there's no effort to maintain it unless it completely breaks down. There's no organized quality improvement effort. Every time I peel another layer from the onion it looks worse.

"And I feel like the Lone Ranger when I talk about making the division profitable. I think they feel that if they just put up with my ravings for a while, I'll be gone just like the others before me. I'm too old for this."

"Could you get your old job back?"

"Sue, too many people's jobs depend on me."

"Well, maybe they ought to depend on someone else this time. I worry about you. You're working long hours and you're not getting enough rest. It's that plant, twenty-four hours, seven days. I can't believe you took the time for a quiet Sunday dinner."

"I'll be all right," Wil says. Her comment takes him back. Thinking about it now, he recalls that his mother used to tell his father all the time that he worked too hard. But he was in the meat trucking business and he had to work hard. Had to be at the Brooklyn packing plant before four in the morning if he wanted a spot at the dock. Will remembers helping his dad with the meat route on Saturdays and during the summer. It was a tough way to make a living . . . had to force your way into a spot at the dock. He can still see that truck — all bent up from the pushing contests in those early morning hours. The meat had to be at the butchers' across town before 5:00 A.M. *Tough business . . . but Dad was tough . . . he never quit . . .*

"I borrowed a young engineer, Alan Updike, from another Allied Division. He's got some good ideas. He told me about this guy named Marcus who really helped them out at his former plant. I've asked Alan to contact the guy. Steaks are ready."

I call it the 'Stuffing the Goose Theory.' Production planning was based on the assumption that if we put orders into the process, somehow we could get the orders through the process. It's like saying that you can just keep shoving food into the mouth of the goose and eventually the goose will pass it all.

– Al Mataliano, retired vice president
Hughes Aircraft

The mind treats a new idea like the body treats a new protein; it rejects it.

– Biologist P.B. Medawar

CHAPTER THIRTEEN

Response and Work-in-Process

*T*he room of the Hunters is scented with burning oak and the wall paintings are alive with dancing flames. "Hunters," Laura says scanning the pictures of men, women, and animals as they walk toward the fire at the far side of the room.

"All Hunters," Marcus says. They move closer to the fire. "Do you remember how the fable of the 'Three Little Pigs' ended?"

"You're kidding," Lou says.

"I remember," Laura says. "The big gray wolf couldn't blow the third little pig's brick house down so he came down the chimney. The third little pig put a boiling pot at the bottom of the chimney, which cooked the wolf."

"That's it, Laura, but I have a sequel to the fable," Marcus says as he seats himself in front of the roaring fire.

....

The fame of the third little pig, Solomon, spread through all Pigland after his brick house withstood the most forceful huffs and puffs of the big grey wolf. Pigs came from distant lands to see the house of brick and to meet the legendary wolf conqueror.

They examined his brick house asking how he made the brick, mixed the mortar, and set the windows. In one of these visits a pig from another village asked Sol if he would build a brick house for her. Since Sol liked to build things, he eagerly said yes. When word got out that he was building houses, others asked him to build houses for them. In time Sol decided to start a business which he appropriately named, Wolforts, maker of wolf-proof homes.

His orders for houses came in at a rate much faster than he could build them, so he began to employ other pigs to help him. His work force grew quickly and Sol could no longer manage all of the activities of his business. He hired three managers. Engin, who would make the drawings for the workers and develop new bricks; Finan, who would manage the money; and Manag, who would supervise the construction crews.

As the business expanded, Engin divided the task of making drawings into three departments, style, design, and layout. The stylists would create the overall style of the house, the designers would develop the house plans, and the layout people would make the detailed construction blueprints. Manag also subdivided his operations into three groups. A group headed by a sow named Clar dug up the clay and ground the lime for bricks and mortar; a second group supervised by a pig called Brice fired bricks; and a third group managed by an older pig named Rocky did the construction.

Finan hired financial and business graduates from Pig Ivy U. These wizards, with their connections to Newpork arranged for the financing of Wolforts's rapid expansion. In its third pig-year Wolforts became a public corporation and declared its first dividend to its shareholders. Engineers were hired from Ham State who were trained in matters of efficiency and return on investment.

In time, Wolforts Inc. became a model of the great wonders of Pigland genius. From other villages and other lands, a constant stream of visitors oohed and aahed as they were shown the vast brick house factory. They toured the clay making and mortar grinding operations at the distant edge of Pigville. There, the workers cut the clay and loaded it onto flat rail cars that transported it to the firing and mixing plant a half mile to the south. From there, the bricks and mortar mix were trucked to the building sites all throughout Pigland.

Sol prospered. In time he built a very large brick house on the largest hill in town. His financial advisors urged him to acquire and he did. He bought railroads and restaurants, banks and bakeries, stockyards and studios, until, as his advisors advised, his portfolio was properly diversified. In order to manage his vast financial empire, Sol promoted his most trusted manager, Finan, to be president of Wolforts. As his advisors advised, Sol needed to spend his time managing his money.

The first hint of trouble surfaced a pigyear after Finan assumed control. At a luncheon at the local Mudclub, Winn, Sol's good friend and mayor of Pigville, asked Sol how he felt about the new brick houses that the wolves were building. He said that the wolves advertised them as wolf-proof and man-proof.

"Harrumph." Sol had a very commanding way of clearing his throat. "False advertising!" Sol said stridently. "And besides, pigs will never buy from wolves."

"I've heard people say that the bricks the wolves use never crack and the mortar never separates from the brick," Winn said meekly.

"Nonsense!" Sol's voice was beginning to rise. "Everyone knows that occasionally a brick will crack or some mortar will separate."

"I'm sure you're right, Sol; all that talk is probably rubbish," Winn said returning to his lunch.

"Rubbish is right," Sol said as he pounded the table with his hoof.

But that evening Sol couldn't get it out of his mind. So the next day, he secretly visited the south plant where the bricks were fired. Without speaking to anyone, he began to pick bricks from the brick pile and drop them to the ground. Of the first 10 bricks he dropped, one broke in half. So he continued, picking bricks from another pile dropping them and counting the number that broke. By this time, the yard pig was yelling at Sol. "Put down those bricks, get the — " The yard pig stopped short when she recognized old Sol.

"What do you make of this?" Sol said, pointing to the pile of broken bricks. "Some of them break when dropped to the ground."

"I guess we don't make 'em like we used to, sir."

"We'll see about that," the old pig said as he flared his nostrils and strode rapidly toward the furnaces where the bricks were being fired.

"Get me Brice," he said to the first pig he encountered. The pig began to run toward a large office building to the east of the furnaces. Before Sol could reach the office area, Brice was running toward him.

"The bricks are brittle; no wonder they crack," Sol was fuming.

"They satisfy our specs, sir. I'll get the reliability reports for you to see."

"Reporting rubbish," Sol bellowed. "The bricks are brittle."

"Sorry, sir, but with all due respect, Clar's people make the mix."

"Bricks didn't break before," Sol snarled. "Take me to Clar."

The old pig was quiet, except for an occasional mutter, as the truck bounced and bounded through the countryside. When they came to the clay pit, Clar was there to greet them with volumes of reports.

"I told Engin's people that mixing bog mud in with the clay would weaken the brick," she explained, "but they said it was

required to allow the new cutting machines to be efficient. I have the memo I wrote to him right here, sir."

"Make no more," Sol said with a sweep of his hoof. "Inform the construction crews that they are not to use brittle bricks."

"But sir, there are six pigweeks of clay cuts already finished," Clar said.

"And four pigweeks of fired brick," Brice chimed in. "If we stopped using bog mud today it would be ten pigweeks before the construction crews got the new bricks."

"Ten weeks? Nonsense. It only takes a few pighours to cut clay and fire bricks."

"Yes, sir, we could expedite new bricks to the construction crews in a pigday, but then what will you do with the ten weeks of inventory in process?" Brice asked.

Sol's head was grinding away. Finan would be flapped if they disposed of all those clay cuts and bricks. The new cutting machine had reduced pig labor dramatically and he knew how the inventory smoothed over the problems of production. Everybody was studying Sol. After what seemed like many pig-minutes, Sol smiled.

"Drop test all bricks, dispose of the ones that break."

Everyone marvelled at the wisdom of the older pig. If each brick were inspected for brittleness, then no brittle bricks would find their way into houses; the new cutting machine could be used; and they wouldn't have to scrap all that material. Every-one was happy with the decision.

The second hint of trouble came about a pigyear later. Salespigs had been saying for sometime that the wolves were offering a variety of colors in their bricks and Wolforts was los-ing some customers because they offered only basic red.

"Why would anyone want anything but basic red?" Sol asked.

"It's the wolves, sir," the sales manager said. "They're putting all this nonsense in people's heads. But we have to respond. We should develop at least two color options."

*"It will take three or four pigmonths to develop new colors,"
Engin said. "We are understaffed in the engineering area. We
just can't respond to each and every customer wish and still do
cost savings, redesign, and provide support to production operations. I'll need to hire more engineers —but until they are on
board, we'll have to set some priorities here."*

*"It would be inefficient to have all those colors in the brick-
making area," Manag said. And we'll lose a lot of our capacity
on changing over from one to the other. It also means lots of
kiln time to run the engineering pilots; and the kilns are already
bottlenecks."*

*"The increased mix will increase overhead costs in every
area; I'll get budget increase requests from every department,"
Finan said. "Our internal cost accounting is not set up to handle it. Maybe it's just a passing thing; I think we ought to wait
and see."*

*"But we must do it, or we may lose our customers," Sol said
resolutely. "Have a plan worked out by next management meeting," Sol ordered and everyone again marveled at the wisdom of
their founder.*

*The plan for adding two new brick options was introduced at
the next staff meeting. There would be three pigmonths of engineering development, half of a pigmonth of prototype and pilot
firings, and then they would be ready to prepare the mix for the
first production. With the average brick manufacturing lead
time of half of a pigmonth, the new options would be available
in six months. Sales was the only group unhappy with the plan,
saying that they would certainly lose more sales in the next few
months. The plan was passed.*

*But Wolforts's troubles were just beginning. Customers were
complaining about variation in color and exterior texture; Sol
agreed with Engin and Brice that there would always be variation.*

*Sales said that the wolves had much better quality consis-
tency.*

One day a pig visited Wolforts with a preposterous tale. He had been to the wolves' factory and thought that the wolves' methods were quite impressive and that Wolforts could learn from them. He said that clay that was cut in the morning was fired the same afternoon and put on the truck to the building site the next morning. The wolves had less than one day of inventory in their whole process. He told of the wolves' claim that they could change color or style of brick in their production line in just a few minutes and they could supply any color and style from a list of thirty-seven styles within three days after an order. He also told of a new machine the wolves had which mixed the clay, fashioned it into bricks, and fired them in one continuous operation, untouched by wolf paws. He also related the wolves' claim that the lower inventories helped them identify defects faster, and they intended to rid their process of all defects.

"Wolfwash," Sol said. "Exaggeration is the wolf's way."

But secretly the old pig was worried. He longed for the good old days when things were simpler and wolves were really wolves. In those days the big gray wolf did what wolves are supposed to do — huff and puff and try to blow pigs' houses down.

"That was great," Laura says, applauding.

"Lou, what do you think is the point of my fable?" Marcus asks.

"I guess the point is that a process cluttered with excess work-in-process has a poor response to customers."

"Good, Lou. Wolforts's manufacturing system cycle time had increased to half a month, and the time for them to bring a new product to market had increased to six months. The bottom line is that as Wolforts's system cycle time increased, it started downhill. Lou, what was the average time from receipt of order to delivery at Continental?"

Chasing Your Tail

When the average system response time is much greater than the average market expectation, all orders will be assigned a priority when they are received. An order that receives a low priority will wait at each process center as other orders of higher priority are processed first. Eventually that order will become due and it will then be assigned a priority. By this system all orders will be prioritized and expedited eventually. All this valueless activity will still leave customers less than satisfied, because prioritizing and expediting does not improve the system's average response time. If something is moved ahead, something also is pushed back.

"Well, first it would take over a month to get it through the office. After we got the schedule in the mill it might take another month," Lou answers.

"What if the customer wanted a slightly different alloy of steel?"

"Add another month if it's an easy one. If engineering got involved, it might never happen," Lou says, smirking at Laura.

"It sounds like you didn't need engineering's help to have poor response to customers," Laura snaps.

Lou scowls, restraining himself. Damn, she has a smart mouth, he thinks. If she were a man he'd be tempted to . . . .

"Just like Wolforts," Marcus says. "Your mill had backlogs of work-in-process — in the office, in the plant, and in the engineering department. An order had to work its way through each of those backlogs, waiting at every operation. This was partly because you were organized like Wolforts, as a series of process centers with stacks of inventory between each process center, and partly because you had the mental model that the inventories were useful."

"So what's the point?" Lou asks.

"The point is that instead of fixing the causes of excess work-in-process and then controlling work-in-process, managers often try to manage their way out of the problems. They build ahead by scheduling material to be built earlier. They develop elaborate priority systems for different levels of urgency; they establish committees to make detailed decisions about what is produced at each operation on a daily basis; and they add expediters to track priority material through the process.

"So they build even though there's a shortage of parts. As the system cycle time increases, the probability that parts at any operation will arrive in time gets worse. To compensate, operations will build what they can and then finish the operation when the other parts arrive.

"If the cause is poor quality, they provide additional capacity and separate repair and rework facilities for the defects. They start additional material, services, or information to cover the loss.

"These responses are necessary because the system is so slow that it must be facilitated and bypassed. But, these reactive efforts add no value, and they use resources that would be better applied to increase capacity, and eliminate defects and errors.

"Beginning to sound like the mill," Lou says.

"These same reactions were common in the engineering groups we studied in school," Laura says. "Inadequate design

---

There Are Always Exceptions — the Business of Alcohol

Work-in-process reduction does not always favor the bottom line. In a restaurant that sells alcoholic beverages, intentional delays are designed into the customer service system, because alcoholic beverages are a high-profit item and more total revenue per person can be realized. To design for high profit, the ratio of dining room table space and bar table space must be optimized so that there is some wait for a table. During this period, the host will seat the customer in the bar. Restaurant waitstaff is often trained in a process that encourages drinking in different stages: at the bar, before the meal, wine with dinner, and after-dinner drinks. All of this increases the system cycle time and work-in-process but increases profits.

capacity, poor information transfer between departments, mistakes made that aren't caught 'til much later, lots of worthless paperwork, and meetings — sounds familiar."

"Suppose that later we have to help a business reduce work-in-process. What's the best way to go about it?" Lou asks.

Marcus hands them each a document. "Here's a reference listing of the remedial actions that the best in the business take to remove excess work-in-process. Refer to these later as we confront the problems of excess work-in-process. We will now study a company that realized that it had a life-threatening problem with their Process Model and with large work-in-process. We'll make the trip to Harley-Davidson in the morning. Hold on to your hats; this one's a thriller!"

Removing Excess Work-in-Process

The following actions are generic to administrative, manufacturing, engineering, service and distribution systems. Administrative, engineering, and service work-in-process is less tangible than work-in-process in the manufacturing or distribution business. In general, work-in-process (WIP) is any work that has been initiated that has not finished processing. Inventory is a broader term including all work that has been expended and/or materials that have been processed or paid for by the producer and that have not been paid for by the customer.

Operations Level Actions

Design with Process Models that Operate Efficiently at Low WIP Levels

High WIP Process Models	*Low WIP Process Models*
operations in series	parallel operations
process center flow	product flow
functionally focused	customer focused
chain of command	network/simultaneous communication

Minimize Interruptions to Continuous Flow

- eliminate defects, errors, and variance
- eliminate need to move or transfer, or if necessary, develop timely, dependable transfer:
  - transfer more often
  - reduce transfer distance
  - eliminate valueless activity at the capacity-limited operation
  - reduce transfer lot size
  - increase available capacity at operations that produce less than the customer demand level
  - add resources (people, machines)
  - use overtime if justifiable

- reduce downtime due to
  - material shortages
  - repair process cycle time
  - changeover

- reduce downtime by reducing the cycle time of the repair process
- increase uptime by using preventive maintenance (train machine operators to perform routine preventive maintenance and repair if possible)
- reduce large differences in operator or machine cycle time in series processes
- release in smaller quantities

Inappropriate Actions

As the system's problems accumulate, schedules will be missed and quality crises become commonplace. If a more responsive, higher quality competitor invades the market, frustrated management will look for quick fixes. These fall into four major categories: organizational, control, technological, and programs.

Organizational: Replacing top or middle managers is the first step, and massive reorganization may follow when that doesn't fix the problem.

Technological: State-of-the art material handling systems and advanced production control software are usually promoted as solutions to the problem.

Control: Management installs systems which provide detailed data; they try to micro-manage themselves out of the mess.

Programs: Employee participation, team building, total quality control, statistical process control, just-in-time, etc. are piloted. Many of these will produce isolated successes, but the bulk of the business continues as usual.

As system cycle times become longer than market expectations, even all the prioritizing and expediting won't get the job done. The business will not be able to quote satisfactory delivery times to the customer and will miss the delivery times they quote. Eventually, the Hunters with the short delivery times will take the business, which will increase the costs per unit on the remaining volume.

A business with these problems may survive a new competitor when markets are strong. But if a general slowdown in business takes place along with the increased competition, the business will be in trouble.

Removing Excess Work-in-Process — System Level Actions

System Level Action 1. Stop using the mental model that work-in-process is useful — that it smoothes production and is there just in case something goes wrong. People must understand that WIP slows response, covers up problems that should be solved, and is the cause of a great deal of waste in the workplace.

System Level Action 2. Adopt reward systems that place higher priorities on system objectives that satisfy customers by promoting system quality, response, and productivity. As sales increase, the reward system should be designed to increase throughput compared to expense.

System Level Action 3. Eliminate periodic load variance such as weekly, monthly, and yearly load cycles in your operation. Common cycles are monthly, yearly, seasonal. At the end of the month, inventories become bottlenecked toward the end of the process. At the beginning of the month the operations are inefficient due to low work levels, and at the end of the month the operations must be worked overtime to meet month-end quotas. Materials tend to go through in lumps.

System Level Action 4. Level load in-process operations by forecasting demand and leveling schedules (pull forward, push back). Plan capacity for the average load level (increase or decrease it), and by monitoring and revising as necessary.

System Level Action 5. Reduce system cycle time and thus reduce reaction delay. Reaction delay effects were described by MIT's J.W. Forrester and by Peter Senge.[1] In long, linear-dependent chains of events, a change in demand may cause production increases at the beginning of the process which will not reach the end of the process for a long time if the system cycle time is long. For example, if automobile sales suddenly decrease, dealer inventory will begin to go up. Because the average car inventory is about seventy days from completion of a car to its sale and because another thirty days may have elapsed from the of some of the components to the completion of the car, any changes in production at the front end of the process will not affect the output for a month or more. By the time a reduction in schedule begins to take effect, sales may have rebounded. Auto manufacturers try to level this situation by offering spot discounts and incentives on the sales end and temporary layoffs on the production end. This lack of synchronization produces bubbles of inventories floating through the system and causes constant increases and decreases in schedules at the individual operations.

System Level Action 6. Reduce cumulative variance in processing. If a typical process has an average cycle time of 100 days, it may have a variance in process time of ten days. If the average cycle time is reduced to ten days, the variance will be proportionately lowered to one day. If the average cycle time is reduced further to one day, the variance will now be in hours.

System Level Action 7. Eliminate the false belief that backlogs mean job security. Job security is increased by increasing customer satisfaction or increasing throughput in response to demand. Small backlogs and work-in-process are sometimes useful. For example, when system cycle time is much faster than customer expectation, it is possible to maintain a small order backlog prior to start of processing and still be highly responsive to customers. A small backlog prior to processing can help to level load the production system at the highest utilization level the demand requires.

Yea, though I walk through the valley of the shadow of death, I will fear no evil.

– Psalm 23, verse 4

CHAPTER FOURTEEN

Valley of Death

*I*t was New Year's Eve, 1985," Marcus begins next morning as they make their way toward Milwaukee, "and the banks were closing early.[1] Rich Teerlink, Harley-Davidson's chief financial officer, and Thomas Rave, vice president of First Wisconsin National Bank of Milwaukee, were frantically trying to transfer money from Heller Financial in Chicago to Citibank. A few days earlier Heller Financial had agreed to provide the last-minute funds to save Harley-Davidson from bankruptcy. But to make the terms of the last-ditch agreement, the money from Heller and other lenders had to be transferred to Citicorp Industrial Credit by midnight or the company would be forced to file for Chapter Eleven, the first step to an orderly liquidation and death of an American legend.

"The closing minutes would make a good script for a movie. Rich got a call from Heller Financial saying that another key player, Walt Einhorn from Mellon Bank East in Philadelphia, couldn't, at that late hour, find anyone to authorize the transfers. And — as if the level of anxiety weren't high enough already — Heller was closing early because it was New Year's Eve.

"Teerlink pleaded with Heller to stay open until he could reach Einhorn. He got through to Einhorn and pleaded that the very existence of the company was at stake. Einhorn hand-carried the transfer authorization until he found the signatures needed and got the money wired while Heller waited. Harley-Davidson had its stay of execution."

"How did they get in that position?" Lou asks. "They were on top of the world in 1970. You had to put your order in weeks ahead if you wanted a Harley then."

"Lou, the path to bankruptcy is sometimes swift and merciful, but usually it's a long painful process. Harley sales were good in 1970, but they were already the Hunted. At seven this evening we're going to meet with Vaughn Beals, the CEO who led Harley-Davidson from death's door to a major turnaround."

"In 1959," Vaughn Beals begins his story, "when Honda advertised the small mini-cycle no one at Harley-Davidson paid much notice. How could a cheap piece of junk from Japan compete in our quality-oriented market?

"The late sixties brought a motorcycle boom and our volume tripled, but our market share didn't go up. More and more people were buying Japanese bikes. From 1969 to 1972, under our new owner, AMF, volume was increased from 27,000 to 60,000 units per year, but unfortunately, quality suffered as a result. We were spending money to increase production but not on new product development or improvement of our product technology. While we were allowing quality to take a back seat, the Japanese were improving theirs.

"So in 1975, when Honda came out with the Gold Wing and its smooth-running 1000 cc engine, they started to take big chunks of the touring bike market. With an equivalent model requiring years to develop, we were helpless to stop the onslaught.

"The market slowed at the end of the seventies. Instead of tapering off their production as the boom slowed, the Japanese makers continued to produce at the higher rates. Making more bikes then they could sell, they exported the excess to this country at heavily discounted prices. Harley-Davidson filed a dumping suit against the Japanese in 1978. The Japanese were found guilty of dumping and were forced to end the excessive discounting, but this was a short-lived victory.

"In retrospect it's a wonder that the company held together through these times. One of the key factors was our brand loyalty. As one T-shirt read at the time 'I'd rather see my sister in a whorehouse than my brother on a Honda!'"

Lou glances at Laura for a reaction, but she only laughs.

"But things continued to get worse. By 1981, because of the competition from Japan, our share of the market — which we had once dominated — slipped to under thirty percent. As you know, the economy was also beginning to slide then, and many blue-collar workers — our core customers — were facing layoff. That, combined with high interest rates, made it hard for them to buy our product. We were very vulnerable because we had a very high breakeven point.

"Another problem was that our manufacturing systems and product quality simply were not up to world-class standards. We had high inventories which gobbled up cash and reduced productivity, and the prevailing attitude toward quality was that if it met specifications, it was okay.

"Other problems? There were lots," he says, beginning to count them off on his fingers. "First, our product line was seriously out of date and was stereotyped with a rough, tough image.

"Second, our Japanese competitors were exporting to this country thousands of high-quality, low-cost machines that competed directly with ours. Third, AMF wanted to sell us, but nobody wanted to buy us. Fourth, an evaluation done by the Boston Consulting Group said that we could stay viable only if we invested sixty to eighty million in a Porsche-designed NOVA engine family with a resultant negative cash flow for two or three years. Fifth, we thought we could go for a quick fix by bringing in computers and state-of-the-art machinery to improve productivity. And finally, we didn't understand what, if anything, we could do to fix the whole mess.

"So you can imagine why they thought I had flipped when I called the top thirteen managers together in early 1981 and proposed that we buy the company. I told them it was the only way to keep Harley-Davidson alive.

"At the time I suggested the buyout, I was convinced of a number of things:

- Anyone outside the company who bought Harley-Davidson would not be willing to invest in its future.
- If Harley-Davidson was to be saved, a leveraged buyout by the executives at Harley was the only way.
- The $80 million price could be leveraged with $1 million in cash.

"Convincing the other board members wasn't easy, but on June 16, 1981, in our black leather jackets, with Willie G. Davidson at the head of the victorious pack, all thirteen of us rode our motorcycles back from Harley's headquarters in York, Pennsylvania to Milwaukee. The plant was ours!

"Then it sank in. We owned the company, but we were deeply in debt. It was no longer the company's financial position and our jobs at stake; it was our money and our homes at risk. And it got much worse before it got better.

"The motorcycle market went into a downturn. The onslaught of new Japanese models even included a Harley look-alike, the Yamaha Virago. Our dealers began to desert us. Remember, it was a soft market to begin with; and people weren't buying Harleys because the quality of the Japanese bikes was higher and the cost lower. With no cash to carry us through, we were dying. And then as if this weren't bad enough, two of our Japanese competitors got into a war of 'honor.'

"It all started in 1981 when the smaller competitor, Yamaha, increased its market share to thirty-seven percent, one share point less than Honda. The president of Yamaha, Hisao Koike, announced to the world that within one year they would over-take Honda and become number one in the world. Honda's president, Kiyoshi Kawashima, counterattacked, vowing to crush and destroy the impudent Yamaha. Honda's counterattack with new models, increased promotion, and price cuts not only battered Yamaha into submission but nearly brought us down, too.

"It was clear that if we didn't cut costs and improve quality, we'd never regain market share. We knew that what we were doing wasn't good, but we didn't really know how to fix it. Looking back, it wasn't a very pretty picture. Let me describe our manufacturing process in 1981 as we would view it today. Our manufacturing process was laid out with similar machines grouped together. Here's a layout of a typical part flow in 1981.

"If you followed a piece through the operations, you might see it first being turned on a chucker and then put in a bin until an entire batch of 1000 parts were completed. Sometime later, a forklift would move this bin of parts to a staging area in the grinding department. The bin would sit there until the bins ahead of it were processed or until it was given a priority by the production control department. Then the thousand parts in the bin would be removed from the bin, ground, replaced in the bin, and moved to the broach area. Here the

Old Gear Process Layout

Source: Peter Reid, *Well-Made in America* (New York: McGraw-Hill, 1990), copyright © 1990. Reprinted by permission of McGraw-Hill.

parts would wait some more, then they'd be removed from the bin, broached, and so on through ten to twelve more process centers. If you actually followed a single part it would take about three months to go through all the operations — three months to do operations that if done continuously might take less than one hour.

"And if a problem occurred in the early processes, it often would go undiscovered for months. By that time there could be hundreds of defective parts in the pipeline. Sometimes we had to compromise our quality to keep production going. The emphasis was on clearing bottlenecks, cost reduction, keeping it patched together. All of our energy was being spent just on making it.

"To adjust for fallout due to quality problems, more than the required amount of material was started at the beginning of the process. A certain amount of scrap, rework, and quality problems were considered part of the cost of doing business.

"Because we knew it took months to go through the manufacturing process, the scheduling system had to start parts at the chuckers three months ahead of time. And since the time through the process was highly variable because of machine downtime, process fluctuations, and quality problems, it was necessary to prioritize, expedite, do special setups and handling to move some parts through the process in time to avoid shortages at the final assembly.

"Even with computer scheduling, expediting, and crisis problem solving, fifty percent of the new motorcycles came off the line missing at least one part. In addition, fifty to sixty percent failed to pass first-time quality inspection.

"So here we were drowning in inventory and up to our neck in parts shortages, putting enormous efforts into inspection and crisis problem solving, but still producing bikes of inferior quality. We knew our system produced lower quality and higher cost bikes than the Japanese. However, up to that time, we had concluded that their lower wages, supportive government, restrictive trade practices, highly disciplined work force, low-cost capital due to a high savings rate, and many cultural advantages were the causes."

Lou feels his face turn red and he checks the urge to say something.

Vaughn continues. "It wasn't until we visited the U.S. Honda plant in Marysville, Ohio and saw an American work force dramatically outperforming us that we realized we had to fix our system. What we saw in Marysville set a new benchmark for us. We had seen similar approaches in Japan but had decided they wouldn't fit in our environment or that these approaches on the manufacturing floor were a small part of their competitive advantage. This time we saw it for what it was — a superior manufacturing system.

"At Honda, there was very little material at the line, no computer, very little paperwork, very few inspection people, very few management people, and very few rejects at the end of the line. Most of the people were engaged in directly adding value in a very simple, uncluttered manner.

"But the big difference was quality. They were achieving ninety-five percent first-time acceptance at the end of their line compared to fifty to sixty percent at our plant. They had only a few hours of work-in-process between final build and pack to ship; we had four days because of missing parts and quality problems.

"As Pogo said, we found the enemy and it was us.

"The most important revelation at Honda was that it wouldn't take big capital investment to close the gap. As a matter of fact, we could visualize a positive cash flow as the improvement process took place.

"There are few advantages to poverty but this time our lack of money was an advantage. We would have tried to invest our way out of the mess we were in if we'd had the money. We would have bought a lot of computer-automated equipment and more sophisticated computerized control systems and installed them in the existing process-centered system I described earlier.

"But our lack of money, our need to act quickly, and our new-found perspective from Honda steered us in the right direction. We defined three thrusts that we call our Productivity Triad. All of these thrusts had the potential for generating cash to give us some breathing room, service our debt, and provide funds for development."

"Didn't it hurt your pride to take an idea from the Japanese? I couldn't handle that," Lou says to Vaughn.

"Lou, you can't eat pride. We had our money at stake here."

"Wouldn't matter to me."

"Believe me," Vaughn explains, "if you were in the position we were in you would learn from anybody who had a better idea."

"Not me."

Vaughn looks curiously at Lou and then continues. "Our first thrust was material as needed or as we called it 'MAN.' MAN redefined waste for us. In the MAN philosophy, waste was anything that didn't add value for the customer. Excess inventory, setup, rework, moving and handling parts, inspection, time that parts sat in queue, expediting, and prioritizing were all considered waste.

"Going to continuous flow manufacturing dramatically reduced all these wastes. Instead of the flow and layout I showed you earlier where we would group components that had a similar set of processes performed on them, we laid out the machines in work cells so that a single employee could manufacture a gear from beginning to end. Our system cycle time for producing a part was now hours instead of months. The savings in inventory were important, but the truly important improvement was in quality."

Gear and Sprocket Department — After

Source: Peter Reid, *Well-Made in America* (New York: McGraw-Hill, 1990), copyright © 1990. Reprinted by permission of McGraw-Hill.

Gear Cell

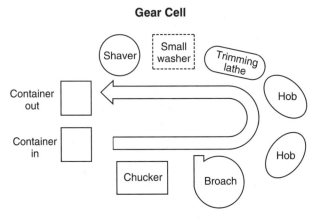

Source: Peter Reid, *Well-Made in America* (New York: McGraw-Hill, 1990), copyright © 1990. Reprinted by permission of McGraw-Hill

"The quality improvement is directly related to the time factor. The shorter the total cycle time, the sooner a defect is discovered, giving faster feedback to the operator and greatly reducing the number of parts run before corrective action can be taken at an operation. In the case of frame-build, we reduced the total cycle time from seventy-two days to three hours.

"In addition, we controlled the inventories produced in these cells by a pull system. In the old system a processing department like lathes would receive an order from our computerized scheduling system to turn a thousand parts. The lathe department would then find the material, find an open lathe, setup the lathe, and run the thousand parts.

"In the pull system, when the final assembly line uses the parts they return the container to a cell that can produce that part. This constitutes the order or signal to build more parts. The number of containers for a given part determines the amount of inventory maintained between the cells and the final assembly lines."

"What happens if you get a sudden change in schedule with this approach," Lou asks.

"It depends on whether it's a volume change, or a change in the mix of products. First, let's look at volume changes. All manufacturing systems are more productive if the schedules are held relatively constant. We keep the next thirty-day schedule as unchangeable, the second thirty days we hold to around ten percent, and the third thirty days at around twenty percent. This allows us to set a pattern for our work flow that changes slowly. The production people and our suppliers can then plan for the changes and accomplish them productively.

"Our second thrust was employee involvement or, as we call it, EI. This was a cornerstone of our turnaround because it provided a greater contribution level from all of our employees. To achieve this we had to first get top-down commitment."

Laura turns to Vaughn. "I hope you didn't do some of the things I saw at Motorola."

"What did they do?"

"Practically turned the place over to the employees. They let the hourly people decide what they are going to work on next, solve problems, decide on line layouts — in other words, they just displaced responsibility to a lower level."

Marcus winces. "Vaughn, a lot of this is new to Laura."

"I understand. A lot of our managers felt that way when we started, but they had to buy into some fundamental changes if we were going to survive. We had to get managers to agree that quality was the goal and that continuous improvement of quality was to be a way of life. They had to agree that all employees should be empowered, encouraged, trained, and supported to solve problems and control quality in their jobs. Managers had to understand that their jobs involved helping to increase every employee's ability to solve the problems of the business, encouraging active generation of continuous improvement ideas, and responding to these ideas by either supporting action on them or by having good reasons for not doing so."

"Hey, I'm not against listening to people's ideas, but I still believe managers decide and employees do," Laura comments.

Vaughn looks Laura directly in the eye. "We don't think of white-collar thinking and blue-collar doing anymore. We need ideas from everyone and we need everyone to be involved in the improvement process. It's a new way of life for us. It isn't just listening to their ideas but acting on them, helping them implement their ideas."

"She thinks that the worker is brainless", Lou says.

Laura glares at Lou, then regains her composure and says, "Hey, I've read some Harvard business cases about some tough union negotiations where the union proposed that management turn the factory over to them and the employees. The question here is who's in control."

Vaughn sighs. "We all share in the final outcome, so we share control. But let's get out in the factory so you can see how it actually works. Mark Cunningham, our Head Hog, will take you through."

As they walk to the factory, Laura asks Mark how he got the name Head Hog.

Mark smiles. "In 1983, Harley-Davidson established Harley Owner's Groups (HOG) in every region of the country to establish a bond with their customers. We organized rides and other activities for Harley owners. I took the job to head that group in 1988, which made me the Head Hog."

"I went on one of those rides in 1985 and it was great," Laura says.

"Eighty-five? You were alive in eighty-five?" Lou whispers to Laura.

"That was my last year."

"And you got accepted for guardian training so soon. Who do you know?"

"Lou, I don't own this circus, I just travel with it," Laura says, smiling.

"What were you doing on a Harley anyway?"

"Why not?"

"Unladylike!"

Mark continues. "Here in the plant you can see examples of our third thrust — statistical operator control, or as we call it, SOC.

"Most of the other quality improvement approaches we tried in the late seventies and early eighties didn't really improve quality a lot," Mark explains. "The problem was that feedback and corrective action took forever. Let's take a typical example. Suppose we have a problem at one of the tube benders in making frames with too little bend in about ten percent of the parts. Well, two months later those bad bends will show up as a problem when they are used in the assembly of the engine. So now we have a hundred frames that have an interference in the assembly process.

"First we would try to find a way to make the frames work with a bend here or there. Then if that didn't work we would quit building with the bad frames, sort out the bad ones from the stockpile, disassemble and put a good frame on the bikes already assembled with the bad frames. If we were not overwhelmed with other crises, we would go back through all the frames in the various stages of frame build and purge the system of bad frames. Since the bender has been operating for two months since the problem started, this could amount to a lot of bad parts.

"Of course we would go back to the tube bending operation and try to solve the problem if the problem still existed. To complete the feedback we would have to find the particular machine that bent the parts and the operator that worked the machine for that lot. Two months later it was an almost impossible task to gather the necessary data: on machine setup, how used, pressures, and stroke speed."

"Didn't you keep data on the process?" Laura asks.

"Even if we had, Laura, how good is data that's two months old? Today, because of the much shorter cycle times, those bad frames would be discovered in less than a day and corrected immediately.

"Before SOC can work well, the feedback time must be reasonably short and the quality of information must be good. We had to provide our people with the tools to measure and analyze their process so they could take immediate corrective action. We now have hundreds of people dedicated to continually improving the process."

"Mark, how is it that Harley employees are willing to improve productivity? To many employees, productivity improvement means more money in the company's pocket and fewer jobs for them," Laura asks.

"We're very up front with everyone. Our goal is to be at least as good as the best competitor on quality and productivity. We had to design teamwork into the system, including teamwork between management and the union. We took our union officials to Marysville so they would know the competitive benchmarks for quality and productivity. We're all united on the goals. As our competitiveness increased we started making some parts that we had been buying, and created sixty new jobs. Our people have seen our market share increase and they know that improved quality and productivity were major factors. That convinced everyone that improvement by employees will *increase* job security.

"Since the leveraged buyout we have:

- increased productivity   50%
- reduced inventory   75%
- reduced scrap and rework   68%

"But how does this relate to the bottom line?" Lou asks.

"Here are our financials for the last five years. Judge for yourself."

Harley-Davidson Financial Figures

Harley (HDI)	'88	'89	'90	'91	'92
Revenue (millions)	$709.4	$791.0	$864.6	$940.0	$1105.3
Net income (millions)	23.9	32.9	37.8	37.0	54.2
Earnings per share	1.50	1.91	2.12	2.08	3.0

"Increased profit percentage," Lou muses, "Hunters again," he says.

"It's the only way to go, Lou," Mark says as they leave the plant.

"Now that you're in good shape again, how are you going to keep the fire going?"

"Laura, we are never going to forget what we went through. We're never going to be complacent again. We're dedicated to continuous improvement from here on in. As Jeff Bluestein, our V.P. of Engineering, has said: 'The day we think we've arrived is the day we should all be replaced by managers of greater vision.'"

As they leave the plant, Marcus removes his light stylus from his pocket. "Let's refer to the Transformation chart as it refers to the Harley-Davidson turnaround."

Transformational Change at Harley-Davidson

Significant trauma	**Mind Changes** New mindsets New mental models New measures	**Delivery Systems Redesign** ⇨ New Process Intent (First-time quality, low system costs) ⇨ New Process Model (Customer-focused flow, pull systems) ⇨ New L & I Systems (Source feedback & correction, SOC, EI)	**Continuous Improvement** Reduce • Valueless time (MAN) • Valueless activity • Valueless variance (SOC)
Performance gapping	**Non-linear**	**Non-linear**	**Linear**

"Lou, describe the continuous improvement system that they installed."

"MAN had two of the linear improvement elements as I see it. In the MAN philosophy, the process is redesigned to move the product continuously from operation to operation. Lot sizes and inventories are lowered which reduces valueless time in the process. Since defects were detected over one hundred times faster after they put MAN into place, fewer parts were run before they could take corrective action; and this reduced valueless activity. The SOC thrust was aimed primarily at controlling processes and reducing variance, and it worked. They had all three of the linear improvement thrusts covered."

"Excellent, Lou. You didn't miss anything." Lou smiles.

"Laura, how did they go about redesigning their Delivery Systems?"

Laura refers to her notes. "They established a new Process Intent; they didn't just meet specifications at the end of the process. Instead they eliminated errors and defects from the process, reduced volume breakeven points on all products by reducing costs, and reduced inventories that gobbled up cash and adversely affected productivity. They established a new Process Model, which, as Lou already said, was continuous flow of small lots of parts with a pull system to minimize inventories. Quality was to be assured at every point of the process by establishing statistical operator control."

"Do either of you realize what they changed in their Delivery Systems to increase the rate and quality of learning and improvement?" asks Marcus.

"They said that having the operators control and improve their own operations was a big factor," Lou says.

Marcus smiles. "You say that like you don't believe it, Lou."

"I'm still thinking about it. Hard to argue with guys that are down to earth like that."

"The short cycle times to detect and the fast correction policies they put in place also increased the rate of learning and improvement," Laura says.

"Good. What change took place in their collective mind-set, mental models, and measures?" Marcus asks.

Laura answers immediately: "They had a mind-set that lower wages, supportive government, restrictive trade practices, a more highly disciplined work force, low-cost capital, and many cultural advantages were the reasons behind Honda's lower costs and better quality. They also believed that the way to fix their problems lay in doing more of what they had done in the past. They changed to the mind-set that their manufacturing processes were inferior to Honda's, and that nothing short of a complete redesign of their system would do the job.

"Their mental model," she continues, "was an operation-centered one, and they believed that state-of-the-art machinery and computer systems would fix what ailed them. They changed to a product flow model and a pull system in which parts were manufactured in small cells with very short manufacturing cycle times and extremely low errors and defects."

"Their measures were quantity, utilization, and efficiency. They felt they were performing well if they continually improved over past performance. But the trip to Honda blew all these measures," adds Laura.

"I can't believe it, but I'm beginning to see this mind-change stuff," Lou says. "As long as everyone thought that they would never close Continental, they didn't come to grips with reality."

"You've got it. You're both another step closer to understanding the Non-Linear Solution. We'll be heading back to Guardian Command this evening. Now let's summarize the lessons we learned from our Harley-Davidson visit."

Lessons Learned

- *From a perilous position, Harley-Davidson fought its way back to regain market share. To accomplish this they transformed themselves by completely revising their mind-set, mental models, and measures; by redesigning their Delivery Systems; and by installing a high-performance, continuous-improvement system with a high degree of involvement of all employees.*
- *They changed their Process Model for manufacturing from a process-focused model to a product-focused model. This change reduced their manufacturing time from weeks to hours.*
- *They changed their philosophy about work-in-process, developing a materials as needed (MAN) discipline, which assured that materials arrived at work stations just as they were needed — in small quantities at short intervals. This pull system reduced inventory, parts, shortages and expeditions.*
- *They trained operators in statistical quality control which the operators applied to their individual operations.*

"I've got to go now; I'm meeting with some friends," Marcus says.

"Are you saying that Harley-Davidson has discovered the Non-Linear Solution?" Laura says.

"Yes, but they need to continue to rediscover it," says Marcus, walking off.

Laura and Lou cross the street to a small cafe with a quiet dining area in the front and a secluded bar in the back. They sit in the front and order coffee.

Minutes later Laura rises. "Lou, I'm going to go over and talk to the guys at the bar in the back," Laura says.

"I think I'd better go with you."

"Not necessary, Lou. Order me another coffee."

Lou fidgets as he watches Laura talking and laughing with the bikers across the room until he can stand it no longer. He walks across the room and approaches their table. He positions his big frame between Laura and a massive bearded man. "Laura, you ready to go?" Lou asks gruffly.

"Lou, let me introduce you to some great guys." Laura makes the round of the table, introducing Lou to everyone and invites Lou to join them.

Lou gives her a disgusted look. "I'll catch you later," he says, heading back toward the cafe.

Later, as they leave the bar, Laura says. "Lou, you should have lightened up and talked to those guys, you might have learned something."

"What am I going to learn from a bunch of bikers?"

"They told me why they ride Harleys."

Lou frowns, "I'll bet they did. I know damn well why they ride. A buddy of mine used to say, 'If you can get a woman to ride behind you, you can get anything you want from her.'"

Laura frowns. "They said things like they liked the thump of the engine on their bottom, that a Harley looked like a motorcycle instead of a torpedo, and that they like the image and the trade-in value. There was only one reason for owning Harleys that they all agreed on."

"What's that?" Lou asks skeptically.

"Cause they're made in America, Lou."

"Now you're talking!"

Aerospace is one business we don't intend to surrender to foreign competition.

– John Wolf, vice president & general manager,
MD80/90
Douglas Aircraft

CHAPTER FIFTEEN

Capacity Constraints

A s they head north along the coast of southern California, the morning clouds are clearing. A flock of gulls swarms around a fishing boat a mile from shore. The mid-morning sun streams through the clouds.

"The scene below you was very different in September a few years ago. We're going to go back to view it as it appeared that day. As they look down on Lakewood Boulevard in Long Beach, the scene changes to show a huge crowd of people filling the boulevard. Traffic is detoured. Over two thousand people, carrying a huge banner, are parading across the boulevard and pulling a fuselage of an MD80 commercial aircraft.

"This parade of employees at mid-day signifies a major turn of events at Douglas Aircraft.[1] The American Airlines fuselage you see is fuselage #1673. To fully understand the significance of this fuselage, we'll get a firsthand account from John Wolf, a vice president with Douglas Aircraft. Remember, although you saw a quick flashback to 1989, we're in 1992."

Laura is surprised that John Wolf's office is simple and austere, not what she expected of a vice president of a large corporation. Quality and production charts line the walls. John is tall and tanned, with the lean, hard-muscled look of a runner.

"There's nothing quite like building planes," are the first words from John after introductions. "In what other business does your customer take delivery, get into the product and fly it home? It sends chills up my spine when that plane roars down the runway, clears the fence, climbs sharply, and does a slow bank to the right, heading to its home base. At that moment I think, 'We built that plane,' and I'm proud. People who work here feel just like I do; they can't imagine doing anything else; nothing else would measure up."

"John, Marcus told us a little about #1673. What was so significant about that particular fuselage?" Lou asks.

John leans back in the chair. "To appreciate #1673, you would have had to have been here in late 1987 when we had just ended a very disruptive strike. The outlook was bleak. Because of its superior features, demand for the MD80 was high, but we were losing money on every one. We had been missing deliveries before the strike, but during the strike we lost customers. At this point, faced with major losses, we restructured to reduce costs, and at the same time we were in the process of redesigning the way we build planes.

"Responsibility and accountability for overall customer satisfaction and financial performance was clearly defined in the new organization by organizing manufacturing, production control, purchasing, quality control, and personnel functions together on product teams. A product team couldn't get just part of the job done, they had to get the whole job done — while paying attention to quality, schedule, and cost.

"Just after we cut costs and began the redesign, the axe fell. It started with a 90-day notice to American Airlines that another slip in schedule would take place by the end of 1989. Airlines must plan additions to their fleet months ahead so they can add scheduled flights, lease hub space, hire pilots and flight attendants, and begin selling tickets. The same day that

American Airlines was given notice, Bob Hood, our president, got an angry telegram from Bob Crandall, president of American Airlines. With that telegram in hand, Bob Hood confronted me. He was fuming mad; the veins of his neck were bulging; his face was all red. Needless to say, I was shaken.

"Immediately after that, we took a very close look at our entire process for making a plane from concept to delivery. It took one hundred fifty days in assembly to build a plane. We knew if we could increase throughput we could get back on schedule and lower our costs. The big bottleneck was identified as the nose cone assembly area. It was obvious to us that we needed to increase the rate of assembly in this area. But the big question was, would the union and the workers buy this as a job-saving solution or just another management ploy to get more work from them?

"What followed was unprecedented in my time at Douglas. In the past, management had always set the goals and then tried to get everyone to meet them. This time we, the company and the union, explained the company's situation and asked the people doing the work to set the goals. The people said that as long as they had parts shortages, insufficient hand tools, and inadequate training in some areas they couldn't set realistic goals. I agreed to provide the nose cone team whatever it needed to complete the job on time and with first-time quality and they could set goals based on my guarantee. The nose cone crew was skeptical. They set a goal to be back on schedule by September, but they doubted that management would follow through with the support we promised.

"But we did respond. And so did the nose cone team. Some workers were so committed that they cancelled vacations to help the team meet the goal. It was a very emotional experience, because all the care, dedication, and teamwork paid off: they reached a goal that they had created themselves. And on

September 11th, they delivered nose cone #1673 to the fuselage assembly area along with a huge sign that said, 'We did it, now it's up to you.'

"That they delivered the nose cone by September 11th meant not only that they had increased output by thirty percent, but also that we were definitely going to be able to meet our year-end delivery schedule. So although we still have a long way to go, that was a turning point for us," John says. "The MD80 is one of our main sources of income today. Ready for a plant tour?"

Later, as they leave the plant following the tour, Laura says, "That won't work, having the workers set their own production rates."

"But they set them higher than management did," Lou says.

"But what will keep them from lowering them again?" Lou shakes his head and shrugs his shoulders.

"What was the major factor that reduced the system cycle time from 155 days to 105 days on the MD80?" Marcus asks.

Laura sighs. "I'd say there were two factors." "The first was the change in Process Model. They integrated all the functions along the flow of the MD80 Delivery System which focused everybody on the customer. Second, they focused on relieving the bottleneck in the nose cone assembly area."

"Right! When they designed the organization around Delivery System flow rather than functional flow, the system delivered more value in a shorter time. What do you think were the most important factors in increasing the nose cone assembly rate, Lou?"

· "Solving the parts shortage problems."

"That, plus getting people to work harder," Laura says.

"The key was increasing throughput at the capacity constraint. The effect of capacity constraints is to limit the output of the whole process to the output at the constraint. We're going to study this effect in more detail by visiting L.A. International Airport, one of the busiest airports in the world." Marcus says.

"Sounds like a lesson coming," Lou says.

"You've got it Lou. It's lesson time."

They arrive at the Los Angeles airport terminal at dusk.

"What a mess of people," Lou says as they walk through the automatic doors. Ticket counters stretch along the back wall, and there is one long line doubling back and forth in roped-off aisles. At the front of the line, people are being called by the next available agent. Another agent with a clipboard is moving down the line, talking to people. In the background there's the periodic roar of a departing plane.

"We have a capacity constraint here," Marcus says. "More people are getting in line than are being served; the line is growing," he says as they get in line. "How could we estimate how long we'll be in the line?"

"By observing the average rate at which people are being serviced and multiplying that by the number of people in line." Laura says. "If the fifteen people in this line are being serviced at one person per minute, we will have to wait fifteen minutes. Conversely, if you divide the total wait time into the number of people in line, you will find the rate at which each is being serviced." She writes on the back of her airline ticket and hands it to Marcus:

$$\text{wait time (system response time)} = \frac{\text{number of people in line (WIP)}}{\text{rate of service (output rate)}}$$

Lou frowns. "You're complicating things again. They just don't have enough computer stations and agents here at this airport," he says impatiently.

"Lou, how would you increase the service rate with just the number of computer stations they have in use right now?" Marcus asks.

"They can have other agents find people in line that can go directly to the check-in counter at the plane or who can be taken care of without the computer," Lou answers.

"Good idea. But even with that, suppose the line grows so long that people may miss flights," Marcus asks as they walk toward the gate.

"A service agent can suggest to people in line that if they are passengers on a soon-to-depart flight, they should go to the front of the line." Laura says.

"That's what the agent with the clipboard is doing," Lou says. "But that's costing them to do that."

"You've got it, Lou," Marcus says. "When a system has a capacity constraint and can't process work as fast as it's coming in, the response time to a customer increases until the response is so poor that expediting and prioritizing are necessary. These activities not only produce additional costs but they usually require the talent of the best people in the business."

Lou nods, "The worse it gets, the more wasted effort; and the more wasted effort, the less time spent in permanently fixing it. We used to say that when you're up to your rear in alligators, it's hard to remember that you came to drain the swamp."

"Someone may never have told the alligator fighter that draining the swamp was an objective at all," Marcus says.

That afternoon in the room of the Hunters, Marcus begins the formal part of the lesson begun earlier at the airport. "Capacity constraints have dramatic effects on the performance of business systems. They limit output rate, slow response, reduce quality, and cause a great deal of valueless activity. Let's examine each effect of a capacity constraint starting with its effect on output rate.

"First, the output rate can be no higher than the rate of the lowest rate operation that the output depends on directly. Second, to improve system response time, either you must reduce work-in-process or you must increase the output rate." Marcus hands them each a document. "Please read these three short case histories and then I have some questions for you."

....

Capacity Constraints and System Response Time

Case 1: Provide the Resources — Loaner cars

Carl Sewell, the famous Dallas Cadillac dealer, improved response to his customers by eliminating a capacity constraint — not enough cars. This case comes from his book, Customers for Life.

> *Sometimes it's worth paying attention to a comment, even if only one person makes it. I remember a focus group where a man said he hated our loan car program, because when he showed up for service he was told we didn't have any loan cars. He was the only person who said that had happened to him, and our general manager swore he always had cars available, but there was something about the way the customer said it that rang true. I couldn't figure out why he would make up something like that.*
>
> *So I did a little checking and found out that a number of times the general manager was turning people away. Instead of ordering more loan cars, he would tell people to come back when one of the loaners he had was available.*

We replaced that general manager and now, if we tell you there
will be loan cars available, there will be.[2]

Case 2: Provide the Resources — Trained People

Boom. It was hard to believe that in just five short years
People Express, founded in 1980, had become the fifth largest
airline in the United States. This spectacular success had been
achieved by providing heavily discounted fares and no frills service. It cost less than a bus ticket to fly between many eastern
cities. Passenger seat miles doubled in 1982, and founder
Donald Burr was able to brag that in the third quarter of that
year, People Express had more departures from New York airports then any other airline. In 1983 passenger seat miles doubled again. In 1984 revenues doubled. The sky was the limit for
this Hunter. Or so it seemed.

Bust. People Express acquired routes, bought planes, and
hired people fast enough to support the sales demand, but one
critical resource was not developed fast enough. Because of their
highly flexible, wide-scope, individual job design, the training
time that was needed to achieve quality was long. The number
of people operating at a high quality level was inadequate.

In 1982, service quality began to deteriorate and by 1984
delays in reservations and ticketing, delayed or canceled flights,
and overbooking began to take their toll. Harried service people
and flight attendants were treating customers like luggage.
When customers began deserting and employees saw their stock
tumble in 1985, service deteriorated further. As sales deteriorated, the company went from a profit in 1985 to a $20 million
loss per month in 1986. They would never recover before a
takeover by Texas Air in September, 1986.

From Hunter to Hunted. The failure to supply enough
capacity, in this not so tangible area of quality service, had
weakened the company so they were standing on only one leg —

low price; and that's where the Hunted counterattacked. In 1984, American Airlines used their Sabre reservation system to offer advance purchase discount fares. As other airlines offered the same discounts to maximize their revenue per mile, the effect was devastating to People Express.[3]

Case 3: Provide the Resources —
Engineering Design Time

Delco Remy, a division of General Motors, faced a serious dilemma during 1991. GM was restructuring due to market share losses, and personnel cuts had been mandated across all of GM, including Delco Remy. Reducing engineering resources at a time of business expansion in the controls market proved problematic to the controls engineering department.

Despite the personnel cuts, the controls group at Delco Remy was expected to reduce development time, improve quality, and reduce costs. New work was coming in faster than the engineers could complete it, however, and the backlog of jobs that resulted meant that ultimately there were delays getting products to customers. Also, efforts to increase quality and lower cost proved minimally effective. Even under normal circumstances engineers were constantly having to wait for things: information from sales, design details, parts from suppliers, tools, the completion and testing of prototypes, etc. Of course, as the system became overloaded it became less efficient; the engineers' time was consumed even more by various non-value-adding activities, such as tracking missing parts and information, coordinating with others with whom they were to meet, juggling sudden changes in priorities, reviewing nonconforming material, doing design estimates, writing memos, and so on. Each engineer was responsible for more projects than before, and understandably, each project therefore received less attention and took longer to complete.

To cope with this dilemma, Ron Pogue, chief engineer, and Dan Crishon, assistant chief engineer, led the redesign of their controls engineering Delivery System. Their analysis of the work flow revealed large backlogs at product concept and at product design. The backlogs consisted of:

- *design jobs not yet started*
- *design jobs for which the engineers were waiting for information before they could proceed*
- *redesigns*
- *ongoing product or process improvement jobs*

They didn't have the option to add engineers. But they reasoned that they could still increase design output and reduce development time if they were to:

- *reduce the number of design iterations by the following means:*
  - *define customer requirements better prior to design*
  - *allow engineers more time at the concept stage to fully develop the design and perform all appropriate calculations*

Response of Engineering Development Systems

Information for Redesign

This loop may be repeated many times

Back-log → Concep-tion → Back-log → Engineering design → Back-log → Materials procurement → Back-log → Prototype build and test

Quality and cost improvement jobs

Backlogs at Engineering design are caused by:

- Waiting for test results on a prior iteration
- Lack of timely information
- Engineers occupied with non-engineering activities
- Inefficient tools
- Waiting for tool availability
- Waiting for authorization from finance or management
- Waiting for work to be checked
- Complex communications that must be executed
- Insufficient people

> – *design for more tolerance to variation in processing*
> – *involve suppliers early in the design phase to improve manufacturability*
> – *design for simplicity of assembly*
> • *reduce the time it took to build a prototype so that feedback to the designer was faster and corrections made sooner*
> • *establish guidelines to prevent interruption of a designer when that person was on the critical path*
> • *increase engineering throughput by eliminating valueless activity and improving design tools*
>
> *Since each redesign required the same engineering resources, reducing the number of iterations reduced the net workload on the designers.*

"So you didn't say what happened in the Delco Remy case," Lou says.

"Too early to say," Marcus answers, "but they have made some important progress. They've reduced the average number of iterations, increased engineering throughput, and reduced their development time with no increase in people."

Marcus asks Lou and Laura to identify the capacity constraints in each case.

"An insufficient number of cars in Sewell's case," Laura says, "an insufficient number of trained people in the People Express case, and insufficient engineering time in Delco Remy's case."

"Let's use these cases to understand the very important mathematics of response," Marcus says.

"In Sewell's case, the fewer cars, the lower the loan rate; the lower the loan rate, the more people waiting. Both the lower loan rate and the increase in customers waiting cause the customer to wait longer for a car.

"In the case of People Express, fewer trained people resulted in a slower, lower-quality service rate. The result was long wait times at the counter and delays due to confusion.

"Let's formulate the mathematics of response for Sewell, People Express, and Delco Remy," Marcus continues as he flips the switch on an overhead projector. "You can see here that all three capacity problems have the same mathematical form.

The Mathematics of Response

$$\text{Longer wait for loaner} = \frac{\text{More people waiting}}{\text{Fewer cars, lower loan rate}}$$

$$\text{Longer wait time for ticketing and baggage} = \frac{\text{More people waiting}}{\text{Lower service rate}}$$

$$\text{Longer time to build plane} = \frac{\text{Fuselages waiting}}{\text{Low nose-cone rate}}$$

$$\text{System response time} = \frac{\text{Work-in-process}}{\text{Output rate}}$$

"Let's do a simple calculation from what we picked up at Douglas Aircraft. Douglas was building about three planes per week before the turnaround and I counted about sixty-six planes in their whole process. We can calculate the average time to build a plane by dividing the planes in process by the output rate." Marcus writes with the light stylus.

$$\text{Average Build Time} = \frac{66 \text{ planes}}{3 \text{ planes per week}} = 22 \text{ weeks} = 154 \text{ days}$$

"That closely matches the 155 day number that John gave us for their average build time before the turnaround. Now let's compare that with the build time after the turnaround. If the number of planes in process dropped to 60 and the build rate was increased to 4 planes per week, then . . .

$$\text{Average Build Time} = \frac{60 \text{ planes}}{4 \text{ planes per week}} = 15 \text{ weeks} = 105 \text{ days}$$

"Can you see the effect that output rate has on build time?" Marcus asks.

"I can also see that if they could reduce the number of planes in process by temporarily increasing their output rate above their order rate, they could offer a faster response to the airlines," Laura says. "The excess in-process inventory they are carrying is not only expensive but also causes poor response to customers."

"Very good. John Wolf is aware of that potential," Marcus says. He hands them each a sheet of paper.

....

Improving Customer Response

- *If more work comes in than can be processed (output rate lower than input rate), the amount of unfinished work (WIP) in the system increases, which means that it takes longer (response time) to process any job coming into the system.*
- *To reduce the average time (system response time) to do a job, the system has to process jobs faster than they are coming in (output higher than input), until the backlog and work-in-process are lowered.*
- *If customers have to wait longer than they expect, input will eventually go down as customers find another supplier, but only after a time delay. This delay time is*

dangerous, because by the time you become aware that you are losing business, you will lose much more before you can improve your response and you may not be able to regain the lost customers.

After Lou and Laura have finished reading, Marcus says, "I'll leave you with some questions to think about. Which of these approaches was used at Douglas Aircraft, at the airport, and at Sewell Cadillac? Which one should People Express have used?"

"Now let's review what we've learned," Marcus says as he writes with the stylus.

Lessons Learned

- *System response time equals work-in-process divided by output rate.*
- *If the Delivery System has a capacity constraint that limits the output rate to less than customer demand, the time to respond to a customer increases. These capacity constraints must be removed.*
- *To improve response time, the output must be higher than the order input for a period of time to remove work-in-process. Once response time exceeds customer expectations, the output rate should equal the input order rate.*

"Here's a list of ordered actions that can be taken to improve customer response time."

Ordered Actions for Improving Customer Response Time

1. *Focus on the customer end of the process. If there are customer backlogs and there is sufficient capacity in the final processing operations, increase the output rate until your customers are totally satisfied with your response.*

2. *If capacities are insufficient in the final processing area, focus on increasing capacity at the bottleneck areas by one or more of the following methods:*
   - *Increase productivity through technological enhancements, increased knowledge and expertise, elimination of valueless activity, and increased motivation.*
   - *Add or redistribute human, machine, and external resources.*

3. *When and if there are no customer backlogs, you should stabilize the output at the average demand rate. A small finished-goods inventory (days, hours, or in the case of McDonald's, minutes) can sometimes be justified if the inventory improves average response to the customer. A small backlog ahead of the process may be justified if customer response capability exceeds customer expectations and the small backlog level loads operations that have marginal capacity.*

4. *To further reduce system cycle time and improve customer response, the Process Model should be optimized to be efficient at low quantities of work-in-process.*

5. *If you can control the input rate (not possible in fast-service businesses), reduce it while maintaining the output rate at the average customer demand rate. This*

will reduce work-in-process. For example, in the case of Douglas Aircraft, they maintained an output of four planes per week while holding the input rate at three planes per week, which reduced the in-process inventory of planes by one plane every week. In two-and-one-half months, the planes in process dropped by fifty.

6. *Reduce process variance and rework by getting it right the first time.*

   - *In manufacturing:*
     - *improve quality of incoming materials*
     - *use design of experiments to identify most significant variables*
     - *install process controls for early detection and control of variables*
     - *rework defects immediately at the station that added the value*
     - *use error prevention devices*

   - *In engineering*
     - *use quality function deployment to define customer attributes*
     - *involve suppliers and manufacturing early in the design effort*
     - *use design for manufacturing and design for assembly techniques to simplify the design and assembly*
     - *identify the key product characteristics and key process characteristics that must be maintained*

7. *Improve quality of input:*

   - *consider business value*
   - *reduce rework*

- *improve the rates of supply, and response of the support systems that supply information, services, people, tools, and materials*

"The crucial lesson you must understand," Marcus says, "is that system throughput cannot be increased unless the throughput is increased at the worst bottleneck in the value-adding chain."

Backwards Is Sometimes Better

A general product development process is charted below. Assume a typical time to market of two years. Time to market may be six months to six years depending upon the company, the product and process complexity, volumes, and availability of technology.

Most people involved in the process would agree that the activities in the development process that most influence the time to market, quality, and costs are the early activities. These include: defining what the customer values and at what price; developing and evaluating concepts; and designing for manufacturability, quality and reliability.

However, if the total development time is two years and customers need the product in two years or less, the engineer will be confronted with a need to hurry in the front end of the process. This occurs because the design, prototype tool development, and sample build times are so long that the design activity must be started almost immediately after first customer contact. But if you are already late, how can you afford to take the time to do more analysis up front? Because of this chicken and egg dilemma it is usually best to start the time compression process by reducing the prototype build time.

To reduce the time to produce the first prototype, focus on the post design process, including tooling and process development, sample build, test, and evaluation. Typically this part of the process is one third of the total time to market. For example, if the total time to market is two years, production of the first prototype will be about eight months. Redesigning this portion of the process to reduce valueless time will typically reduce the time to three to four months. As this is progressing, additional time of one to two months is added to the front end, which allows acquisition of better information from the customer, analysis of competition, more flexibility in developing concepts, and more time for supplier, process engineering, and manufacturing involvement. Time can be taken to design for manufacturability, quality, reliability, and cost.

Putting the additional time up front not only will increase the value-to-cost ratio for the customer but will reduce the number of design iterations required to a maximum of two and will reduce the second year of development to four months. The total time to market can typically be cut in half with this approach and the value-to-cost ratio can be markedly improved.

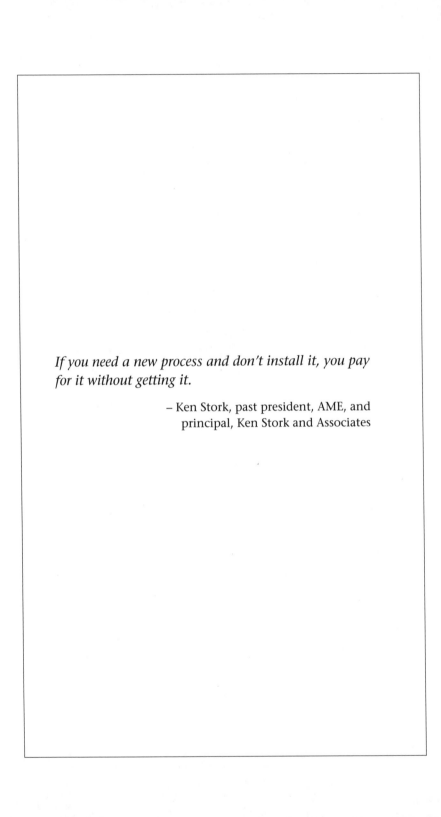

If you need a new process and don't install it, you pay for it without getting it.

– Ken Stork, past president, AME, and principal, Ken Stork and Associates

CHAPTER SIXTEEN

Continuous Improvement Drivers

M arcus gives Lou and Laura the next day off for study and contemplation but tells them lessons will resume after dinner.

"Quite chilly tonight," Julia says as they gather in the main room. "Thought we could do with a bit of fire, so I asked Gregory to make one for you. I must tell you, Marcus, that I don't think I can stand to hear one more time how he saved your life when the emperor's aides were plotting to kill you . . . and the war stories about your Roman military campaigns together seem to grow each time he tells them. And since you gave him that title of chief of intelligence, he's gone overboard. Last week he tried to fingerprint me. Can you imagine? Well, he got a piece of my mind."

Marcus smiles as he walks toward the fire. Light from a huge fire blazing in the corner dances upon the domed ceiling. In the center of the room, a huge olivewood table is set with very old dinnerware — from 450 A.D. if he's not mistaken. "What's the occasion?" Marcus playfully asks Julia.

"No occasion. Just thought you travelers might like a hearty meal. Laura, I've set your place over here."

"So all I have to do is bring a female into Special Forces and I can expect this kind of treatment?"

"It never hurts to recognize where the real talent is," Julia says as she disappears into the kitchen.

Lou laughs. "You should know better than match wits with that old woman, Marcus."

"I like Julia," Laura says. "English, isn't she? Bet there's a story there."

"English she is. And quite a story," Marcus says.

He removes a light stylus from his pocket and motions for them to join him at the fire.

"Let's start our lesson before dinner. A linear improvement process like Henry Ford had and Motorola has today is a foundation in any company's transformation process. To understand how to install a linear improvement system in a business, we need to understand the three linear Drivers and how they work to continually improve system response time, quality, and value-to-cost ratio. Let's look at the First Driver, the reduction of valueless time in a process."

With the light stylus Marcus begins to draw a figure to the right of the fire. "On a routine appointment to a doctor, how much time would you actually spend with the doctor?"

"Probably five to ten minutes," Laura says.

"How long are you there altogether?"

"Maybe an hour and a half."

"What's happening the rest of the time you're there?'

"You're waiting in a room full of sick people reading two-year-old *National Geographics,*" Lou says, laughing.

"That means that only a very small part of the time you're in the doctor's office is value added time. I'll show that this way." Marcus completes the figure.

"The dark band at the bottom is the short time with the doctor. You can see that the value-added time is only a small part of the total time you're there. Is that clear, Lou?"

"Clear."

"Now let's diagram the flow in a way that gives some further insights." Marcus sketches another diagram with the light stylus.

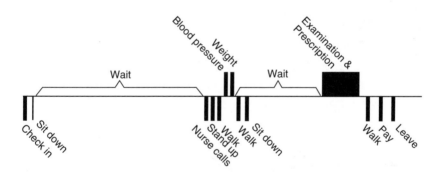

"The activities above the line add value as perceived by the customer and the activities below do not add value."

"So what's the point? Everyone knows doctors keep you waiting a long time."

"What would we have to do to improve the average response to the patients in a doctor's office, Lou?"

"Cut down the wait times."

"That's the point. The average patient cycle time would be reduced if we scheduled patients to arrive just before the doctor is available."

Lou shakes his head. "Sounds good, but not practical."

"Why not?"

"Why should doctors improve response?"

"I'll leave that one be," Marcus says, smiling. "Let's look at another example. Here's a timed flowchart of an oil change and lube at a typical auto dealership around 1970, compared to the process used at a business such as Jiffy Lube." Marcus sketches with the light stylus.

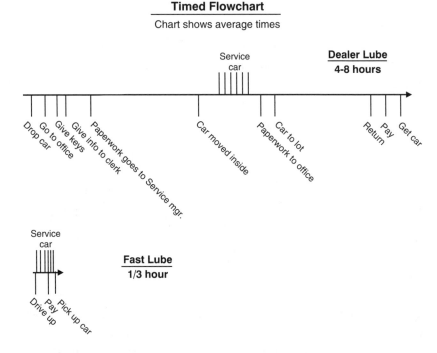

Timed Flowchart

Chart shows average times

"Laura, is any less value added in the second process?"

"Probably more."

"Any less quality?"

"No, I think it's better. I took my car there."

"How about response time improvement?" Marcus asks.

"From four or more hours to twenty minutes," Laura says.

"There's virtually no waiting with the fast lube process. All of the value is added in a continuous flow, just like at the Ford plant."

"Comparing the two flowcharts," Lou observes, "the fast lube places also eliminate some activities that add no value, such as taking the customer to work, shuffling paper, and moving the car from one place to another," Lou says.

"Good point, Lou. Much of the valueless activity in a process is often due to the same bad design factors that cause long system response times. Now, let's compare the two on a physical flow basis. First, the dealer physical flow."

Physical Flowchart – Dealer Lube, Oil

"Compare that to the fast lube physical flow."

Physical Flowchart – Fast Lube, Oil

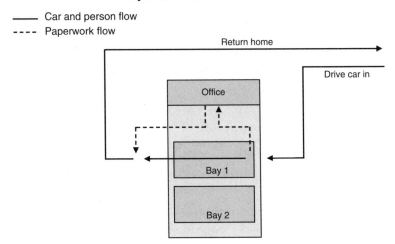

—— Car and person flow
- - - - Paperwork flow

"Could you squeeze some time out of the fast lube process?" Neither Lou or Laura answers. "Get the idea?" Marcus says to both of them.

"The idea that there's no wasted time in their process?" Laura asks.

"I think he means that if they're really good, it's tough to improve them," Lou says.

"That's true. But there is a measure we can use to indicate the potential for improving response. It's called the cycle time ratio. The cycle time ratio is the ratio of the total process time to the value-added time.

"You can see that the dealer cycle time ratio is 18:1 compared to 2:1 for the fast lube process. As the ratio gets down to the 2:1 level, it is very difficult to improve without reducing productivity."

"Marcus, I'm trying to get a whole picture of the Continuous Linear Improvement process that would be used to reduce valueless time and activity," Laura says. "From what we've learned so far, I guess the first step is to analyze the process and identify the largest valueless times and activities."

Cycle Time Ratio Chart

Cycle time ratio = Total process time
compared to Value-added time

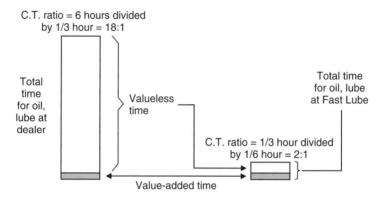

"Essentially correct, but there are some other steps that you should take before you begin linear improvement," Marcus replies. "Linear improvement continuously improves a system, but it doesn't bring about a transformation. Linear improvement is the best approach when you have well-designed Delivery Systems. We'll assume that we've transformed the business like Harley-Davidson did and we now want to improve the system continuously. Then we use a linear improvement process," Marcus says, picking up the light stylus again.

"If you follow the linear improvement process, system response time will go down, quality will go up, and costs will go down." Marcus begins to write.

....

Continuous Linear Improvement Process

1. Use the planning tools first.

- *Do a simple group analysis to identify processes that should be grouped according to common parts, processes, customers, etc.*

- *Identify your customers' needs for the process you're improving, and then identify what needs improvement (e.g., cycle time, quality, cost).*

2. *Analyze the process using linear analysis tools.*
   - *Draw a logic flowchart of the process as it currently operates.*
   - *Make a timed flowchart of the average process by:*
     - *recording above the horizontal axis the average completion times of value-added activities*
     - *placing all other activities below the line*
   - *Draw a chart of the physical flow showing all moves.*
   - *Draw a chart of the flow of information — particularly emphasizing transfers between people, departments, and functions.*

3. *Assemble the team responsible for this process, empower them, and provide them with training in linear improvement methods.*

4. *Develop a vision of what the process could ultimately be and develop goals.*

5. *Focus the team on the First Linear Improvement Driver — reducing the longest times between value-added activities.*
   - *Increase output at the worst bottlenecks.*
   - *Eliminate excess work-in-process.*
   - *Eliminate transfers, moves, unnecessary approvals and other valueless activity. Place value-added activities in parallel as much as possible.*
   - *Shorten looping processes (repeated processes, rework loops, etc).*
   - *Level load operations*

6. *Focus the team on the Second Linear Improvement Driver, elimination of valueless activity.*

   • *Ask why the activity is necessary and whether it can be eliminated.*
   • *Can the activity be consolidated with another activity?*
   • *Use cause and effect diagrams to find sources of valueless activity.*
   • *Use total productive maintenance (TPM) procedures to eliminate waste.*

7. *Keep work-in-process as low as possible by establishing controls to schedule the value-adding activities.*

8. *Focus team on the Third Linear Improvement Driver — reduction of valueless variance, starting with defects and errors. Use statistical problem-solving tools with a heavy emphasis on design of experiments (refer to shaded box in Chapter 22) and process control. Reduce variance in schedules, loading, output, procedures, etc. Use root cause analysis (CEDAC) to eliminate the causes of defects. Use error prevention tools such as* poka-yoke.

"Let's diagram how the First Linear Driver, reducing valueless time, benefits the customer," Marcus says rapidly drawing with the light stylus.

"That's all there is to it?" Laura asks. "How about the quality and cost improvements you mentioned?"

"Here's the light stylus. One of you add those to the figure."

Laura reaches for the stylus. "How do I operate this thing again?" she asks. "I forgot from last time."

Driving Linear Continuous Improvement

"Ever done any computer-aided design?" Marcus asks.

"Some," Laura says.

"Same principle. Try it. Move the whole stylus like a computer mouse. The menus are 3D pull-through."

"Neat!" Laura says, beaming. "Let's see . . . what happens when we reduce system cycle time? Well, for one thing," she says as she draws with the stylus, "it takes less time to find and correct defects, which means that you don't produce as many of them. So you save money on inspection, scrap, and rework — not to mention the lower cost of carrying reduced inventory. Then I'll put in the cost reduction path due to the reduction in expediting prioritizing, and crisis activity. I think that does it."

Driving Linear Continuous Improvement

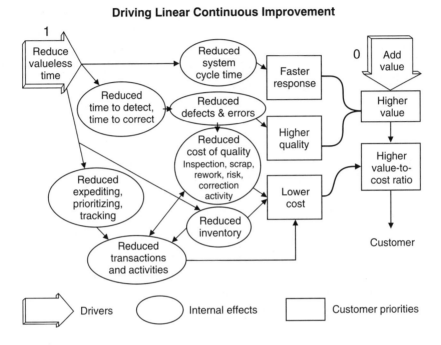

"Dinner is served," Julia says as she enters carrying a tray of salads. "Enough talk for now."

Marcus rises and begins to pace back and forth behind them, his hands folded behind his back. "Valueless time reduction is the Primary Improvement Driver of today's Hunter," he begins. "As valueless time is reduced, three parallel effects take place. Laura, could you please write these for all of us to see?"

....

Effect 1 — Response: As system cycle time is reduced, the business responds faster to customers and markets, forecasts are more accurate, and parts shortages are reduced.

Effect 2 — Quality: As errors and defects are detected and corrected sooner, quality to the customer improves.

Effect 3 — Cost: All the transactions and activities associated with wasteful handling, prioritizing, expediting, inspection, rework, and crisis problem solving are reduced. Expense due to scrap, obsolescence, excess floor space and carrying excess inventory is dramatically reduced.

"I can understand all the effects except the one about reducing parts shortages," Lou says. "I can't see that as system cycle time is reduced, parts shortages are reduced."

"It's hard to understand at first," Marcus says. "When Harley-Davidson had very high work-in-process, they had many parts shortages. After their transformation, they had very low work-in-process and very few parts shortages."

"I noticed that when we were there, but I didn't completely buy it; it just doesn't make sense," Lou says.

"Lou, Harley-Davidson's original process for making gears took seven weeks. With a seven week process, two problems caused the parts shortages. The first was that they had to forecast what should be started into the process at least seven weeks in advance. Secondly, since the gears had to pass through many process centers, it was difficult to determine precisely when a certain batch of gears would be completed. Can you guess how accurately they could predict when a certain batch would be ready to ship to the final assembly lines?"

"Within a week or two, if the forecast was good," Lou says.

"H-D's new process for making gears is less than seven hours from start to finish. If a small group of twenty gears was started into the process, how accurately could you predict when they would be completed?" Marcus says.

"Within an hour, I'd say," Laura says.

"You're demonstrating the point. The longer something takes to process, the greater the variance will be in actual completion date compared to predicted completion date, because there's an increased chance the item will be held up somewhere in the process."

"But a good computer-based material planning system, like material requirements planning, would make corrections in the schedules as the gears went through each process center, reducing the total variation," Laura says.

"MRP helps, but it merely makes adjustments by moving things forward and backward in the schedules. In the new H-D gear cells, the material is prioritized before it begins the first operation, but then it moves rapidly through the operations with no further rescheduling."

Laura raises her head. "That's because it's not necessary in the cell arrangement. The material stays in a single department the entire time it's being processed. It's completed in such a short time that it would take a computer operating in real time to keep up with it."

"You've got the picture. Time to eat," Marcus says heading for the table.

During dinner, Lou brings the conversation back to the lesson. "I believe the results at Harley, but I'm still not comfortable with the notion that less work-in-process leads to fewer parts shortages."

Marcus replies, "Generally, the longer any process takes and the more transfers and handling steps, the greater the variance in the time it takes. As you reduce the time it takes to produce parts or services, the completion time becomes more predictable, and shortages are less likely to occur."

"I can see another reason for reduced parts shortages," Laura says. "With shorter process times, you can catch and correct defects earlier; and if necessary, you can build new parts quickly if a major problem should occur. This will substantially reduce parts shortages due to quality problems."

The following morning over coffee, Marcus says, "Now let's lay the foundations for understanding the Second Linear Driver — reduction of valueless activity.

"Arnold Toynbee, the noted historian, once said, 'Dirt is matter out of place.' Analogously, we can say that valueless activity is activity out of place. These out-of-place activities in a process delay the response to customers, increase the number of errors, and add cost. We're going to take a quick trip this evening to catch the second shift at Simpson Timber in Shelton, Washington. It will help you understand some of the techniques that can be used to eliminate valueless time and activity."

"Marcus, why do you distinguish between valueless time and valueless activity?" Laura asks.

"As Ford said, valueless time is not obvious to people, so it can accumulate in processes without gaining a lot of attention. Since valueless activity can be more readily seen by most observers, and because wasted time or valueless time in processes is not apparent, there is a tendency to focus improvement efforts on wasted effort or wasted material. But I can't stress enough how important it is to reduce valueless time in a process if you're to quickly respond to your customer's needs. Keep in mind also that valueless time has a negative impact on quality and serves as a Primary Cost Driver. So, reduction of valueless time should be the first redesign objective. Valueless activity should be removed as *part* of the process of reducing valueless time."

"So, reducing valueless time is the most important Driver?" Laura asks.

"Not the most important Driver, but the best one to start with — the first Driver."

"Does that mean there's a more important Driver?"

"Yes, we'll get to it. Not yet, but soon. Now, let's get moving. We have an appointment in Shelton."

A. Business Analysis

B. Delivery System Analysis Tools

When Continuous Linear Improvement Won't Work

In 1988, a defense firm named XTER (for the sake of anonymity) began to lose bids that previously they had always won. At that time, XTER employed a bidding strategy based on their technical capability, which was their principle strength and competitive advantage. To exploit this advantage, XTER would design the most exotic version of the product they could envision, using all the latest breakthrough concepts. Because competitors could seldom match their technology, XTER could bid higher and win based on the perceived additional value of their design. This had been a successful approach over the years but was no longer working.

Unknown to XTER, in the late eighties the defense department, faced with declining funds, changed its purchasing policy. To encourage competitive pricing, technical requirements were lowered so that at least two suppliers cleared the requirements. The net effect was to reduce the technical requirements to the technical capability of the least common denominator of the best competing firms. Of course, this significantly reduced XTER's competitive advantage.

Not fully appreciating the effect of the new purchasing policy, XTER continued to offer considerably more than the minimum technical requirements and continued to quote higher prices. But after losing numerous contracts, XTER fought back by lowering quoted prices. They had become the Hunted and were forced to retreat and cut their losses.

XTER's 1988 quote Delivery System, shown on the next page, was not designed for a cost sensitive market.

Their engineers, driven by a design-to-strengths strategy, by tradition, and by personal inclinations to design state-of-the-art products, produced exotic and costly designs which resulted in high cost estimates. When these costs were integrated (usually in the final days before the bidding deadline), the program manager would discover that the total cost was higher than the expected winning bid. In the frenzied final days, the zealous program manager would wrest (with threats, of course) large price concessions from internal and external suppliers. If this didn't get the bid package cost to a competitive level, the program manager might plead to management for concessions on profit. With this approach, XTER was in a lose-lose situation. If they lost the bidding, they would underutilize their resources, resulting in higher overhead on future bids. If they won, they and their suppliers suffered losses.

In 1989, XTER realized that their strategy, based largely on technical superiority, wasn't viable in this new marketplace. To be successful again, XTER would have to offer more cost-effective systems even if that meant less exotic technology. They further discovered that the new ground rules for bid acceptance

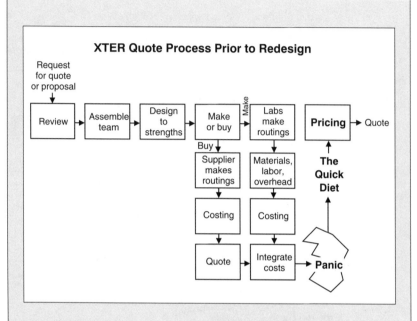

XTER Quote Process Prior to Redesign

allowed for resubmission if a technical bid failed to clear technical requirements. This led to a new strategy among competitors. The new strategy was to bid at the minimum estimated technical level and to resubmit in those categories that failed to meet the minimum. In this way the smart competitors were able to locate the minimum technical requirements of the system, and this gave them an advantage.

Once XTER defined their new strategy, they redesigned the quote Delivery System to deploy the new strategy. They first defined the new Process Intent:

- bid should just clear the minimum technical requirements
- bid price must be low enough to win
- margin between bid price and cost should be 25%

To accomplish this new Process Intent, the design team developed the following process:

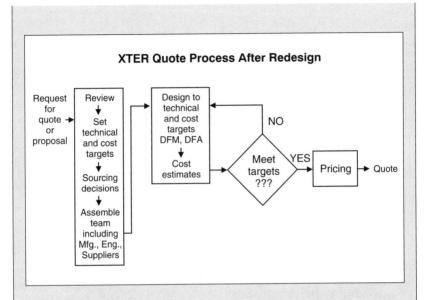

XTER Quote Process After Redesign

In the old process, decisions to reduce technical offerings or arbitrarily cut costs were made at the end of the process. In the new process they are made in the design process.

Using Continuous Linear Improvement methods to improve this process would have been ineffective, because the basic Process Model of the Delivery System prior to redesign didn't meet the strategy of the business.

Meaningful cultural change needs to be viewed and managed systematically. Experience has taught us that people's attitudes and self-esteem are, in fact, changed when they participate in systemic organizational change. The basic learning is that people become what they do.

— John J. Sherwood
Organizational Consultants, Inc.

When a famous sculptor was asked how he could sculpt such a beautiful horse out of a rough stone, he replied, "I simply cut away the extra stone until I get to the horse."

— Attributed to Rodin

CHAPTER SEVENTEEN

———

Valueless Activity

T he view from the third story of Simpson Timber's modern sawmill is spectacular. Outside, they can see the automatic log handlers loading huge logs — forty feet and longer — onto a conveyor that carries them up three stories to the debarker. As a log moves inside, hold-down rollers pinch it and a gang of mean-looking knives revolves around it, stripping the bark. At the cutoff saw, orange laser stripes encircle the log, and like the circular saws in the horror movies, six huge discs, in a whirring shrill unison, cut through the log as easily as if it were a slice of cheese. The clean smell of fresh-cut wood is stimulating. At the chipping edger a computer scans the logs' diameters, automatically sets the saws, and the log is disassembled again. Falling two stories in a river of wood, moving at frightening speeds, the log emerges at the other end of the mill as 2x4s.

"In 18 months," productivity improvement director Paul Everett shouts as they walk along a vibrating catwalk three stories above the floor, "our cycle time through the sawmill, dry kiln, and planer mill dropped from twenty-eight days to seven days. Our throughput at that time was 26,000 board-feet per hour, and today we've increased that rate to 37,000 board-feet per hour. And all this was accomplished by our operators with very little capital investment. The productivity improvement group here at Simpson trained all of our people in the mill in the principles of value-added management. We then organized many small teams to attack and eliminate anything that didn't add value. To do this the teams first identified what did add value."

Value-Added Activity
■ Remove bark
■ Saw to length
■ Saw to width
■ Edge trim
■ Dry
■ Plane
■ Trim and grade
■ Package and trim

"How did they decide what adds value?" Lou asks.

"They asked themselves what they do to the trees that makes them valuable to the customer. Once they decided that, then the objective was to add the value in the shortest time, with no defects and errors, and with the least operational expense. That meant cutting out all time and activity that didn't add value. Here's the list of time and activity that, according to the teams, added no value.

Time when value is not being added	Activity that adds no value	
• Time wood sits as logs	• Unjamming	• Setup
• Time wood sits ahead of the kiln dryer	• Moving wood	• Handling
• Time wood sits ahead of the planer	• Machine repair	• Searching for tools
• Time wood sits in the shipping yard		

"Organizing all this information on a time chart helped us immensely. When we did that we found that the total time to go from logs to finished lumber was twenty-eight days.

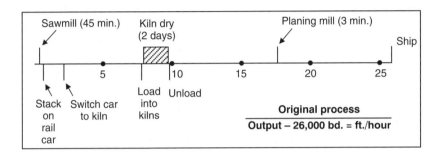

"On these charts we put the value added activities above the line and non-value added activities below the line. The activities are placed along the line at the approximate times when they occurred during the twenty-eight-day cycle. The widths of the lines represent the average time to perform that operation. You can see that sawing and planing takes less than one hour out of the twenty-eight days.

"As each team took responsibility for a part of the cycle and started reducing valueless activity, we came to realize that these little things were not little at all. Not only did we reduce line stops and damaged wood, but as we uncovered the causes of problems like jamming, we also discovered the constraints to increasing the throughput rate in the mill. We reduced work-in-process and increased output rate at the same time. This reduced system cycle time from twenty-eight days to seven days in a matter of months. This not only directly improved our bottom line, but the improved response time allowed us to supply spot markets for lumber that previously would have passed us by."

"Glad to hear it, Paul," Marcus says. "We've got a busy day ahead of us, so we have to be leaving now. But thank you very much for taking the time to show us around."

"My pleasure. Any time."

They continue on in silence until Marcus speaks again. "You now understand why the Second Linear Driver, reduction of valueless activity, provides improvement of all three elements of Process Intent. Costs will go down as activities are eliminated. Quality will increase because fewer transactions mean less chance of error. System cycle time goes down and response improves because each non-value-added activity usually has waste time ahead of it, during it, and after it. For example, if we reduce the number of people who must successively approve an insurance application from five to three, we reduce the processing time. Think about the figure we looked at last night. What would it look like if we added an additional Driver for reducing valueless activity?" Back at Guardian Command, Marcus calls up the figure again and adds to it the Second Driver.

Driving Linear Continuous Improvement

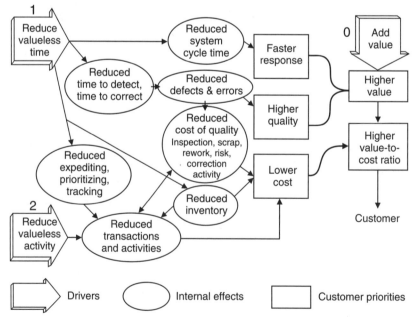

Laura carefully considers the figure and thinks about their visit to Simpson. "What stands out in my mind most from our visit to the sawmill is something Paul said about how their improvements were the result of operators' efforts and had little to do with capital investment."

"I'm glad that made an impression on you," Marcus says, "because it was definitely an important point. In fact, many companies look to computers and automation to make them more competitive. This approach works if the focus is on improving the way that value is added. But when this approach is used prior to the redesign of the Delivery Systems, the investment is wasted. I think you'll appreciate this example," he says.

How Not to Spend $2,000,000

In October, 1986, a $2,000,000 appropriation was approved to automate and improve the chemical plating and cleaning area at Electron Dynamics in Torrance, California. Of that total, $400,000 was designated for a new material-handling system that included the most advanced scheduling software. A task force, headed by Dan Wallace, was asked to review the appropriated hardware and software and assist with getting the new system up and running. In addition, the team was told that the new system should possess the following characteristics: it should allow for continuous flow processing and a total processing time of less than four days; and it should allow for an automated process with improved yield and no required priority levels. Specific objectives were to eliminate excessive overtime, constant crises, 100 priority assignments per day, two full-time people expediting 1,500 parts, and a backlog of two weeks.

From the beginning the group had misgivings. They knew that the work coming into the area had to be stable and predictable for continuous flow to work, but the realities were constant juggling, prioritizing, expediting, and schedule changes.

They first did a group technology analysis. This breakthrough analysis showed that the entire operation really consisted of six different mini-process lines or mini-factories, but the existing physical layout didn't correspond with these six groups. Neither did the proposed layout.

In a second breakthrough, they proposed a major change in the inventory control system, in which inventory was released to the area in small, controlled quantities only as the previous quantities were consumed by the six lines. This suggestion was troublesome to some members of the team, because if the idea worked, the proposed automated material storage and handling system would be useless and the computer hardware and software would be unnecessary. Others on the team felt that reduction in inventory would have disastrous results. In their minds, there were significant reasons for maintaining large amounts of work-in-process, including reduced parts shortages, insurance that work was always available for people, covered losses due to defects, easier scheduling, economies of scale due to large batch sizes, reduced set ups, and motivation for people to work harder.

But a flow analysis indicated that the idea was right on target. If they adopted the six separate flow lines and the inventory control system, they could reduce cycle time from ten days to four hours.

After much debate the team decided to implement the task force's suggestion on a Monday in the near future. On the Saturday before that Monday, they removed all inventories from the area. Four hours' worth of material for each of the six lines was placed in plastic pass-through-the-wall boxes. They set a hard and fast rule that when an individual line used the inventory in the box, an operator would throw a switch on the box and four more hours' worth of material would be retrieved from the stockroom. With this rule there was never more than eight hours of material in process. Although people predicted that such a system would shut the whole place down, the operation started smoothly and by the end of the day it was clear that it was going to work.

By scheduling the six lines separately and controlling the maximum and minimum work-in-process, they avoided a capital investment of $2,000,000, reduced work-in-process by ninety-five percent, reduced cycle time from two weeks to eight hours, eliminated any need to prioritize or expedite, drastically reduced overtime, and increased productivity by twenty percent due to elimination of multiple setups and two expediting jobs. Quality improved because problems could now be identified within hours instead of days.

Quality director Don Carr, who had encouraged and supported many of these projects, later said that he was impressed with the results. But what impressed him even more was that he could think of no other time in his career where a team of people was given $2,000,000 to make improvements and decided not to spend the money!

"So the lesson here is don't make large investments in automation or computer systems until you have simplified the Process Model, eliminated valueless activity, and established flow controls," Laura says.

"You've got it," Marcus says.

"Is this a rare case?" Lou asks.

"Very common."

"So the engineers are spending money like drunken sailors."

"Wrong, Lou. Most engineers and management recognize this pitfall, but there are still many who don't separate the improvement of value-adding activities from the reduction of valueless activities. Improvement of the value-adding part of the activity is typically accomplished through design, invention, or automation, as in the case of Herman Hollerith's machine, which dramatically reduced the cost of tabulation and counting information."

"Or Ford's engine-block machining line," Lou says.

"Wouldn't it be better to go for automation first instead of going through all this process improvement?" Laura asks.

"There's a tendency to do that today," Marcus answers. "It's natural to look for a technical solution early in the transformation process. It is far better to employ the first two Drivers before automating, or you will automate largely valueless time and activity. In addition, although automation is often proposed as a way to eliminate people errors, many variances in process are caused by variables which are not understood or controlled. So it is best to simplify and reduce variance in a process before automating. In many cases automation is essential to survival but the automation will be much better utilized if it is applied to a process already designed for maximum value-to-cost ratio. Here are two examples illustrating the proper use of computer technology in one case and the simplification of information systems in the other case," he says.

"But don't you have to reduce variance to reduce valueless time and activity?" Laura asks.

"Yes, they are all tied together. But in my experience, continuous improvement takes place faster if you start with reduction of valueless time. I need to get you on a different subject now. Last night I received a call from Alan Updike, an engineer I've worked with before. He wants us to come to Torrance, California to talk to his new boss, Wil Danesi, the general manager of Garrett Processing Division. Alan thinks we might be able to help. I want both of you to go with me on this job for the initial analysis, starting tomorrow morning. This will be your assignment to prove yourselves and to qualify you for a Guardianship."

"The enemy you were talking about last night is us, isn't it," Lou asks.

"We can be our own worst enemy," Marcus says. "But what is it about us that makes us our own worst enemy?" They both look puzzled. "Think about it a little longer."

> **Information System Simplification**
>
> A western U.S. corporation applied continuous improvement tools to its corporate information and reporting systems using a four-stage method.
>
> **Step 1.** Eliminate all reports and informational processes that add little value. Recipients of the information and reports were asked to identify reports and information that they seldom, if ever used, or that they could do without. In this manner, fifteen percent of all reports and information generated unnecessarily were eliminated.
>
> **Step 2.** Users were asked if they could accomplish their work with less frequent reports. Frequency of the essential reports was reduced where possible.
>
> **Step 3.** The remaining and essential processes were timed and charted. Valueless time and activity were eliminated.
>
> **Step 4.** Some hard-copy reports were eliminated by making them available at the user's computer terminal.

The following morning, as they arrive in Torrance, Laura says, "With today's faster transfer and processing technologies it should be a lot easier to reduce system cycle time."

"Yes," Marcus says. "But not all businesses have taken advantage of these advances in transfer and processing capability. In fact, the response times of many companies have even increased in the last fifty years."

"Why did they let that happen?" Laura asks.

"They just didn't understand what was happening to them," Marcus sighs.

"Is that the worst enemy — ignorance?"

"The worst enemy is what causes ignorance," Marcus says.

"Failure to learn?" asks Lou.

> **Greatest Enemy**
>
> Arrested learning.

"Close enough. The greatest enemy is arrested learning!"
Lou looks toward Laura.
Laura gives him a thumbs up.

David and Goliath

Since the mid-nineteenth century, when the Bessemer and Martin-Seimens process reduced the cost of steel 90% below the cost of iron, the process had required large amounts of energy to heat the metal to high temperatures three times and required considerable effort to move the heavy metal through multiple operations.

In the early 1970s the big steel makers looked the other way as small mini-mills were installing a new simplified and automated process for steel making. In this new process, molten steel is cast into two-inch slabs and those slabs are immediately rolled into steel sheet. The cost of the development of this revolutionary process was more than dollars. As they mastered the hot and explosive metal, many pioneers at Nucor in Crawfordsville, Indiana lost their lives. They reduced the process time from molten metal to flat rolled steel from a typical industry average of 1 week to 55 minutes, more than a 100:1 improvement in manufacturing cycle time. They increased yearly output to 2,400 tons per person, whereas Big Steel's output remained at 800 tons per person per year.

While mini-mills cast molten steel into slabs and immediately rolled the slabs into sheet steel, Big Steel continued to cast nine to twelve inch slabs and transported the slabs two or more miles to a rolling mill. But by 1990, mini-mills had captured twenty percent of the sheet steel market and could no longer be ignored. Their high-technology Delivery Systems had dramatically reduced non-value-added activity and eliminated what were formerly regarded as value-added steps. Many of the mini-mills, operating on incentive pay with highly flexible work rules and more advanced technology, cut the number of worker-hours to melt, pour, and roll to one hour per ton. Big Steel was still at two to three worker-hours per ton. While mini-mills were expanding in the eighties, Big Steel was undergoing massive restructuring.

In the late eighties, one of the Goliaths, U.S. Steel's Gary works, was fighting back. By that time the Gary works had slipped into deep trouble. General Motors had virtually eliminated U.S. Steel's Gary works from its supplier rolls. Ford's Pete Urchek demanded that the Gary steelmaker find a new way of doing business or they could forget about supplying Ford. Gary was supplying poor quality steel, it was arriving late, and they were arrogant with their customers. In 1987, the Gary works finally woke up and decided to fight, but only when the situation had become life threatening. That was the year that George Lukes and John Goodwin arrived at Gary to face a deteriorating business and low morale. They set to work immediately and eliminated some capacity constraints in the plant. They brought in outside customers to tell the workforce why they were losing customers. They then pulled a team of workers off their jobs on the line and sent them to visit customers to determine what had to be done to achieve customer satisfaction. They were generally empowered to change the way the steel was made, stored, and shipped so that the fifty-ton rolls of steel arrived at the customer sites in perfect condition. The results were astounding. They identified problems with the steel and relayed those back to the plant where they were promptly fixed. Rubber pads were put on the flatbed trucks to cushion the steel sheets; they started using plastic rings to stop crane damage; and they persuaded those who loaded the steel to sign a tag on the roll, verifying the condition of the roll before shipment. The reject rate at the customer dropped from 2.6% to .6%. At the same time they were developing innovative ways to involve and empower all their employees in a continuous improvement and Delivery System redesign process, and they were investing in new technology such as coal injection technology which does away with coke ovens and new coating and forming techniques which improve the quality of steel delivered to the customer.

There have been many small battles between the Davids and the Goliaths of steel in the past few years, and the Davids are steadily gaining ground. This war's not over yet. The point is that investment and development of new technology is an important weapon of the Hunter, but it should not be relied on exclusively.

Of the twenty-five largest industrial corporations in 1900, only two remain in that select company today. Figures like this help to remind us that corporations are expendable and that success — at best — is an impermanent achievement which can slip out of hand.

– Thomas J. Watson, Jr., Chairman, IBM (1963)

CHAPTER EIGHTEEN

A Sinking Ship

*I*f Wil hadn't come along they'd have closed this shop," Alan Updike says as he walks the trio from the guardhouse toward the Garrett Processing Division foundry. The foundry is located in a large industrial area in Torrance, California just southwest of Los Angeles. Across the street are huge oil storage tanks, and idle oil wells dot the landscape. The foundry is housed in one of many nondescript buildings along Van Ness Avenue; buildings that go unnoticed except by the people who spend a third of their lives inside. "I'm glad you said you could help, Marcus."

"Glad to help. Thanks for bringing me in," Marcus says as they reach the entrance. "Wil was telling me over the phone that you've already done some good work."

"I've only been here a few months but we're already making progress. I've explained all the approaches that would help them and Wil is pushing hard. One problem is that everybody is protecting their own turf, so it's difficult to get them interested in what benefits the whole business. Some people are applying these new approaches, but it's like you once said, it's hard to be a prophet in your own land, especially if you're not a foundry man. They want to know where these approaches I've been preaching have been applied in a foundry. Most of them are so busy putting out fires that they won't take the time to try new approaches. They might listen to you a little more closely than to me."

So the marines have landed, Lou thinks. He is loving this. It's his kind of place . . . hot metal. "Where do you buy your ingot material?" he asks confidently.

"Worked with metal, Lou?" Alan asks.

"Spent some time around it," Lou answers, trying to keep a lid on his pride.

They walk rapidly through the foundry without stopping. Lou can see a group of men moving a ladle of molten aluminum in position over a set of molds. He catches a glimpse of a man carefully packing sand into a frame. He wants to stop and watch, but the procession is moving rapidly through some double doors into an office area.

Wil rises from his desk as the four of them are ushered into his office. "Thanks for coming on such short notice, Marcus," he says. He points toward a large oval conference table. His movements are solid and athletic. He begins speaking rapidly in a commanding manner. Dark, heavy eyebrows offset intelligent deep-set eyes. "I'll get right to the point. I just came on the job. I've been given a short time to straighten out this shop or it's going to be closed. We've reduced overhead drastically in the past few months, we've got all the people in the shop and office involved in continuous improvement, we've installed statistical quality control on some of our operations, we're buying new equipment to reduce our labor costs, and corporate management has supported all these efforts. We've improved a lot, but it's been a struggle month to month just to keep the place going. We're losing business to other foundries who offer twenty percent lower prices and faster delivery. We need some fresh approaches, and Alan said you could help."

Marcus leans forward, elbows on the conference table. "We only have this morning to complete our preliminary analysis, so I'll be direct. We should start with your present strategy, the principal strategic thrusts that you feel will make you the supplier of choice and improve your financial performance. Second, we'll need to determine which Delivery Systems in your business are limiting the achievement of your strategic goals, and finally, we'll help you organize teams to redesign those key Delivery Systems. Let's start with response to customers. What is your average time from receipt of order to delivery?"

"Forty to fifty days," Alan says.

"How about your response to a new product initiative by your customer. How long does it take you to design, build, and approve new tooling?"

"Haven't charted that, but we know it's too long," Alan says.

"Probably nine months or more," Wil says.

"How fast do you fix quality problems that customers bring to your attention?"

Wil smiles appreciatively. "Alan said you'd ask some very pointed questions."

"How about quality?" Marcus persists.

"There have been some complaints about quality from our customers, and a significant portion of our cost is due to inspection, rework, and scrap."

"If I went to your customers today and asked them for an evaluation of your performance, on what would they rate you poorly?"

"On schedule, delivery, and cost."

Two grueling hours after they arrive, Marcus is satisfied that the whole performance of the division hinges on one key Delivery System — the manufacture and inspection of castings. Alan suggests they move to his office for the next step of the analysis.

Marcus turns to Wil as he leaves the office, "Can you be available at about 11:00 A.M. to make some future plans?"

"I'll make the time," Wil says.

On the way to Alan's office, Lou asks. "Why don't we just go out and see what they're doing?"

"You might be able to see what they're doing but you will not be able to see what they *need* to do until you understand why the present system is falling short of meeting strategic goals," Marcus says. "You can learn that faster if you get the big picture first."

In Alan's office, they create a timed flow chart for the casting process that traces the flow of the material from the time the mold is prepared until it is ready to ship to the customer.

**Final Processing and Inspection
for Aluminum and Investment Castings**

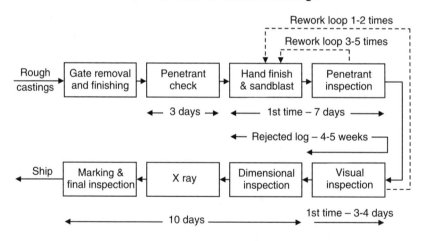

System cycle time for final processing and inspection – 40 to 50 days

Marcus asks Alan to identify the bottleneck areas and questions Alan's calculations of the total process time. An hour later he suggests a tour starting at the shipping dock and working backwards in the flow.

Aluminum Casting Physical Flow
(before redesign)

"Why start at the back end?" Laura asks. "Shouldn't we work on the front end where the castings are made? That's where the defects are caused. All the testing and rework wouldn't be necessary if the castings were made right the first time."

"I agree with you, Laura, but no matter which area we set out to redesign, first I want to understand customer perceptions so that we know what should be improved at the output end. Garrett's customers aren't satisfied with the output and we have to determine the reasons for the poor response and high price. In the final processing and test areas we can learn a lot about the problems that cause poor response, bad quality, and high cost. It's easier to understand a process if you first know what comes out of it. Then we'll redesign the process to improve the output."

Marcus continues, "Alan, what finished goods inventory do you have that hasn't been shipped?"

"None," Alan says.

"Then let's move on to the final inspection area."

"I've arranged for Rich Reynolds, our quality manager, to take you through the inspection and final test area," Alan says.

Rich is waiting for them as they enter the inspection area. There are stacks of material sitting everywhere, waiting to be inspected. Marcus points to the stacks. "How many days' inventory is this?" he asks an operator.

"Five days maybe," the operator says.

"Is that about average?" Marcus says.

"Much higher at the end of the month."

Marcus strokes his chin. "Why?"

"We're always pressed to make end-of-month shipping targets. We go all out at the end of the month to meet the monthly schedule before the books are closed. But it creates bottlenecks at the end of the month and inefficiencies at the beginning of the month."

"Is the inspection area a bottleneck?" Marcus asks.

"I guess so."

As they walk to the X-ray area, Marcus asks Lou what he'd do to level the schedule in the final inspection area.

"Tell everybody that a month from now they'll be measured on a weekly variance to schedule."

"That's all there is to it?" Marcus asks.

"That's what I'd do if I were in charge," Lou says.

"Would that work?" Laura asks Marcus.

"I can't think of a better solution," Marcus says. Lou smiles to himself as they continue to walk.

In the X-ray area, Marcus asks an X-ray reader how much backlog they are carrying.

"About six days," the reader says.

"How about the quality of the X-rays?"

"Sometimes they are better than others."

"How often do you reject material?"

"As often as they make it bad," the X-ray reader says, with a grin, "but it's usually not the parts that are bad, it's the X-rays."

"Why would the X-rays be bad?" Marcus asks.

"Sometimes they're overly exposed, and sometimes the operator shoots the parts incorrectly."

Marcus goes over to a rack of parts with red tags. "Are these parts rejected?"

"Sure are."

It doesn't seem to Lou that Marcus is going to get much from this guy.

Rich pulls a casting off the rack and explains to Marcus that these parts are waiting to be X-rayed a second time.

Marcus stops and talks to an operator doing X-rays. "How often do you have to re-shoot an X-ray?" he asks.

"There're always some to be re-shot. They have a lot of problems in the film developing area."

"Are you saying that none of the bad films are due to incorrectly shooting the part?" Marcus asks.

"Very few," the operator says.

"How much inventory is sitting ahead of the film developer?" Marcus asks.

The operator looks at the racks sitting just outside the film developing room, "Two to three days, I'd say."

"Laura, what would you do about the incorrect X-rays?" Marcus asks as they move again to the visual inspection area.

"I'd find the cause of the incorrect X-rays and fix it."

"What do you think the cause is?"

"I'd have to study the rejects to say."

"How much of the cause is in the way the system is designed?"

"Do you mean for example that the feedback is poor?"

"You got it. How long does it take for an X-ray operator to get feedback after he takes an X-ray?"

"I'd have to make a study."

"You already have all the information you need," Marcus says smiling.

Laura looks puzzled. Suddenly, her face bursts into a smile. "Two to three days," she says.

Lou is puzzled. Marcus looks at him. "Lou, how long does it take for an average X-ray that's just been taken to work its way through the process?"

"I've got it. Since there are two to three days of work-in-process it will take that long on the average to reach the reader. But then you have the additional time for the feedback to get from the readers to the X-ray operators. It could be a long time, if ever."

"Why do you say if ever?"

"I get the feeling that most of the time the operator who takes the X-ray never gets feedback on the same parts he or she X-rayed."

"Laura, what do you think of the quality of the information that is fed back to the X-ray operators?"

"My guess is poor," Laura says

Marcus turns to Rich. "What type of defects are showing up on the X-ray?" "Shrink is the main problem and there are some random inclusions," Rich says.

"What's shrink?" Laura asks.

"After the metal is poured into a mold, if it doesn't cool at a uniform rate, a void can develop inside the casting. We call that shrink."

They pass through the visual inspection area and into an area where many individual booths dot the floor. Marcus stops and picks up a casting just outside one of the booths. "What are the red circles on the castings for?" he asks.

"The red circles identify defects detected by the penetrant inspectors. The part is immersed in a solution of high penetrating oil combined with a fluorescent dye. The "penetrant" material seeps into casting flaws, which become visible when viewed under ultraviolet lighting."

"What happens after the defects are identified?"

"They go back to a grinder who grinds that area to remove the defect."

"Where's the grinder?" Marcus asks.

"Follow me," Rich says walking to another area of the plant.

"All these parts are to be reworked?" Lou asks as they walk into the grind rework.

"Getting the picture, Lou?" Marcus says.

"I think so. We operated like this at Continental but I could never see it as a system."

Marcus bends over and reads a tag. "What's the hot tag for?"

"Rush job," Rich explains.

Lou shakes his head. "Marcus, are you saying that you don't know what a hot tag means?"

"What does it mean, Lou?"

"Just what Rich says it means. It's a priority tag. It means that these parts are to be expedited."

"Why do they have to expedite?"

"Because they have a customer in a hurry."

"It looks like they have a lot of customers in a hurry," Marcus says walking along and pointing to more hot tags.

"Looks that way," Lou says.

"What does that say about their average time from receipt of order to delivery of order?"

"It's longer than the expectations that many of their customers have."

"Is that a problem, Lou?"

"Wil Danesi says it's a problem. Customers think that Garrett takes too long to deliver."

"Rich, I've seen enough of the final processing," Marcus says. "Can we now start at the beginning of the process and work our way forward?"

"Sure can," Rich says. "Where do you want to start?" "Making the cores," Marcus says.

Rich nods and motions for them to follow as he walks through double doors into the aluminum foundry. "Hey Frank," he yells across the shop. Light streaming from a huge door envelops a stocky figure moving toward them with a swagger. "He's built like a small beer truck," Lou says.

"This is Frank Doran, our operations manager for the aluminum foundry," Rich says. "Frank, can you show Marcus and his assistants through the casting shop, starting with the making of the cores?"

Like a surgeon, Marcus picks his way through the preparation of the molds. "How much time and trouble to change from one set of molds to another?" he asks.

"We get the molds from storage well ahead of time so that when we changeover, we can do it in minutes," Frank says.

They watch the final preparation of a large mold. "Do you ever have a problem with the final casting that can be traced to mold preparation?" Marcus asks.

"Last week an operator didn't put one of the chills into a batch of molds and we had some bad castings," Frank answers. "We ought to walk over to the pouring area because they're just about to pour. You can watch a process that started in Egypt thousands of years ago."

As they approach three large metal melting pots, the atmosphere is spiced with an acrid, penetrating smell. The hinged lid of one of the pots is open, revealing molten aluminum. Its silver surface is clouded by sludge. A man deftly skims the sludge from the surface of the melt, revealing a shimmering pool of molten aluminum. Light from a skylight fifty feet above bounces from the shiny surface and dances up on the back wall. The same man, goggled, gloved, and glistening with sweat, moves to the front of the furnace with a tool resembling a large spoon with a narrow handle. The furnace operator dips the spoon into the liquid metal and pours a cupful of hot metal into a small mold. A minute later he knocks the solid sample out of the mold, grabs it with a gloved hand and moves rapidly toward the far corner of the shop.

"He's going to get a lab check on the metal composition before he pours," Frank says.

Another man inserts a temperature probe into the middle of the hot melt.

When the furnace operator returns, he continues to skim the slag until the surface is pure aluminum. He reaches for a six-foot metal rod with a bucket at the end. Frank cautions Laura to step back. The man reading the temperature at the center of the melt nods and the furnace operator dips the bucket into the melt, fills the bucket, lifts it from the furnace and moves toward the spot where Laura is standing. Laura doesn't flinch as the man passes the ladle within ten feet of her and begins to pour the hot metal into the spout at the top of the first mold. Just as the last metal falls into the spout, molten metal rises to the top of the six exits and begins to freeze.

Laura feels a rush of excitement as the operator passes her. *Exciting and dangerous. What huge forearms. There must be eighty to a hundred pounds in that ladle, and he handles it with ease . . .* He stops by Laura on the way back to the furnace, holds the bucket out, and gestures as if to say, "Wanna try it?"

Laura leans toward the operator and speaks in his ear. His eyes almost pop out of his head. The operator stands almost stupefied as Laura casually walks away.

"What did you say to that guy?" Lou asks.

"I asked him if he could handle really hot stuff."

"He didn't have much to say to that," Lou says, laughing.

"He didn't know what to say, would you?"

"Critical process and methods," Marcus says to Frank as they leave the pouring area.

"You have to know what you're doing," Frank says.

"Does the furnace operator get feedback about the shrink?"

"We don't find the shrink 'til it gets to X-ray and that's a month later. It's too late by then," Frank says.

Marcus turns to Lou. "Lou, count the number of times they move the castings as they go through the process, starting right now."

Outside, they watch a worker pick up and roll over the sand mold. Suddenly it crumbles, revealing the metal casting. At three other work stations, the gates are sawed off, ground flush, and sandblasted. At each station Marcus asks the same question. What are the inventories at the input and output of each station, how are the castings transported, how do they know they are producing quality castings at each stage, and how fast do they correct problems.

"How many moves so far, Lou?" Marcus asks as the castings are about to enter the heat-treat furnace.

"Thirty-four," Lou says.

"What valueless activities accompany every move, Laura?"

"Handling, storage, tracking, expediting, and prioritizing."

"Rich, what kind of mood are the operators in? Do they realize that the place is in trouble?" Marcus asks as they walk back to Wil Danesi's office.

"They know it's not good, but they've heard shut-down threats before. I don't think they believe it could really happen to them."

"How about you, Rich, how do you feel about the situation?"

"Hey, I think we've gone critical. We have to do something."

"What do you think it's going to take to turn it around?" Marcus asks.

"Some big changes, I'd say."

"So what do you think?" Wil asks as they enter his office. "Can you help us out?"

"Definitely," Marcus says.

"So when can you get started?"

"Wil, as I told you, I'm booked up, but since you wanted to move right away on this, I could start it off with a workshop on the basic concepts with your staff, but the only opening I have would be a Saturday."

"How about this Saturday?"

"That would be fine with me — how about your staff?"

"They're almost all in here on Saturdays now, so I'm sure it would be all right with them."

"Once we get things rolling, Lou will work with you on this job. Laura will help out. I'll help them."

"If you recommend him that's good enough for me," Wil says looking toward Lou. "Lou, what do you think? Can you help us turn it around?"

"No doubt," Lou answers weakly.

"What do you think, Laura?"

"We can handle it," Laura says smiling at Lou.

"Good, when can you start?"

"We'll spend the rest of the morning walking through the operations and Laura and Lou will do a more detailed analysis starting Thursday. Can you arrange for them to talk to the right people and let those people know we're here to help?"

"Will do," Wil says. "See you on Thursday morning."

"Marcus what do you think?" Lou asks as they arrive back at Guardian Command. "Do you think we can help turn it around?"

"What do *you* think, Lou?"

"I got the feeling that Wil was talking the whole division, including investment casting, aluminum casting, engineering, the office, everything . . . "

"The whole division, Lou, but we'll start with the aluminum casting process."

"That's a lot to bite off," Lou says.

"We can do it, Lou," Laura says. Lou glares at her.

Marcus places his hand on Lou's shoulder. "Remember Continental Steel?" Lou's eyes narrow at the mention of Continental. "But do I know enough to do the job?" he asks.

"Not at this point." Marcus replies.

Lou's heart sinks to his gut. "Will I know enough by the time I start?"

"I hope so. Let's begin by systematically analyzing Garrett's Delivery Systems from the rough grind operation to shipment to customer. Our starting point is to make sure we understand what is driving our redesign.

"Let's start with our full transformation chart so we can put it all in perspective." Marcus flips the light stylus on and retrieves the transformation chart.

"Let's look at the three elements of Delivery System design, beginning with Process Intent. Process Intent itself has three characteristics: response, quality, and value-to-cost ratio. We'll start with response. Do Garrett's existing Delivery Systems provide satisfactory response to their customers?"

"No, Wil said they don't," Laura says.

Driving Transformational Change

Change strategy

| Vision & zeal | **Mind Changes**
 Mindsets
 Mental models
 Measures | **Delivery Systems Redesign**
 ⇨ Process Intent
 ⇨ Process Model
 ⇨ Learning and Improvement System
 ⇨ Value-Adding Technology | **Continuous Improvement**
 Reduction of
 • Valueless time
 • Valueless activity
 • Valueless variance |

Significant trauma

Performance gapping

The Non-Linear solution

| **Usually non-linear** | **Often non-linear** | **Usually Linear** |

"Take out your major influence factors on system cycle time. Which factors would you guess are most significantly affecting Garrett's system cycle time?"

Six Major Influences on Customer Response Time and System Cycle Time

- *Management and work force commitment to fast response*
- *The Process Model*
- *Work-in-process (WIP)*
- *Capacity versus demand*
- *Variance*
- *Valueless activity in the process*

"All six," Laura says. "Work-in-process may be the leading factor."

"I'd say insufficient capacity in the inspection area is the biggest factor," Lou says. "Especially at the end of the month."

"There's a clue there, Lou." Marcus says.

"Do you mean why don't they smooth the work load over the month?"

"They should, but what is the major cause of the bottle-neck?"

Laura perks up: "I would say the level of rejects they generate is a large part of the excess work-in-process, and because these rejects flow through many of the inspections more than once, they contribute to the capacity constraint in the inspection area."

"How much could they reduce cost if they could get it perfectly right the first time?" Marcus says.

"I'd guess twenty to thirty percent," Laura says.

"You're low, Laura."

"Thirty to forty percent," Lou guesses.

"Still low, Lou."

"But making castings is an art, not a science," Lou says.

"To improve the quality of the castings we need to replace the art with science — the science of quality. We'll now begin the second phase of your training with lessons on the second element of Process Intent — the design of Delivery Systems for quality."

"But Wil Danesi said customers aren't complaining much about quality," Lou says.

"They finally get it right, but it takes a lot of inspection. And they rework over twenty percent of what they process," Laura says.

Marcus smiles slightly. "Lou, are you saying that just because customers don't complain, they're happy with the quality from the foundry?"

"If I wasn't happy, I'd complain," Lou says.

"Would a customer that doesn't complain ever buy from a competitor?"

"I suppose," Lou says humbly.

"So lack of complaints may not mean customer satisfaction?"

"You talk in riddles sometimes."

"I'll meet you both here at eight this evening to go over your preliminary analysis of Garrett Processing Division. I want a timed flow-chart and a physical flow chart," Marcus says as he slowly fades.

"When do you want to get together to work on this?" Laura asks when Marcus is gone. "I've taken some notes we can use."

"I have my own notes right here," Lou says, tapping a finger against his temple and walking away. "You do the timed flowchart and I'll do the physical flowchart."

"That's fine with me. Do you want to meet back here at seven-thirty to go over our charts?"

"Nah, I'll just be here at eight," Lou says as he leaves the room.

At ten minutes before eight, Laura returns to the room of the Hunters to find Lou stoking a fire. He doesn't look up as she moves across the room and seats herself at the conference table.

"Finish your flowchart?" Laura finally asks.

Lou doesn't answer but continues to stare into the fire.

"Would you like me to look at your flowchart before Marcus sees it?

"You think you're an expert on everything, don't you?" Lou says.

"You're taking me wrong, Lou. It's just that I've studied business at Harvard. It's my specialty."

"You don't know a damn thing about business. You wouldn't survive a day in a factory. They'd rip you a new ass."

"Who does Marcus listen to, Lou? Not you," she retorts.

Lou rams the poker deep into the fire, spraying sparks onto the stone hearth. "Damn," he mutters as his head drops. Without turning, he hands his chart to Laura. "Do what you want with it," he sighs.

Suddenly, Laura is aware of Marcus standing beside the fire. "Oh, I didn't see you come in. Been here long?" she asks, embarrassed.

"Long enough," Marcus answers curtly. "Are the charts finished?"

"Here they are," she says, handing them to him.

He studies the charts a few minutes, sets them down, and walks over to the bottom of the stairs. He doesn't look pleased. "The timed flowchart is missing some important wait times, and the overall time is at least thirty percent in error. I expected better from the two of you."

The corners of Lou's lips begin to curl, but he stops short of a smile even though he feels pleased at Laura's embarrassment.

"Marcus . . . " She looks from Marcus to Lou and back again. She swallows. "I did the timed flowchart. What wait time did I miss?"

"You got all the storage times at the input of the operations, but you missed many of the storage times at output." He returns the flowchart to her. "Meet you upstairs in five minutes. We're headed to the other side of the planet to pursue the subject of quality and customer satisfaction."

"I can't believe it," Laura grumbles to herself as they follow Marcus up the stairs. "He was really upset," she said loud enough for Lou to hear. "Do you think he heard us arguing?"

"He did," said Lou.

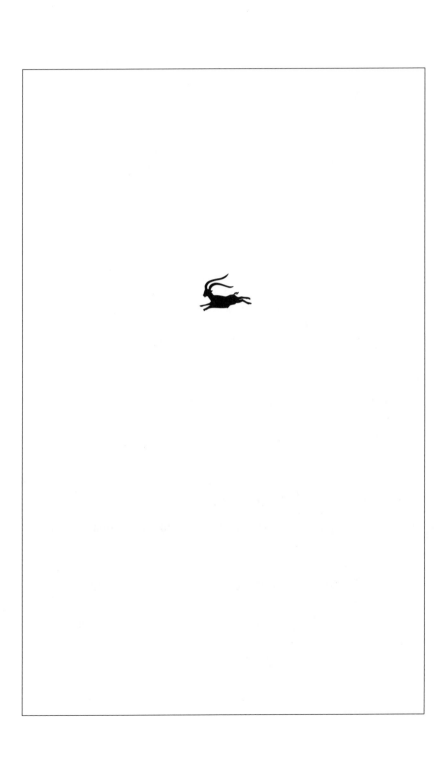

Quality comes not from inspection but from improvement of the process.

> – W. Edwards Deming

Treat the customer as an appreciating asset.

> – Tom Peters
> *Thriving on Chaos*

We lead the industry because we follow the customers.

> – Fred Turner, chairman, McDonald's

Ask the customer what they want . . . and give it to them.

> – Carl Sewell, premier U.S. auto dealer

CHAPTER NINETEEN

Customer Satisfaction

*J*ust moments after they rejoin Marcus, they are in a green valley on the banks of a huge river. "Nice night for a walk," Marcus says.

"Beautiful," Laura says.

"Where are we?" Lou asks.

"That will be obvious when we climb out of the valley at the next bend in the river. Let's talk about customer satisfaction while we walk. Before the Holiday Inns were started by Klemmons, do you think customers were complaining about the cost and services the motels of the time were offering?"

"Klemmons wasn't satisfied," Laura says.

"Before the McDonald brothers offered fast service in 1941, were customers complaining about response?"

"I don't remember that as a concern," Lou says.

"Were customers complaining to A&P in 1932 that they would rather have less service and lower costs?" What about Ford's customers; were they complaining that he didn't offer enough variety in 1925?"

"Until the Hunters came along with the new capability, customers didn't know what they were missing," Laura says.

"But once they did?" Marcus asks.

"Then that became the new expectation," Lou says

"What do you think is the goal of a business?" Marcus says as they round the bend in the river and begin the climb out of the valley.

"To make money," Lou says.

"What has to happen before a business can make money?" Marcus asks.

Laura says, "My marketing professor used to say, 'Nothing happens until somebody sells something.'"

Marcus laughs. "Your professor must have been in business at one time. Let me restate your thoughts in broader terms. To be successful," he says as he writes in the air with his stylus, "a business must":

- *be the supplier of choice*
- *achieve financial gain*

"Would you say that being the supplier of choice is a necessary but not a sufficient condition for success in business?" Laura asks.

"Yes!" Marcus says.

"But making money is both a necessary and sufficient condition for business success," Laura says.

"Right again, Laura."

"Why do you have to make this so complicated," Lou says, impatiently. "You just simply have to make a profit."

"How do you define financial gain?" Laura asks, ignoring Lou's comment.

"Financial gain may mean different things at different times in the history of a businesses, but it would be some combination of long-term positive cash flow, net asset increase, return on investment, profit, and stock appreciation. But the bottom line comes only if the business can sell its products and services. You have to be the supplier of choice before you can have financial gain. To be the supplier of choice the Hunters . . .

- *Go beyond meeting the expectations of the marketplace. They develop strategies that create the expectations in the marketplace by constantly innovating and improving their products and services.*
- *Continuously redesign their Delivery Systems to offer faster response, higher quality, and lower cost.*

"This is the Kano Model for customer satisfaction,"[1] Marcus says, as he creates another chart.

Three Dimensions of Customer Satisfaction

Kano Model

- Achievement of excitement features greatly increases customer satisfaction.
- Achievement of performance features mildly increases customer satisfaction.
- Achievement of basic features is expected and weakly increases customer satisfaction; but failure to achieve these greatly increases customer dissatisfaction.

"What does this suggest about using customer complaints as the only measure of customer satisfaction?" Marcus says, as they approach the plateau above the valley.

"Not good enough," Laura says. She gasps as they reach the top. To the west the immense silhouettes of three pyramids are starkly outlined by the full moon.

"Egypt," Lou says.

"We're in Sakkar, Egypt," Marcus says, as they survey their surroundings. "To our northeast are the ruins of Memphis. We are going to visit a chapel at the base of one of the pyramids. Let's whisk ourselves over there."

"Does either of you have a pocket knife or a nail file," Marcus asks, a massive pyramid looming behind them.

"I do," Lou says.

"Try to put your knife between two of the stones," Marcus says.

Lou opens his knife and tries to insert the end of the small blade.

"Won't fit," he says.

"Each of the blocks is over two tons," Marcus continues. "Over a hundred miles from here the stones were so precisely cut and finished that they fit within a thousandth of an inch. We stand before the work of a giant — Imhotep.

"At the start of Dynasty 3 in 2980 B.C., Imhotep was named 'Chief of All the Works of the King' by the Pharaoh Djoser and was given the responsibility for engineering the construction of the pyramids. Imhotep could have easily satisfied Djoser with the cement and stone construction that had been pioneered before his time, but he had a better idea. An immortal pharaoh should have a tomb that would last forever. He knew of a hard material that had been created millions of years before that would probably last forever."

"Granite," Lou says.

"Right," Marcus says. "Imhotep not only provided something that exceeded the expectations of his customer, Djoser, but he also devised so accurate a system of standards for quarrying and dressing granite that it's not likely it could ever be improved on — even given today's far superior measuring methods and cutting tools. They could measure within plus or minus one thousandth of an inch and control the process of stone production so that the dimensions of the stone were accurate to that degree."

"Impressive, but what's the point?" Lou asks.

"The point is that Imhotep not only exceeded his customer's expectations, he developed an integrated system of quality control almost 5,000 years ago. He carefully determined standard stone dimensions mathematically; he devised uniform methods and standard procedures for the stone cutting process; and he created standard measuring devices as well to make in-process checks.

"So process control is almost 5,000 years old," Laura says.

"At least," Marcus says. "Many of the principles of quality systems are very old, but it's only in recent years that customers have come to expect very high quality — largely because the Hunters are using quality as a weapon.

"Today, all of the great quality wizards agree that to be a Hunter, the Delivery Systems of the business have to be designed for quality from the ground up. And they also agree that customer satisfaction is the ultimate quality goal. In our next lesson we'll learn about existing mindsets, mental models, and measures that must change to achieve high quality. We'll begin by looking back to the quality mindset of 1970. Lou, where did quality fit into your priorities at Continental Steel in 1970?"

"We made good quality steel!"

"Suppose quality control held up a shipment because the quality level was unacceptable?"

Great Weapon of the Hunter

Quality

"We worked it out with quality control."

"Worked it out?"

"We figured out what it took to get it passed so we could ship."

"So quantity was the main priority?"

"Throughput was the name of the game," Lou says, looking down at the floor.

"Most producers today are convinced that improving quality is essential for survival; that quality is the number one priority."

Lou bristles. "If quality is the first priority, then cost will drive you out of business! I was for quality, but I had to live in the real world!"

"What's your definition of 'real world,'" Laura says, biting her lip.

"I mean you do the best you can with bad material, bad designs, and bad equipment. That's real world. No customer is going to want to pay for perfect quality anyway!" Lou says, stridently.

"So you're saying . . . that quality costs more?"

"It doesn't take an MBA to figure that out."

Laura taps her finger on the table. "Lou, my MBA professors would agree with you that cost and quality are tradeoffs."

"Then what the hell are we arguing about?"

"There's a production line. And there'll be a customer. Ultimate customer, I will call him. The one that pays for your product or service. Must pay attention to the ultimate customer. Lead him. You have to tell him what he's going to need three to five years from now, and have it ready . . .

"It is very important, very important to find out what he thinks is right or wrong about your product today. Just to be satisfied — that will not keep you in business. Lead him."[2]

– W. Edwards Deming
Out of the Crisis

"Enough!" Marcus interrupts. "You're both right. Lou, in your 'real world' quality was a tradeoff. Demand for steel was high. The Process Intent of your Delivery Systems was return on investment and profit."

"Nothing wrong with that! Isn't that the ball game?"

"Let's draw your Process Model in 1970," Marcus says, reaching for his light stylus.

Quality Process Model in 1970

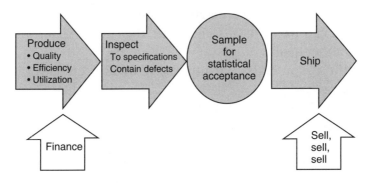

"Looks right to me," Lou says.

"So as long as you could get the material to pass specifications, everyone was satisfied with the quality, except maybe the customer. This Process Model was justified by the quality mindset of the seventies — that quality costs more."

"I feel like I'm being set up here," Lou says. "I was always for making the product better if it could be cost justified. I'm just saying you have to be realistic."

"We're going to get an expert modern viewpoint on the competitive advantage of quality from Ron Gill, a vice president at Delco Electronic, a $4 billion-company."

Suddenly they are standing at a receptionist's desk in a foyer. The receptionist looks up.

"Oh," she says startled, "I didn't see you come in.

> Quality must be defined as conformance to requirements, not as goodness.[3]
>
> – Phil Crosby

"We have an appointment with Ron Gill," Marcus says.

"I'll buzz him," she says.

Seconds later, Ron emerges from his office. "How's the famous Marcus doing?" he says, smiling.

"Not famous, but fortunate," Marcus says.

"There's a little conference room right around the corner that we can use. I have some slides that help explain how we think about quality."

"Ron, Lou feels that increasing quality increases costs," Marcus says.

"Lou," Ron explains, "you aren't the only one who feels that way. The average businesspeople in this country are unaware that there is a best-in-its-class competitor with similar processes that are 100 times more defect-free. If they do discover this gap, it's often quite a shock. They also may not be aware that five to ten percent of their customers are dissatisfied with the product, sales, or service, and will not recommend them to others. They believe that zero defects is neither a possible nor cost-effective goal. This chart compares the low-average producer with the best-quality producers."

"What I hope you'll see," he continues, "is that anything less than the best quality is costly, starting with its impact on profit and market share. A typical U.S. company spends from ten to twenty-five percent of its sales revenue on costs that are quality related, such as inspection and test, scrap and rework, analysis and problem solving, warranty, and customer returns. That's two to five times the profit on sales of an average U.S company. The best-quality competitor spends less than one percent of sales revenue on quality costs.

Quality is Profitable

Average Quality Supplier
Cost of quality 15-25% of sales
Dissatisfied customers 5-10%
Lost sales 2-5% per year

High Quality Supplier
Cost of quality 1% of sales
Dissatisfied customer <1%
Lost sales <1% per year

10,000   1000   100   10

Defects or deviations from specifications
for one part process step in parts per million

"This means that the typical company is going to have a difficult time competing with the best-quality producers for a couple of important reasons. First, the typical company, because it has not made quality a priority, is going to create dissatisfaction among its customers. As you know, dissatisfied customers will be less likely to buy products or services from that company again. The second thing to consider is pricing. The best-quality businesses can underprice their competitors by as much as fifteen percent while still providing customers with a product of superior quality. Furthermore, if we include the cost of lost sales due to poor quality and delivery delinquencies, some have estimated that the cost impact may be as high as fifty percent for some companies.

"They should also know, Marcus, about large-scale studies, like the PIMS study, which shows that companies producing the highest quality products and services have the largest growth in profit and market share.[4]

"Here's another thing to keep in mind: the greater the quality variance, the greater the cost. The top-quality producers in the world no longer believe that just meeting specifications is a reasonable final objective. The top-quality producers have abandoned this traditional view," Ron says, handing them each a chart.

The Traditional View of Quality

"For years, of course, we lived with the assumption that if a product was within specification, it was good enough; and if it was outside specification, it was bad. In some industries it was common practice for manufacturing to ask for an engineering okay to use material that didn't meet specifications. But over the past twenty years the Hunters have realized that any deviation from the best target value causes loss. Genichi Taguchi portrayed the concept particularly well," he says, handing them another chart.

The 1990s View of Quality

Regardless of specifications, any departure from target value is a cost
1) Cost of inspection, rework, and test
2) Cost of increasing customer dissatisfaction

"What Taguchi suggests here is that any variation from target value increases cost of manufacture and costs to the customer, thus creating customer dissatisfaction and ultimately loss of market share and profit."

"But will people pay for perfection?" Lou asks.

Ron turns to Lou. "It doesn't cost more for zero variance, Lou; that's what I've been trying to show you! It actually costs less if you redesign the product and process to eliminate variance. It does cost more *if* the only means you have to reduce it is test and inspection," he says.

"Lou," Ron continues, "you and I were brought up believing that if you want better quality, you have to pay for it. In the fifties, most U.S. companies assumed that to optimize cost we should provide the customer with products of the lowest acceptable quality. There are two things wrong with this assumption. First, the customer simply may not be satisfied with this level of quality. That means that you lose customers, which is far more costly than fixing the quality problems. Second, the assumption that quality costs more is wrong. As I said before, quality only costs more if you achieve it by increased or unnecessary inspection. Most U.S. companies now believe that quality is essential to survival, and that improving quality reduces costs, increases market share, and increases revenues. And remember this: Management must embrace quality improvement efforts wholeheartedly.

"Delco Electronics is a good example. In the past ten years, we have had to dramatically improve our quality to meet the tough requirements of Buick, Cadillac, Ford, Toyota, NUMMI, and Saturn.

"We listened to all the quality wizards: Deming with his fourteen points, Crosby with his twelve points, and Feigenbaum with his seven points. We concluded that they all worked. But the critical factor was not the message; it was the zeal and leadership of the managers who carried it out. We set goals of fifty percent reduction in field failures per year, and we are meeting our goal."

"But customer satisfaction is not just a product-quality issue. The customer must be satisfied from first contact through the life of the product. For example, to improve our response to a customer's request for quotes, we started with a timed flowchart for the process, then systematically set out to reduce

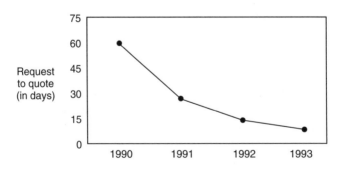

valueless time and activity within it. As a result, we've reduced the time to quote from sixty days in 1990 to four days in 1993."

"You can win a customer with a low cost, but you retain their loyalty through quality. So, I'll leave you with that thought and this last chart," he says, passing them more paper, "which shows the changes in attitudes regarding quality over the last twenty years."

Quality Mindsets 1973 to 1993

As they leave Delco Electronics Lou is frustrated and perplexed. "I don't understand something. If I'm so far behind the times, why was I chosen?"

"You were chosen because you have zeal. You care about people and you care about the work. You can teach us that, Lou."

"That's a good one. This is beginning to sound like *The Wizard of Oz*. Am I providing the heart or the courage?"

> Narrowly interpreted, quality means quality of product. Broadly interpreted, quality means quality of work, quality of service, quality of information, quality of process, quality of people, quality of system, and quality of company.[5]
>
> – Kaoru Ishikawa

"Both, Lou."

"I can't believe this. You're really serious. Are we going to follow the yellow brick road to meet the Wizard?"

"Something like that. But instead of one wizard, we're looking for the many wizards who will help you discover the Non-Linear Solution."

Lou's laugh comes as an explosion.

When they return to Guardian Command, the room of the Hunters is dark. A layer of fresh snow covers the skylights, and when Marcus pushes a button at the entrance, the west skylights open, creating a wave of falling snow. Sunlight beams down, brightening the east wall. Marcus moves toward the spiral staircase at the far end of the room.

He leads them down farther than they've ever been before, until they reach a dimly lit tunnel that leads to a cavern. As they enter the cavern, the sound of their footsteps echoes off the stone walls. Marcus immediately walks to a large, ancient trunk in the corner and unbuckles its straps, which clatter against the floor. He slowly opens the lid, reaches in the trunk, removes two large leather pouches and hands one to each of them. On the outside of the pouches, in gold-embossed letters, is written:

Great Quality Principles

"You may open your leather pouches," Marcus says, and they begin to untie the gold braid and remove a set of smaller silk pouches. Each pouch is beautifully embossed in gold letters.

"Old pouches," Lou says.

"They go back to at least my time — 500 A.D.

"You're kidding, these principles were around then?" Laura says.

"Oldies, but goodies, Laura. If you are ever to become full guardians, you must understand the deepest meanings behind these great ideas. They are the principles with which the great Delivery Systems were designed. There are three sets of great principles: value-adding principles, quality principles, and system principles. You may open the pouches marked 'GQP#1,' 'GQP#2,' and 'GQP#3.'"

"Marcus, there's a pouch marked 'Greatest Principle' and one marked 'The Non-Linear Solution.' When do we open those?" Laura says, as Marcus closes the trunk and walks slowly toward the circular stairway.

"We'll open the pouch marked 'Greatest Principle' when you discover it yourselves. The pouch marked 'Non-Linear Solution' has a blank parchment in it. After you discover the Non-Linear Solution, you must articulate it in writing in twenty-five words or less. Let's go back upstairs now and start talking about the great quality principles."

Lou and Laura follow him back up to the room of the Hunters, remove the first three parchments from their silk pouches, and unroll them.

Great Quality Principle #1

Quality can be improved and costs reduced at the same time.

Great Quality Principle #2

Improving quality increases competitive advantage. Therefore, the goal should be ultimate quality performance.

Great Quality Principle #3

All variance results in loss to the system as a whole and loss to society. Therefore, variance must be reduced.

Marcus moves now to a picture of a Cro-Magnon woman who is crafting spear points. "For early woman, quality may have simply meant usefulness. In the Middle Ages, a craftsman placed a mark on his work, and that mark was perceived as an indicator of its quality. Although the meaning of the word 'quality' has changed over the centuries, there are fundamental principles that have transcended these changes. Take out the pouch marked GQP#4 and open it now, please."

Great Quality Principle #4

Quality is perceived in the mind of the customer. Discover what customers value now and what they may value in the future. To be the supplier of choice, exceed their expectations.

"Lou, do you agree that this is a fundamental principle?" Marcus asks.

Regardless of the exact definition of quality, quality and satisfaction are determined ultimately by the customer's perception of a total product's value or service compared to its competitors.[6]

– Ronald Fortuna

"If you mean that the customer decides what quality is, I agree."

Marcus moves to the portrait of Thomas Jefferson. "To Jefferson, quality was the consistency and interchangeability of parts of a musket. This led Eli Whitney to develop standardized interchangeable parts and standard processes for producing them. This concept of cookie cutter reproducibility, or minimum variance between parts, lay at the heart of the Industrial Revolution and the development of mass production. Almost all suppliers today use standards for their processes. Now let's look at the contents of the fifth pouch."

....

Great Quality Principle #5

Design products and services according to customers' values, and standardize the processes that produce this value.

....

"I'm not sure that this applies so well to the service business, where everyone wants personalized service," Laura says. "If I'm buying a suit, for example, I want the tailor to take care of my individual needs."

"I know what you mean," Marcus responds, "but when you stay in a hotel, for instance, there are certain expectations that you have about what you're going to get. You expect the room to be cleaned daily, towels to be replaced, and the bed made with clean sheets. You may expect fresh coffee and Danish in the lobby each morning. If these are standard expectations, then the hotel must have standardized operations, which include training all its employees to provide these standard services."

"What Laura is saying is that you can't always go by the book," Lou adds. "An old general like you should know that. Once the battle starts, you make it up as you go."

"That's true, but even in the chaos of battle, you're relying on standard operations: clearing, loading, sighting, and firing a cannon. But I agree with what you're saying. A service business is an interactive one, and it must be flexible enough to adapt to individual customer needs right on the spot. However, Laura, one of the strengths of mass suppliers like McDonald's, American Express, Federal Express, and Buick is quality consistency. You know you'll get what you expect."

"But one of the strengths of the custom suppliers like Wendy's is you can get it any way you want it," Laura says.

"As long as you stay within their range of standard customized offerings. You can't get a filet mignon at Wendy's. Wendy's will customize your hamburger right on the spot, but they have many standardized processes that ensure quality consistency. Maybe we should revise the fifth principle," he says, turning on his light stylus.

Great Quality Principle #5

Design products and services according to customers' values, and standardize the processes that produce them while also accommodating the specific needs of customers.

"Did we just change a great principle?" Laura says.

"We improved it," Marcus says.

Laura laughs. "Just change 'em as you go?"

"Continuous improvement," Marcus says. "Management must lead the way in quality improvement. The foremost thrust in the philosophy of the legendary quality guru, Dr. W. Edwards Deming, is that the system is the cause of bad quality, and since only management can change the system, they are ninety-five percent of the problem. This brings us to the sixth great quality principle:

Great Quality Principle #6

Management controls the system; therefore quality improvement must begin with management.

"The systems approaches taken by Deming and Juran are widely used today. They both agree that a total system approach is essential, because a system is optimized by optimizing it as whole, not by optimizing its parts or subsystems. Juran has said that we've actually 'planned' our quality problems," Marcus

Juran's Quality Planning Roadmap

Reproduced with permission from the copyright holder, Juran Institute, Inc., Wilton, Connecticut 06897 USA.

says, handing both Lou and Laura a chart. "This is what he calls a roadmap for planning quality into the design of products and services, and ultimately, into the design of the processes that produce them."

Marcus removes his light stylus. "To sum things up for you, first management must commit to ultimate quality. Once they've made this commitment, as our great quality principles suggest, they must focus on the kinds of activities that allow for continuous improvement and redesign of the Delivery System. Here's a chart that lists such activities:

Three Levels of Quality Transformation

Mind Level

Create new mental models and measures by:
- *knowing the costs of poor quality and the opportunities of superior quality*
- *committing to surpassing customer expectations*
- *initiating a quality-improvement plan*
- *setting goals and measuring progress*
- *providing quality-improvement knowledge and tools*
- *rewarding quality improvement*

Delivery System Level
- *targeting system*
  - *quality planning*
  - *quality function deployment (QFD)*
  - *design for manufacture*
  - *design of experiments*
- *feedback system*
  - *reduce time to detect*
  - *improve quality of feedback*

- *feed-forward system*
  - *reduce time to correct*
  - *improve the quality of problem-solving processes*
- *prevention system: install and improve processes that prevent defects*

Continuous Improvement Level

- *organize teams to improve quality*
- *measure and set goals*
- *perform Pareto analysis of defects*
- *determine source and cause of defects*
- *change process or design to eliminate defects*

"What's this 'time to detect' and 'time to correct' stuff?" Lou asks.

"You're going to learn about it shortly," Marcus replies. "In fact, it's just part of much more you have to learn about management's role in helping to establish the changes in understanding necessary to achieve ultimate quality, but we must move on now to the next quality — the Delivery System level. The next lessons will deal with some of the basic fundamentals of the design of systems for quality, feedback, feed-forward, and defect prevention. We will begin with feedback system design by going back in time to 1925."

> I worry that whoever thought up the term 'quality control' believed if we didn't control it, quality would get out of hand.
>
> – Lily Tomlin

Dr. Deming and the Red Beads

For years, Dr. W. Edwards Deming toured the United States demonstrating the lessons of systems, management, and statistics. He used a demonstration with red and white beads to teach that to manage effectively one must carefully discriminate between that part of performance that is inherently due to the system design, and that part which can be attributed to people performing within the system. In his bead demonstration, the percentage of undesirable beads in the incoming material is 20 percent. No matter how much the workers try to scoop only white beads (using a fifty-hole paddle Dr. Deming provides) from the box of mixed beads, each time they scoop fifty beads they get an average of around ten red beads per scoop. Deming explained that workers' performance is determined solely by the system in which they are working. Management, he said, must not only recognize that most of the failure for a system to produce desired results is due to the system itself, but that management must change itself, and the system, to improve outcomes.[7]

PIMS (Profit Impact of Market Strategy)

In the long run, the most important single factor affecting a business unit's performance is the quality of its products and services, relative to those of its competitors. A recent PIMS study shows how a quality edge boosts performance in two ways:

- In the short term, superior quality increases profits via premium prices. Of the businesses included in the PIMS study, those that ranked in the top third on relative quality sold their products or services, on average, at prices five to six percent higher (relative to competition) than those in the bottom third.
- In the long term, improving relative quality is the more effective way to grow. Quality leads to both market expansion and gains in market share. The resulting growth in volume means that a superior-quality competitor gains scale advantages over rivals. As a result, even when there are short-run costs connected with improving quality, over a period of time these costs are usually offset by scale economies.[8]

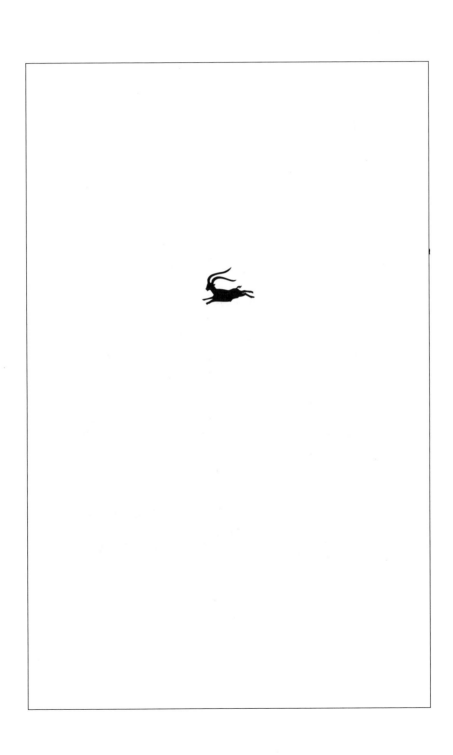

The Progress Principle: Any process of exhaustive search can be greatly reduced if we possess some way to detect when "progress" has been made. Then we can trace a path toward a solution, just as a person can climb an unfamiliar hill in the dark — by feeling around, at every step, to find the direction of steepest ascent.

Many easy problems can be solved this way, but for a hard problem, it may be almost as difficult to recognize "progress" as to solve the problem itself. Without a larger overview, that "hill climber" may get stuck forever on some minor peak and never find the mountaintop.

– Marvin Minsky
Professor of Mathematics, MIT
Society of the Mind

CHAPTER TWENTY

Feedback System Design

*L*ou wonders where they're off to now. Marcus always has something up his sleeve; everything's a big mystery with this guy. As thick cloud cover starts to thin, Lou sees a large body of water, a farm, some horses, and a plow.

"Where are we?" Laura asks Marcus.

"Canton, Ohio, 1925."

"Lived in Canton before we moved to Kokomo," Lou says. He looks around and everything is just as it was. There's Myers Lake . . . Ninth Street . . . and he's not prepared for what he sees next: his father . . . and himself as a young boy. They are playing catch. Lou watches the trajectory of the ball and the intent but happy face of the boy he used to be.

"Lou, you spent a lot of hours playing catch," Marcus says.

Lou begins to move closer, but Marcus grabs him by the arm. Still, Lou feels drawn to them. "Are they real? Can I talk to them?"

"No, Lou, we best not . . . sorry. I brought you here for a lesson on the design of Learning and Improvement Systems. Our first lesson is on feedback design."

Lou is distracted. He remembers nights at that upstairs window, listening to the trains in the distance, thinking about far away places . . . running secret messages from his window to his buddy Jim's window . . . 500 feet of string and two pulleys. If he looks under the porch he knows he'll find the sun-baked mudballs that he and Jimmy stored there for the big war. Lou smiles.

"Lou, snap out of it! We can't stay long and I've got a point to make."

"Sorry. What's the point?"

"Observe yourself pitching the ball to your dad. How long after you throw it do you detect where it's going?"

"Less than a second."

"How is the quality of the information you get about where it hits?"

"Good. I can see where it hits myself."

"How long does it take you to correct?"

"As fast as Dad fires the ball back, I'm ready to throw again."

"Okay, let's leave."

"Wait a minute. What's your point? Why the hurry?"

"The longer you stay, the more you're going to want to interfere with the past. We are not allowed to interfere."

"But you did it with Henry Ford."

"No, Lou, I was there in the 1920s. I was present when I helped them. This is different. Let's go!"

As they leave, Lou feels a sweet sadness as he looks back and sees his mother walking out onto the back porch, from where she calls her family in for supper. In a flash, they are no longer in Canton but back in the room of the Hunters. "Lou, have you thought about the point I was making?"

"You were talking about feedback design, right?"

"Right, but I didn't think you were listening. When you were watching that pitch and catch between you and your dad, you were observing a Learning and Improvement System. To learn how to pitch a ball you must have feedback, and the way the feedback system is designed determines how fast and how well learning takes place.

"As you remember, it took about one second for you to detect where the ball hit, and the quality of the information you had was very good, because you saw the trajectory and the point of impact." Marcus removes his light stylus and begins to write.

Time to Detect

A measure of the time it takes for a person or machine to become aware of the effect of an action.

"We'll mark the time of the first throw as zero," he explains. "One second later we have detection. So how long is the time to detect?"

"One second?"

"I'll draw a chart of the feedback system for a supplier and a customer."

Ideal Feedback Design

"Where would you say the very best feedback takes place?"

"Immediately as it's produced by the people who produce it," Lou says.

"Very good. Why is that the best feedback," Marcus says.

"Because the providing person or persons can detect immediately and the information would be high quality," Lou says.

Laura shakes her head in disagreement. "They need feedback from their customers. That's the best feedback."

"You're both right. The trick here is in obtaining both immediate feedback from the next customer for your product or service, and feedback from the ultimate customer. Then you must translate this information into a well-designed feedback system right at the source of production or service."

"But you're saying that the person doing the job should get the feedback directly. I'm still not convinced that workers at that level care enough," Laura says.

"Why not?" Lou says. "How about the way statistical operator control was designed at Harley-Davidson."

"That was different; they were threatened with losing their jobs."

Marcus tenses. "All workers are threatened if the company they work for doesn't produce quality."

"But I don't think the worker can comprehend that," Laura says.

"Motorola and Harley-Davidson educate the worker on the whys, wheres, whats, and hows, and I assure you, they do understand," Marcus says. "It's an imperative — an unconditional imperative — to produce zero defects."

"Zero defects is nonsense," Lou says. "Something is always going to go wrong! It's Murphy's Law."

"The late great Japanese manufacturing expert Shigeo Shingo had some interesting thoughts on that subject," Marcus says.

He explains how Shingo made a distinction between errors and defects. Shingo saw that there is a cause-effect relationship between the two: Defects arise only because people make errors. And while it's impossible to eliminate all errors from any task performed by humans, it *is* possible to prevent errors from becoming defects if operators get the kind of feedback that allows them to take corrective action right away.

"That's what the concept of source inspection is all about," Marcus continues. "Lou, at Continental, what happened if an error occurred?"

"Defects. Then once we knew we had a defective product, we could make corrections."

Management Correction Cycles

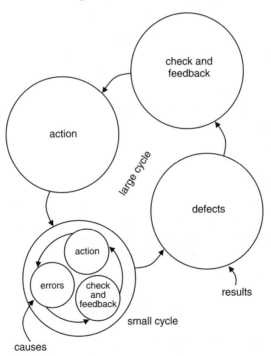

Source: Shigeo Shingo, *Zero Quality Control: Source Inspection and the Poka-Yoke System* (Cambridge, Mass.: Productivity Press, 1986), 82.

"Precisely. This is what Shingo referred to as large-cycle control or management.[1] Source inspections, on the other hand, allow control to be carried out in small cycles. This is how it works," he says, writing with the light stylus:

Source Inspection

- *an error (cause of defect) occurs*
- *operator receives feedback before the error causes a defect*
- *operator takes appropriate corrective action*

"Traditionally, inspections did nothing more than uncover defects after the fact," Marcus continues. "But by using source inspection and *poka-yoke* devices that prevent errors from becoming defects, it is absolutely possible to achieve zero defects."

Lou is amused. "*Poka-yoke* devices?"

"Shingo was referring to devices like jigs, limit switches that prevent overtravel, sensors that indicate presence of a part."

"I'll buy that," Lou says.

"Now let's talk about correction, the second important characteristic of a well-designed Learning and Improvement System. Let's go back to the pitching lesson. You already said that the time to detect was one second. How long did it take you to make a correction before the next pitch?"

"About five to ten seconds," Lou says.

Marcus writes with the light stylus:

Time to Correct

A measure of the time that elapses from the discovery of a problem until that problem is solved with no chance of recurrence.

"If we say that correction time was about ten seconds, then the sum of the time to detect and the time to correct would be eleven seconds. This completes one cycle of learning." Marcus draws a chart with the light stylus.

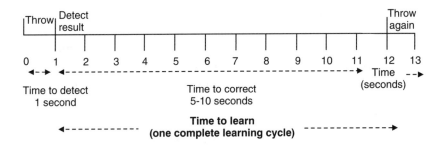

"You will notice I have introduced an additional characteristic — time to learn — which is the sum of the time to detect and the time to correct. The time to learn is the time for one complete learning cycle." He writes with the stylus:

Time to Learn = Time to Detect + Time to Correct

"You were a pretty good ball player in your time, Lou. How many times did you throw that ball as you were growing up?"

"Thousands," Lou says.

"Laura, suppose we design the feedback system differently. Imagine that after he released the ball, he couldn't see the trajectory or the impact. Imagine that everything would go blank in front of him immediately after he threw."

"Then he wouldn't get any feedback."

"But suppose that after his father caught the ball, he would draw a picture of the impact on a postcard and mail it to Lou. Lou would then wait until he got the card in the mail before he would throw another pitch to his dad. Now how long is the time to detect?"

"Two days."

"Is the quality of information as good as it was before ?"

"No."

"How long is the time to correct in the second case, Laura?"

"It's going to take a little longer to recall the memory of what happened and make a correction."

Marcus turns to Lou. "So what's the time to learn in this case?"

"Over two days."

"How long would it take to learn to throw well if one learning cycle was over two days?"

"Forever," Lou says.

"The point is that the rate at which we learn and how well we learn depends a great deal on how long it takes us to detect, the quality of the information detected, the amount of time it takes to correct, and the quality of the problem-solving process. Was the correction process in your steel mill a fast, high-quality process like the one you had with your father — catching and immediately returning the ball to you to throw again? Or was it more like the second case where you have to recall what you did days before and then try to correct?"

"More like the second case."

"How would you reduce the time to detect in the Garrett casting shop, Lou?"

"By inspecting immediately after each operation," Lou says.

"How would you do it, Laura?"

"I'd first reduce the system cycle time which would reduce all of the times to detect. The bottom line is that the shorter the system cycle time, the lower the average defect and error level in the process. Long system cycle time also lengthens the learning cycle and reduces the accountability which can be assigned to the person or process that introduced the error. I would also reduce the variance they have in casting quality, if I could."

"Good. Now open the seventh great-quality pouch."

....

Great Quality Principle #7

Detect defects, errors, and variances immediately, and provide high-quality feedback immediately.

....

"Up to now, we've focused on feedback time. Let's now focus on the quality of feedback and the quality of problem-solving processes. We'll start with feedback. There are three characteristics of good quality feedback," Marcus says, as he writes with the stylus.

....

Characteristics of High-Quality Feedback

- *useful*
  - *provides data on key outputs that produce customer satisfaction*
  - *provides data on key process variables*
- *facilitates quality improvement*
  - *has action rules*
  - *depicts trends*
  - *provides history and audit trail if required*
- *user friendly*
  - *communicates directly with the person or group whose actions are reflected by the data*
  - *visible or conveniently available*
  - *simple but informative*

....

"Lou, the feedback you got when pitching to your father was of high quality. The source operator or machine that receives feedback directly from the operation and directly from the customer has the best of both worlds. This is the simplest and most effective feedback.

"When time to detect is excessively long in systems, the very life of the business may be threatened. For example, the system cycle time for designing, manufacturing, sale, and customer use of an automobile is four to six years. If any miscalculation of future customer values is made in the early stages, five years may elapse until customer reaction results in lost sales and correct interpretation of the losses. This chart, which we've looked at before, shows this clearly."

**Time to detect a miscalculation of customer values
or a failure to deliver customer expectations**

"Although the customers have problems with the car, they may not complain, or worse, they complain but they're ignored. You've heard people say that you'll always have a few complainers or that you can't please everyone. Such attitudes obviously reduce the usefulness of the feedback and contribute

---

Feedback That Facilitates Quality Improvement at the Source — Precontrol

Once you've set the design target and the upper and lower specifications, you can then precontrol limits halfway between the specification limits and the design target. Take two consecutive samples. If either sample measured falls outside the specification limits, shut down the process until you're able to find the problem and take corrective action. The zones between the specification limits and the pre-control limits are called the yellow zones. If two samples fall into the yellow zone, stop and adjust the process. The remaining possibilities, one yellow and one green, or two greens, allow the process to continue.

---

to complacency; and then, the only feedback that shakes them from their complacency is the realization that their customers are now purchasing a competitor's product. So while some managers will continue to rationalize data until conditions reach such a critical stage, Hunters reduce the cycle time of their learning by designing their systems to provide fast, unfiltered feedback from their customers and fast, unfiltered feedback from the sources of errors and defects.

"Let's discuss the fourth element of our detection and correction systems — the quality of the correction process. Laura, how would you measure the quality of a correction process?"

"First measure whether the right problems were solved," she says, fingering her Harvard ring.

"Good starting point. Lou, how would you measure it?" Marcus asks.

"I'd measure whether the process fixed problems so that they never happened again."

"Excellent! Let's put it all together. Solving the *right* problem is first. Solving the problem correctly is a close second. High-quality correction processes do both well. Laura, how would you ensure that the right problems are solved?"

"I'd prioritize them by urgency and by the potential value that the solution would have for the business."

"Let's list the characteristics of a high-quality correction process."

Characteristics of a High-Quality Correction Process

- *solves the right problems*
  - *prioritizes what needs to be corrected*
  - *determines what the real problem is*

- *solves problems correctly*
  - *produces the best solutions: develops alternatives; has algorithm for selecting best alternative; has good test for validating solutions*
  - *no recurrence (eliminates root cause)*
  - *anticipates and prevents future problems: maintains records of lessons; systematically applies lessons learned to future problems*

- *is productive*
  - *high return for the effort*
  - *everyone contributes*

User-Friendly Feedback — Visible Control

Feedback should be highly visible:

- performance measures posted where everyone can see them
- maintenance records and machine settings attached to equipment
- alert lights standing high above the operations, signaling a need for immediate attention at that station
- markings on floors and walls indicating what should and should not be there
- safety guidelines and rules posted

"On our next visit," Marcus says, "we're going to learn about the very important relationship between system cycle time, time to detect, and time to correct. Our teacher will be Leo Moore. We'll be meeting him in the morning. I expect you to rework your timed flowchart and physical flow analysis from Garrett and have those ready for me to review tomorrow evening. Meet you here in the morning."

"Lou, what do you have against me?" Laura asks moments after Marcus leaves.

"Nothing."

"It seems that every time I open my mouth lately you jump on me."

Lou says nothing, but continues to stare into the fire. Finally, after a few tense moments he answers. "You're just like the rest of them."

"The rest of who?"

"Ivy leaguers with their big educations."

"You resent the fact that I went to Harvard?"

"It's the attitude," Lou says rising to leave.

"It's really that I'm a woman who isn't keeping her place, isn't it?" she says with a tremor in her voice.

"See what I mean? You even think you know what I'm thinking. Don't lay that male chauvinist stuff on me. I'm going outside," he says.

"At night, on the mountain?" Laura asks softly.

"There's a full moon."

"Do you want company?"

"Suit yourself."

"Can you wait a minute while I change clothes?"

"I guess."

Laura returns in less than five minutes in a khaki jumpsuit, carrying a parka. Lou glances at her but self-consciously looks away.

They hike quietly in knee-deep snow. About a hundred yards down the side of the mountain Lou stops.

"It was just about there a few months ago that I saw a cougar," Lou says, pointing to a ledge.

"Beautiful animal," she says.

"Beautiful and deadly, probably a female," Lou says, with a twisted grin.

"You just don't get it, do you, Lou?" she says, sadly. And then: "Shadows in the moonlight. Don't see that very often."

Lou turns toward her. "My mother used to say that it's hard to dislike someone who walks with you in the moonlight."

Laura smiles. No more than twelve inches separate them. "A penny for your thoughts," she says.

"I guess we'd better start back."

"What's the hurry?"

"We need to go over those charts. I'll make a fire."

"That would be nice," she says. "And by the way, I agree with your mother."

Feedback That Facilitates Quality Improvement at Suppliers

In 1983 at Delco Electronics, it could take weeks before a supplier was notified that material they had shipped to Delco was defective; and it could be months before final disposition of the material was made. Because the process took so long and material stayed in limbo so long, often the defective material would be sorted or modified for use in shortage situations. If shortages were severe, engineering would be asked to allow deviations from specifications to permit use of the material. As Jim Brock, manager of incoming inspection, sarcastically put it, "the longer materials sat the better they looked." To solve the problem, Jim put a team together to redesign the process of notification, disposition, and return of defective material. The team was facilitated by Charlie Mays.

The team set a goal to drive down the percentage of defective material from suppliers at least 10:1 by redesigning the feedback systems for suppliers. Very early into the redesign process they found the major culprit — an old procedure called the material return authorization (MRA). The MRA process flow is diagrammed below.

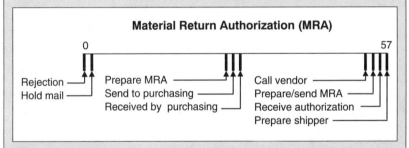

Material Return Authorization (MRA)

With this procedure, the average time to get a material return authorization was almost two months, during which time the material remained in locked storage. By examining the documents associated with each defective shipment, they found that two to three weeks elapsed before the receiving clerks would fill out the MRA form and send it to purchasing. Because the clerks were overloaded, they were compelled to handle only emergencies like production shortages, billing errors, receiving and shipping, lost material, and material movement. Recognizing this as a capacity problem, the team worked together to simplify the clerks' job and put some of it on computer. The time to go from rejection to purchasing was reduced to one day.

To eliminate the wait time in purchasing, the clerks in the receiving inspection area were authorized to request an MRA immediately from the supplier; and suppliers were required to respond immediately with a correction. The process time from rejection to MRA and return to supplier was reduced to two days. The quality of incoming material increased and the inventory in locked storage was almost eliminated, saving over $3 million.

By 1992, the procedure was almost unneeded because most of Delco Electronics' suppliers were certified and didn't require incoming inspection.

Environmental Feedback

Martin Marietta Energy Systems dramatically improved the process of reporting to their state environmental agency. A team led by John Stanley, Dan Lineham, and Ann King streamlined the process for reporting stream test results, eliminating half of the building moves, 30 percent of the transfers between people, and reducing the time to report by 50 percent.

Feedback from the Customer and the Source

Carl Sewell, the phenomenal auto dealer who grew from $10 million in sales per year in 1968 to $250 million in 1990 with corresponding profit increases, tells how his dealership achieved one of the highest CSIs (Customer Satisfaction Indexes) in the General Motors dealer system by creating systems that get it right the first time.

Inspectors make people sloppy. If you know someone is checking your work, you might not check it yourself. We learned that lesson the hard way. After going for years without having quality inspectors, and getting scores on the General Motors Customer Satisfaction Index (CSI) in the high nineties, we decided that the best way to ensure 100 percent quality was to do 100 percent inspection. That way, we would be able to catch the few problems that were getting by. So we started adding inspectors. Eventually we got up to seven, and we inspected every job at every turn. And you know what happened? Our CSI, and our quality, went down. Because we had all those inspectors, our technicians stopped feeling as responsible for their work. They felt it wasn't up to them anymore to make sure the job they did was absolutely right. That's what the inspectors were for, they said.

The technicians had a lot of pride in what they were doing. The moment we took away all those inspectors, our CSI went up and so did the quality of the work. It's now the best it's ever been because our people feel more responsible for their work, and they like that feeling.[2]

Creating a Learning System for the Learning Impaired

Shares, Inc. in Shelbyville, Indiana, is a sheltered manufacturing house that employs mentally and physically handicapped individuals. The company receives a mixture of short- and long-term contracts that involve light machining and manual assembly.

Many of the employees' learning disabilities stem from short attention spans. They range between three and one hundred percent functional as compared to industrial work standards. The operators are paid "piece rate" based upon the standard. The wide range of worker functionality created huge variations in operation time. Consequently, most of the operations were designed with large batches and large buffers between them. As you might expect, quality was an issue.

The first step was to perform an appraisal of the current system, which included process-flow mapping and boundary-condition assessment. It was apparent that the current systems design was a form of constraint management. Separating the constraining operators through the use of buffers only exacerbated the problem. Poor quality was the result of too little feedback provided not quickly enough to operators who already suffered from learning disabilities.

The solution was to attack the issue of learning and not manage around the constraints. This was done by creating flow-line teams using pull signals with buffers between operators. Crucial to the implementation was the strategic placement of highly capable operators in checkpoint positions. Feedback to learning-impaired operators was immediate, falling into the window of their attention span. If an operator made a mistake, that person was corrected immediately, increasing their attentiveness and learning. Also, attention to the line rate through team motivation and small buffers enabled highly dysfunctional operators to work two or three times faster.

The end result, according to Rick Land, a training specialist at Shares, was beyond their wildest expectations. Dramatic improvements in quality was only one of the benefits. Productivity, cost, work-in-process, and average employee earnings all showed significant improvements.

The result also has significant social implications. With the right system design, the learning disabled can earn a good wage while creating value to society by producing a quality product. It also disproves the age-old paradigm that the result of poor quality lies with the operator, even if the operator is learning impaired.

– Mike Louis
Manufacturing Consultant
Technical Assistance Program
Purdue University

I shall try to correct errors when shown to be errors, and I shall adopt new views so fast as they shall appear to be true views.

            – Abraham Lincoln, August 22, 1862

Every thing was coming this way — immigrants, railways, water traffic . . . there were things about the country to learn and the ones who learned the fastest, fared the best.

            – Marshall Field, 1901

CHAPTER TWENTY-ONE

Feed-Forward System Design

*I*t all started in May 1987," Leo Moore, manufacturing supervisor at Hughes Aircraft says, "with a problem we had in the Electronic Instrument Assembly area. It was a Friday afternoon. Seems like it happens every Friday close to quitting time."

"I know the feeling," Lou says.

"I remember walking over to the repair station at the test area where a large number of units were failing final test. The repairman said that the units had been stacking all day long due to a batch of bad capacitors. Many had been sent back for rework, and it looked like we were going to miss the weekend shipment. At that time it seemed something was always going wrong and causing us to miss our schedule. When I checked with Bill Smock, the planner, and he said that we were only nine units short of making the week's schedule, I felt a little better. I asked the operators if they would agree to work overtime to disassemble and repair nine units, and then I went back to my office to call my wife to tell her I'd be late.

"The next thing I remember is a repairman at my door saying, 'You'd think receiving inspection would have caught those capacitors.'

"That got me thinking about something you said in your workshop, Marcus. You talked about time to detect — the time from the introduction of a problem into the system until it is detected. I wondered how long that bad capacitor was in our process before we discovered it at final test. To get some idea of how long, I tagged a couple of instrument chassis that were just starting in the process and forgot about the problem, until a few months later, that is.

"Two months later, someone brought me the two tags I had put on the chassis. The tags had a note that said, 'Notify Leo when this chassis finishes final test.' I had completely forgotten about those tags I had put on to measure the system cycle time to build an instrument. When I figured the time, I couldn't believe it. It had taken forty-nine working days to go through the line. As I was guiding a customer on a tour through the plant that afternoon, I couldn't help wondering how it took forty-nine days for that supply to be processed from start to finish. There are only six hours of labor in each unit. How could it take forty-nine days?

"But it did explain the capacitor problem. With the long total cycle time, it took a long time to detect errors and defects. Although those capacitors had passed receiving inspection they were in our process many weeks before we discovered another problem with them at electrical test. It also partly explained why delivery time was three months from receipt of order. I found later that it also explained many other costs like scrap, rework, repair, additional inspection, expediting, prioritizing, crisis-solving, and wasteful management actions.

"The next morning I set out to solve the mystery of the forty-nine days. First, I observed that there were a number of weeks of backlog before and after kitting, and about three weeks inventory on the flow rack. There were two more weeks partially assembled on the shortage rack waiting for the parts that we were missing when we released the kits. And there were units sitting ahead of visual inspection, final test, and rework stations."

"Could you explain to Lou why you released kits if all the parts weren't there?" Marcus says.

"Sure, two reasons. One, we used to think that if the assemblers had a lot of work stacked ahead of them, they worked harder. If the stack got smaller, they would slow down. Second, a stack ahead of the assemblers made sure they didn't run out of work. Besides, if we had enough parts to build them up to ninety-five percent complete, we could quickly complete them when the rest of the parts were acquired."

"Those sound like good reasons to me," Lou agrees.

"But that meant they had to sit three weeks on the flow rack and two more weeks on the rack where they waited for the rest of the parts," Leo says. "I know it sounds crazy now, but it made sense at the time." He hands out a diagram. "This is the layout and process flow we had then. We found that our forty-nine days resulted from parts being stacked at every station.

Instrument Assembly Flow

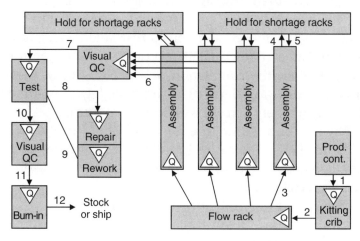

"We then put a team together to rethink the way we were doing things. In the next few weeks, although many team members had serious reservations, they all agreed that we had a poor Process Model and a poor Learning and Improvement System. We decided to start with continuous improvement approaches that reduced the system cycle time, and defects and errors. Starting with the overall flow diagram, the team focused on the wait times, starting with the largest and proceeding to the smallest. The longest time was on the flow rack and the second largest was the wait time on the shortage rack. The action plan to reduce these two wait times involved three steps:

- release only complete kits
- stop releasing kits until all inventory on the flow rack and on the incomplete rack was completed, except for selected hot jobs
- release only one week prior to scheduled time for power supply completion

"Everyone agreed that we were not going to be driven by the size of the stack of inventory, but instead by the need to meet customer requirements. System cycle time dropped from forty-nine days to fifteen days within two months.

"To address the third longest wait time, a visual inspection was immediately moved adjacent to the build table, and a rule was established that visual inspection would be performed immediately on the completion of a power supply. Feedback and correction was taking place immediately. First-time test yields rose to ninety percent within three months.

"By the third month, the team had gained confidence and decided to change the basic Process Model. After they designed a new layout and put it in place, the system cycle time dropped to less than eight hours."

"Leo, could we see the new line?" Marcus asks.

"No problem, I'll get Rosie, our union rep, to show you around. Let's head that way."

"Won't the union let you show us through? Have things gotten that bad?" Laura asks.

Leo laughs, "No, there's no problem there. I just want you to see it from the workers' point of view. I'm not even going to go with you; we've developed real trust here."

Laura is skeptical, but she tries to keep an open mind. She is introduced to Rosie and the tour begins.

"You can see here," Rosie says, "that the power supplies are moved from one assembly operation to the next along this U-shaped table. The people who work on the line and the engineer made the layout, but the line operators did the final balancing of the jobs. They inspect their own work and the work of the preceding operation."

Instrument Assembly After Redesign

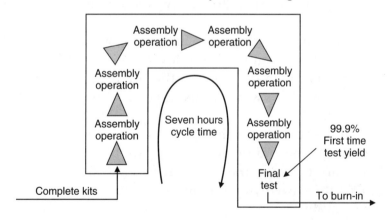

"The operators balanced the jobs?" Laura asks.

"After our engineer did a rough balance, some jobs still required more effort than others, so the operators divided them evenly."

"But if you let people do that, they'll make the jobs too easy," Laura argues.

Rosie flashes Laura a disdainful look. "We know what we're up against in the electronics business today. We want to keep our jobs and we're willing to work."

Laura manages a weak smile. "Don't take me wrong. I only meant to say — "

"I know what you meant to say!" Rosie interrupts. She motions to some square outlines on the tables. "The line is U-shaped and there is a square between each operator to control inventory build-up."

"How does that work?" Lou asks.

"There's one square between each operator. When one operator finishes the work at his station he moves the supply to the square in between. If the first operator finishes and there is still a power supply sitting on the square to his right, he stops working until that supply is moved."

"But wouldn't that stop the whole line if one operator stops?" Lou asks.

"Yes, and that sometimes happens if we have a quality problem that we can't solve quickly. We've learned that if there's a problem, in the long run the best policy is to stop, fix it, and go on. That's why our first time inspection yield is 99.9 percent today.

"All of the problems the operators found today are on this flip chart. At the end of the day we have a meeting with the whole team to assign the problems to someone to follow up and fix within twenty-four hours — and fix it so that it never happens again."

Lou shakes his head. If he were the boss, he'd straighten them out on this one. He can't believe Leo would let them have a list up like that when a visitor comes through. *Looks bad. What if I were a customer?*

"We used to hide our problems," Rosie says, as if she's read his thoughts, "and that's where they stayed — hidden. By encouraging people to expose problems and then help fix them, everyone's attitude has changed. People on this line believe that management wants top quality, and we're proud that we make top quality. Customers see the list when they visit, but they also see this chart showing a quality improvement of one hundred to one. That's the bottom line. And besides, customers are smart enough to know that if we immediately correct our problems in-house, we're going to do the same for them."

"Can your operators be objective when they inspect their own work?" Laura asks.

"Our quality has improved over one hundred to one," Rosie says.

"Can't argue with that," Laura says.

"Lou, what do you think about what you saw?" Leo asks when they return to his office.

"Impressive, but how did these changes affect the costs?"

"Lou, when I prepared my first presentation for upper management, the full impact of these changes finally settled on me. Everything was better. As I looked at the last slide in my presentation, I thought they would never believe that this kind of improvement occurred in just six months. Let me give you the overall results." Leo goes to the chalkboard and begins writing.

- *average manufacturing cycle time reduced from 49 days to 1 day*
- *first-time test yield increased from 60 to 99.9%*
- *productivity increased 80%*
- *costs reduced 30%*

"In your words, Marcus, we're no longer one of the Hunted. We now can deliver a customer order in two weeks. Our costs have improved thirty percent and we have achieved a new level of quality."

"You're a Hunter, Leo. I appreciate the time you spent with us, but we have to move on. Keep in touch."

"Hey, Marcus, you're the hard one to find."

"Can you now say which of the six major influences on system cycle time was most responsible for the big reduction in time to detect?" Marcus asks, as they arrive back at Guardian Command.

"Their new Process Model," Lou says immediately, "including the new layout and reduced work-in-process."

Marcus beams. "Good! They not only reduced work-in-process by ninety-five percent, they put controls in place to keep it at the new level."

"Leo sold me on low work-in-process. He's a straight talker and I can't argue with the bottom line," Lou adds.

"Laura, what factor do you think was most important?"

"I think that management's commitment was number one. I agree that the new Process Model was a major factor but it was their understanding of the link between system cycle time and quality that was impressive. When the system cycle time was reduced, the time to detect was reduced, rework went down, nonvalue added activity went down, and productivity went up. I made a diagram of the connection," she says, showing Marcus and Lou her notebook:

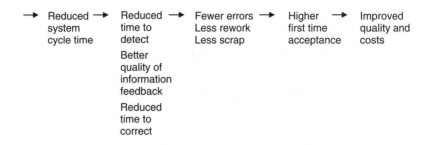

"Laura, you're in good company. Let's compare your graph to W. Edwards Deming's chain reaction, as he calls it."

Deming Chain Reaction

Source: W. Edwards Deming, *Out of the Crisis* (Cambridge, Mass.: MIT CAES), copyright © 1986 by W. Edwards Deming. Reprinted by permission of the publisher.

"Marcus, I'm confused," Laura says. "Deming says start with quality. Another expert says start with quality and cycle time reduction. And you seem to emphasize cycle time reduction first."

"Since time to detect and time to correct are reduced when cycle time is reduced, I tend to start with cycle time reduction, but variance reduction should be close behind."

"I was impressed that Leo and his team had a time limit on solving problems," Laura says.

"Yeah, twenty-four hours they said, but that's not realistic," Lou says, shaking his head.

"But they were doing it on almost all problems, Lou," Laura says.

"I'll give them an A for effort," he says, reluctantly.

"A good feed-forward system," Marcus says, "such as the one Leo designed, has a short loop where the correction of problems and errors that cause defects takes place in less than twenty-four hours."

"I sense that we've arrived at another great quality principle," Laura says.

"You've got it," Marcus says. "Open up the eighth silk pouch."

Great Quality Principle #8

Correct errors within the process immediately and prevent their recurrence.

"Of course," Marcus says, "good feed-forward systems must also have long loops where customer dissatisfaction is solicited and corrective action is taken at once. Take a look at this chart," he says, pressing a button on the light stylus.

"The short loop, which Leo and his team designed, has a correction time of twenty-four hours after an error is detected, because the team has all the resources necessary for solving short-loop problems. Solving these kinds of problems is absolutely crucial to the pursuit of quality. But you also have to remember that if you're to achieve total quality, you can't ignore the larger loop. That's the lesson I want you to learn

Ideal Feed-forward Design

- Designing for customer satisfaction
- Relentless pursuit of dissatisfaction
- Fast time to correct
- High quality correction processes
  Non-recurrency of errors

from this," Marcus says, as he hands them each a printed page. "This is a summary of an article recently published by a manufacturing consultant named James Cameron. Please take a few minutes to read it."

When Lou and Laura are done reading, Marcus continues: "Another important point to take away from this example," he says, "is that prevention activities fall into two categories: prevention at the planning and design stage and prevention at the execution stage. In the planning and design stage, effort is made to anticipate all potential risk of customer dissatisfaction or problems of producibility using customer-use simulation, failure-mode analysis, and overstress testing. The design is then made as insensitive as possible to the conditions that pose the risk. Designing so that the product or service is not sensitive to processing variables is called designing for robustness. In the execution stage the science of errorproofing is called *poka-yoke*, which I referred to before.

"This leads us to the next great quality principle," Marcus says.

Great Quality Principle #9

Anticipate and prevent the introduction of errors and defects.

"We have now identified the major factors influencing quality," Marcus says. "Let's do some review."

Seven Major Sources and Causes of Bad Quality

- *insufficient commitment by management*
- *reward systems based upon efficiency and quantity*
- *poor planning for quality*
  - *customer requirements poorly defined*
  - *design targets not optimized for customer and supplier*
  - *product or service is difficult to produce (unforgiving designs and processes, too many parts, difficult to assemble, etc.)*

- *designs and processes not capable of requirements*
  - *key variables and variable interactions not identified*
  - *processes not standardized*
  - *people insufficiently missioned and trained*
  - *inadequate variance reduction*

- *poor design of feedback systems*
  - *high times to detect*
  - *poor quality information*

- *poor design of feed-forward systems*
  - *high times to correct*
  - *poor problem-solving capability*
  - *recurrence of problems*

- *poor prevention systems*

"Let's get on with our lesson," Marcus says. "We'll be leaving soon for Schaumburg, Illinois to meet with the modern quality wizard, Keki Bhote. He'll provide more insight into the methods Motorola and other top-quality producers use to continuously improve manufacturing processes, reduce variance to target standards, and eliminate defects."

Lou still doesn't completely buy it. He folds his arms, cocks his head, and peers at Marcus. "I just don't see how it's possible to eliminate defects completely. You talk like you've never worked in a manufacturing operation before."

"As part of my education, I worked as an oarmaker at the Arsenal in 1405 for six months, as a machinist at Singer Sewing Machine manufacturer in 1880, as a telephone inspector at a Western Electric plant 1892, as a foreman over running board manufacturing at the Ford Rouge plant in 1925 for three months, and at Yanmar, a Toyota supplier for two months in 1980. By the way, Lou, you're going to get an opportunity to extend your manufacturing background, also. I've already set it up for you to work on the line at Honda in Japan as part of the training for your guardianship."

"Me work for the Japs? I'd rather be dead."

Marcus and Laura exchange smiles. Lou looks at them strangely, then suddenly erupts in laughter. "A little late for that alternative, isn't it?"

If Our Bodies Detected as Our Businesses Do

"Security officer inside second finger, left hand, calling Central Pain Control Center."

"Come in 2LF."

"Got a Bodcon 2 down here. Host placed finger on hot object. Temperature over 400 degrees at epidermis. Need an immediate command for withdrawal."

"I'll put you right through to Reticular Activating System."

"RAS here. Please hold . . . RAS. Sorry to keep you waiting; what can I do for you?"

"This is security and safety at station 2LF. Host put finger on hot object. It's 600 degrees at endodermis. We're going to have permanent damage!"

"Giving finger 2 on left hand rapid withdrawal signal. Hang on."

"Whoa! What a ride! That did it. Now I need a couple divisions of skin repair crews."

"That's outside our jurisdiction. Would you like me to give you the call code for Central Repair?"

"Yes, thank you."

If Our Bodies Corrected as Our Businesses Do

"Control Center, do you read me?"

"Control Center, hold please. Whom do you wish to talk to?"

"Region H director."

"Whom may I say is calling?"

"External security officer, left hand region."

"One moment please . . . "

"This is Region H director."

"This is security officer, Patrick. Host lacerated second finger, left hand, on a garbage pail. Need two divisions of antibodies."

"All available antibody production units are busy. Right now it's about a two day wait."

"But this one looks bad to me."

"I'll put it on the priority list. Keep me informed."

• • •

"Control Center, Control Center, please come in."

"This is Control Center, hold please."

"Don't put me on hold, it's getting out of control down here. Have to talk to Region H now!"

"I'll connect you immediately."

"Region H director."

"Got a Bodcon 4 on my hands down here. Bacteria entering main blood supply."

"Are you sure?"

"I'm sure — worst I've seen in thirty years — need ten divisions minimum."

"Alright, I'll go for an emergency priority. Hang in there."

"How long?"

"First, I'll have to get an okay for an emergency priority from Cerebral Center. It'll take awhile to identify the virus and produce the antibody, and then we should be able to get your ten divisions to you shortly after that."

"Please hurry . . . "

Seeing the Big Picture

Shortly after the introduction of its new-model-year product, a large original equipment manufacturer's customer began experiencing severe electrical failures with the new unit, both in-house and in the field. The failure rate was extreme, but no single failure mode was evident or apparent. Different parts of the circuitry and discrete electrical components seemed to be failing randomly; and conventional responses of specification tightening via emergency engineering changes had little or no effect. Late in the model year, patterns of failure began to emerge which were confirmed early in the second year of production. The problem appeared to be cyclical in nature and field failures were occurring with greater frequency in the hot, dry regions of the U.S. From this data, the supplier determined the root cause of the problem to be electrical overstress due to electro-static discharge (ESD) voltages.

Three main sources of ESD were identified — electrical transients from other customer systems, customer interface with the unit in the field, and ESD voltage in the manufacturing build process itself. The supplier addressed each of these problems by redesigning its circuitry and incorporating newly-developed shielding materials. These changes eliminated the electrical transients and customer interface problems. The manufacturing build process was redesigned from a batch to a synchronous-build process, which incorporated ESD protection and an outstanding internal feedback and feed-forward system. Time to detect and correct problems was short. Extensive and redundant product assurance testing confirmed that these measures had eliminated the ESD problem.

The customer was assured that, concurrent with its new-model-year introduction, this problem would be completely eliminated. One month into the new model year, the customer was still experiencing ESD failures. The supplier was stunned. All its data indicated that the problem no longer existed, but the customer was still having ESD-related defects.

In desperation, the supplier sent a small team of hourly workers, along with a quality-assurance engineer to the customer's plant to help with rework and retesting of failed units. Within minutes after arrival, one of the hourly workers suggested a complete review of the customer's build process, and immediately found the source of the failures. No antistatic protect measures were being used by the customer during handling and installation of the supplier's product. ESD related failures were being induced at several points during assembly. Once discovered, the "problem" was rectified by the supplier, who immediately provided the customer with antistatic protection devices, ESD training, and the methodology to assure their continual effectiveness. This three-year problem was finally solved!

What is significant about this story is not that the supplier solved a quality problem and retained a major customer's business; but rather, that the supplier recognized that the ESD problem was a symptom of a larger system-design problem, and then took the necessary and immediate steps to redesign the system. The supplier's initial narrow definition of the problem unwittingly reinforced an age-old adage which is the bane of manufacturing — "It's their problem, not ours" — the belief that the manufacturing system ends at the shipping door, rather than in the hands of the ultimate customer.

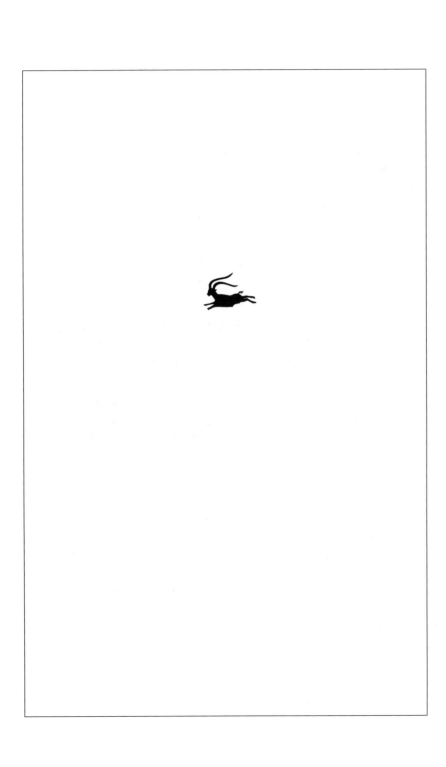

In cycle time management, it is often said that inventory is evil; that inventory is the graveyard of poor management. Similarly, in quality control, variation is evil, and large variation is the graveyard of poor quality management.

– *World Class Quality*, Keki R. Bhote
Senior Corporate Consultant
Quality and Productivity Improvement
Motorola, Inc.

CHAPTER TWENTY-TWO

The Variance Graveyard

B efore we meet with Mr. Bhote," Marcus says, walking toward a portrait in the room of the Hunters, "I want to talk about the history of the development for improving quality. This is Richard Sears," he says, gesturing toward the nearest painting. "What was his contribution? you ask. The average consumer of the late nineteenth century didn't expect perfection. And Sears, a mass retailer, didn't promise perfection. But he did promise 'Satisfaction Guaranteed or Your Money Back' — whether that required repair, a new part, total replacement, or your money back. To the rural catalog purchaser who didn't trust big business, quality meant standing by your guarantee, and Sears did that.

"In 1892, Western Electric published a manual for inspection procedures titled *Inspection Plan*.[1] This landmark book presented some very powerful concepts concerning the need for quality in complex systems. The manual described the phone system as a series of components starting with one handset and extending through more than a thousand components to the handset at the other end. The failure of a single component could cause the whole system to fail. Thus, the first concept demonstrating the need for quality was that a phone system is only as good as its weakest link. A second powerful concept was that every part of the system must fall within certain specifications to achieve quality at the system level. To achieve such quality, components of the system would require inspection — with limits for acceptance at each stage of manufacture. By the end of the nineteenth century, inspection was on its way to becoming an institution.

"In the early twentieth century, scientific management further standardized the work process. The goal was to develop optimum work processes, establish management control of these processes, and minimize any variation that could be attributed to the worker. With this control, the mass producers could be reasonably certain that all the parts would fit and work properly when assembled. But some variation occurred in spite of these standard processes. Producers like Ford and Western Electric would station inspectors at various points in the assembly process, including a final inspection prior to shipment, to weed out defects. This contained defects within the department that produced them.

"Although economists of the time could justify these inspections purely on a cost basis, they still were regarded as a necessary evil. At the Western Electric Hawthorne plant, inspectors accounted for thirteen percent of the work force, and at the Ford Rouge plant, inspectors made up five percent of the work force." Marcus points to a portrait of a man on the south wall. "The industrial world was ready for an alternative to this costly approach when on May 26, 1924, this brilliant but unknown theoretician at Western Electric headquarters in New York asked to see his boss. We're going to go back to 1924 to witness that extraordinary event. We'll bypass the scenic route and place ourselves immediately at the scene."

They are in an office overlooking a busy Manhattan street. Marcus assures Lou and Laura that they cannot be seen or heard. A large man standing in front of the desk hands a memo to another man seated behind the desk.

"A *two*-page memo . . . " The man behind the desk smiles as he takes the document. "Not like the Walter Shewhart I know." After he begins reading, the man continues: "You say that we can improve the uniformity of our telephones?"

Shewhart clears his throat and begins to speak very softly.[2] "Not only can we improve uniformity, we can reduce the cost of inspection, reduce the cost of rejection, and attain maximum benefits from quantity production."

"Those are big claims, Walter. Can you explain them to me?"

Shewhart walks around the desk to point to a chart. "This chart shows the variation in the resistance of the carbon element in the mouthpiece of our telephones. It shows that the process for making carbon elements is in control and that the quality of this process can be assured simply by taking samples periodically," he says.

"Do you mean this chart eliminates the need to inspect every part?" the man behind the desk asks as he rises and looks out the window. "Are you saying we can eliminate 100 percent inspection?"

An In-Control Process

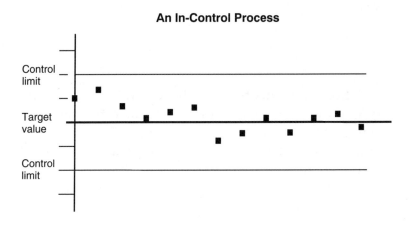

"Only on processes that are 'in control.' A year ago the process for making carbon elements was not 'in control,' and we had to inspect every part."

"What's changed? What was done to get the process 'in control'?"

"As I studied the variation in process in the plant, I observed that there seemed to be two types of variation. The first type was random and seemed to be inherently due to the process. For example, you can see that the measurements of resistance on this chart randomly vary around the target value. There are no measurements that stand out from the rest. This process is in control. Here is a chart of this same process six months ago."

Process Before Elimination of Assignable Causes

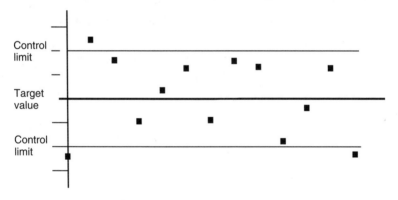

"Notice the points that are above and below the control limits. The causes of these outliers were discovered and eliminated until no more outliers were produced. Thus the process is in control and can be depended upon to produce a predictable distribution of resistance within the control limits."

"I can see that, but I also notice that the random variation is larger in the original chart. How did you reduce the random variation?"

"We reduced variation by finding its major causes and eliminating them through a lot of trial and error experiments. It's not just eliminating 100 percent inspection that we're after. We can learn how to make telephones more uniform by controlling and reducing variation through the use of statistics and scientific experiments."

Shewhart's boss turns and looks directly at Shewhart. "What do you recommend we do with this method, Walter?"

"We need to teach these statistical methods throughout our plants, starting at Hawthorne."

"They are back in the room of the Hunters now and Marcus explains that what Walter Shewhart developed was the world's first quality-control chart. "He defined two general causes of variation — random causes and assignable causes. Random causes, sometimes called common causes, are inherent in the design of the process. Assignable causes, which are sometimes referred to as special causes, are the result of a specific definable source.

"The stage was now set for a young engineer at the Hawthorne plant in Chicago. This man had a new family and was looking for part-time work at night to supplement his income. He discovered that the Hawthorne Club Evening School, supported by Western Electric, offered pay for teaching night courses. He needed a subject to teach and Shewhart's statistical methods were the most recent idea that interested him. In 1926, this engineer launched a series of night classes in Shewhart's methods and in 1928, he published a manual titled *Statistical Methods Applied to Manufacturing Problems*. These methods would come into widespread use at Hawthorne in the early years, reducing average defect levels in the plants by forty percent. The percentage of processes 'in control' increased from sixty-eight percent to eighty-four percent."

"That engineer was Dr. Deming, wasn't it?" Laura says.

"No, the young man's name was Joseph M. Juran. But Hawthorne was to be a breeding ground for other pioneers. Deming was working at Hawthorne in those years as a summer student while pursuing his Ph.D in physics at Yale. He would also meet Shewhart, but not until he was at the department of Agriculture in 1927. He adopted and used Shewhart's methods at the Agriculture Department and later for the Census Bureau. In the fifties, both Juran and Deming would make enormous contributions to Japan's dramatic quality turnaround, and in the eighties they would provide the leadership for a quality renaissance in the U.S. One last note on Shewhart: Deming wrote in 1988 that another half century would pass before people in industry would appreciate Shewhart."

Marcus continues. "Please open now the tenth and eleventh quality pouches. These are two more principles that have developed in the last hundred years that have advanced quality. And they were first developed by Shewhart."

Great Quality Principle #10

Use statistical tools to measure the degree to which a process is "in control."

Great Quality Principle #11

Variations from standard can be separated into two categories: random and assignable causes. Random causes are normal statistical variations that originate in the basic design of the system; assignable causes are special causes that are not part of the normal expected statistical variation.

"Now we're ready to visit Mr. Bhote," Marcus says.

The meeting takes place in Keki's office at the Motorola Corporate Headquarters in Schaumburg, Illinois.

"Marcus, after your call the other night, I did a little thinking about your question of how Motorola improved quality over 100:1 in ten years," Keki says. "Our *first step* to quality improvement was to establish measures so people would know how they were doing. If a typical process has 1,000 parts and process steps, the average producer will have something go wrong in the process ninety-nine percent of the time they run it. This means that some part in the process will be either reworked or scrapped almost every time the process is run. The best producers in the world rework only one out of every three-hundred units. Motorola decided to measure the number of defects produced per million chances of producing defects.

"The *second step* was to measure ourselves against the competition. When we benchmarked ourselves we found that not only did most of our manufacturing operations produce errors and defects at over one percent, but payroll, order write-up, and journal vouchers had errors at similar levels.

"As we looked around the world in the early eighties we found that it was a one to five percent defective world, including the service industry. Restaurants err at that rate in the bills they charge customers, airlines have three to five percent baggage handling mistakes, and doctors write prescriptions at that error rate. A little scary," Keki says, laughing. "We searched for anybody better than that. We found that U.S. airlines have a fatality rate thousands of times less than that. We found a watch manufacturer and two TV manufacturers that had error rates of less than .001 percent.

"The *third step* was to set goals so high that business as usual wouldn't cut it; goals so high that the teams would have to totally rethink their processes. Back then a goal of thirty percent quality improvement per year would have been outstanding. At Motorola today, that would seem like a puny goal. In 1981, our top management set a goal of ten-to-one improvement in quality in five years. When we met that goal in 1986, our top management ratcheted up the goal to 10:1 improvement by 1989, 100:1 improvement by 1991, and less than .0004 percent defects by 1992. By and large, we have achieved all these goals to date.

"Our *fourth step* was to institute teams and empower them to make changes in their work to improve quality and reduce cycle time. We trained these teams, had them set goals consistent with our key corporate initiatives, and provided expert support people to assist them."

"Our *fifth step* was to reduce variation in all our processes."

"But what's the bottom line?" Lou asks.

"By improving our quality, in the last five years we have saved more than $3 billion what we would have spent if we had not had the quality improvement.

"Three billion dollars?" Lou says incredulously.

"Three billion!" Keki says. "These are conservative estimates, too, and do not include the increase in profits that have resulted from increases in market share. Lou, there are a number of things that we firmly believe today at Motorola: Quality improvement is necessary for survival; it is one of the best ways to lower costs; it is one of the keys to maintaining and increasing market share; and it is best achieved by empowering the entire work force to participate in meeting the goals."

"Keki, Lou and Laura have your book, *World Class Quality*, which is a great reference for them. But now we have to be going, and I'd like to thank you for your time."

"Anytime, Marcus. Stop by more often and see us."

"I will."

Back at Guardian Command, Marcus says, "Let's sum up what we've learned. The development of modern quality concepts began with the standardization of parts that Eli Whitney and others pioneered. In the late nineteenth century, manufacturers set limits on the acceptance of parts and removed unacceptable parts from the process through inspection at early stages, and quality became an economic tradeoff. In the 1920's, Shewhart showed that statistics could be used to improve and control quality. In the last twenty years, there has been a revolution in the way we think about quality. This new way of thinking about quality emphasizes commitment to ultimate quality and the design of Delivery Systems that achieve it.

"Now that you're familiar with these ideas," Marcus says," we're ready to add the third and final Driver — valueless variance reduction — to our continuous improvement process. I said before that a continuous improvement process is a foundation block that every company must have. The entire transformational process rests on this block, so it's important that you fully understand how to help a company establish this foundation." Using the light stylus, he adds the third Driver to the Continuous Linear Improvement chart.

"Looking at this chart, I think it would also be a good idea for us to list all the great quality principles we've learned to date."

Driving Linear Continuous Improvement

Drivers	Internal effects	Customer priorities

The Great Quality Principles

Great Quality Principle #1

Quality can be improved and costs reduced at the same time.

Great Quality Principle #2

Improving quality increases competitive advantage. Therefore, the goal should be ultimate quality performance.

Great Quality Principle #3

All variance results in loss to the system as a whole and loss to society. Therefore, variance must be reduced.

Great Quality Principle #4

Quality is perceived in the mind of the customer. Discover what customers value now and what they may value in the future. To be the supplier of choice, exceed their expectations.

Great Quality Principle #5

Design products and services according to customers' values, and standardize the processes that produce them while also accommodating the specific needs of individual customers.

Great Quality Principle #6

Management controls the system; therefore quality improvement must begin with management.

Great Quality Principle #7

Detect defects, errors, and variances immediately, and provide high-quality feedback immediately.

Great Quality Principle #8

Correct errors within the process immediately and prevent their recurrence.

Great Quality Principle #9

Anticipate and prevent the introduction of errors and defects.

Great Quality Principle #10

Use statistical tools to indicate the degree to which a process is "in control."

Great Quality Principle #11

Variations from standard can be separated into two categories: random and assignable causes. Random causes are normal statistical variations that originate in the basic design of the system; assignable causes are special causes that are not part of the normal expected statistical variation.

"This concludes our study of the first two elements of Process Intent — response time and quality," Marcus says. "Before we begin our study of the bottom-line element of Process Intent — the value to cost ratio — let's see what you've been able to do with the timed flowchart and physical flowchart that you made for Garrett Processing Division."

Laura hands Marcus a package of papers. "We worked together on these."

"Teamed up?" Marcus asks, nodding.

And we think it's pretty good," Lou says.

"Then it's good enough for me," Marcus says, returning the papers to Laura.

"But you didn't even look at it," Laura says.

"You worked on it together and you say it's good. That's good enough for me.

"Let's walk to the room of the Hunters to talk about value and cost — the bottom line," Marcus says, as he rises abruptly and walks toward the spiral staircase.

"Can you believe that? After all that work we did, he didn't even look at it," Laura says, as they follow Marcus.

"Old military trick," Lou says, as they round the last turn in the staircase.

"Trick?"

"He pitted us both against himself to get us to work together."

"Do you think he'd do something that devious?"

"I think he knows how to get the job done. It's working, isn't it?"

Design of Experiments (to Reduce Variance)

To reduce process variance, you must discover the variables in the process that are responsible for most of the variance. In cases where the total number of variables in a process is large, or where the important variables are not known, or where interaction effects are important, the methods of Dorian Shainin are very effective. Pioneers in over 2,000 American companies have demonstrated that the Shainin methods dramatically reduce variance, scrap, and rework, often down to zero failures and 100 percent yields. There is usually one variable, or an interactive set of variables, that causes most of the variance. Dorian Shainin calls this variable or set of interacting variables the "Red-X." Once you discover this variable, you can determine its ideal value and set realistic tolerances (tolerances that dramatically reduce output variance and are achievable) for it.

Another design of experiment method focuses on finding process parameter settings that will minimize the effect of the variables that are more difficult or more costly to control.

Variance is measured by dividing the specification limits by the range of values the process produces. This ratio is defined as C_p. The processes of the best quality producers produce a total variation that's less than half as wide as the specifications or C_ps of two or better. A more refined measure of variation is C_{pk}, which includes a measure of how far the average process value is from the target or design center.

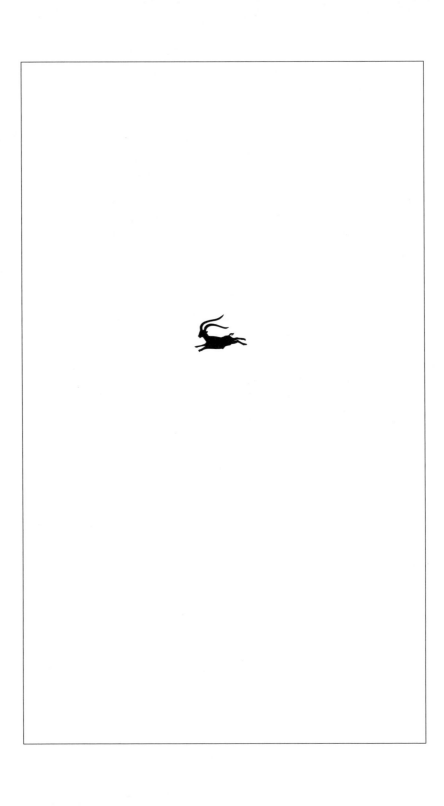

CHAPTER TWENTY-THREE

System Value/Cost

Marcus sits in silence for a few minutes before he speaks. "Tell you what," he says. "Change of plans. I just realized that I have to catch up on my mail and make some very important phone calls. What I would like you to do in the meantime is open your pouches marked 'Great Value-Adding Principles.' We'll pick up our lesson tomorrow morning at eight, and I'd like you to be prepared to tell me why you think I emphasized the word 'whole' in the first principle. So . . . until tomorrow," he says, as he moves toward the stairs.

"Curious about what's in the pouches?" Laura says, holding one of them by its drawstring.

Lou shakes his head. "Not really. Probably no big deal. Marcus just likes to be mysterious."

Laura laughs. "Likes to be? He *is* mysterious."

"He plays it to the hilt. All very dramatic, you know? Like the old-time radio shows I used to listen to as a kid."

"Admit it. You're curious."

"About Marcus? Or what's in the pouches?"

"Both."

"Not that curious."

"Well I am." She carefully unties the leather drawstring on the pouch marked 'Great Value-Adding Principles' and takes out seven small parchments, which she places upon the table, unrolls, and begins to read.

Great Value-Adding Principles

Great Value-Adding Principle #1

Take great care to discover the customer's whole-value expectations, including performance, response, quality, cost, and flexibility.

Great Value-Adding Principle #2

Design the whole Delivery System to deliver what customers value.

Great Value-Adding Principle #3

Design the process with value-adding activities in parallel if possible.

Great Value-Adding Principle #4

Design the process to minimize the time between linear-dependent activities. (If an activity cannot take place until another activity occurs, the second activity is said to be linear-dependent.)

Great Value-Adding Principle #5

Design the process so there are no valueless activities or valueless expenses.

Great Value-Adding Principle #6

Minimize variance.

Great Value-Adding Principle #7

Maximize value throughput compared to expense.

"Heavy!"

"Heavy? What's heavy?" Lou asks.

"Just an expression. What do you think of the great principles?"

"Just common sense."

"Uncommon sense, I'd say. Think I'll get to bed early. Sounds like a big day tomorrow."

As Laura starts to climb the stairs to her room, she begins to unwind. At the top of the stairs she notices the sweet smell of burning incense. The door to her room is ajar. Julia is tucking in a bed sheet as Laura enters. "I usually make up my own bed — not sure I can get used to this, " she says.

Julia continues to make the bed. "You'll get used to it, dear; it's a pleasure to serve a lady." She gives the pale blue quilted comforter a flip to align it.

Laura stops and sweeps the room with her eyes. On a table by her bed are a beautiful antique lamp, a silver pitcher, and a burning stick of incense stuck in a small ceramic bowl filled with white sand. Small porcelain figurines in the west window are silhouetted against the glow of the setting sun, which is bright enough still to cast light upon a painting of an English landscape on the east wall.

"Julia, the painting is beautiful. Thank you so much. How did you know I liked blue?" she says, feeling the comforter.

"My business to know things. Just threw the drapes together. Yellow to cheer you and blue to calm you. Hope you like 'em."

Variance Versus Variety

"Variety" means different product targets for customers and can be a competitive advantage if variety costs are minimized.

"Variance" is deviation from target values and should be minimized through product design, process design, and process control. Principle variances are quality variance, delivery time and location variance, cost variance, and loading variance at operations.

"I love them. You made them?"

"Nothing to it, luv. Glad to have someone who appreciates. You know men — a bed, a chair, a desk, a lamp, and they're happy. But not us. We need to be more civilized. I'd of done it before you came if Marcus had let me know a lady was going to be with us."

"Am I the first?" Laura says.

"The first, luv. About time I'd say."

Laura laughs. "But not the last."

"The first of many I'm sure," Julia says.

"You act like something troubles you, dearie. What's the problem?" Julia sits on the settee and motions for Laura to sit beside her.

"It looks like there's an assignment coming up tomorrow and Lou thinks it's his. Marcus says we're a team but Lou doesn't see it that way. It's going to be a battle."

"My husband, bless his soul, was like Lou," Julia says. "Lots of bluster 'e was . . . but a kind man. And Marcus can get imperious at times and when 'e does, I give him a bit of my mind. It's his background, you know."

"How do you mean?"

"Acting imperious, I mean. Marcus was a general in the Roman Army."

"Really! He told us he was in the Roman Army but he didn't say he was a general? Maybe Lou's met his match. This will be interesting."

"Lou's met his match alright." Julia says, standing and collecting her cleaning equipment. "You're better than a match for any man as I see it. Goodnight, dearie — sleep tight."

At dawn, Laura dresses and makes her way to the morning room. As she descends the stairs she's greeted by the smell of freshly brewed coffee. Julia is on the back porch in her parka watching the sun as it finishes its climb above the mountains to the east.

"It seems to be sitting on the top of the mountain," Laura says softly.

"Dearie, it's just resting itself before it climbs again . . . there it goes again. I think I hear the boys."

"'Whole' means zoom out so that you get the big picture doesn't it?" Lou says, as he and Marcus enter the breakfast room.

"It means that and more," Marcus says. "Whole means that the whole system — from the mines, oil fields, and farms, to the final customer — is optimized by designing all the parts to optimize the whole. It also means that all of the customer priorities — response, quality, value/cost ratio, and flexibility — are optimized."

"We were taught that different market segments are sensitive to some priorities more than others," Laura says, as she seats herself. "For example, the upscale markets are more sensitive to perceived value and quality than they are to costs. We were also taught that when a product is first introduced with superior performance, the market is less sensitive to cost, but as time goes on and competitors come to the market with equal performance, the market now becomes cost sensitive."

"Those are correct teachings but there may be a blind spot there."

"How so?" Laura says, curiously.

"Anytime there is a performance gap between what a business offers and what is ultimately possible, the business is vulnerable. If a business believes they can accept higher costs of design and manufacture because they have superior performance, they are at considerable risk to the Hunters who set ultimate targets for response, quality, and value/cost. The Hunters determine the sensitivity of the market place when they offer it faster, better, and for less. The Hunted try to simplify the problem by emphasizing certain priorities and de-emphasizing others. The Hunters exploit the Hunted's narrow vision; they turn it into a competitive advantage.

"This morning we're meeting in Denver with two men — Ken Stork, whom you've already met at Motorola, and Dr.

Robert Hall — at an Association for Manufacturing Excellence meeting. Our focus will be on the value-to-cost ratio and we'll learn how the design of the whole Delivery System affects this ratio. We'll leave as soon as we finish our breakfast. Bob Hall, by the way, is a professor of operations management at Indiana University and the author of several excellent books on improving manufacturing processes. Bob and Ken are two of my most treasured teachers."

Marjoline's Lounge is in the Marriott in downtown Denver. Roses are etched in the windows and varied flower arrangements are everywhere. Soft classical music can be heard between the conversations of business people going about their work.

"Tried to get a table in a quiet area but this is the best I could do," Ken says, after introducing Bob Hall.

"This is fine," Marcus says. "We're on a tight schedule, so can we just dive in?"

Ken laughs. "You're always on a tight schedule. Just fire away."

Marcus hands them each a value and cost chart.

"Bob, we'd like to focus on the cost part of the value-to-cost ratio. The question is: What do the best companies in the world do to reduce system costs and increase profit margins?" Marcus says.

Bob pauses before he begins to speak. He has a youthful, handsome face, which, as it turns out, complements a quiet intelligence. He speaks softly and articulately in a pleasant southern Indiana accent. "There are three general approaches used to reduce cost. First is continuous linear cost improvement. Many companies motivate their employees to reduce costs through suggestion systems and cost-improvement programs, and they have trained and empowered their people in continuous improvement methods. Second, if a company is fat, restructuring is necessary.

"But beyond restructuring, if we study how companies like Harley-Davidson, Xerox and Tokai Rubber have survived the Hunt and are now holding their own in tough, world competition, we find a third, even more powerful approach common to the superior cost performers: First, they are always working toward providing better customer service; second, their quality-improvement efforts result in superlative processes that produce superior products; third, they continuously redesign their Delivery Systems to reduce system cycle times and eliminate nonvalue-adding activities; and fourth, they increase both responsibility and skills at lower levels of the organization.

"In general, the leading companies believe that if they serve their customers well and remove valueless activity, time, and variance from their operations, then cost will take care of itself.

"Traditionally costs have been categorized by material, labor, and overhead, where overhead includes management, investment, debt service, and other expenses. But these categories don't identify major cost Drivers and opportunities for cost reduction. To identify the Drivers and opportunities we must understand how cost is added from the acquisition of raw materials to the distribution of finished products. Each stage adds value, but the direct cost of adding the value is a small part of the costs at each stage.

"Less than ten percent of the final cost of the components we buy is the cost of adding value. So if we can measure and manage the system cycle time, system quality, and system cost throughout the entire value-added process all the way back to the acquisition of raw materials, then it gives us an enormous opportunity to reduce costs."

Marcus interrupts "It's useful to understand that cost reduction opportunities are the same at suppliers as they are in our internal Delivery Systems. Here's a chart which shows opportunities at both sources."

The Opportunity Cost Challenge

Opportunity costs   Cost of value-adding activity   Profit

1st supplier   Immediate supplier   Final producer   Price to final customer

Marcus hands them another chart. "This next chart shows a detailed listing of the cost opportunities in four groups: cost of lost people-potential, cost of poor quality, cost of long cycle times, and cost of suboptimum design."

"The first group, lost people-potential, is the cost incurred when we don't get the full contribution possible from people. Motorola, Cincinnati Milacron, and Harley-Davidson achieved

Reducing Costs and Increasing Value

Cost Categories	Cost Opportunities	Cost Reduction &
With cost focus & restructuring	With delivery system redesign and continuous improvement	Value-Adding Drivers

Cost Categories	Cost Opportunities	Cost Reduction & Value-Adding Drivers
People	Cost of lost people potential	Unalignment with mission Lack of participation Inferior tools or technology Failure to develop potential
Materials & services	Cost of poor quality	Lost customers Warranty & returns Inspection & controls Rework & scrap Management time
Investment & debt	Cost of long cycle times	Delay in getting to market Expediting & prioritizing Missed schedules Overstock, stockouts Cost of inventory Floor space

Expense	Cost of sub-optimum design	Lack of customer appeal
		Product Non robust design
		    # part numbers & # parts
		    complexity of parts
		Process # steps
		    # control points
		    # suppliers
		    # support people
		    difficulty of assembly

large cost reductions by increasing the contribution of their work force.

"Keki Bhote and Ron Gill helped us appreciate the second group, the cost of poor quality. Ten to fifty percent of a typical company's costs are wasted on inspection, scrap, rework, warranty, crisis firefighting, and quality problem-solving. In addition, untold losses are incurred when customers are lost.

"We've also explored the costs associated with long system cycle times, including the cost of prioritizing, expediting, crisis activity, excess inventories, premium freight shipping, and lost customers.

"Ken, could you show how system costs go down as system cycle time is reduced?"

Ken reaches in his briefcase. "Sure can," he says, as he holds a chart for them to see.[1]

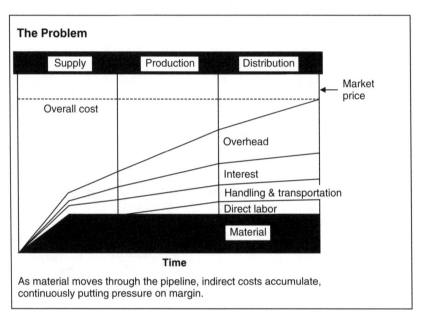

The Problem

As material moves through the pipeline, indirect costs accumulate, continuously putting pressure on margin.

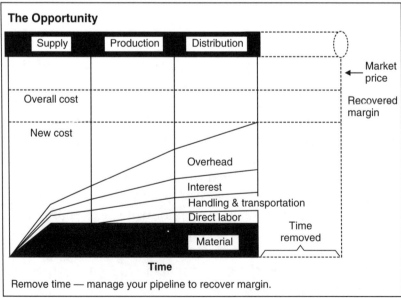

The Opportunity

Remove time — manage your pipeline to recover margin.

"When you consider the whole value-added process," Ken says, "a large part of indirect costs are related to the system cycle time from the mines, oil fields, and farms, all the way through to the final customer. There are two important lessons here.

"First, the major cost-reduction opportunities are also major sources for increasing the value to the customer.

"Second, one-half of the cost reduction and value-increasing opportunity is in the supplier system."

"Ken, how do the best companies reduce their supplier cost?" Laura asks.

"To accomplish this well the supplier must be involved from the very beginning. The sources of supplier costs are the same as the sources of the customer's costs, and the opportunities to reduce supplier costs are the same opportunities that the customer has. This chart shows a breakdown of supplier or customer costs. You can see that value-added costs are a small part of their costs.

Sources of Cost Reduction Opportunities

"That means the chosen supplier has an inside track in establishing their components in the new design," Laura offers.

> ### Ford Motor Company's Efforts to Include Suppliers in Product Development
>
> The Ford Motor Company has successfully redesigned their product development process to include the expertise of their suppliers. First a multi-functional team of buyers, quality engineers, and design engineers decides which suppliers offer mutual competitive advantage because they are world class in quality, technology, service, etc. Purchasers are then directed to these few suppliers who then become part of the team. They become involved in the early development, adding their expertise to the expertise of Ford's engineers. They make suggestions on material, process, and design, which shorten the development process, improve the quality, and reduce total product cost.
>
> At Motorola, all recent product development teams have used this approach.

Bob speaks: "If a customer expects to have good relationships with its suppliers, it cannot expect a supplier to have its engineers working for years on a new design — and then let the production contract go to the lowest bidder."

"Yes, that's right," Ken says. "It must be a long-term, continually beneficial partnership."

"But how can suppliers with limited resources manage to provide this kind of support?" Laura asks.

"Both customer and supplier will have limited resources," Ken replies, "so there has to be an optimization for mutual benefit. This means fewer suppliers to any one customer. We call this supplier-base optimization for mutual benefit. The fact that there will be fewer suppliers for each customer will mean that the smaller number will each have a larger volume with that customer. Some suppliers will lose the business because of response, quality, or total price. Those suppliers will improve their capability and return to bid the job again. The competitive pressures will still be there to be the best. In general, however, supplier-customer relationships of the nineties will be longer term; more like successful marriages where both parties win. Here's a chart showing the transformation of the supply system."

Transformation of the Supply Delivery System

"Smart suppliers are going to reduce their customer base just as customers are reducing their supplier base; and they'll get rid of their bad customers."

Lou is amused. "I thought that the customer was always right."

"A company not only should become the supplier of choice," Ken explains, "but it also must do what it takes to be customer of choice."

"If a supplier is an only supplier, doesn't the customer risk being shut down if that supplier has a serious problem in delivering. I think I would be against single-sourcing," Lou says.

"Lou, we only depend on a single source as a supplier if the supplier has a long, proven record of on-time delivery. Also, that supplier must have short lead times so that if they experience an internal problem, they can recover fast. Only suppliers with world-class response will be selected."

"But suppose the single-source supplier has a quality problem?" Lou argues.

"Same answer, Lou. We will choose suppliers who have total control of their processes.

"To sum it up," Ken says, "to be the supplier of choice, a company must not only have the best designed internal operations in its competitive arena, but must also have the best suppliers in the business."

"Let's examine the fourth group of opportunities for reducing cost and increasing value," Marcus says, after Ken and Bob leave. "Product or service design has a major effect on both value and cost. In order to obtain the highest value-to-cost ratio, the engineering development Delivery System must be designed to provide high value and then to produce that value at minimum cost. Such a Delivery System must include five important activities.

"The first activity is to design the product and process with manufacturing, engineering, finance, quality, and suppliers.

"Second, discover and deliver what the customer values. Product developers should make an intensive effort, using quality function deployment (QFD), to list and prioritize the attributes that customers value most. This will help developers determine how what they can provide compares to what competitors can provide — as perceived by customers. QFD also helps determine target price and target value, which guides the efforts of designers.

Elements of a Mutually Beneficial Supplier-Customer Partnership

An Association for Manufacturing Excellence Survey identified the following key elements of customer strategy for a mutually beneficial supplier-customer partnership:

- encourages early supplier involvement in product development
- views a good partnership as a two-way street
- is proactive and committed to helping suppliers improve dramatically
- uses supplier rating systems that are consistent
- uses benchmarking to set goals for suppliers
- listens to suppliers — and is willing to take corrective action
- rewards the best suppliers

To appreciate this activity, you should understand how the Hunted have determined price in the past. They first determine what they think the market wants. They then design the product and determine the cost of manufacture. They then add overhead costs and profit, and that determines the price of the product or service. In other words, this is a bottom-up approach where the price is determined by the cost of the design. Hunters take a top-down approach which begins with a determination of the price-to-value ratio that will give them a competitive advantage. They then design the product and process to deliver value at a cost that will allow a strategically satisfactory profit. Here's a drawing illustrating the two approaches."

**Pricing as Determined by Cost of Design
vs. Design for Competitiveness**

"Now, on to the third activity: Develop a product and process concept to consistently and reliably provide the product or service value — function, performance, and features — at a minimum cost and variance. In this phase you develop a conceptual model for test. Then you design components and select suppliers for them. Suppliers assist in developing the highest value-to-cost ratio. It's important to balance technological risk against benefit at this point. Although new product and process technology can provide breakthroughs in cost and performance, they may also increase the time to get the product to market, adversely affect quality and reliability, and increase costs during the start-up phase.

"Fourth, you must consider the number of different parts, ease of assembly, manufacturability of the parts, and reliability of the assembly. In the concept stage, you should conduct an analysis to predict potential failure modes so the attention can be focused on designing for prevention. Design products to be insensitive to process variation; design processes so that they are capable of producing the product or service with minimum variation.

"Fifth, establish operations, standards, procedures, training, monitoring, and controls to ensure that the process meets its optimum capability.

"I'm meeting an old friend for dinner tonight and then I'm heading east on a job tomorrow. You have reservations at the Portofino Inn. Tomorrow, you will analyze the Garrett operation in detail. I want you to carefully analyze their systems for feedback and feed-forward. To do that, collect some data on their most recent quality problems and analyze them for time to detect, quality of information fed back, time to correct, and whether any of these problems have occurred before. Also, get some data on the variance at critical operations for my review before the workshop for the staff at Garrett Saturday morning."

"Do we need to prepare anything else for the workshop?" Lou asks.

"Just the data you collect tomorrow. I'll handle the rest. See you later," says Marcus, as he walks away.

Lou shakes his head. "Sometimes he acts like a ten-year-old school kid with a frog in his pocket. Very mysterious guy."

"Mysterious, but interesting," Laura says.

"I'm not complaining. It's one hell of a good deal we've got, or should I say one heaven of a good deal? Do you know how to take this data he's talking about?"

"Did it once with Marcus, but I'm a little shaky about it."

"Great, just great. The blind leading the blind," Lou says, shaking his head in disbelief. "By the time tomorrow's over I'll be ready for a beer."

"That might be nice. Count me in."

"I don't know about that. What would Marcus say if I took you to a bar."

"You won't be taking me, Lou, I'll be going with you. And don't worry about Marcus. I'll handle him. We should probably check in. Do you know where the Portofino is?"

"No, but Marcus said it was right on the ocean, just south of Hermosa Beach."

Cost Strategies over the Years

Experience curve strategies. Experience in many industries shows that costs decline by 20 to 30 percent with each doubling of accumulated volume. Realizing that increased experience and/or volume reduces the cost, many companies have adopted experience-based strategies adding capacity ahead of demand and then slashing prices to stimulate sales. Increased demand and hence production volume serve to drive down costs, therefore allowing market share to be captured from competitors.

Portfolio management. This strategy is based on managing businesses within a corporation as a portfolio of businesses instead of as individual profit centers. A corporation with this strategy adopts an internal resource allocation scheme which is based on investing heavily in high-growth businesses, maintaining position in stable businesses, and phasing out less profitable businesses.

Strategic use of debt. A debt strategy is used by a company when normal profits from a product are not enough to fund the growth required to remain competitive. Typically this occurs in price- or investment-sensitive markets where one competitor's cost structure is higher than another's. In this case, the disadvantaged company will use debt to fund growth in the face of lower profits created by price cutting and comparatively high costs of production.

Strategic assignment of overhead cost. High-volume, low-complexity product lines require lower overhead costs per unit than do high-complexity, low-volume product lines. As product complexity increases, costs must be assigned on the basis of the resources they use. Otherwise complex, low-volume products or services will be underpriced. If management knows the real costs of adding value for each of their product or service groups, they are better positioned to strategically price products and services. They can then decide what cost-to-price margins should be to fulfill their strategy in the market place. They may also decide to focus on fewer products to reduce overhead costs.

Restructuring. Direct reduction of costs by reducing people (accomplished through layoffs, suspension of hiring, firing, shutdowns, early retirement and reorganization), reducing investment and expense, and reducing material inventories.

Strategic advantage of quality and time. Many companies today use faster response and higher quality to improve market position and reduce cost.

Cost Sub-Optimization

Focusing directly on cost reduction is an important management function, but if you don't consider whole system costs, the results can be counterproductive, as in the following case (company's name withheld by request).

In 1986 a large video repair business in the eastern United States was in serious trouble. Dealers were deserting them. Analysis of the difference between customer perceptions and customer expectations showed that dealers were unhappy with the service delay in getting their video equipment repaired. The mindset of the management had been to focus on achieving one hundred percent efficiency (hours paid to repair compared to standard hours to repair) and minimum expense to support the repair department.

In order to try to turn the business around, a new service manager set out to change the mindset of his staff and repair people. He convinced them that their single-minded focus on efficiency costs had cost them the most important asset they had, customers. He convinced them that response and customer satisfaction must be the top objective.

Prior to the redesign it took up to fifteen days to fill an order for a service part, ten days for responding to an inquiry letter, and four days for a repair turnaround. When the service manager analyzed the process and made a timed flowchart, he discovered an important fact: The average time actually spent in repair for an average job was less than one hour. This is a timed flowchart for the repair process.

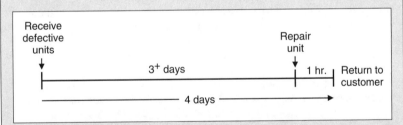

The largest valueless time was the backlog ahead of the repair operations. Analysis showed that the backlog had three causes: repair parts not in stock, the supervisor's mindset that the backlog keeps his people from running out of work, and the repair-workers' mindset that keeping the backlog provides job security.

After he convinced everyone to reduce the repair cycle time, the sales manager solicited ideas from all workers on how the backlogs could be eliminated. As a result of these ideas they now keep a computer-optimized inventory of repair parts, which allows for fast repair with minimum inventory. When the UPS truck arrives today, seven employees meet the truck, and within thirty minutes they have all units to be repaired out of the shipping boxes and on conveyors headed to the repair stations. Backlogs at the repair station are kept to less than one day and the units are reboxed and returned by the next day. They can now guarantee a twenty-four-hour repair turnaround compared to the best competitor's average of forty-eight hours.

Today they have the fastest response in the business in all customer areas and they are getting faster. Management attributes their recent impressive recovery in market share in part to the redesign of their Delivery Systems.

General Motors: Process for Choosing Suppliers

When Jack Smith assumed a commanding role in the 1992 General Motors shakeup he brought Dr. Inokai Lopez from GM Europe to North American Operations. Dr Lopez created a massive change in the North American purchasing policy, modeling it after the successful approach used in Europe.

The new GM purchasing policy provides lifetime contracts to suppliers who provide the best global quality, service, and price (QSP). In the new GM purchasing process, bids are solicited from a large number of suppliers worldwide. Based on the lowest bid and some estimates of what is ultimately possible, the central staff sets a target price which is usually lower than the lowest first bid. In the second bid round, suppliers who also meet the quality and service requirements are asked to quote the target price or better. This process is continued until the purchasing staff has determined the supplier who is not only best at the end of the bidding, but that has agreed to additional yearly improvements.

The intent of the GM process is to push inside and outside suppliers to their ultimate capability. Since the combination of inside and outside suppliers have sales of over $50 billion, the successful implementation of this approach would be a major factor in returning GM North American Operations to profitability.

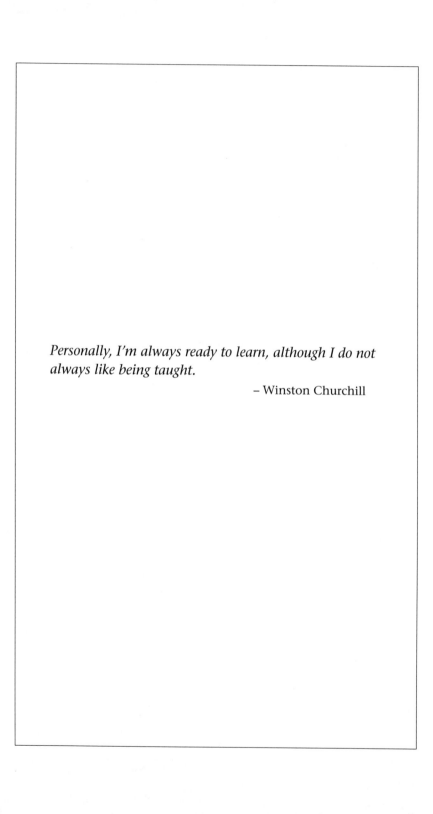

Personally, I'm always ready to learn, although I do not always like being taught.

– Winston Churchill

CHAPTER TWENTY-FOUR

The Vision

*L*ou is enjoying the salt air, the feel of the sand between his toes, and the view from Hermosa Beach. To the south, the cliffs of Palos Verdes, which jut out into the ocean, are studded with thousands of lights glowing softly in the darkness of early evening. The ocean-front homes are tiered like doll houses on the hillside as far as he can see.

He's getting a kick out of watching Laura. The way she moves down the beach — down with the receding water, up just in time to avoid a crashing wave — reminds him of a sandpiper.

"What are you thinking about?" he asks, when he catches up to her.

"Not much," she says, flipping back the hood of her sweat-shirt and combing her hair with her fingers. "Just happy to be here. Spirits in the material world," she says, playfully, and Lou laughs, because that was the title of a song that had been on the music television station in her room when he stopped by to pick her up before they went to dinner. "You call that music?" he'd said.

"I enjoyed being at Garrett today," he says.

"Me too. I was surprised that everyone was so helpful."

"I know what you mean," he says, nodding, "I thought they'd be real defensive when we asked for information on quality problems. But they answered our questions openly."

"And they let me use their computer to make those flow-charts I gave you," she says.

Roller skaters, cyclers, runners, and walkers move up and down the strand in a moonlight ballet. There's a soft ocean breeze and gulls hover almost motionless above them.

Lou reaches down for a small shell, brushes off the sand, and bounces it in his palm. The salt air feels good. Such a simple pleasure — the kind of pleasure he never appreciated before. Up ahead, he spots a tavern on the pier. It might be good to have a beer or a soft drink. He's enjoying spending time with Laura; he doesn't want the evening to end yet. "How about a drink before we go back, Laura?"

"Sounds good to me."

"The only table I have open is in the front," a man at the door says.

"This place makes me feel about a hundred years old," Lou says, after they're seated. "Bet I'm the only one over thirty in the whole place.

"Things sure change," Laura says. "I don't exactly feel like a teenager myself. Everything's different. The music, the clothes . . . everything."

"Ever hear a big band, Laura?"

"My dad used to play Harry James a lot."

"Can't beat the big band sound."

"I'd like to see one sometime," she says.

"All gone, Laura, they're all gone! What kind of work was your dad into?"

"He did some hunting, fishing, trapping, and a little prospecting. He had a little shop in our home where he and I repaired radio and navigation equipment for bush pilots. Anything to make a living."

"You repaired radios?"

"Started when I was nine."

"I had you figured all wrong," Lou says, plaintively . . . "Did you say he did some prospecting?"

"For gold."

"And I had you figured as a rich kid, but how could you afford MIT and Harvard?"

"I won a scholarship, and I worked repairing radios and televisions while I was in school."

A soft expression comes over Lou's face. "I really had you figured wrong."

She nods. "I know you did. I had you wrong, too."

"How so?"

"Do you want the truth?"

Lou lifts his mug and takes a sip. "Maybe not. Your dad seems like my kind of people."

"Lately, I've been thinking a lot about him. You remind me of him. He loved his work, the land, and the animals that fed us. He knew how to survive in the Arctic."

Lou beams. "How was he like me?"

"You care about people who work for a living. And there's no doubt that you know how to survive."

"It seems to me that you can take care of yourself all right," Lou says, as he motions to the waitress for another round of beers.

"Had a great teacher who taught me how to be independent. Like you, he was a tough guy with a big heart. I'll bet you think I don't care about people."

"I think you have the impression that the workers in a factory work just for a paycheck. But it goes beyond money. The people I worked with at Continental spent a great part of their life working with metal, and they loved it. Many of them, like me, knew that they weren't cut out to be engineers or doctors or investment bankers. But they felt important when they did the work; they were proud to say they worked at the mill."

"You really loved your work, didn't you?" she asks.

"When Marcus first brought me back to earth he took me to Continental. It was gutted. For days it rolled around in my mind. It must have been hell for the guys who worked there. I was thinking that maybe I got off easy. Those men were part of the work itself. Hard to tell where one left off and the other started. Know what I mean?"

"Like the work was their life?" she asks.

"Their life. Have you ever felt that you were part of something much larger than yourself? Were you ever part of a group that was proud of itself? After you and fellow workers go through the ups and downs of the business world together, you get close. We helped each other — shared when one of us was laid off. Do you know what I mean?"

"I hear what you're saying. I didn't think you felt that deeply about things," she says. "We come from very different points of view."

"What's your point of view?" he asks, shouting above the music.

"Do you really want to hear it?"

He nods.

"From my viewpoint it takes more than dedication and commitment to the work to make it in the business world. I know that you think I don't have much to contribute because I have very little experience in business. I can appreciate how you feel. But because of my background I have to ask certain questions about Continental. Were you analyzing your systems continuously? Were you really looking at the competition objectively? Were you changing fast enough to keep up? Were you pressuring yourself to do the ultimate, or were you just satisfied to meet your efficiency goal and budget? You've gotta be tough on yourself to make a good profit, to increase market share, to make a good return on investment, to increase the stock value for the stockholders. If you don't do that, there aren't any jobs left."

"You're right. But it isn't right to sell the people short. The people's jobs are management's responsibility."

"I agree."

"We're all here to take care of each other," he says, wistfully. "I guess you're right about one thing. If management doesn't continuously transform the business, they hurt everyone who depends on them for their jobs. When I look back now, a lot of things are clear. I was spending all of my time just keeping the mill running. I wasn't improving our response to customers and our system cycle time. We carried excess work-in-process, scrap rates were high, equipment downtime was high, and we moved, handled, and stored materials too many times. We were too busy putting out fires instead of fixing the system. I get damn mad when I think about the takeover people and the Japanese dumping, but I can see now that we might have saved the mill if we had done some of the things we're learning now. I can see it today. The mindset of most of the people at Garrett is the same as we had at the mill. Wil Danesi and Alan Updike have their heads on straight, but most of their people think just like I used to think — that the only important measure is how much they produce."

"That's why what we're doing is important," she says.

"I agree," he says. "I don't have a fancy education like you and I don't learn as fast as some of you whiz kids, which makes this job really frustrating. But when I set my mind to something, I get the job done. I'm going to be good at this Guardian business, you'll see."

"I think that you'll be *great* at it."

He blushes, then grins broadly. "You too, Laura, you too."

They watch as the small band sets up their instruments. "This isn't going to be Harry James," he says. "Can you believe Marcus stuck us with this foundry job?"

"I thought you wanted an assignment? And besides, Marcus has a lot of faith in us."

"I'm glad somebody does."

"We can do it, Lou, and we're not alone in this. I think that Frank Doran, Rich Reynolds, and Ron Schultz want to redesign the business. And Marcus said he'd help."

"Hey, Marcus takes off for points unknown, " Lou says, "just when we're really getting into the thick of things. I'm afraid we're going to do the wrong thing. And you'd think he'd match us up with experienced partners. I mean, let's face it, we're both a couple of greenhorns; you with no experience and me coming from a company that went belly up. It's critical right now and he ought to be here." Lou's voice rises as the band begins to play, "Let me show you a plan for reorganizing the shop that I was going to show to the foundry staff tomorrow. I used your flowcharts to come up with it."

"I don't think we're supposed to do that, Lou."

"Not supposed to do what?"

"Marcus says we're facilitators. We're not supposed to tell them what to do."

"Sounds like Marcus. He's never run a factory."

"I'd talk to Marcus first, Lou."

"Yeah. I was planning to show him the layout in the morning, but he'll probably shoot it down."

"Confidence, Lou."

"He doesn't think much of my ideas. I think he's only impressed by people like you who have fancy degrees from places like MIT and Harvard."

"He told me that you had a good head for business."

"He told you that?"

Laura lays her hand on the back of his. "I agree with him, Lou."

Her touch sends a rush through his body, but just as quickly as she places her hand, he pulls his away, reaching for his beer.

"I'd better walk you back to the hotel," he says, very matter-of-factly.

The walk back along the strand is quiet except for the breaking waves. He's intensely aware of her presence, her perfume, her femininity, and he's embarrassed by his feelings. *Can't allow this to happen . . . she's so young. Funny . . . I'm dead and I'm worried about age difference. But right now I'm alive . . . what a crazy situation. She's definitely a woman . . . better forget it! She wouldn't be interested in me anyway . . .*

At the Marina Laura stops walking. "Cat got your tongue?" she says.

Lou is looking down, dragging his foot back and forth in the sand. "I was just thinking . . . pretty girl like — "

"Woman, Lou."

"Right. Woman. I was just thinking that a pretty woman like you must have had to chase guys away with a stick."

She shrugs. "Actually, a lot of guys were intimidated by me. But that hardly matters now," she says, with a smile.

Not another word is spoken until they reach her room. "Thanks for a great time. See you in the morning," she says, as she opens the door. She slowly closes it behind her, leaving Lou standing in the hallway.

He has trouble getting to sleep. Thoughts of Laura fill his head. Finally, he drifts into a deep slumber but then is startled by the ring of the phone beside his bed.

"Hi, Lou. Sorry I'm so late. Hope you didn't wait up for me," says the voice on the phone.

"Oh, hi Marcus," Lou says, groggily. "What time is it?"

"Almost midnight, just got in. Sorry, it sounds like I woke you. How about coffee at six in the Marina Cafe?"

"No problem. See you then." After tossing restlessly for a long while, he finally turns on the light and reaches for the flowchart that Laura made earlier in the day. He's still amazed that she did this in an hour on the computer. He starts to jot notes and begins drafting his plan. By five in the morning, he has it completed. He showers, dresses, and goes to the window, which overlooks the entrance to King Harbor Marina. Several fishing boats are moored to a bait barge a few hundred yards across the channel. The bark of a seal cuts through the morning air.

"Good morning, Lou," Marcus says.

"Good morning. You sure can pick the motels. This is first class."

"If we have to endure the discomforts of being human, we might as well enjoy the pleasures. Sorry I woke you last night — sleep well?"

"Well enough. I have that data you asked for on recent quality problems in the foundry. Do you want to go over it?"

"Sure do — just tell me briefly what the problems were, where they were introduced, and where they were detected."

"OK." Lou hands Marcus a sheet of paper. "I have four examples here."

Example 1. Shell thickness on investment patterns was too thin and the molds cracked. The problem was detected at final layout inspection.

Example 2. A customer drawing change was not communicated to manufacturing which resulted in unacceptable castings. The customer detected the problem after receiving the parts.

Example 3. An entire lot of castings had a condition called 'shrink.' The bad castings were caught at x-ray. Cause unknown.

Example 4. Insufficient cleaning of the wax pattern resulted in flash at the dimensional check.

"Lou, what are some of the common characteristics of these four problems?"

"I have the common characteristics listed. I figured you'd ask." Lou says, as he lays a list on the table. Marcus reads it out loud.

Common Problems

- *Time to detect is long (five to fifteen weeks).*
- *Quality of feedback is poor.*
- *Scrap and rework costs are high.*
- *A great deal of expediting is required to meet the original schedule. In the case of the drawing errors, corrected parts arrived at the customer very late.*
- *Problems reach crisis state because they go undetected so long.*

- *Time to correct is long. Problem solving is hampered by the lack of timely information.*
- *There is no permanent prevention effort. Time to prevent is forever.*

....

"Very good, Lou. Where did you get that 'time to prevent' buzzword?"

"I figure that if you can make them up, I can too."

Marcus laughs. "I like that: time to prevent. I might start using that. Are the people at Garrett lax in attitude about quality problems?"

"No, Wil's made believers of all of them. They want quality."

"Then what's wrong?"

"I did a lot of thinking about that last night while I was waiting for you," Lou says, lifting his eyebrows.

"I'm glad you got that off your chest, Lou."

"The problem at Garrett is just what you've been preaching — the system is not designed for fast response, high quality, or high value-to-cost ratio. Feedback and feed-forward systems are not designed well for learning and improvement."

"You've discovered the greatest principle of all, Lou."

"I have?"

"Take out your pouch marked 'Greatest Principle.'"

....

The Greatest Principle

The rate and quality of learning and improvement is designed into the system.

....

"Lou, is it clear how the system design influences the rate and quality of learning and improvement?"

"Yes, and I think I know what should be done about it."

"What?"

"I have a flow design all laid out right here that will reduce the system cycle time by weeks. It improves feedback design to reduce defects and errors. It should also eliminate over fifty percent of the valueless activity in the process. I wanted you to look at it before we showed it to the staff tomorrow morning."

"Hold on, Lou, slow down. That's not what we do. We do *not* provide answers."

"You're kidding? What's the point of learning all this if I'm not going to use it. I'll bet Laura told you about my plan," Lou says, hotly.

"No, Laura didn't tell me a thing. I'm pleased that you developed a plan; but your job is to get them to develop their own. People support what they create, Lou."

"But how do I do that? Can we afford to take the time?"

"Slow down some. We have to take the time. It has to be their vision, not yours."

"Good morning, everybody. Isn't it a beautiful day?" Laura says, as she walks in.

"Good morning," Marcus says, as he stands to pull a chair back from the table for Laura. "We were just about to talk about getting everyone in the Foundry involved in the redesign process."

"Then I'm glad I came early. How long have you guys been at it?"

"Not long." Lou says, before turning to Marcus. "So how do we get them to come up with the vision?"

"To understand that, Lou, you need to remember the process we went through to get you motivated to come up with the vision you have. What were the first steps you went through in your learning journey."

"We studied Whitney, Ford, McDonald's, and Motorola."

"Before that, Lou."

"You mean the visit to the mill?"

"Even before that. We established your mission — your reason for learning. Then your education began. You learned what the Hunted do to turn themselves around. Last came your assignment. I had to help you transform yourself so that you would be able to help them transform themselves. They can then transform their business."

"But that isn't practical with all those people. Besides, I think there are some real hardheads in that shop."

Marcus laughs, "Lou, I can't believe you said that. Do you mean harder heads than yours?" Lou manages a weak smile.

"I agree with Lou. They're not prepared to redesign their Delivery Systems," Laura asserts.

Marcus stares intently at them. "It's our job to get them ready. We have to get them to commit to a company level mission. If they're not involved at the mission level, they won't be willing to make changes that are best for the whole business."

"Can that be done in two days?" Laura asks.

"You've a lot of work to do," Marcus says.

"So what do we do next, General?" Lou says.

"We have to prepare the leaders in the foundry so they can come up with the action plans," Marcus says. "We facilitate the process. We don't give people fish; we teach them to fish."

Lou rolls his eyes.

"You don't buy it, do you Lou?"

"Hey, mine is not to question why, mine is just to do or die."

"All right, let's look at your plan. Could you explain how your thinking developed?"

"Well, I started with Wil Danesi's strategic needs. He said their major goals were faster customer response and lower cost."

"Good starting point," Marcus says." Defining Process Intent is the first step. Did you come up with some targets for response and costs?"

"I didn't have any competitive benchmarks, so I went for ultimate possible performance targets. I figured if they can do the ultimate, they can't lose. I started with the flowcharts of the aluminum casting process that Laura made yesterday. Here they are." Lou lays a sheet of paper with two flowcharts in front of Marcus.

Aluminum Casting Physical Flow
(before redesign)

"Laura, why don't you explain your chart to Marcus," Lou says.

Laura flashes a smile at Lou. "Sure. On this chart I use a dashed arrow to show a move and a triangle to show where material is stored temporarily. If you follow the numbers on the

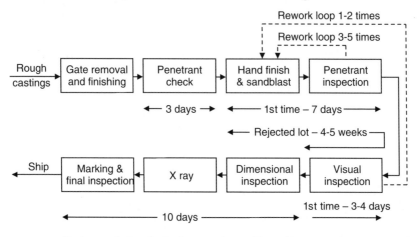

**Final Processing and Inspection
for Aluminum and Investment Castings**

System cycle time for final processing and inspection – 40 to 50 days

arrows, you can trace through the process. During the process, the material is moved over fifty times. It's moved twelve times between buildings. It's stored over thirty-five times. It's easy to understand how it takes fifty days to get through the process."

"How long should it take?" Marcus asks.

"Alan Updike had all the value-added process times. We added up the time it would take to process a casting if there were no times when it was waiting between processes, and that was about three days. So I figure five to six days would be a good goal."

"How would you reduce the time, Lou?"

"There are some things they have to stop doing. I made a list of those."

"Interesting approach, Lou. Do you have the list with you?"

Lou hands it to him.

Practices That Must Be Stopped to Reduce System Cycle Time

- *carrying large work-in-process*
- *making over 50 moves, over 100 handling steps, and 12 moves between buildings*
- *separating process centers that saw, grind, sandblast, weld, inspect, and test*
- *varying build schedules*
- *loading key value-adding operations without regard to capacity and demand*
- *prioritizing or expediting*
- *processing in large batches*
- *maintaining over 35 in-process storage areas*

"Then I made a new Process Model for the Foundry that will solve their problem," Lou says, handing Marcus a package of papers.

Marcus reads through the documents. "You're going Non-Linear, Lou!"

"What! What's wrong with it?"

"Nothing's wrong. It's great. I just said you're starting down the Non-Linear road."

"I am?" Lou says, with a half-pleased, half-puzzled look.

"It's very important to understand what is beginning to happen in your thinking, Lou. You're on the verge of a breakthrough. Let's take the time now to talk about the very powerful approach to redesign that you're just beginning to understand. It's an important part of the transformational change process." Marcus checks his watch. "We have about an hour before we need to be at Garrett. Let's instantly go to the room of the Hunters and talk about Non-Linear Transformation."

"But what about the new Process Model I came up with?"

"That's your Process Model, not theirs," Marcus says.

"I don't get it," Lou says.

"How many people wash and wax their rental car?" Marcus asks.

"No one."

"Think about that."

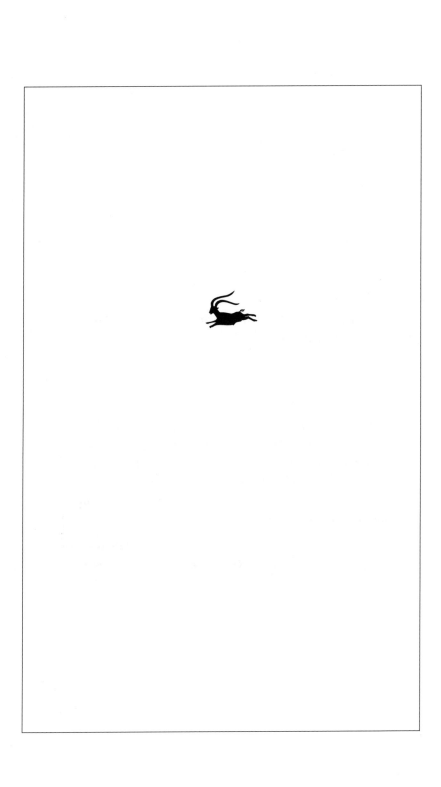

A national daily newspaper seems like a way to lose a lot of money in a hurry.

– John Morton
The Making of McPaper

When our frames of reference are fixed and rigid, they become a substitute for thinking. Learning takes place when we have the flexibility to change our frames of reference. The most creative efforts of human beings involve departing from existing frames of reference and constructing new ones.

– Moshe F. Rubinstein
Tools for Thinking and Problem Solving

CHAPTER TWENTY-FIVE

The Transformation Process

*I*n the room of the Hunters, Marcus begins. "We're going to listen in for a few minutes on a board meeting of the Gannett Company, a $1 billion media company, at their Rochester, New York, headquarters. It's a cold November morning in 1979."

As the scene develops in the board room, Lou and Laura see a man pacing back and forth in front of a roaring fire. "The man pacing is the Chairman, Al Neuharth," Marcus explains. "How would it affect the company if we set aside a special kitty next year for research and development," he says.

"How much of a kitty?" a staff member asks.

"A million dollars. That's enough to find out if this company has what it takes to publish a national newspaper," Al replies.

The questions come in a torrent. "How will the money be spent?" "Who will do the research?" "How will we go about the task?"

"I didn't ask how we would spend it," Neuharth says. "I asked how it would impact us."

"Neuharth sure made that clear," Lou says.

"His mind was made up, Lou. He had been thinking about a national newspaper for a long time. I'm sure that no one at that table, including Neuharth, could have imagined what would develop from that Monday morning decision."

"So what did happen after that?" Laura asks.

"Before I describe what happened, let's understand the process of transformation that Neuharth initiated. Transformation takes place at four levels," Marcus explains, as he begins to write with the light stylus:

Transformation Levels

- *transformation Drivers*
- *changing the mindsets, mental models, and measures*
- *Non-linear redesign of Delivery Systems*
- *continuous improvement*

"Major transformations are initiated or driven by five principal Drivers."

Transformation Drivers

- *strategic changes prompted by market changes*
- *significant trauma*
- *the vision and zeal of the inventor or entrepreneur*
- *performance gapping*
- *the Non-Linear Solution*

"Al Neuharth started with vision and zeal, but his vision and zeal could not be transferred instantly to his staff. To establish the new mindsets, mental models, and measures that would be needed to publish a national newspaper, a non-linear mind change would be required. That was the purpose of the research study he proposed.

"To conduct the research, Neuharth selected five young executives and cloistered them in a small cottage in Boca Raton, Florida. They were given four questions to answer: Can we produce and print a national newspaper? Can we distribute and sell a national newspaper? Can we design a daily newspaper that will grab readers around the country in sufficient numbers to make the effort worthwhile? Can we get the necessary advertiser support for a national newspaper?

"The team first took stock of the Delivery System that Gannett already had in place. At that time Gannett had eighty-one newspapers, and thus, the largest circulation — 3.6 million copies per day — of any newspaper group in circulation. Gannett also had the nation's largest network of journalists — more than 4,000 — production and distribution facilities within two hours of forty large markets, and their own news service bureaus in eleven state capitals. Even so, to establish a national daily newspaper, the Gannett Delivery System would require massive redesign.

"They calculated that the newspaper would be sold initially at 105,000 outlets, most of them news racks that must be designed, built, and placed. They would have to use computer composition and satellite transmission to transmit full pages so that the newspaper could be laid out in only one location.

"At a Gannett board of directors meeting in October 1980, the first two of the four questions that Neuharth had asked his research team were answered satisfactorily. They showed, first, how with known computer and satellite technology, they could produce the paper and transmit it to existing printing presses in sixty-four cities. They also explained how the difficult task of distributing the papers could be done. It was agreed that the project should go forward to the prototype and testing stage.

"But the team continued to struggle with the third question: Could they get the readership? What did they have to offer that the *New York Times* or the *Wall Street Journal* didn't already supply? Neuharth's vision of gaining readership was clear: thirty-two to forty pages with full color on each section front, extensive sports coverage with daily results, as much as a full page of weather, top news stories from every state, and lots of timely news coverage of national and international events. They decided on a name: *USA Today*.[1]

"Al Neuharth closely directed the prototyping and testing. The first prototypes were sent to 4,500 opinion leaders across the country. Unfavorable reaction came from journalists who called the prototypes shallow and posing little threat to community newspapers. Madison Avenue advertising agencies advised them that major purchasers of national advertising were accustomed to magazine-quality color, a capability that would require new skills at the printing plants and millions of dollars in new presses. Trade publications agreed that the paper would be a tough advertising sell. By the summer of 1981, many Gannett executives were leaning toward cutting their losses.

"The public thought otherwise, however. A Louis Harris poll found that newspaper readers who saw the prototypes loved them. A Simmons Market Research poll found that the paper appealed to the toughest readership — single copy buyers in big cities. The evidence was mounting that *USA Today* would sell, so question three was partly answered.

"But now a fourth and even bigger question began to dominate the debate: Was there profit in it? A financial analyst assigned to the team estimated that the publication would lose $90 million in the first three years, then turn profitable. Corporate finance viewed the sales projections as unrealistic. They felt that the national newspaper would bring financial disaster to Gannett and was a very poor return on investment. Unfortunately, the only way they could prove the sales predictions was to launch the paper.

"On December 15, 1981, Neuharth convened the Board of Directors and key members of his staff for a vote to launch or not to launch. The vote was twelve to zero for launch. Neuharth had achieved a change in mindsets and mental models.

"In the next nine months they completed the redesign of Gannett's existing Delivery Systems to accommodate the national paper. In September, 1982, the first edition of *USA Today* sold out as it hit the streets in the Baltimore area.

"Gannett stock rose to 60.25 in December of 1982, up from 30 in the spring of that year.

"On June 15, 1987, while Neuharth was on the road, he received a telegram from John Curley, Gannett's CEO, informing him that they had done it — *USA Today* had broken into the black for the first time. The announcement of a profitable fourth quarter in 1987 was a turning point for the paper. The unbelievable numbers that the team had dreamed up years earlier were now fact."

"That's an interesting story, but what does it have to do with the problems we have at Garrett?" Lou asks.

"Garrett's transformation also started with a transformation Driver," Marcus replies. "Roy Ekrom and Frank Geldert provided the significant trauma when they threatened to shut down the plant. Instead, they convinced Wil Danesi to take over as general manager — to provide the vision and zeal. Just as Al Neuharth did, Wil now has to change the mindsets, mental models, and measures of his management team. He's already started the process by setting far-reaching performance expectations. Our first job for Wil will be to open the minds of his staff and help them acquire the knowledge they'll need to meet these expectations. That will lead to the Delivery System redesign that will provide convincing evidence that the new ideas work."

Driving Transformational Change

"Let me get this straight," Laura says. "You're really starting at the Delivery System redesign level because you can't really get a mind change in many staff members until they see a result."

"That's essentially true," Marcus says.

"If I were the boss, I would make them do the right thing no matter what they had in their minds," Lou says.

"Wil Danesi knows better than to do that," Marcus replies." He knows he must transform the people's thinking, not by edict, but because they believe in it. Our job is to facilitate some early successes in the redesign of their Delivery Systems to establish that belief. Finally, your job will be to help put a process in place for Continuous Linear Improvement to ensure that the rate and quality of learning and improvement are maintained at a high level. Let's describe more about what happens in the redesign level of the transformation process," he says, as he switches on the light stylus.

Delivery System Redesign

Delivery System redesign begins at the level of strategy. Management should have measures that provide early detection of uncompetitive Delivery Systems. Such measures should monitor the vital signs of Delivery System competitiveness. We can classify the vital signs according to their level of seriousness.

Early Vital Signs

- *Customers seem harder to please; they want faster response and seemingly unreachable quality levels.*
- *A great deal of management's time is spent prioritizing work, solving various crises, and expediting to meet customer delivery expectations.*
- *Time to obsolescence is decreasing faster than time to bring new products to market.*
- *Quality levels are not improving rapidly, and customers claim that competitors offer higher quality.*
- *Customers are asking for product or service performance features that the business doesn't provide.*
- *More inspection is necessary to meet customer quality requirements.*
- *Prices must be reduced constantly to meet competition.*
- *It seems that competitors are using unfair tactics to take your customers.*
- *There are continual surprises from competitors and customers.*
- *Blame-placing and in-fighting are rising.*
- *Management is arrogant about the superiority of their system and they create a "no-bad-news-or-criticism-is-welcome atmosphere" for their subordinates and customers.*

When management ignores the early vital signs, more serious vital signs emerge. Months or years may transpire between the two.

Serious Vital Signs

- *reduced customer satisfaction index*
- *reduced sales or loss of market share*
- *declining profit margins*
- *long-term negative cash flow and the sale of profitable assets*
- *increased liabilities compared to assets*
- *discounts or incentives must be used to maintain customers*
- *market share can only be maintained at a loss (often the investment is so high and costs to quit the business are so high that it's tough to quit)*

If dramatic action isn't taken at this juncture, the business will go critical.

Critical Vital Signs

- *profit losses*
- *stock value decline*
- *cash deficits*
- *reduced credit rating*
- *debt restructuring to stay afloat*

When the business goes critical, restructuring is essential for survival.

Redesign of Delivery Systems is best undertaken when the early vital signs occur, or at worst, when serious vital signs emerge.

"It's tough to take the early vital signs seriously when they seem to be a natural part of the business," Lou says. "If you're inside the mess, it's tough to see it as a mess."

"Just like doctors, we have to get people to examine their own vital signs before they need major surgery," Marcus says. "Do you think the past management at Garrett acted on the early vital signs?"

"Definitely not."

"The part I'm concerned about is that we're teaching them to do surgery on themselves," Laura says.

"They must learn preventive medicine,"Marcus says." Non-linear redesign is preventive surgery, like removing colon polyps before they become cancerous, or reducing fat intake to prevent heart disease. The Hunters have a systematic approach to non-linear redesign of their Delivery Systems. In other words, they stay in a continuous process of transformation."

"It's useful at this point to again clarify the difference between Delivery System redesign and continuous improvement. Continuous improvement takes place continuously at individual operations or at a small series of operations. These changes are *linear* in that they don't usually require large departures from traditional thinking."

Systematic Continuous Linear Improvement

Linear approaches start with the existing process and make systematic improvements. The assumption is made that the existing Process Intent, Process Model, and Learning and Improvement System are the best for the deployment of the strategy; otherwise, non-linear techniques are appropriate. Goals and achievements are usually modest with Continuous Linear Improvement — normally ten to fifty percent improvement per

year. These operational changes take place in the micro-struc-
tures of the Delivery Systems.

In the Continuous Linear Improvement Process:

- *improvement is measured against past performance*
- *the Process Intent of the existing process is assumed to be essentially correct*
- *the Process Model for the existing process is assumed to be essentially correct*
- *valueless time, valueless activity, and valueless variance are systematically reduced to improve response, quality, and costs*
- *the focus is on identifying and solving problems and identifying and reducing constraints*
- *deduction and reduction are the principal modes of thinking*

Present   **Improved**

Process ————————▶ *Process*

Continuous Improvement

"The non-linear approaches used to redesign Delivery Systems are more powerful," Marcus continues, "but they usually require a major break from traditional thinking. A systematic redesign should take place along the following guidelines."

Systematic Delivery System Redesign

- *First, redefine or update the business strategy to meet the present and future needs of the business. Once you've determined the new strategy, give first priority to redesigning the Delivery Systems that have the highest impact on the future of the business.*
- *Use group technology techniques to define separate Delivery Systems within the whole Delivery System.*

- *After you designate a Delivery System for redesign, you must examine and align it with the newest strategic thrusts of the business.*
- *Determine the performance gap of the existing Delivery System by measuring present performance (system response, quality, and value-to-cost ratio) and comparing it to ultimate performance. The larger the gap, the more revolutionary the redesign must be.*
- *Analyze the existing Delivery System and develop a rough vision of what can ultimately be designed.*
- *Choose a team capable of both designing the new Delivery System and making the changes necessary to implement it. Train the team in redesign principles and empower them to develop an action plan to present to top management for approval.*
- *The team develops an entirely new Process Model designed around the Core Value-Added Model.*
- *The team redesigns the Learning and Improvement System. To do this, it designs processes to reduce feedback time and improve the quality of the feedback. The team should design feed-forward or corrective action processes into the front end of the Delivery System to provide faster and higher quality preventive action systems. In many cases the fundamental measurement and reward system is redesigned to increase the rate and quality of learning and improvement. The team also puts into place systems for training and developing workers.*
- *The primary modes of reasoning are induction and reconceptualization; deduction and reduction are employed as necessary.*
- *The team presents their action plans for approval, and begins to implement them immediately.*
- *Management follows up to facilitate the implementation.*

"How does the team change the existing measures and reward systems?" Laura asks.

Marcus moves under the skylight. "Let's start with measures. Wil Danesi said that they needed major improvement in customer response and large reductions in costs. The teams should design new measures which support that strategy."

"Like measuring the average time from receipt of order to shipment?" Laura asks.

"Yes," Marcus says.

"They already have cost measurement systems," Lou says.

"Their cost measurement systems are designed for cost control and not cost reduction," Marcus says.

"How's that?" Lou asks.

"For cost reduction, we need to have measures that best relate to the largest opportunities for cost reduction. We need to learn to measure the costs of lost people-potential, the cost of poor quality, the costs of long cycle times, and the costs of sub-optimum design. Which of these opportunities to reduce costs is the largest?" Marcus asks, looking at Lou and Laura.

"I'd say that besides restructuring, reducing the cost of poor quality is their largest opportunity," Laura says.

"Why do you say that?" Marcus asks.

"They ship good quality to their customers but they have a lot of inspection, rework, and scrap. Wil Danesi sees that," Laura says.

Group Technology

Motorcycles may be grouped according to the displacement of their engines (1100cc, 750cc, 550cc, and 250cc) or according to their primary intended use (street, off-road, and on/off-road).

Grouping Delivery Systems for redesign is an art. Gear manufacturing, sheet metal, and cabinetmaking are obviously different groups because they employ essentially different processes.

"A lot of that is due to long detection and correction times. I'd start by reducing the system cycle times," Lou says.

"You're both right on target," Marcus says.

"But Wil Danesi's managers have to be open to change to bring about the transformation," Laura says.

"It goes much further than that," says Marcus, as he begins to write again.

***

All Successful Managers of the '90s:

- *can no longer be merely open and adaptable to change*
- *can no longer be merely progressive about change*
- *must be ultimately flexible*
- *must anticipate and drive both linear and non-linear change*
- *must sense the vital signs, search for the performance gaps, create the overall vision, facilitate the implementation process, and provide follow-up support*

***

"Let's summarize the transformation process," Marcus says.

***

Transformation Process

Begin with strategy at the business level. Recognize that this strategy is deployed through Delivery Systems. Recognize that the capability of your Delivery Systems determines the limits of your possible strategic options.

If you must change strategy, critically re-examine your mindsets, mental models, and measures. Change these 3Ms to fit the new strategy.

Keeping the new strategy in mind, designate Delivery Systems for redesign that will have the greatest impact on the success of the strategy. Divide the Delivery Systems into natural groups, either by customer, technology, like processes, or similar design. Also consider strategy in terms of the process's output requirements (customer values, competitive benchmarks, internal and external requirements). This will suggest changes in the Process Intent and Process Model that you can design into the new Delivery Systems.

Finally, put in place a continuous improvement system that draws upon contributions from everyone in the business.

"So, is the Non-Linear Solution that management must drive the transformation process?" Laura asks.

"That's part of it."

Laura smiles. "We've got a lot of parts, but no chicken."

"Keep examining the parts from this non-linear perspective and eventually you'll see the chicken," Marcus says, with a smile.

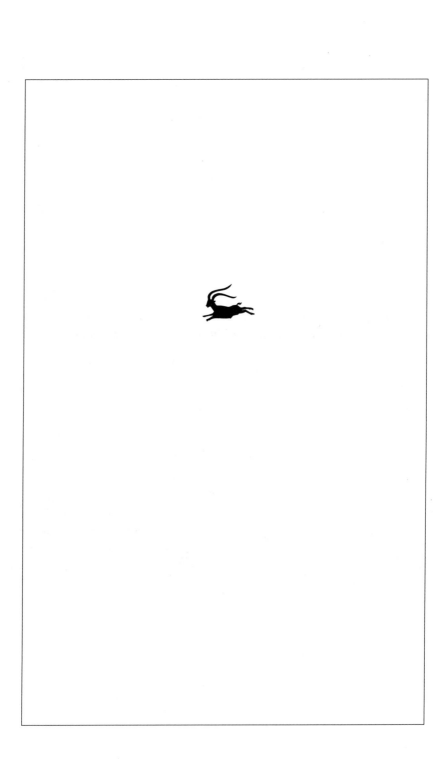

People sometimes stumble over the truth, but usually they pick themselves up and hurry about their business.

– Winston Churchill

CHAPTER TWENTY-SIX

Learning Organizations

*F*rom the moment the workshop starts at Garrett that Saturday morning, Lou can't believe that this is the same Marcus. Weaving and bobbing, sometimes logical, sometimes emotional, first in a soft voice, then in a loud, resonant tone, the usually softspoken Marcus pounds the message home. He speaks adding value and age-old quality principles. He teaches the major influences on response, the major sources of poor quality, and the major opportunities for cost reduction. He also teaches them the system principles that Hunters use to design their businesses:

....

System Principles for the Design of Value Delivery Systems[1]

1. *A system is optimized by optimizing it as a whole, not by optimizing its parts or subsystems. This might be called the "house-divided-against-itself principle."*
2. *To improve the output of a process without tradeoff, we must improve the process itself. (You learn to hit by improving your swing, not by watching the scoreboard.)*

3. *Value Delivery System design must be targeted to the basic goals of a business: to be the supplier of choice and to achieve financial gain.*

4. *Strategic planning and Value Delivery System design cannot be independently executed. Value Delivery Systems must be designed to deploy business strategy. Because a great deal of the strategic strengths and weaknesses of a business derives from the capability of its Value Delivery Systems, improving their design enhances strategic options.*

5. *There are subsystems whose improvement will produce dramatic improvement in the performance of the whole system. Peter Senge calls this the "Trimtab Principle," referring to the large leverage that a small change in the rudder trimtab has on the maneuverability of a large boat.*

6. *Derive Process Intent (response, quality, and cost/value requirements) from the business strategy, then develop the Process Model to optimally meet the Process Intent.*

7. *There are no universally optimum Process Models, but for a given Process Intent there is an optimum Process Model.*

8. *System response and delay is designed into the system. A system's average response time follows Little's Law: SRT = WIP/OR (SRT is average system response time, WIP is average work-in-process, and OR is average output rate). Expediting and prioritizing does not improve average response time but usually makes it worse. The need to prioritize and expedite is an indicator that the average response time of the system is worse than the average market expectation for delivery time.*

9. *Reducing system cycle time and valueless activity improves customer response time, improves system quality potential by reducing time to detect and time to correct, reduces operating costs by eliminating the need to prioritize and expedite, reduces the cost of excess inventory, improves the accuracy of forecasts, and reduces variance in delivery date. This may be called the "no tradeoff principle."*

10. *Complaints are just the tip of the iceberg of customer dissatisfaction. There is a delay between the time that a customer is dissatisfied and the occasion of lost sales.*

11. *The potential for learning and improvement to take place within a system is designed into the systems that provide feedback, feed-forward, learned lessons, pre-ventions, and rewards. Ideal feedback is fast and provides high-quality information. Ideal feed-forward is fast and provides solutions which eliminate recur-rence of the problem.*

12. *There is a tendency for people to blame their problems on outside causes. On the contrary, the source of their problems is either in the design of the system of which they are a part, or in the way they react to the system or its outside forces.*

13. *The design or redesign of a system should involve those who operate the system, those who control the resources of the system, those who have a stake in the system, and those who have system design expertise or knowledge.*

14. *The reaction of a system to intervention is predictable only if one knows system principles. Accordingly, the result of an intervention can be the opposite of the desired result due to fundamental laws and principles*

designed into the system. You'll find many examples of this principle in Peter Senge's The Fifth Discipline.

15. *System throughput ≤ bottleneck throughput. If a product must be processed at a certain operation and that operation has the lowest throughput in the value adding chain, then that operation is called a bottleneck. This might be called Goldratt's Law, after Eliyahu Goldratt, who developed the concept in his book,* The Goal.

To demonstrate these principles, influences, sources, and opportunities, Marcus sets up a simulated factory. Step by step, applying these principles, the team reduces the total cycle time from twenty-six minutes to one minute; reduces defects and errors from 10,000 parts per million to 400; and reduces nonvalue-added activity from fifty percent to less than ten percent. For the first time, it all comes together for Lou. He is amazed with the results.

Marcus speaks of the ways that Hunters continuously transform themselves, how they redesign their Delivery Systems and install continuous improvement systems. He emphasizes the need for a balance of Continuous Linear Improvement and non-linear redesign of the Value Delivery Systems of the business. He speaks of flexibility, performance gapping, the six components of learning systems, and urges each of them to drive the change necessary to turn Garrett into a Hunter.

Now, by the end of the day, Lou and Laura are exhausted from watching Marcus conduct the workshop. Marcus has said he has a fifty-five-year-old body, but it seems to Lou and Laura that he has the energy of an eighteen-year-old. For every question the workshop answered for them, it generated two more. But just as they get to Marcus to ask him questions at the end of the day, Wil Danesi ushers them off to his office.

"Your workshop was very good," Wil begins, "but it generated more questions in my mind than it answered. I realized in the workshop that there are many levels in the design of Learning and Improvement Systems. There are the individual level, the group level, and the organizational level. What's your definition of learning compared to improvement?"

Marcus begins speaking and writing on Wil's board simultaneously:

....

Learning: The process of acquiring knowledge and skill. Inquiry, problem solving, and memory are parts of the learning process.

Improvement: The attainment of more desirable outcomes.

....

"These two processes can take place independently or dependently. Learning can take place without improvement. For example, your people hopefully learned something today, but until they apply this learning there is no improvement."

"But how can you have improvement without learning?" Wil asks.

"Next Friday we'll use today's lessons and apply them in order to improve your aluminum casting process. But the whole organization will not learn from this unless everyone begins to apply the lessons to their own areas."

"In the workshop, you talked about how our mindsets, mental models, and measures inhibit our development," Wil says. "What mindsets do you think we have here at Garrett that hold us back?"

Marcus considers the question for several moments before answering. "Many have the mindset that if they had a new computer system or replaced machines that are old, they could fix their problems. Most have the mindset that management would never shut the place down. Some have a mindset that they are already doing everything they can to turn this place around. Almost everyone has a mindset that these new ideas I've presented to you don't apply to this business because it is different."

"What mental models do we have that we need to change?"

"Your managers believe that the end of the month push is the only way you can achieve monthly production requirements. You deplete inventories and human energies in the last week of the month to make up what you weren't able to build in the first weeks of the month. This ensures that the next month will start with insufficient inventories and that your work force will probably be too burned out to make average schedule requirements. Lower output at the first of the month again leads to the necessary push at the end of the month. This is a self-perpetuating, destructive, mental model."

Wil leans back in his chair. "I have the managers agreeing to change because I say so, but they aren't convinced. How do we get them to want to change?"

"There are two ways to change the three Ms. In the first approach, you must convince them that it's in their own best interest to do so. Otherwise, the company won't remain competitive and people won't have jobs. This approach works best when it is accompanied by significant trauma. If there is little trauma, a second approach is more useful. In this approach management must be convinced with hard evidence that redesign improves the business. So you redesign one or more crucial Delivery Systems, and as these redesigned Delivery Systems are successful and the managers who supported the redesign are rewarded, thoughtful managers will be more receptive to new mindsets, mental models, and measures.

"Then you can put other models in their minds — models that have the potential to operate on a level schedule and still put out the total monthly requirements. Then you have to get them to change their Process Model in the casting operation to fit the new mental model."

"Do you think that an improvement in the aluminum process would be that convincing?" Wil asks.

Marcus smiles. "Let's envision what ultimate performance in the aluminum Delivery System would be compared to today's performance. Right now it takes an average of over fifty days to process a casting order through the foundry," Marcus says.

"Where did you get that number?" Wil asks.

"Lou and Laura came up with it by analyzing the process. Laura, show Wil your timed flowchart."

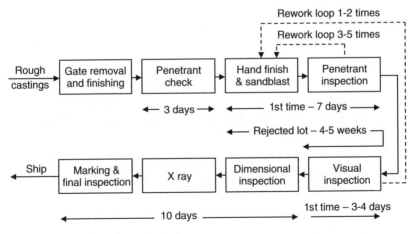

**Final Processing and Inspection
for Aluminum and Investment Castings**

System cycle time for final processing and inspection – 40 to 50 days

"Wil, this Process Model has some designed-in features that your managers must come to understand. Let's begin with response. With this model, what's your average response to an order?"

"Fifty days."

"How about your response to a reduction or increase in orders from a customer?"

"Depends on where the orders are in the process when the change comes in."

"Suppose an order is at the breakout operation when you get a request to delay shipment two weeks? Also, tell me what you would do if they asked you to deliver the order two weeks early."

"In the case where it's delayed, we would either stop processing the order or continue processing if we think the customer will buy it later," Wil says. "If the expected delivery date is moved up two weeks we would move the order for that product up in the schedule."

"What if the customer asked for earlier delivery of an increased order?"

"We'd put a priority on the orders we had in process and expedite them through the process. We would also start the additional quantity right away."

"Suppose at the end of the month you are short of dollar volume requirements?"

"We'll find a high dollar order that we can expedite through the process."

"How often do jobs in process get reprioritized and how does this reprioritization impact the accuracy of your scheduling process?"

"Marcus, obviously we do a lot of reprioritizing, and I guess that says that our scheduling isn't too accurate. We're planning to set up a new computerized scheduling system to fix that."

"Let's imagine that we could change your Process Model in such a way that the casting can go from core build to shipping in five days instead of fifty and the order can be processed through the office in a single day instead of five."

"That would be magic," Wil says.

"But if it were possible, let's reask the questions we just went through. What would your average response be to an order with this new model?"

"One week."

"Suppose that a customer asks you to delay shipment a few weeks?"

"No problem, because we probably haven't started the job in process yet."

"And, if they ask you to deliver two weeks earlier?" Marcus asks.

"Probably no problem. We can move the order up to start it immediately and finish it without expediting it. I'm getting the picture. With this model we don't start the order into the process until five days before the ship date. With the Process Model we have now, we start the order at least fifty days before shipment, which means our forecast has to be ten times better with our model than with your magical model. With the model you're envisioning, most of the changes in priorities, increases, and decreases would occur prior to starting it in the process. No doubt about it — the response of the new Process Model is far better."

"What happens to an order that isn't expedited with the present process?" Marcus asks.

"It will either sit or move very slowly through the process until it becomes hot enough to receive a high priority."

"Are you saying that eventually everything has to have a priority or it will be a long time moving through the process?"

"Not quite everything, but you make an interesting point. If we could move everything through the process in five days we could prioritize orders before they started into the process, and once they started we could process them in a first-in/ first-out order. That would eliminate the need to decide daily at each station what to run, and in what order."

"What do you do today if you discover a major problem with an order at the X-ray inspection?" Marcus asks.

"First, if we can rework the parts we would process them back through grind, weld, finish grind, penetrant inspection, heat treat, and then regrind and X-ray; it would take expediting at every station to get them ready to ship in about a week. If we have to start additional castings because we can't rework the defects, it will take four weeks to expedite enough to make up the requirements. I get the point. In the new process we would discover problems faster. We would learn what causes the problem faster."

"Enough of that," Marcus says. "Let's go to measures that are inhibiting you. I've asked your managers which performance measurements are the most important. What do you think they answered?"

"Dollar output, meeting schedule requirements, utilization, efficiency."

"That's pretty close. Some of your managers consider utilization more important than throughput or system cycle time. They choose to keep expensive machines, such as X-ray equipment, busy at all times, even if keeping the machines busy has no relation to demand. Would you agree that the equipment is generally underutilized, and if you do, why is it underutilized?"

"I agree. We could be operating two full shifts and a partial third if we had the business."

Marcus pauses. "Do you think that your people realize that."

Wil looks intently at Marcus. "I don't know. I feel that output, meeting schedule requirements, and return on investment are very important. But I agree that achieving high utilization or high efficiency isn't important if it doesn't make you the supplier of choice and generate more sales and profit."

Marcus gives a thumbs-up signal to Wil.

"You haven't mentioned overreliance on inspection, over-focus on fixes rather than elimination of defects, and the overly large-batch mentality," Wil says.

"Don't need to if you already see those problems," Marcus says. "But it's a long way from understanding what needs to be done and doing it. That's the difference between learning and improvement. One more thought on the three Ms. Your managers see more advantage than disadvantage to in-process inventory, and they are focused more on output than on the process that produces the output."

"I heard someone say that that's a little like playing tennis by keeping your eye on the scoreboard instead of on the ball," Wil says.

"Or on the process of hitting the ball."

"So we must improve the process to improve the output to improve the score?"

"Exactly!"

Wil stands. "About the Transformation Drivers . . . I understand how changes in strategy, vision and zeal, performance gapping, and significant trauma can drive the transformation of a business. But what do you mean by the Non-Linear Solution?"

"We're part of the Non-Linear Solution at this moment. We're transforming our minds by choice, not because we are compelled to do it."

Wil eyes Marcus intently. "What's the next move?"

"Wil, we've set the stage. All we need is a breakthrough to get it going, and we'll do that Saturday," Marcus says, as he leaves.

"Is that all?" Wil asks jokingly. "Just one small miracle?"

The Organizational Learning Process

To meet the challenge of technological acceleration, firms must learn faster and more effectively, because the most successful innovative organizations are also high-performance learning systems. Moreover, firms must create different ways of learning and of learning how to learn under these unfamiliar, dynamic, environmental conditions.

In summary, the following premises about organizational learning can be derived from a rich and varied literature:

1. Organizations learn in ways that are different from and possibly greater than the sum of the individual learning of organizational members.

2. Organizations engage in different learning processes, ranging from the relatively simple to the more complex, depending in part upon the degree of change that learning stimulates in the organization and the norms of the organization regarding change. Another influence upon learning mode is the level of change that is detected in the external environment.

3. More routine and simpler forms of organizational learning involve incremental regulation of, and small adjustments to, ongoing systems. Such learning can be called linear because actions are adaptations of past practices.

4. More radical and complex forms of organizational learning involve changing the ongoing systems and the underlying norms and values within the organization in substantial ways. Overall approaches and the necessary preconditions to generating and interpreting learning may also change through a creative process of self-organization. This learning is non-linear in the sense that future actions depart significantly from past procedures and norms.

5. Transitional learning phases exist when learning cycles are incomplete and when firms are moving from one learning mode to another. Here, a process of unlearning established and accepted ways is often necessary before new learning forms can take hold.[2]

– Dr. Patricia Myers
Syracuse University

Learning, Improvement, and Profit

As the following example shows, the rate and quality of learning and improvement is designed into a Value Delivery System.

By the early 1990s, the printing plate service business became intensively price competitive. As a result, net profit margins for one company eroded until early in 1993, and it posted monthly losses. In addition to the losses, over ten percent of the orders delivered to customers had errors and had to be redone, and thirty percent of deliveries were late. A great deal of management's time was spent prioritizing and expediting orders and a great deal of time (about twenty percent) was spent on rework.

At that time the plate-making process was designed as in the following timed flow diagram:

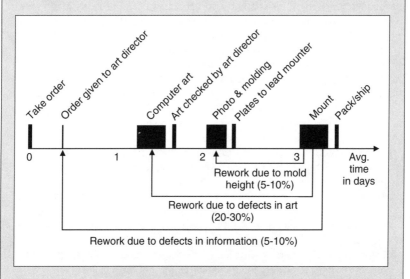

The salesperson took the order from the customer at the customer's place of business. Either later that day or the following day, the salesperson gave a completed order form to the art director along with available drawings and an explanation. After determining a priority for the job, the art director filed the package on a rack. The package sat with other jobs on the rack for typically a day, until its priority came up and a capable artist became available. The art director then assigned the job to a computer artist who, in an average time of three hours, designed and produced black-and-white computer print-outs of the art and assembled the art into a complete package. The complete package was then passed to the art director who, after a few hours, would check the art for quality and note any corrections to be made by the artist. After correction, the package was moved to the photographic area to be photographed and developed into negatives. The negatives were then moved to the polymer area where they were checked and cleaned. After about a day in queue the plates were produced in an average of two hours. The art department, photographic, and polymer departments all worked two shifts, while the mounting department worked three shifts.

The individual plates were then moved to the mounting department where after a wait of about one day, the individual plates were mounted. During the mounting process, all defects and errors that had been previously made were detected. Over fifty percent of the jobs required substantial rework due to the errors that could be traced to inadequate or faulty information supplied by the salesperson, to errors in the computer art, and to defects in polymer molding. An analysis of the system revealed the following basic deficiencies in the design of the learning system. First, defects were detected days after they were made (e.g., *time to detect* was one to three days). Second, because the errors were corrected by whoever on either shift had the time, errors were not usually detected or corrected by the individuals making them. Third, no one felt personal responsibility for a customer's order except the salesperson.

The process was redesigned to improve the learning system. In the new design, when the salesperson arrives with the daily orders, a computer artist and mounter are assigned on the basis of backlogs and capability to do the work. The computer artist and mounter temporarily suspend work on what they are doing and meet with the salesperson to review the order requirements. Typically, the computer artists kept backlogs at less than one day and therefore were able to begin work on a job within twenty-four hours. When they finished, the mounter selected to do that job checked the work of the artist against the order to ensure correctness and mountability. Most of the remaining errors were detected at this point — a source of learning and improvement for both artist and mounter which instilled a sense of responsibility toward the customer. Because this team caught errors early, quality improved immediately. Because of the reduction in rework, the capacity constraint at mounting was eliminated and third shift mounting was eliminated. On the basis of this design the company turned profitable.

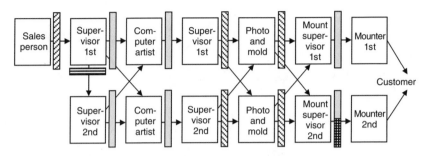

Information interface diagram before redesign

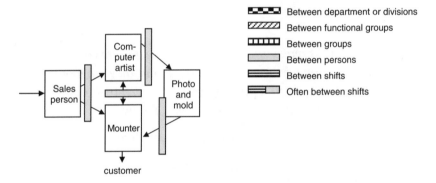

Information interface diagram after redesign

Nowadays, I make it a practice to call them into consultation on any new work . . . I observe that they are more willing to set about a piece of work on which their opinions have been asked and their advice followed.

– Columella, Roman landlord, 100 A.D.

Effective delivery systems should be designed by those who manage them.

– Lynn Shostack, "Designing Services that Deliver"
Harvard Business Review, Jan.-Feb., 1984

CHAPTER TWENTY-SEVEN

The Expert

*T*hat was one hell of a discussion between Marcus and Wil," Lou says, as they disassemble the simulation materials that Marcus used in the workshop.

"Powerful I'd say," Laura says.

"It's starting to clear up," Lou says. "He wasn't just talking about mind changes in the foundry. Did you notice that Marcus looked directly at us each time he referred to mind changes?"

"I noticed."

"Are you going to go over with me what we need to do in the action-planning session next Friday?" Lou says.

"Marcus said we'll be visiting with a Ms. Somers, director of organizational development and training at McDonnell-Douglas, to get a lesson on team empowerment."

"Empowerment?"

"On Friday the team will be given the power to analyze, develop action plans, and implement those actions, but we need to know more about the process. Somers is going to meet us at the Red Onion tonight in Sunset Beach. We'll take the shortcut to get there immediately."

The Red Onion is a Mexican restaurant with white stucco walls and hot pink accents. It has an open view of Huntington Harbor.

"You must be Lou," says a smiling lady with a cherubic face as she approaches Lou.

He has a feeling he has met her before. But she seems very young to be so far up the organizational hierarchy.

"Ms. Somers?" Lou says.

"I knew you immediately from Marcus's description," she says. "And you must be Laura. Table for Somers, please," she says to the man at the reservation desk.

"Marcus says that you're a master and can help us get ready for an implementation next Saturday," Lou says. "He says you've been through dozens of implementations and he's learned a lot from you."

"He said that? He exaggerates."

"Can we explain our situation to you?" Lou asks.

"Sure."

"We're both new on the job and we've never done an implementation. Laura, could you talk about our progress to date?"

"The Delivery System that we're going to redesign has already been chosen," Laura says. "The team has been chosen and trained in the design principles. They've each received a letter explaining the purpose of the session. The general manager will start the session in the morning by chartering the team."

"Sounds like you're all set," Somers says.

"But I don't see how we're going to come up with a set of action plans that everyone agrees on in a day and a half," Lou says. "These guys are far apart right now."

"We have to bring them together."

Laura says, "We've made a physical-flow layout, a timed activity chart, an organizational interface flowchart, and a quality-potential analysis. We've benchmarked time and quality performance and prepared a customer perception analysis. Marcus said that's all we need to do to prepare for the action planning session."

"Did you get the data from the people who are going to be in the action planning session? It's important that the action planners recognize the data as authentic."

"I think we're all right on that one," Lou says.

"Do you have the feedback and feed-forward information plotted on a quality-potential diagram?" Somers says.

"I have it right here," Laura says, as she hands her a chart.

Quality Potential Diagram
For Aluminum Casting Process

TTD = Time to detect
TTC = Time to correct
TTP = Time to prevent
FTA = First time acceptance
√ = Statistical process control

⟶ Material flow
------▶ Information flow
– – –▶ Correction flow

"Looks good. We'll use this chart in the implementation. Now let's talk about the heat treat," Somers says.

"How many different heat profiles do they use?"

"Six," Lou says.

"How long does the average heat treat take?"

"Sixteen hours."

"How many average castings can they put in one furnace load?"

"Fifty or sixty."

"How many are in a typical lot?"

"Ten to fifteen."

"Then I understand the wait time."

"I'm not sure I understand," Laura says.

"Think of it this way, Laura: Suppose you are a casting a lot of ten parts that has to be heat treated using profile number three of the six profiles. And suppose that to meet the total customer demand, they have to run full furnace loads only, which means you must wait until they have fifty other castings that need the same heat treat profile before they can heat treat your parts. So you'll have to wait a few days."

"I understand," Laura says. "Since there is only one furnace, if they're running sixty castings per furnace load and the heat treat cycle is twenty-four hours, I could wait as long as a week to have my parts heat treated."

Somers nods. "Let's move on to the inspection area. How long does it take to completely inspect a casting if it is run nonstop through the process?"

"I would guess a few hours," Laura says.

"But how long on the average does it take for a casting to move through the whole inspection process?"

"Ten to fifteen days," Laura says.

"And I suppose there's a lot of prioritizing and expediting in this area?"

"They have people doing that full-time," Laura says, reaching for the corn chips.

"Have the two of you come up with a good vision of what can be done?"

"Lou developed a concept of long-range vision that's marvelous," Laura says.

"Very good. But remember, Lou, it has to be their plan. It's important that you can see what is possible but you can't provide them with the answer. We have to start where they are and help them go as far as they can go. Would you show me your vision?"

Lou immediately removes another folder from a leather satchel and enthusiastically reviews the vision concept.

"Excellent," Somers says, after he finishes. He settles back in his chair with a sigh.

"What will happen on Friday and Saturday?" Lou asks.

"We'll spend the first two hours of the action-planning session reviewing all the data you've collected and getting the team to understand the complete process as it's done today," Somers explains. "Have individuals on the team explain to the others that part of the process about which they are most knowledgeable. Encourage everyone to ask tough questions regarding the reasons for wait times, waste activity, defects and errors, and anything else that increases cycle time, defects and errors, and cost.

"Next will come an introduction to the concept of performance gaps — starting with a customer-perception analysis. This will get everyone acquainted with how they fall short of customer expectations. Following that, we'll present the ultimate performance standards for total cycle time, defects and errors, and nonvalue-added activity ratio. These benchmarks compare their Delivery System with the world's best. Finally, we'll encourage them to think of ultimate benchmarks: Can they respond instantly? Can they reduce defects and errors to zero? Can they get valueless activity to zero? These questions raise the team's level of discontent with the existing Delivery System.

"After that, we'll break the group into teams of seven to ten members and give them one hour and fifteen minutes to develop a new, visionary Process Model for the Delivery System that will give ultimate performance. We'll provide them with a basic model to get them started — usually a Core Value-Added Model.

"To use the Core Value-Added Model, you must first identify the few activities that must be performed to produce the added value that will satisfy your customers totally.

"Then the model is constructed by placing the core value-added activity at the center of our Process Model, with the customer and suppliers at the input of the model and the customer at the output." She hands them each a piece of paper from her briefcase.

Core Value-Added Model

"At Garrett," Somers continues, "the ultimate Process Model will go instantly and directly from the customer order to pour, and will provide defect-free materials and information for pouring. After the pour, the ultimate Process Model will deliver totally satisfying output to the customer instantly. So this suggests that you can pose several ultimate challenges to the teams." She asks Lou to write down the challenges as she states them.

Challenge #1. *Nothing should be added to the core Process Model unless it adds value. The challenge is to not add an activity that doesn't contribute value.*

Challenge #2. *Go from customer order to pour in twenty-four hours or in twice the value-added activity time between order and pour, whichever is less.*

Challenge #3. *Go from pour to customer satisfaction in the same time frame.*

Lou has some doubts. "But how do you know that a team will be able to come up with anything close to these goals? And even if they do, will they be able to pull it off?"

"People support what they create," Somers says as Marcus walks up to the table.

"Candace, what's your background?" Lou asks. "How did you decide to get into management?"

"I'd say my father was the biggest influence. He encouraged me to develop my potential."

"Was he an executive at McDonnell-Douglas?"

"No, he was a general superintendent at a steel mill in Indiana."

Lou is so surprised he spills salsa on his tie.

"He died when I was ten. Is something wrong, Lou?" Candace says, concerned by the look on Lou's face.

"Marcus, can I talk to you for a few minutes?" Lou asks, wiping his tie with a wet napkin.

In the men's room, Lou asks, "Marcus, is this Candace . . . *my* Candace?"

Marcus nods. "She's your daughter, Lou."

Lou slumps into a chair and drops his head in his hands. "I knew there was something about her. She was just a kid the last time I saw her. Looks just like her mother, now that I think about it."

"Looks a lot like you," Marcus says.

"She does? You say she's an expert on this stuff?"

"An expert, Lou."

"Will I see her again after tonight?"

"You and your daughter will be facilitating the implementation on Saturday."

Lou smiles and shakes his head. "You son of a gun. You had this planned all along."

Marcus nods smugly. "I always have a plan, Lou.

"Just me and my daughter? What about Laura?"

"I need Laura's help on another job, involving the redesign of an engineering department. Let's get back to the table."

"Thought you guys got lost in the powder room," Candace says, as they return. Laura and I had a nice talk."

"About what?" Lou asks.

"Laura was telling me about her father. Quite a guy."

"Candace, tell us about your father," Marcus says.

"I was just in the sixth grade when he died, and I adored him. Everybody looked up to him. He was always helping people at the mill who had problems."

"Soft on people?" Laura says.

Candace looks thoughtfully at Laura. "Everybody who knew him said he was a tough man; if there was a tough job they gave it to my dad. But he was big-hearted. He used to say that if you take care of people, they'll take care of you."

"It's late, and Laura and I need to run," Marcus says. "We're starting the redesign of an engineering department in Dallas in the morning."

"I guess we'll be seeing a little of you on Saturday," Candace says to Marcus. "Hope I've been some help."

"More than you know," Marcus says.

"Lou, until next Saturday, Candace will be your teacher. She'll give you some reading to do and answer your questions. See you then," Marcus says, as he and Laura leave.

"I'm hungry, how about you?" Candace asks, as they settle in their seats again. "I guess the job's ours."

Lou is staring silently at Candace.

"Something wrong?" she asks.

"No, nothing wrong. I was just thinking."

"What are you thinking?"

"I was thinking it's a lot easier to change when you're young."

"My father used to say that you never grow old if you keep learning and growing in your mind."

"You sure you're okay?" Candace asks. "Nothing's the matter?"

"Nothing," Lou says. "Nothing."

"Lou, I have to go," Candace says, reaching for the check after dinner. "Got a staff meeting at seven in the morning."

He snatches the check. "Marcus said we might get together before Saturday."

"What are you doing Thursday night?"

"Anything you say."

"How about six-thirty P.M., right here?"

"I'll be here."

There is nothing more difficult to take in hand, more perilous to conduct, or more uncertain in its success than to take the lead in the introduction of a new order of things.

– Niccolò Machiavelli, 1469-1527
Florentine statesman and philosopher
Discoveries

Leadership is the capacity to translate vision into reality.

– Warren Bennis, President
University of Cincinnati

CHAPTER TWENTY-EIGHT

A Small Miracle

*I*n the closing minutes of the workshop on Saturday, Marcus became very emotional, saying that all the great changes he had ever seen were the result of a heroic move by some member of management. His closing was like a call to battle. Rich Reynolds took the call to heart.

All day Sunday, the Process Models that Marcus presented rolled around in his mind. Would these apply to the biggest problem area he had — X-ray? Rich managed the entire inspection department at Garrett, including X-ray. The X-ray work group was divided into five specialties: production control, which decided priorities and moved material; "shooters," who set the parts up and inserted them into the X-ray machines; film processors, who loaded the film cassettes for the shooters and processed them after the shooting; readers, who viewed the exposed film for any defects in the castings; and supervisors, who directed the work and solved problems due to bad paperwork or inadequate process instructions. In general, the Process Model started with production control-setting priorities. When a group of parts had sufficient priority, the shooter would X-ray them, the film processor would develop the film, and the reader would read the film. There were always backlogs at each operation.

The Process Intent in the X-ray department had always been to achieve high asset utilization and operational efficiency. But Marcus had convinced Rich that those were the wrong measures to worry about when customers were saying that their response was slow. The new Process Intent should be based on quicker customer response, higher quality, lower costs. With the old Process Intent there was great pressure to X-ray parts even if the X-rays couldn't be developed or read because the X-ray units were a large capital investment. At the reading stations where capital investment was low, the emphasis was on efficiency of the readers. To get efficiency at the read stations the work was stacked ahead of the readers, so the readers did nothing but read X-rays all day long.

The Process Models that occupied Rich's mind that Sunday morning were the instant-service model, the pull model, and the one-mind, one-mission model.

In the workshop, Marcus asked the staff at Garrett how many weeks of customer backlog Domino's Pizza carries. When the staff answered zero weeks, Marcus asked them how many days and how many hours. The answer of course was zero. Marcus then smiled and said, "That's the instant-service model." Although the instant-service model was theoretically appealing, it seemed far-fetched for the x-ray area, considering that their average response to a work order was nine days. But if they could achieve response within hours, the beneficial impact on the entire plant operation would be tremendous. As Sunday passed, Rich became more and more excited. What if he could get everyone in X-ray to buy in?

When Marcus described the push and pull models, it was clear to Rich that they were using a push approach. The jobs were pushed into the X-ray shooters as fast as they came in, and the X-rays stacked up in front of the readers. With a pull system, jobs would not be X-rayed until a few hours before the readers were able to read them. But Marcus said that a pull-system model works best when there is no capacity constraint. If every operation had minimal excess capacity, then the parts could be processed immediately at each operation. Marcus also said that eliminating valueless activity at an operation increases available capacity at that operation to do value-adding work. It was clear that if they could adopt a Process Model that helped reduce valueless activity at the same time that the system cycle time was reduced, they would have a winner. Marcus also said that one of the biggest sources of valueless activity was rework and scrap. Since fifteen percent of their X-rays had to be reshot, redeveloped, and reread, if a new Process Model or a redesign of the Learning and Improvement System would reduce the number of reshoots, there would be excess capacity.

The model that Marcus described as the one-mind, one-mission model seemed like the best model to reduce rework. In the simplest form of this model, one person acts with sole responsibility for the whole mission. In a more complex version of the model, a number of people with sole responsibility for a single mission or multiple missions act as if they are a single mind on a single mission.

Marcus said that the one-mind, one-mission model worked very well in work situations where feedback and feed-forward systems were slow or nonexistent. That was certainly the case in X-ray. When a reader got a bad film, he blamed it on the shooter, who blamed it on the film processor, who, in self-defense, blamed it on the shooters for bad instructions. Over fifteen percent of the X-rays had to be reshot.

When Marcus described the traditional process-center model, which organizes work according to similar processes, Rich could see that that was the way the X-ray department was organized. All parts to be X-rayed were staged in a single area, all X-ray machines were arranged in one area, the film processing was in another area, and the read stations in yet another area. Marcus said that arranging people and machines along the product or service flow, as Honda and Harley-Davidson had done, facilitates faster customer response, lower system cycle time, and improved quality.

In a customer-focused Process Model, machines and people are organized along the flow of the Delivery System. Although Rich could see some advantage to that model, he felt he could achieve significant response as well as quality and productivity improvements by using a simpler form of the model. He envisioned a model in which a single person would handle a complete job from X-ray through read.

It's been a good day, Lou thinks as he walks from the Garrett foundry toward the front office. "Everything is coming together and the data package is nearly complete." Someone calls his name as he passes the reception area. It's Rich Reynolds. "Got a minute?" he says as he approaches Lou. "I need to have you talk with Vince." Lou nods and follows him back into the foundry.

"Vince doesn't buy the idea that we should have the operators do the whole job from X-ray through read. He's convinced it'll hurt efficiency and utilization. Could you explain it to him. Maybe he'll listen to you — you being an old steel man and all."

As they enter the X-ray area, Vince greets Lou with a grateful smile. "Jesus, am I glad to see you," Vince says, rising from behind his desk and taking Lou's hand.

Damn, if only Marcus were here! Lou's not sure he's ready to handle what he thinks might be about to happen. *Better hear him out and think carefully before I say anything.* "What's on your mind, Vince?"

He motions for them to take a seat. "Well, Rich here came away from the workshop last Saturday with some crazy ideas."

Vince has stopped smiling and he begins, warily, "He thinks we ought to have the operators learn all the jobs, and then do all the value-added activities all the way through from X-ray to film development and read."

"And what would that mean for you?"

"Are you kidding? It'll kill my efficiencies. And you know damn well I get measured on equipment utilization."

"I've been trying to explain to him," Rich says, impatiently, "that utilization and efficiency will be just as good with the new system."

Lou decides that the best way to handle this situation is to try to think of what Marcus would do. He'd remain calm, that's for sure; and he'd ask questions. "Vince, why do you think your utilizations will go down?"

"To get the utilization we have today, I have to keep people on the X-ray machine all the time."

"But utilization *can't* be any higher than demand," Rich says, emphatically. "Marcus explained that in the workshop."

"Marcus doesn't have to meet my utilization figures each month!" He turns sharply to face Lou. "I thought you understood; I thought you were one of us—"

"Vince, I — "

"Do you know how much these X-ray machines cost? Long after you're gone, those boys in corporate will be on my back, making me explain why my utilization and efficiency figures are low."

"But what if — "

"You think you can come in here, try this, try that, change everything around. I'll tell you what: You're playing with people's jobs — that's what you're doing!"

"Dammit, Vince!" Rich shouts, "Don't you understand that if we don't make these kinds of changes nobody's gonna have a job? There isn't going to be a company if we don't do this!"

"Look," Lou says, "what if we could find a way to keep your utilization the same as it is now while we're increasing your efficiencies?"

Vince's face is twisted with cynicism. After a long, uncomfortable silence, he stands. He's a huge man, and he towers over them. "Why the hell are we focusing on the X-ray department anyway? Why not start with the real problem — bad castings? If you can't make a good product, don't blame it on inspection." His face is flushed with anger.

"Don't be so defensive, Vince. Relax," Rich says.

Vince slams his fist on the table. "This is bullshit! Focus on inspection? The problem's in manufacturing!"

This guy is a heart attack waiting to happen. Lou wonders if he behaved the way Vince is behaving now. Probably. Only Lou guesses that he was worse. How can he let Vince know that they're not attacking him? "We're not focusing on inspection," Lou says calmly. "I'm only here to help, and I promise you I won't do anything to hurt your efficiency or your utilization. I agree with you. You wouldn't need so much inspection if quality was improved."

"So why not start with manufacturing?" Vince asks. He exhales sharply and sweeps his sleeve against his sweaty brow.

Rich stands. "We are," he says, "and that's where the majority of the effort is being concentrated. But like Marcus says, we have to consider the whole system."

Vince shakes his head and walks to the door. "Look," he says, pointing his finger at Lou, "when you get manufacturing straightened out, come back and talk to me." He walks out the door.

Lou catches up with him just before he reaches the lobby, and together, they walk out into the warm, dry air.

"Can I buy you a beer?" Lou asks.

Vince shakes his head. "Promised my wife I'd be home a half hour ago."

"Long drive?"

"About forty minutes . . . Lou, I don't have anything against you . . . "

"Hey, believe me. I understand. When I was a plant manager, if somebody had suggested to me the changes that Marcus is suggesting to you guys, I'd have thrown his butt out of my office. I know this is a lot to take in at one time. I've been around Marcus for a while now, and I'm just beginning to understand what the hell he's talking about."

Vince stops beside his van. "Rich is a good guy. And he's a good boss. But I think he's gone off the deep end since that workshop with Marcus."

"Rich wants very badly to see Garrett turn around, and he wants to do everything he can to make it happen. Can't blame him for that, can you?"

"I'm not against progress. I just don't like it shoved down my throat . . . I must have looked a little bit like an asshole in there."

"You were just standing up for what you believe in. When I was managing a plant, my boss called in some people to help. And you know what? I gave them such a hard time that they never came back. I wish now that I would have listened. Maybe we could have saved the place."

"Belly up?"

Lou nods. "Beautiful sunset."

"Sure," Vince says, vaguely. "Well, see you tomorrow . . . and thanks."

"Hey, Vince!"

He rolls down the window. "What?"

"So how about you give it a try?" Vince's face is a mask of uncertainty.

"Tell you what . . . I'll think about it."

Lou nods, smiling, as Vince pulls out of the parking space. The setting sun hangs just above the roof of the van, and Lou continues to gaze at the glowing orb.

For years the glow of the open hearth was his sunrise and sunset. Continental . . . Lou remembers standing in the corner of the conference room years ago. Three men in suits are seated at the table. "We've been running the mill this way for twenty years," Lou hears himself saying, "and we've done pretty well. You come in here and tell me what other steel companies have done, and I'm not against change, but this doesn't make any sense."

"Lou," one man says, "would you just give it a try?"

On Tuesday morning, Vince did decide to talk to all the operators about reorganzing the inspection area. Not all of them were thrilled about being responsible for the whole job, but a majority agreed to try it.

Those who agreed were cross-trained on all of the jobs and then assigned to carry out the process from start to finish. They loaded their own film, X-rayed the castings, developed the film, analyzed the developed radiographs, and wrote the reports. In case of error, a correction would be made on the very next run, all within one hour. The figure below shows the feedback (solid lines) and feed-forward (dashed semicircles). In the system before the redesign, feedback took place many days later and was given by the supervisor, if at all. The feed-forward was intended to fix blame rather than correct. In the new, simplified short-time system, learning and improvement take place in short, closed loops.

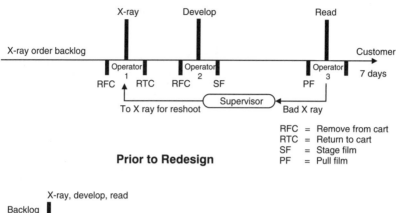

Prior to Redesign

RFC = Remove from cart
RTC = Return to cart
SF = Stage film
PF = Pull film

After Redesign

The results surprised even Vince. In six weeks the output rose from an average of eight jobs per day with ten people to twelve and a half jobs per day with eight people, which equates to a productivity increase of ninety-five percent. The average system cycle time was reduced from six or seven days to three hours. Customer backlogs dropped to less than one hour. Vince referred to the new system as Domino's X-ray, and the number of reshoots dropped drastically. When he and Rich compared the original and final processes, they were able to make up the following chart to show to Wil Danesi.

As Vince described it to Wil Danesi, before they redesigned the system, a shooter who made a mistake in setting up the parts to be X-rayed would typically not have to reshoot that lot because it would likely come back to another X-ray shooter. In the new system, if the films are not good, the shooter has to go right back and re-shoot. This is further incentive to get it right the first time.

Comparing the Two Systems

Cycle time	6-7 days	3 hours
Defective X-ray rate	15%	.5% 30:1 improvement
Productivity	.8	1.56 95% improvement

Feedback		Prior	After
• Time to detect for manufacturing		7 days	4 hours
• Time to detect for X ray & develop		2-3 days	1 hour
• Quality of feedback information		poor	good
• Number of people required to communicate feedback		many	1
Feed-forward			
• Time to correct for X ray		1 wk→∞	hours
• Quality of correction process		poor	excellent
• Incentive to correct		low	high
• Number of people to correct		many	1
• Chance of recurrence		high	low

For Wil Danesi, it was the needed breakthrough. Here was a success of significant proportions that could be used as a example for changing the staff's minds. Further, it substantiated his assertions that the new approaches were the answer. If throughput and quality could be increased in the other inspection areas as much as it had increased in X-ray, the division would be on its way. His hopes increased for the implementation that Lou, Candace, and Alan would be conducting the following weekend. If they could just do the same for the remainder of the aluminum casting Delivery System, the transformation would be on its way.

CHAPTER TWENTY-NINE

Test Before the Lesson

The improvement they've made in the X-ray area is tremendous," Lou says to Alan Updike as he lumbers into Alan's office Wednesday morning. "That should convince the doubters on the staff."

"But we still have some who feel that the changes will hurt efficiency and capital utilization," Alan says. "Wil is pushing, but a lot of managers are dragging their feet. That's why the action planning session on Friday is crucial. If the results are good the momentum will grow. If not, the opposition will come out on top. It's a critical point in the transformation."

"I wonder if we should have started with something safer," Lou says, "where failure would not be a serious setback. If we try to take on the whole process, there'll be serious financial repercussions if we don't make it work."

"That's the way Marcus operates," Alan says. "He believes the bigger the venture, the bigger the gain. And besides, we don't have time to mess around with small, safe pilots. We have to show divisional-level results fast or we're dead. Did you finish the time chart of the process flow?" he says.

Lou nods vigorously.

"Do you think we have all the information we need for the implementation tomorrow?"

"I'd say so. I've seen Marcus do at least ten of these at our Kansas City division. If you do it like Marcus does, we have enough information. How many times have you conducted one of these sessions?"

"Never have, but Candace Somers from McDonnell-Douglas will be leading the session, and she's an expert."

Lou can tell by the look on Alan's face that he's worried. "Have you seen her work?" he asks.

"No, but I've met her, and I'm sure she can handle it. Last night we planned tomorrow's session in a lot of detail. She asked to walk through the process tomorrow morning before the session. Can you walk her through?"

"Sure," Alan says tentatively. "I hope she knows what she's doing."

When she was a child, Lou worried about her walking to school by herself . . . and now, it's as if she's leading him on a mountain climbing expedition. Hell, he's not worried about if she can handle it. It's himself he's worried about.

He has trouble getting to sleep that night. He paces his hotel room, nervous about the level of responsibility — people's jobs, their lives — resting on his shoulders. When he finally falls asleep, it seems only a minute later that he hears the alarm blaring. He panics, certain that he's overslept. But it's only 5:30. By 6:00 he has showered, dressed, and is on his way to meet Candace and Alan at the foundry. His mind races all the way there.

Candace asks a barrage of questions as Alan walks her through the factory. Later in the conference room Candace is clearly in charge. "We need to get the data charts taped high on the walls. Can you start by taping this one over here?" she asks. Lou nods and starts to answer, but Candace continues. "And Lou, can you make the name tags? And when you get that done, we need to find four more chairs."

"Yes Sir!" Lou says, with mock respect. He sees the humor in the situation: ordered around by his own daughter! Marcus is probably having a good laugh over this.

The staff starts filing in about 10:15 A.M., and by 10:55 everyone has coffee and is seated. One of the early arrivals has been watching Candace direct Lou and is clearly amused. "Candace, how's your assistant working out. Can he take direction?" the man asks, laughing.

"Hard to get good help nowadays," Candace says, turning and giving the man a mischievous smile.

"And sometimes good help isn't appreciated," Lou says, with a grin.

An air of anticipation sweeps the room as the clock reaches eleven. Wil Danesi rises and walks to the front of the room. There is an abrupt silence.

"We have a great opportunity here," Wil says, pausing to look at everyone purposefully. "We simply can't expect to stay in business if we keep doing things the way we always have. I'm not saying there haven't been a lot of improvements in recent months, but we need major overhauls of our Delivery Systems. I hope that this group will do some spectacular things for the whole foundry.

"You are not here today to make recommendations. I expect this team to analyze, dissect, challenge, and reach, to come up with action plans which all of you can agree to implement. We need action, and we need it now!

"Let me spell out what I think we need out of the aluminum processing area. Marcus calls this the Process Intent. The cycle time in that area is now over fifty days. We need to cut it to less than ten days to set a new industry standard for customer response. To cut costs we need to dramatically cut rework and scrap. We need to make it right the first time."

Wil points to Candace and Lou, then introduces them. "I understand that Candace will be our main facilitator today. Lou will assist her. Candace, it's all yours."

Just as Wil begins to walk away, Candace turns to Lou and whispers, "Show time, Lou." A smile bursts on Lou's face and a chill runs up his spine as he watches his little girl move to center stage and take charge.

"Good morning! We don't have a lot of time so let's get right to it." She walks to the first chart hanging on the wall and points to an area adjacent to the breakout table.

"After the gates are removed at the sawing operation, the castings are lifted from the saw table and placed on a cart, right here," Candace says, pointing to a triangle on a layout of the foundry where the castings are temporarily stored after sawing. "When the cart is full it is moved down to the grinders where it sits, waiting. Why don't the castings go immediately from saw to grind?"

"A grinder or a grinding machine may not be available immediately after saw," someone answers.

"Takes a lot longer to grind than to saw," someone else says.

"This morning I saw only two grinding machines operating, but there were three or four machines sitting idle. Is that typical?" Candace asks. A few heads nod.

"Let's move on. After grind the castings are again placed on carts, and when the carts are loaded they are pushed into another building where they sit waiting to be hand finished."

As Candace leads them through the analysis of the data, Lou is dazzled. He wonders how she gets away with asking such penetrating questions. *If I asked those questions, they'd throw me out of here.* At 11:50 she stops the questioning. She silently paces, then stops and faces the group. "It's your turn," she says to them. "Now you need to ask the tough questions of yourselves. If this is going to work you have to get into the act. You have to question your current way of doing things or you're not going to come up with ultimate performance."

"I have a question," Rich Reynolds says. "Why doesn't the penetrant inspection operator who finds a defect, regrind it immediately and retest it?

"Great question, Rich," Candace says. "That's the kind of question you need to ask. Can someone answer Rich's question?" With that a floodgate of questions opens and for the next hour and a half there is no letup. As Candace encourages them, they rip apart their own process.

"Lou, when we break into individual teams, I want you to facilitate the red team. I wrote a short set of instructions for you," Candace says, as she hands him a 3 x 5 card.

Role of the Facilitator

- *Keep the team on track toward meeting its goal.*
- *Do not contribute any personal ideas. Focus on the process of helping the team meet the goal.*
- *Encourage everyone to participate. Manage the vocal few so that everyone's ideas are heard.*
- *Draw ideas out of people.*
- *Work to get team consensus; that is, everyone on the team "owns" the action or is willing to support it even though it may not be exactly the way each would do it.*

- *Record the team's results for presentation to the entire group.*
- *Remember, it must be 100 percent their ideas.*
- *See that a spokesman, other than yourself, is chosen to present the team action plans.*

"Do you have any questions?" Candace asks.

"Gonna be tough to hold my ideas back."

"Lou, my dad used to say that the three toughest things in the world to do are jump a fence that's leaning towards you, kiss a girl that's leaning away from you, and help someone who doesn't want help. They won't support your ideas, Lou, but they'll support their own. So bring the group members to agreement before you write one of their ideas on the chart."

"I don't know about this, Candace. I'm not prepared."

"'Life often gives the test before the lesson,'" she says.

Lord it's tough to hear my own words of wisdom.

"You can do it," she says, patting Lou on the back. "Refer to your facilitation instructions every fifteen minutes and grade yourself."

"Grade myself." He laughs. "You're something else!" His little girl has the tenacity of a drill instructor. But she knows how to be tough and charming at the same time . . . as if she can make him appreciate being ordered around. He smiles and shakes his head.

He catches himself a dozen times during the first action-planning session. For the first time he realizes how he tends to dominate others with his ideas and decisions.

"How did you do?" Candace asks Lou, as they come back to the conference room.

"Okay. I think we've come up with a great Process Model."

"Without your ideas?" She asks, smiling.

"I slipped a few times and injected an idea or two. It scared me when they immediately accepted my ideas."

"Only a few slips — that's good for a first time. You'll get better as you go. Do you think the team's Process Model is as good as the one you developed on your own?"

"Better!"

"Well, I'm sure the blue team came up with the best Process Model," she says, winking.

Lou pulls his head and shoulders back squarely. "We'll see about that."

As each team presents its Process Model, Lou is amazed. The two Process Models are almost identical. Within an hour Candace has them agreeing on a common Process Model that incorporates the best ideas of both teams.

She takes charge again. "Tomorrow morning, I'd like each team to detail the Process Model and write the action plans. Think about it tonight and we'll see you in the morning," she says, as they file out of the conference room.

As they leave the foundry, Lou invites Candace to dinner. "I have plans tonight, Lou, but you can come along. I have an extra ticket."

"For the Lakers game?"

"It's Christmas time, Lou. *The Nutcracker* — a ballet. You'll love it."

"You're kidding," Lou says, laughing.

As the ballet approaches the finale, dancers dressed like blossoms begin the "Waltz of the Flowers." They leap and weave to the music as a petite ballerina, Dewdrop, flits among them. The Sugar Plum Fairy dances with her cavalier, and all the inhabitants of the Kingdom of Sweets dance a waltz. Finally the music fades to a lullaby as Marie and the Nutcracker Prince are borne into the sky in a sleigh.

"That's synchronous, Lou," Candace says, as they leave the theater. "Not push, not pull, but synchronous."

"Synchronous?" Lou says.

"Everyone was synchronized to the music, just the way a Delivery System should be."

"Is that possible?" Lou asks.

"It's a great goal and it is possible," she says. "The first step is to get all system cycle times as low as possible."

As Candace drops Lou at his hotel, he says. "Why the overnight break? Wouldn't it be better to start and finish in one day?"

"Incubation time, Lou. They'll have some great ideas by morning."

By 9:30 the following morning, the teams have their action plans, and they reassemble in the conference room. After they settle down, Candace first asks the blue team to present its action items.

Rich Reynolds is spokesman for the blue team. "We're going to make it one continuous process from saw through weld in a single area, arrange the machines in a U-shape, and design a continuous flow through that part of the process. Here's our proposed layout for the casting finish cell."

"They stole our idea but we have a better layout," Frank Doran says.

"No way," Rich Reynolds says, grinning.

"Let's compare the two layouts," Candace says. Thirty minutes later she has both teams agreeing on a single layout.

"Let's go to the red team for an action item," she says.

Frank Doran stands and points to an action item on the red team chart.

Wil Danesi reviews and approves the action plan. Candace stands in front of the group and asks Lou to come forward.

"First, let me congratulate all of you! The Process Model you developed is a powerful one. The actions which you have committed to are aggressive," she says. She pauses and intently scans the room. "The next thirty days are critical, because what you do in that time will determine your success."

She continues to explain that the completion of the action plans should both reassure them that transformation is possible and give them confidence that they can implement the necessary changes. "The improved results you get will spur you to redesign other Delivery Systems in your business. Dedicate yourselves to this effort so that you won't just go back to work on Monday morning and revert to putting out fires and patching up problems. Spend the time and effort to complete the actions and there will be smaller fires and fewer problems. Thanks for inviting me and I wish you success."

She turns to Lou. "Lou, would you like to say something?" Lou isn't prepared, and he falters for a few moments before he finds the words: "I'm proud to be a part of this — and I'm relieved. How about a hand for our workshop leader. Isn't she great?"

As the applause dies, Candace says, "How about a hand for the man who had the leadership to begin the transformation?" She points to Wil Danesi. Wil stands and over the applause he says, "Give yourselves a hand. I started it, but you've made the commitment to make it work. Anybody who needs my help with their action items — you've got it. Now let's get out of here and rest tomorrow before the big push on Monday."

CHAPTER THIRTY

The Greatest Cost of All

*T*he old man is stooped from years of working at a bench. His coveralls are faded and worn and his safety shoes are comically large. A kind, wrinkled face surrounds sad eyes — eyes that have seen better times. As Lou seats himself at the other end of the breakfast counter, the old man rises, walks over, and sits down next to him.

"Give the man a coffee, on me," the old man says.

"Thanks," Lou says.

"Gonna be a nice weekend for fishing. Do you fish, Lou?"

"Used to, but got so busy in my last years. How do you know my name?"

"Heard some people talking about you. Said you're doing some work over at Garrett. God doesn't deduct the time spent fishing from a man's life," he says, winking.

"Maybe I should have done more fishing. I didn't catch your name?"

"Just call me Joe. Never too late. You look like you could use a break. I've been watching you. You're pushing it all the time, and you worry too much."

"Yeah, I do. There's a big load on me, right now."

"You're okay, Lou. You're my kind of people — hot metal man."

"Thanks. Steel and metalworking's been my life."

"Where did you work steel?"

"Midwest, mostly Indiana."

"Any good fishing out there?"

"Crappie, some smallmouth."

"Mean to travel back there sometime."

"Joe, what kind of work do you do?"

"I'm recently retired — just in time too. It's changed, Lou. Things are different now. Came out here in the fifties, everybody was expanding then, more and more business all the time. With the layoffs in the last few months and the turmoil . . . well, I was getting tired. It wasn't much fun going to work anymore." The old man stares off into the distance as the conversation slows. He has a faraway look, as if he's caught up in another time and place.

Across the aisle the waitress is taking an order, and Lou is deep in his own thoughts. It's hard to believe that two months have passed since he and Candace did the final processing project. The teams they put together not only came up with great action plans, but they implemented them. In the first sixty days, manufacturing cycle time dropped from over fifty days to nineteen days, and it's still dropping. Quality's also improving due to the better feedback and feed-forward designs, and productivity's up over fifteen percent. The big surprise came on Monday when Marcus promoted him and Laura to Journeyman Guardians. Now they just have to discover the Non-Linear Solution. He wonders if Laura's already got it figured out. He also wonders if Marcus is really serious about sending him to work in Japan. He doesn't know if he'll be able to handle that.

"Things really started changing when Danesi took over at Garrett, didn't they," Joe says, interrupting Lou's thoughts. "Some of the things they're doing now they should have done years ago and they wouldn't be in this trouble," Joe says.

"Like what?" Lou says.

"Well, I hear that a couple of weeks ago Wil started these meetings with people, encouraging everybody to openly discuss problems they were having. A lot of the ideas people had in these meetings were old ideas, but this time management listened. Sure has impressed the people in the plant. But they need to do something cause the guys are beginning to pull back."

"Why are they pulling back, Joe?"

"They come in here and talk about it. Some are saying that they can't win. If they don't improve, they lose the business — if they improve, they cut jobs. Danesi says that they've got to be competitive to keep their jobs, but not everybody's listening. They feel like they're damned if they do and damned if they don't."

"How do you feel about it, Joe?"

"My background's different from most of these guys in the shop. My dad had a business and I worked in the business when I was young. Today I think a lot about what he said then. He'd say, 'Joe, the biggest cost of business is not the cost of materials, or labor, or overhead.'"

"What did he mean by that?"

"He meant there is a cost much greater than the costs of people, services, material, tools, equipment, capital, and facilities."

"Like the cost of poor quality, long cycle times and suboptimal designs?"

"Much greater than those," Joe says.

"I give up," Lou says.

Joe stands up, looks down at Lou and says, "The cost of lost opportunity."

"Lost opportunity? You mean like grabbing the brass ring?"

"There are two parts to lost opportunity, Lou. The first part is that new opportunities are constantly developing and you gotta take advantage of them. The second part is that the

> **Greatest Cost of All**
>
> The Cost of Lost Opportunity
> - loss of existing customers
> - lost share, sales, and profits
> - missed market potential
> - lost jobs and lost technology

business you already have has gotta be constantly renewed. A business that's not prepared for new opportunities, that's not creating new ones, or at least renewing its present business, is dying. When Danesi took over the business, they were dying."

"How did it get to be in such bad shape?" Lou asks, not believing he's hearing this from a machinist.

"For many years I saw it coming. They were operating cost plus and there was plenty of business."

"Cost plus?"

"Whatever the costs were, they added a profit and that's what the customer paid. But then the competition came with their higher productivity and quality, and the customers were demanding more from them. Garrett's sister divisions, who had always bought from them, started to buy from outside foundries as soon as the cost pressures hit them. That's when the foundry started losing business, losing money, and losing jobs. They were dying because they weren't developing new products fast enough, they weren't responding fast enough to customers, and their price was high.

"Joe, I think the shop got that message for a while, and they've made some big progress, but they aren't the best in the business yet."

"Maybe they believe they've done enough already," Joe says, fiddling with a pocket watch.

"But they haven't! And if they don't believe that, they're in trouble. What is it going to take to get them to understand?"

Joe stands and places his hand on Lou's shoulder. "Son," he says, "I'd like you to have this watch."

"I can't accept this," Lou says, looking at the gold watch. "It's an antique." There's no answer. He looks up but Joe's gone. Even his coffee mug is gone. But he's left money on the counter to cover the bill.

Lou signals the manager. "That guy I was talking to? Do you know him?"

The manager shakes his head. "I didn't see anybody with you."

"Small man about sixty-five, gray hair, kind of stooped over, says he hangs out here — wears a red carnation?"

"No one here like that."

Bewildered, Lou slowly stands and heads for the Garrett complex. Why in the world would the guy give him an antique gold watch. It nags at him. He digs it out of his pocket and holds it in his palm. The sun glints off its surface. Turning it over, he sees an inscription etched on the back:

....

When the student is ready the teacher will appear.

....

Lou recognizes it as an expression Marcus has used. Marcus . . . probably up to one of his tricks. But Lou wonders: Is he the student? Or the people in the foundry? And who's the teacher? And why is Marcus so obsessed with talking about businesses as being involved in a war? One thing is certain: The cost of lost opportunity could put Garrett out of business. He wishes Laura were around. He'd really like to talk to her now.

Jonathan Seagull spent the rest of his days alone, but he flew way out beyond the Far Cliffs. His one sorrow was not solitude, it was that the other gulls refused to believe the glory of flight that awaited them; they refused to open their eyes and see.

He learned more each day. He learned that a stream-lined high speed dive could bring him to find the rare and tasty fish that schooled ten feet below the surface of the ocean; he no longer needed fishing boats and stale bread for survival. He learned to sleep in the air, setting a course at night across the offshore wind, covering a hundred miles from sunset to sunrise. With the same new control, he flew through heavy sea fogs and climbed above them into dazzling clear skies . . . in the very times when every other gull stood on the ground, knowing nothing but mist and rain.

– Richard Bach
Jonathan Livingston Seagull

CHAPTER THIRTY-ONE

Hitting the Wall

S eppuku mono da!"

Lou turns to face his supervisor. *"Domo sumimasen,"* Lou says. Different than the POW camp, he thinks. If he had screwed up then, he would have been dead. This is the second time he's made the error of letting down the team. And it's the second time he's had to apologize. If someone had told him during his days in Bataan that he'd some day willingly humble himself before a Japanese man, Lou would have said, "Never!" But he has a mission now, far too important to let those old, complicated feelings stand in his way.

He reaches for the next engine block. He checks the seating of the front bolts and installs two alternator brackets. He's learned a lot in the past few months and can't believe it's his last day. He's actually going to miss this place. Never in a million years would he have believed that he'd ever have a Japanese friend like Jiro. Lou is to meet him at the Sakura at seven tonight.

"*Komban wa,*" Jiro says, as he approaches Lou at the Sakura. Jiro smiles, his angular features appearing to be chiseled from a golden stone.

"*Genkidesu ka,*" Lou says, reaching out to shake Jiro's hand.

"Look behind you," Jiro says. Lou turns just in time to greet three more fellow workers as they approach his table. "They came to wish you *sayonara.*"

"You came to see me?" Lou says, incredulously. Touched by the show of affection, his mind drifts back to the Steel Inn and the Friday night get togethers. What would Ken think, Lou wonders, about his new friends? Or about his even beginning to like raw fish?

"Most of us have to catch the eleven o'clock train," Jiro says later, as he stands.

"We will miss you, Lou," Jiro says for the group, as he holds his glass in a toast. "To Lou, our very good friend from America."

"Any time you visit the U.S., look me up," Lou says, as he shakes each of their hands.

"I will," Jiro says. "*Sayonara.*"

"*Sayonara,*" Lou says.

As Laura closes the door of her hotel room she sees the light blinking on the phone. She decides that she'll find out who called and then return the call after she rests a while.

"A man named Lou called at 4:00 P.M. He left his number," the operator says. "He says it's urgent."

The operator at Lou's hotel informs Laura that Lou is gone but that he left a message for her. He asked if she could meet him at 6:30 in the restaurant at her hotel.

As she changes clothes, she realizes that she hasn't seen Lou in over five months. She also realizes that she has missed him. For all the tension between them, she has become quite fond of him. Yes, at times he's unbearable, and God knows he's sometimes stuck in his ways, but they do have their good moments; like the little game about who opens the door for whom. And when she grabs the check after dinner, he always raises a huge fuss. Or he loves it when she asks for the check but the waitress automatically gives it to him. And he adores his daughter so. He has many endearing qualities. And besides, they complement each other on the plant floor. Looks like they're becoming a team after all.

"We need to talk," he says urgently, even before he's seated.

"Lou, my mother would say you look like the wrath of God. How was Japan?"

"I feel like the wrath of God. You won't believe what's happened."

"In Japan?"

"No, I'll tell you all about Japan later. I mean after I got back."

"The implementation failed," she guesses.

"No, it went great. I was at Garrett yesterday. The team figured out how to drop the total process time from fifty days to five days. I brought comparison flowcharts," he says, handing a sheet of paper to Laura.

"In the new redesign process, the same person who does the penetrant check also grinds castings immediately to eliminate flaws. This shortens the feedback loop from a few weeks to

**Aluminum Casting Physical Flow
(after redesign)**

△ 37 Storage areas
- -► 57 Material moves

While parts are queued on conveyor for batching into heat treat, they are sample x-rayed and penetrant checked for feedback.

less than an hour. Problems are now corrected immediately as they're detected. The percentage of castings that are good the first time is rising fast.

"The front part of the process, from breakout to finished casting is improved by ten to one in process time, and productivity has improved by over twenty percent. No prioritizing or expediting is needed in the process now. Work moves through the process on a first-in-first-out basis."

"That's great. So then what's the urgency."

"You won't believe it," Lou says, shaking his head. "Right after I left for Japan they had to lay off some people. And after the team came up with all those good ideas and put them into effect."

"But not due to the work you did, I'm sure."

"No it wasn't due to what we did. The effects of the recession are finally hitting Garrett. After all that work they did, they're still not going to make it into the black. I can't believe it. What timing."

"You should have expected it then, with the recession going on."

"I know, I know. But it's still bad news. I think we're dead in the water."

"You mean our Guardianships? Have you talked to Marcus about it?"

"No, I'm not worried about the Guardianships; I'm worried that people will think it's not worth trying to improve if they're going to get laid off anyway. When I talked to Marcus about it, he gave me one of those 'it all comes with the territory' speeches."

"Hey Lou, I'm sure this isn't your first layoff."

"I've had to lay off people when our steel sales dropped, and I was laid off myself a couple of times when I first started. But this is different."

"How's that?" she says. The waiter brings a club soda for Lou. "I'll have one of those, please," she says.

"I don't know why, but this one shook me," Lou says. "Maybe I feel responsible for the people's jobs."

Laura is somewhat astonished. She's never expected him to open up to her like this. "You need to worry about the success of the project first," she says.

Lou looks at her incredulously. "Do you have ice water in your veins?" he asks. "I can't believe you don't care — "

"Wait just a minute, Lou. I never said I didn't care about people."

"You're right," Lou says, rubbing his chin. "Sorry."

She suggests that he start over.

"Okay. Let me put it this way: My first project is going down the tubes, and I feel helpless to stop it. With the defense budget shrinking, a lot of people feel that maybe the recession in the defense business is permanent . . . the airlines have delayed orders . . . I don't know why I wanted to see you. There's nothing you can do." He hangs his head and rolls the sweating glass between his palms.

"Wait a minute, Lou. Is it really that bad? Let's assess the situation. Haven't they made big progress?"

"Couldn't be better. That's what upsets me. They've all busted their butts to make it all work and now this."

"Why can't you be satisfied with the end result. Garrett is turning around. They're going to make it and you did a good job, Lou."

"Yeah, that's the frustrating part. I feel like the marathon runner about to win the race, when he reaches the last hill and finds he's out of gas. They call it 'hitting the wall.'" Lou tells Laura about the old man, Joe, who first got him thinking about the cost of losing the whole foundry. He also shows her the watch, and although the inscription is as inscrutable to her as it was to Lou, they both agree that Marcus must be up to something.

Lou takes a long drink and sighs heavily. "Geez, it must sound like I'm whining," he says. "Let's get something done here. We've got this Non-Linear Solution thing to work out. Do you have any idea what it is?"

Laura reaches for her brief bag and removes some notes. "I've kept a list of the main things Marcus says when he refers to it," she says, handing him a sheet of paper.

General Attributes of Companies That Have Discovered the Non-Linear Solution

- *They go further than defending the markets they wish to keep — they attack competitors in their markets when and where they choose.*
- *They respond faster, provide more quality for the price, and offer more value for the price than competitors.*
- *They are flexible. They anticipate and drive linear and non-linear change.*
- *They are dedicated to transforming themselves.*

Specific Initiatives of Companies That Have Discovered the Non-Linear Solution

- *They have measures in place that provide a high awareness of the early vital signs.*
- *They continuously identify performance gaps using all four performance improvement measures:*
  - *comparison to past performance*
  - *comparison of customers' expectations of performance to their perceptions of performance*
  - *comparison of their performance to the world's best performance (competitive benchmarking)*
  - *comparison of performance to the ultimate possible performance*

- *They strive for ultimate possible performance.*
- *They search continuously for knowledge that will improve their competitiveness.*
- *They continuously revise their mindsets, mental models, and measures to remain the Hunter in the marketplace.*

- *They continuously drive non-linear redesign of their Delivery Systems to be the most competitive in the marketplace.*
- *They have a continuous improvement process which requires that everyone be dedicated to learning and improving themselves, and the business, to the greatest extent possible.*

....

"You've really done your homework," Lou says.

"Thanks," Laura smiles.

"But how do you say that in twenty-five words or less?" Lou asks.

"That's a problem. Do you think Marcus is serious about the twenty-five words or less?"

"He seemed serious to me. I was wondering if it wasn't something simple like a decision to transform the business to a Hunter."

Laura cups her hand in front of her mouth. There's a long silence . . .

"What are you thinking?" Lou asks.

"I think you have something there. Let's build on that," she says, as she writes on a note pad.

....

Proposed Non-Linear Solution

The decision to transform your business into one that is characteristic of a Hunter.

....

"Let's analyze for completeness by comparing with the list I generated. She places her sheet of attributes and initiatives below Lou's proposed Non-Linear Solution. "By using the word Hunter you cover all of my general attributes. That's impressive. Let's look at specific initiatives. What do you think, Lou?"

"Now that I think about it, the word 'decision' is weak. Marcus is always saying that it takes more than a decision; it takes commitment and action."

Laura smiles. "It also takes wisdom. I love puzzles," she says, as she writes.

....

Proposed Non-Linear Solution

The wisdom, commitment, and action to transform the business into one that is characteristic of a Hunter.

....

"There's still something missing," Laura says. "I think we have to examine the word 'non-linear' that Marcus keeps using. Scientifically, 'linear' means that there's a simple relationship between independent and dependent variables. For example, if the number of egg-laying chickens doubled, you would expect egg production to double. If the relationship between egg-laying chickens and egg production were non-linear, you might triple or quadruple egg production by doubling the number of egg-laying chickens."

"I think it goes further than that," Lou says. "I think Marcus is saying that you can keep the number of chickens the same and still double egg production."

"Right." Laura laughs. "He's saying that the rate of improvement in a business can be dramatically improved."

Lou laughs. "Marcus would ask the chickens for sunnyside up."

"Yes, he would," Laura says, with a smile. "Let's look at what we have."

Proposed Non-Linear Solution

The wisdom, commitment, and action to transform a business into one that is characteristic of a Hunter through linear and non-linear learning and improvement.

"I added the part about learning, because Marcus says that improvement usually follows learning," Laura says. "Let's test it. Is there anything Marcus said when he mentioned the Non-Linear Solution that we left out?"

"I can't think of anything."

"I can," Laura says as she writes again on the note pad.

Proposed Non-Linear Solution

The wisdom, commitment, and action to be the Hunter, to transform our systems through the use of both linear and non-linear means, and to dramatically increase the system's rate and quality of learning and improvement.

"I'll go with that," Lou says, "except that 'transform' is redundant with linear and non-linear and we have too many words."

Laura smiles broadly. "I agree. Another try."

Proposed Non-Linear Solution

The wisdom, commitment, and action to be the Hunter; to transform our systems so that their rate and quality of learning and improvement is maximized.

"Looks good," he says. "Twenty-five words."

"Then let's test it on Marcus when we see him next."

"Don't you see him regularly?"

"No, I haven't seen him in two weeks."

Lou shakes his head. "He just throws us in and expects us to swim." He's silent for several moments before he turns to look at Laura directly. "I don't know how to thank you," he says, putting his arm around her shoulder.

"For what?"

"For helping me see the big picture."

Laura reaches toward her shoulder and gives Lou's hand a squeeze. "Any time," she says. Then she kisses his cheek, and immediately he feels the blood rushing to his face.

"Gotta get back," Lou says. "Gonna give 'em hell in the morning. Got an urgent call from Wil's secretary that he wanted me to be in his office at seven."

"Have you decided what you're going to do?"

"No, but I've decided what I'm not going to do."

"What's that?"

"Let it beat me! I'm a Hunter."

"Right on. I'll be finished here in the morning. If you'd like, I can come out to help."

"Sounds like a good idea," he says, as he lays a twenty on the table and rises to leave.

"I'm buying," she says, handing the twenty back to Lou.

"Not tonight. From here on let's alternate. You get the next one."

"That's a deal. See you tomorrow afternoon on the floor. I'll find you. Will you tell me about Japan?"

"Sure will. There's lots to tell." He walks to the door, hesitates, then comes back. "You look very beautiful in that dress, by the way."

"Didn't think you noticed."

"Hey, I'm dead, but I'm not *dead*," Lou says, as he walks away.

There is an old and popular idea that we learn only what we are rewarded for. Some psychologists have claimed that human learning is based entirely on "reinforcement" by reward: that even when we train ourselves with no external inducements, we are still learning from reward — only now in the form of signals from inside ourselves. When we try to use this idea to explain how people learn to solve hard problems, we encounter a deadly circularity. You must be able to do something before you can be rewarded for doing it!

Few animal experiments of Pavlov or Skinner have shed much light on how humans learn to form and carry out their complex plans; the trouble is that other animals can scarcely learn such things at all. These twin ideas of reward/success and punish/failure do not explain enough about how people learn to produce the new ideas that enable them to solve difficult problems that could not otherwise be solved without many lifetimes of ineffectual trial and error.

In addition to producing new ideas, we must use various kinds of memories. At each moment, we must keep track of what we've just done — or else we might repeat the same steps over and over again. Also, we must somehow maintain our goals — or we'll end up doing pointless things. Finally, once our problem is solved, we need access to records of how it was done, for use when similar problems arise in the future.

– Marvin Minsky
Societies of the Mind

CHAPTER THIRTY-TWO

The Mind of the Hunter

*F*rank Doran is waiting in Wil's office when Lou arrives the next morning shortly before seven.

"Good morning, Lou. Wil's out in the final inspection area. Asked me to talk to you. Cup of coffee?" Frank says, as he walks to the coffee table. "Just made a fresh batch."

"I can smell it," says Lou. "Wil says you're manager of operations in the aluminum side of the business. Been around casting long?"

Frank smiles as he pours a cup for Lou. "I was pouring hot metal for boat anchors when I was eight years old. At eleven I set my family garage on fire with an exothermic reaction that got out of control. Thought my dad would beat me; instead he asked if I had learned anything. It's in my blood, Lou. My ancestors in Ireland have been casting metal for four hundred years."

"Wil says the competition's tough these days," Lou says.

"Tough isn't the word for it. It won't be my first plant shutdown if we lose this one."

Lou looks distressed. "Do you really think you might lose it here at Garrett?"

"Not if I have anything to do with it. That's what I wanted to talk to you about. I've come up with an idea to increase sales in the September time frame, but I need you to tell me if you think it can be done."

497

"I'm all ears," Lou says.

"I've been pushing our sales department to come up with orders to make up for that ten percent reduction we're anticipating for September. They've hit all our customers again to milk some more sales but haven't come up with much. They say that we are picking up some new product sales but these won't impact our schedule for as much as a year. They say that our development time for new castings is too long. It takes us an average of nine months to get a new pattern designed, built, and approved. Marcus says that you guys can help us redesign our new product process to speed it up."

"I'm sure we can," Lou says. "I don't have much experience in that area, but I'll give Marcus a call right away."

"How about Laura," Frank says. "She's an engineer, I understand."

"She's coming in today. She might be able to help," Lou says. "I'll get a hold of Marcus right away and see what he says. I'll get back to you as soon as I have an answer."

"Great," Frank says, standing. "I've got to get back to my office for a staff meeting."

When Marcus returns Lou's urgent call an hour later, Lou explains the situation to him. Marcus suggests that Lou begin the data collection process. When Lou expresses doubt about his ability to work in engineering, Marcus laughs. "Just treat it as a Delivery System, Lou."

"Wil asked if Laura could help," Lou says.

"She has her hands full at Motorola. And besides, I heard about the great job you did with Vince. You have great insight there, Lou. You can help the Vinces of the world."

"It was nothing, really. I've walked in Vince's shoes. So, about Laura . . . She was planning to come back here today. She says there's a break in her work back there."

"That's fine. I'm sure she can help. Have all the data ready by Friday evening. I'll meet you at about seven. Set up an implementation for next Saturday, all day. Gotta run. I'm counting on you."

"I'll give it my best shot."

Lou and Frank are heavily into the data analysis by the time Laura arrives just before lunch. Alan Updike joins the three of them later that afternoon. During the rest of that day and all day Friday, they continue to put the data together. By late Friday evening they have a timed activity chart of the process, quality data, and an organizational interface chart.

Millie Rierra's Restaurant is located just across the street from the beach. On a clear night, the outline of Catalina Island can be seen to the south across thirty miles of Pacific Ocean. The restaurant is packed when they arrive. Lou requests a window table overlooking the beach.

"It takes an average of thirty-five weeks to get new tooling designed, built, and approved," Laura says. "Selected high priority jobs have been approved in half the time, but they're the exception."

"I'd say that's typical tooling time for casting patterns," Lou says.

Laura nods in agreement. "The problem as I see it is that a few weeks reduction in the time isn't going to help. It'll take a huge reduction to have any kind of significant impact on their fall schedules. We also need to improve the quality of the process so that the first samples run at Garrett are good."

"Tall order," Lou says.

"Thought I'd catch you two here. Have it all figured out?" Marcus asks, as he approaches their table.

"Did you have any doubts?" Lou asks, as he makes room for Marcus to sit between them.

Marcus smiles. "None, absolutely none. Fill me in."

"Do you want to start with the flowchart?"

"No, let's start with some questions. What's the output of the process?"

"An approved tool for production," Laura says.

"What are the core value-added activities in the process?"

"Tool design, tool build, and approval," Lou answers.

"Are each of those a core value-added activity?"

Both Lou and Laura have puzzled looks. "Tool design and build are," Laura says.

"But why do you say they add value?"

"Can't build castings without tools, and the customer pays for the tools!" Lou says.

"That's it," Marcus says. "Next question: Any quality problems with the castings from this tooling Delivery System?"

"No, unless you call the rework part of the process a quality problem," Laura says.

Marcus has no reaction. "Let me see the timed activity chart."

Lou hands it to him.

Tool Acquisition Process (Castings)

Prior to Redesign

Marcus studies it for less than a minute and hands it back. "And how about the organizational interface chart?"

Laura raps Lou on the arm. "We guessed that one right. We figured you'd ask for that. Here it is."

Tool Development – Original Process
Interface flow chart

Marcus looks briefly at the drawing and hands it back to Laura. "So they need a big improvement fast?" he asks, rhetorically.

"Need the Non-Linear Solution," Lou says, with a Cheshire grin.

"No other way. How would you do it, Lou?"

Lou sighs. "I thought about it last night. It seems to me that we're going to have to start from scratch on this one. I'd ask what it takes to go directly from the part drawing to the building of the pattern."

"What about tool design?" Laura asks.

Lou shrugs. "Maybe that can be done in parallel as the tool is being built."

"Lou has definitely gone non-linear on us, Laura," Marcus says.

"No choice. We need big improvement fast."

"How big? Have you decided what the Process Intent has to be?"

"They need a process so fast that they can underbid all their competitors on the time to develop a new casting," Lou says. "We're shooting for ten weeks from the time the customer has a part drawing until the pattern is approved by the customer."

"From thirty-five weeks to ten weeks. Tough goal," Marcus says.

"We think it can be done," Laura says.

"How about a Process Model?"

"We've played with a few models but couldn't decide," Laura says.

"Here you would use the Core Value-Added Model as your design base. What is the Core Value-Added activity in this process?" Marcus asks.

"Pattern design," Laura says.

"Pattern build," Lou says.

They both look at Marcus. Marcus is quiet as seconds pass.

"Lou's right," Laura says, nodding her head. "The core value-added activity is pattern build." Lou is astonished.

"Good. Let's draw the Core Value-Added Model for this process," Marcus says, as he begins to sketch on a legal pad.

"Of all the pattern shops you deal with, is there one that is superior in response, quality, and cost?" Marcus asks.

Core Value-Added Model
for Casting Tooling

New Process Intent {
• 10-week cycle time
• First-time quality
• Reduced process cost

Value requirements
• Application information
• Casting drawings
• Specifications
• Timing requirements

Engine manufacturer

Build pattern

Value delivered
• Approved tool for prototype and production
• Tool that optimizes value to cost ratio in minimum time

"Precision Pattern in Phoenix is faster and has the best quality, but they're slightly higher in cost," Laura says.

"Would the cost come down if they got the biggest part of the business?" Marcus asks.

"I didn't ask that question," Laura says. "Does a little more cost in the pattern build matter if it results in getting more business?"

"It's insignificant compared to the advantage of increased sales."

"Let's change subjects. Who will have to be on the team to pull this off?"

"Purchasing and engineering for sure," Laura says. "And maybe a pattern shop."

Lou sits back in his chair as Marcus and Laura make the list of team members that will be needed in the action planning session the following Saturday. Lou's glad Laura knows what she's doing. He couldn't do this without her, and he's grateful.

"Will they be able to get a representative of Phoenix Precision Pattern to attend the Saturday session?" Marcus asks.

"Wil said it would be no problem," Laura says.

"Is purchasing tuned in on this one? Are they in a creative mood?"

"I talked to them," Lou says. "They're ready to do whatever it takes."

The Saturday session is full of surprises. For the first two hours, Laura and Lou ask questions, with Laura leading the way. She's every bit as impressive as Candace. At times her questions are so pointed that Lou winces.

"Why does tool design take two weeks," Laura asks Frank. "How long does it take if you stay on it nonstop after you start?"

"About eight to twelve hours," Frank says.

"After you finish the tool design it goes out for quotes. Why?" she asks.

"To get price and delivery quotations so we can get the best price," someone says.

"It shows two weeks to get a quote back. Why two weeks?" she says.

"Mail time, estimating time at the pattern shop, more mail time, and getting all the approvals here at Garrett," someone says.

"This indicates a one-month backlog at Precision Pattern. Any way around that?" she probes.

The president of Precision Pattern sits up in his chair. "We need that to buffer ourselves against fluctuating demand. We can't afford to lay off a pattern maker if our orders take a dip, because we'll lose them to another shop. And we can't afford to keep them if we don't have work. Keeping a month backlog is a minimum. We can do it faster on overtime and expedite it around other jobs, but that would cost more."

"But that means the average job is delayed a month before you start it," Laura says.

"Yes, unless it's a high priority."

"Shows here that it takes ten weeks to make the pattern," Laura says. "Can that be reduced?"

"It can be reduced if the pattern is built on two shifts, but most pattern makers want to do the whole job themselves," the president says.

"After the pattern is complete, it's shipped from Phoenix to Torrance to build a sample. This sample goes through all the inspection and test that a production part does, and then proceeds to the layout department for dimensional checks," Laura says. "All of this takes seven weeks — one week in shipment, two weeks in processing, two and a half weeks in backlog at layout, and half a week for the layout process. What questions come to mind?"

"Why doesn't Precision do the sample casting, layout, and tool rework before they ship the part to us?" Alan Updike asks. "You have the facilities to do it, don't you?"

"We have the facilities, but your people have always argued that the part must go through the production process before the pattern can be approved!"

By the end of the day, they've developed a drastically new Process Model and approved action plans to implement it. In the new Process Model, the part drawings go directly to the pattern shop, which begins work immediately: building the pattern, casting a sample, performing the first layout with correlation to Garrett, and correcting the pattern as necessary. The first sample will be built, checked, and sent to Garrett for evaluation and approval in eight weeks — twenty-seven weeks less than it took with the old process.

After the session, Lou and Laura present their Non-Linear Solutions to Marcus. He says they're close but that they're missing one very important element. Lou and Laura look puzzled and ask for a clue. Marcus says: "Think about what people must do before they can transform a business."

"I met a guy named Joe at breakfast the other morning," Lou says, looking suspiciously at Marcus.

Marcus smiles. "Retired Master Guardian. Smart old guy — likes to put in his two cents. He's worth listening to. Just runs around poking his nose in other Guardians' business. He recommended you as a Guardian. He's just protecting his interest."

"How did he know me?"

"He met you at Continental years ago."

"You know, I thought he looked familiar. That was nagging at me. Was he one of the three guys the company sent down to help us? So he was a Guardian . . . only stayed a couple days."

"Nobody listened, so he left."

Lou bows his head. "We *didn't* listen . . . I didn't listen. Geez, maybe we could have saved the plant. What do you think?"

"You've come a long way, Lou."

CHAPTER THIRTY-THREE

Recession

W il Danesi's boss, Frank Geldert, raises a champagne glass and practically shouts above the drone of the engine and the sound of water lapping against the hull of the ocean cruiser. "I know what you're going through. I know about the long hours you're spending at work. Thank you. And I also want to thank those of you who have waited long hours for your husbands and wives to come home. But this has been an extraordinary turnaround. Congratulations."

It's a beautiful afternoon in May, and through her conversations with other wives, other staff members, and Frank Geldert himself, Sue Danesi has pieced it all together. The plant is approaching breakeven, and they expect to break into the black by August. She hears about the X-ray area turnaround, the final grind and inspection success, the major improvement with the turbine blade cell, the improved scheduling and sales order-entry systems. She's proud to be part of it. Frank Geldert said it well when he said it wasn't easy to be the wife of a dedicated manager.

Wil set the pattern for their life together just after their first child was born when he came home one day and said he had quit his job at General Motors because he wanted to be a metallurgist. When she asked him where his new job was, he said that he would look for a new job starting in the morning. For the past thirty years it had been a new city, new home, new friends, and new schools every two to three years. It was lonesome at times, but never boring.

As they drive home late that evening after the cruise, Sue senses there is something troubling Wil. "Something wrong?" she probes.

"No, nothing that can't be handled," Wil says.

"What can be handled?"

"We're starting to get cutbacks in orders and delays in schedules from some of our customers," Wil sighs. "It's the recession finally hitting us. Each division in the corporation has a major program to cut inventories, and we're at the tail end of the cutbacks."

"All I heard on the cruise was how great you're doing."

"We are doing great but these cutbacks and delays are going to hit us in September. The problem is that I've projected to Frank Geldert that we'd be in the black by August."

"Does Frank know this?"

"He knows."

"He sure didn't act like it."

"He didn't want to put a dark cloud on our celebration."

"Isn't there ever a happily-ever-after?" she asks, smiling and patting Wil on the shoulder.

Wil smiles. "Last Saturday, Alan Updike, Lou, and Laura worked with some of our people to reduce our new tool development time. I think what they came up with will work. When it does, it will reduce new tool development time from thirty-five weeks to eight weeks. So maybe there will be a 'happy' in September, but there's no 'ever after' in this business. There is no end to the need to constantly transform ourselves and the business."

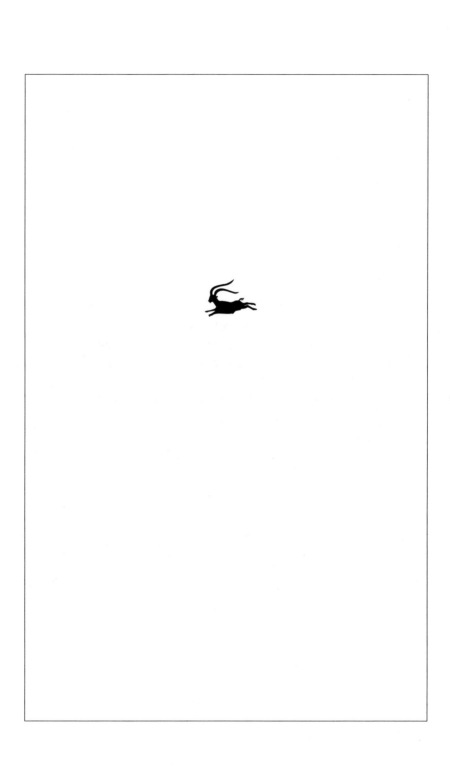

I know that most men, even those at ease with problems of the greatest complexity, can seldom accept even the simplest and most obvious of truths, if it would be such as would oblige them to admit the falsity of conclusions which they have delighted in explaining to colleagues, which they have proudly taught to others, and which they have woven thread by thread into the fabric of their lives.

– Leo Nikolaevich Tolstoy
War and Peace

CHAPTER THIRTY-FOUR

The Finish Line

*F*or Laura, there would be many projects and many successes in the years to come, but the smell of hot metal would stay with her. It would always recall for her the beginning of her career as a Guardian. It would always return her to the foundry and to that moment in Wil's office, the last time she saw him.

"We're going to make it, thanks to you," Wil says to the trio. "We're now doing every pattern job in eight weeks; not just priority jobs, but every one. And this has brought in some new sales. Ron Schultz is leading a complete redesign of the investment casting part of the business, and they are showing some good progress.

"We're starting to come back in spite of the recession. We're seeing some lost customers returning."

It seems to Laura as if some of the stress in Wil's face has vanished.

"Hunters," Lou bellows. "You're Hunters again. You can do it faster and better than an outside shop. Sky's the limit."

"We're gonna stay that way from here on out, Lou," Wil says.

Lou . . . still the bull in the china shop, Laura observes. But not the same bull . . . a different bull . . . not so contentious . . . more like a true believer. Laura realizes that she too has changed — that some of his ways have rubbed off on her.

"I hope you'll come back to visit from time to time," Wil says, interrupting her thoughts.

"That would be nice," Laura says as they stand to leave.

"I'll be back," Lou says.

"Lou and Laura are both starting new assignments tomorrow," Marcus says, as they walk toward the lobby.

"Good for you." Wil says. "Good luck." They shake hands and walk through the lobby door.

Marcus pauses in front of the Garrett lobby, reaching down to pick a wild violet. "Spring is a time for renewal," he says, as he walks toward the parking lot. "It's time for the Non-Linear Solution. Have you figured it out?"

Laura looks at Lou as if to suggest that she hasn't come up with the missing part. "Can Laura and I talk this over by ourselves?" He asks Marcus.

"Sure, I'll be in the parking lot."

As soon as Marcus is out of range, Lou begins: "Something's been gnawing at me, Laura. Marcus keeps talking about American businesses being involved in a war. 'But where's the enemy?' I keep asking myself. Marcus says it's *not* Japan; that it's not the European Community . . . What do you think?"

"I'm still thinking about it."

Lou suddenly remembers a book that Marcus recommended to him. Despite the afternoon warmth, Lou feels goose bumps spreading over his chest and down his arms. "Have you read *The Art of War*, by Sun Tzu?" he asks excitedly.

"No, why?"

Lou feels an adrenaline rush now. He digs in his pocket, takes out Joe's watch, and holds it out so Laura can see the inscription on the back. It occurs to him now that Joe could most definitely have helped him save Continental. But even if Lou had lived, he wouldn't have listened. He ignored the vital signs — even in his own body.

He thought everyone else was the problem.

"It's been in front of our noses the whole time," Lou replies. "It's like Sun Tzu says: a soldier has to know both the enemy *and* himself."

"So what are you trying to say?"

"I'm saying that we're our own worst enemies — that most of our problems are right above our shoulders!"

"I've got it!" Laura says excitedly. "We must transform ourselves before we can transform anyone or anything else. That's the missing part of our Non-Linear Solution."

Lou gives Laura a bear hug and lifts her off her feet.

"You've got it, Laura!"

"We've got it!"

They compose themselves and take a few minutes to add the missing part to their previous effort. Then they show the result to Marcus.

The Non-Linear Solution

Become the Hunter by transforming yourself and then the business in order to maximize the rate and quality of learning and improvement.

"Well, what do you think? Are we close?"

"Close enough. I'm satisfied," Marcus says with a broad smile.

"I don't believe it. We got it!" Laura exclaims.

"It was mostly you, Laura," Lou says.

"But you were the one who simplified it."

"It takes both analysis and intuition," Marcus comments, walking toward the Garrett parking lot.

Laura feels a rush of excitement. "It's great to be part of this — to save people's jobs and secure their future," Laura says as they cross the parking lot.

"We didn't secure their future, Laura. This isn't a Walt Disney production," Marcus warns.

Laura wears a puzzled look. "What does that mean?"

"Let's take a look into the future, and then you'll understand."

There is a sudden swirl of wind through the parking lot. Laura's fingers tighten on her briefcase. "Turn around. Look back at the Garrett Foundry," Marcus says.

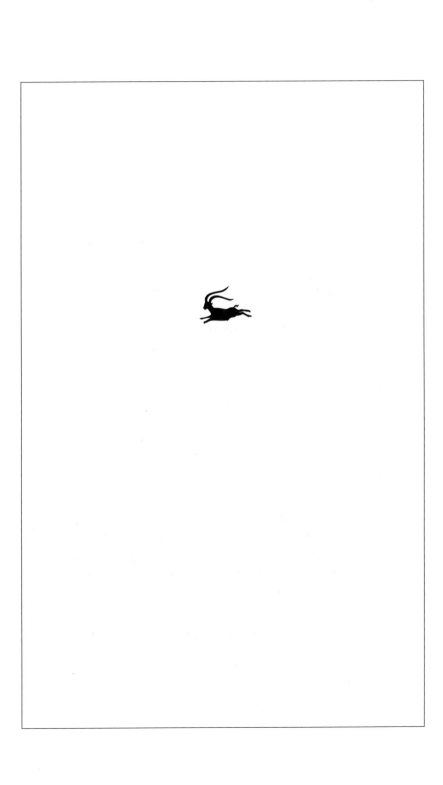

The grand projects undertaken by Europe and Japan to remake themselves — and their belief that such reinvention is necessary for survival — suggest that the twenty-first century has begun — everywhere but in Washington.

– Alvin and Heidi Toffler, "Grand Design,"
World Monitor, October, 1988

America is addicted to foreign investment. The Japanese finance the U.S. budget deficit through their purchase of U.S. Treasury bonds. Certain industries once dominated by U.S. corporations — industries that contributed to this nation's high standard of living and made it the best place on earth to live — have already been taken over by foreign competitors. More Americans than ever work for foreign employers.

– Remarks by Congressman John D. Dingell, Chairman,
U.S. House Committee on Energy and Commerce
from the Foreword to *Selling Out*
by Douglas Frantz and Catherine Collins, 1989

CHAPTER THIRTY-FIVE

2022

"Oh my God!" Laura gasps.

Lou says nothing as he begins to walk toward the abandoned foundry. Trash litters the empty parking lot. Weeds are growing tall along the fence line.

"What a disaster," Laura says. "What's happened?"

"We're in the year 2022," Marcus explains.

"Is Garrett gone, or did they move?" Laura asks.

Lou nods resolutely. "Gone like Continental, I'd guess."

"The whole American commercial and military aircraft industry went belly up shortly after the crash of 2005," Marcus says.

"The crash of 2005?"

"First you need some background to understand why it all fell apart." Marcus walks over and sits on a parking lot curb. "The seeds were sown for the crash in the seventies and eighties, and by the turn of the century, the situation was irreversible. We'll review the period from 1972 to 2022 to help you understand how it all unraveled.

"During the seventies and eighties U.S. productivity increased at significantly lower rates than most other industrial nations. As American industries became less competitive,

Americans purchased more and more imported products, exacerbating the downward spiral.

"In the eighties, the United States, led by President Ronald Reagan's assistant Donald Regan, pressed the Japanese to strengthen the yen to make U.S. products more competitive. The dollar was subsequently devalued by forty percent compared to the yen, which virtually doubled foreign financial resources and brought a wave of foreign investment. The foreign investment inflated the price of real estate, stocks, and business assets in the United States. By 1989, Japan was the richest nation on earth with $43.7 trillion in land, factories, stocks, and other wealth, surpassing the United States for the first time in history.

"As profits went down and unemployment rose in the late eighties, the U.S. had the largest federal budget deficits in history. To finance these huge deficits, the United States increased its borrowing rate and in less than eight years fell from being the largest creditor nation on earth to the largest debtor nation. The U.S. debt surpassed the combined debt of Brazil, Argentina, and Mexico, whose debts had frightened world bankers at the beginnings of the eighties. During the eighties the United States borrowed a trillion dollars from the Japanese, and by the end of the eighties the Japanese were financing one third of the U.S. budget deficit.

"While this was taking place in the seventies and eighties, there were other changes taking place that would turn the tide in the aircraft industry. In Europe, a French and German consortium with billions in government backing developed the Airbus, a commercial airplane. In 1978 they sold thirty-two planes to Eastern Airlines, establishing a commercial aircraft beachhead in the U.S. By 1989, Airbus had captured twenty-three percent of all new orders for aircraft in the world, pushing Douglas Aircraft to third place in the world market. In July 1992, the dam broke. United Airlines, after fourteen years of loyalty to Boeing, awarded a $3 billion-contract to Airbus Industries for 100 twinjet A-320s.

"In 1970 and 1980, the Japanese Ministry of International Trade and Industry (MITI) designated Aerospace as one of the three key technologies for the twenty-first century. In the early eighties, Japanese government aid to jet engine development exceeded aid to telecommunications, energy, and computers. Although the Japanese had been producing engines and components, they did not have the technology or infrastructure to produce an advanced aircraft. In June 1988, U.S. and Japanese negotiators approved the joint development of a new jet fighter for the Japanese Air Force, the FSX. The FSX would be based on the design of the advanced technology F16, produced by General Dynamics. In a single stroke, the Japanese gained access to technology at a fraction of the cost it would take to develop it and we trained them technically to assemble and test these very sophisticated components."

"And from what I've seen, they'll do it very well," Lou says.

"I agree," Marcus continues. "In the early nineties, financially pressed companies such as McDonnell-Douglas lost the ability and interest to finance business investments in new products, plant revitalization, and expansion. Once U.S. business profits had eroded to the extent that they could not finance investment themselves, they had few options. They could cease investment, sell part of their assets, or surrender control of their core assets to whoever provided financial help. A significant amount of capital flowed from Japanese and European banks and the money came with big strings attached to the technology that would potentially develop. By 1993, of the top twenty valued companies on earth, forty percent were Japanese.

"In 1992, as you know, a European trade pact was signed making the European market the largest trade block on the planet, with a gross national product of some $5 trillion. With significant opposition to a North American trade block, it was not until the year 1995 that major trade barriers were lowered in North America.

"By the late nineties, American steel, electronics, semiconductor, auto, machine tool, and heavy equipment industries were either devastated or unprofitable. Although the Japanese economy and stock market suffered due to the worldwide recession of the early nineties, they recovered by mid-decade. Japanese factories were generating enormous wealth, which they invested in new plants and prime assets in the United States. The net effect was that while Americans were purchasing products from the Japanese that depreciated in value, the Japanese were taking the profits from those sales and buying U.S. assets that would appreciate and exact rental income from the United States.

"In the late nineties, the living standard in the U.S. continued to decline while living standards in Japan continued upward. The U.S. government, faced with financing ever-increasing social programs and with cities in bankruptcy, began to systematically reduce social benefits. At the same time, revenues were decreasing due to rising unemployment, lower average wages, and unprofitable businesses. The Treasury was borrowing more and more at higher and higher interest rates, causing annual inflation to hit the staggering rate of twenty percent. At that time the U.S. government was paying $60 billion in interest payments per year to the Japanese and had become virtually dependent on them to purchase the bonds necessary to finance their deficit spending.

"By the year 2003, Japan was manufacturing advanced technology fighter planes that had superior performance and quality, and they were taking sixty percent of the world's new orders for military aircraft. These aircraft were sold with Japanese-designed and manufactured engines.

"Meanwhile, to avoid financial disaster, the U.S. Congress began to cut spending for the military, education, and services. There were demonstrations that led to riots in major cities. Social Security managed to elude the axe until the year 2000. By that time the country was beginning to split between the elderly and the young; the former felt entitled to benefits that kept pace with the twenty percent inflation, and the latter considered the increased taxes an unbearable burden. With increased unemployment, reduced social-welfare payments, and slashed police budgets, crime seemed out of control at times.

"A major event occurred on a Friday in August, 2005. Early in the day Japanese investors started selling enormous quantities of U.S. government bonds because of a trade report indicating that imports had risen dramatically and that exports had fallen for the previous four months. During the last two instances where trade figures were that bad, the United States had devalued the dollar. Hedging against a dollar devaluation, the Japanese were dumping bonds. The U.S. Treasury reacted by increasing interest rates on bonds to twenty-two percent to avoid a shortfall in government funds. Then it all began to unravel.

"It was not in the Japanese interest to destroy the U.S. economy because at that time they owned most of the country's banks, many businesses, most prime real estate, and the two largest TV networks. But once the first domino had fallen on that Friday, there was no stopping it. At this panic state, the Japanese began massive sales of real estate, and real estate values plummeted. Individual and institutional fortunes were lost overnight, accelerating the spiral downward.

"When the dust cleared, the dollar had fallen dramatically and most U.S. businesses were in serious financial trouble. The world went off the dollar standard and onto the yen standard. This was the final blow to the American aircraft industry.

"There were casualties in every industry. Within a year, with sales devastated, IBM went into Chapter 11. Nippon Telephone and Telegraph bought AT&T for a song and formed Global Communications Company. General Motors, which had made a major recovery in the late 1990s by offering top-quality cars and world-beating designs, staggered and fell victim to a hostile takeover by Japanese interests connected to Toyota.

"Anti-Japanese feeling, which had been festering for years, was now widespread, and in the off-year U.S. congressional elections, 'stop the Japanese' campaigns were essential winning a seat. In the presidential election of 2008, it was a contest between candidates to come up with the best Japan-stopping approach.

"By the year 2009, due to the increased financial pressures, U.S. military presence in the Middle East had been virtually eliminated. The U.S. public, with enormous domestic problems, drifted towards isolationism. So when war broke out in the Middle East late that year, there was no support in America to become involved. Japan had by this time converted all of its power sources to nuclear and solar energy and thus was not affected by the sudden cutoff of oil. Pressured by environmental groups, over half of the U.S. nuclear power plants had been closed by that time. American oil producers had lacked the money to invest in developing new domestic sources of oil, so the U.S had become dependent on the Mideast for sixty percent of its oil. Only the European Block struggled to arbitrate the conflict. Oil prices tripled overnight. Transportation in the U.S. ground to a virtual standstill. The U.S. fell into a great seven-year depression."

"Does this have to go on? I've heard enough," Laura says.

"If this is the way it's going to turn out, what's the point of what we're doing?" Lou asks.

"Have you read *A Christmas Carol*, by Charles Dickens?" Marcus asks.

"Ebenezer Scrooge," Laura says.

"This is the way things are headed right now. It doesn't have to turn out this way. If Americans can just learn the lessons of history, it can be turned around," Marcus says.

"What lessons?" Laura asks.

"That no nation can remain the economic leader of the world once its productivity growth stalls. It happened to the Dutch, it happened to the English, and now . . . well, today, the United States ranks dead last among the advanced nations of the earth in productivity growth. American industries are no longer the suppliers of choice in many core growth businesses abroad and here at home. Americans are buying more imports than we are exporting and American companies are fighting to survive. Increased imports, lower market share, lower profits, layoffs, and lost tax revenue will follow. This has been the way all nations have fallen from economic power."

"Would you say that government, education, and business are all in a linear mode?" Lou asks. "Seems like the whole country needs the Non-Linear Solution."

"I would say that, " Marcus says, soberly.

"I'd like to take issue with your scenario," Laura says. "I've been doing my homework on American industry after you shot across my bow a while back. U.S. exports of manufactured goods have almost doubled to over four hundred billion since 1985. Lower interest rates in 1991-92 have reduced corporate debt load. Manufacturing productivity increased 1.6 percent in 1991 — which is very good. The average cost of manufacturing U.S. steel has fallen from $600 per ton, to $480 per ton which is twenty to twenty-five dollars below Japanese averages. American railroads are carrying thirty percent more traffic than in 1982, with forty-six percent fewer employees, representing a freight traffic per employee gain in productivity of one-hundred-fifty percent in nine years. And as I explained earlier, the United States is staging a comeback in electronics.

The U.S. food production and distribution system is still the most productive in the world. Ameican manufacturers of Fords, Buicks, Cadillacs, and Chryslers are on the comeback trail with world-quality products. And besides that, the Japanese aren't doing too well right now. Their stock market has taken some major losses and their corporations profits are down. And I have a lot more examples here if you want more."

"That's enough. I agree," Marcus replies. "I've painted a worst case scenario. There is a lot of evidence for a U.S. renaissance, but it will take a sustained effort."

"But can we really win?" Lou asks.

"You're talking like the Hunted, Lou. It's our job to help companies and individuals discover the Non-Linear Solution and become Hunters."

"I agree with that," Laura says. "But Lou has a good point. Are there enough people like Wil Danesi and enough of us to turn it around? If the government doesn't do something and American consumers don't start supporting their own industries, can we still turn it around?"

"There are thousands of heroes like Wil Danesi and there are many Master Guardians to help them discover the Non-Linear Solution."

"So you mean we can actually change the future?" Laura says.

"That's the idea," Marcus says, as he presents them with the platinum shield of the Master Guardian. "That's what we Master Guardians do."

Notes

Hunted

1 Historical and statistical information is drawn from C. Jackson Grayson and Carla O'Dell, *American Business: A Two-Minute Warning* (New York: Free Press, 1988) and Stephen S. Cohen and John Zysman, *Manufacturing Matters* (New York: Basic Books, 1987).

Chapter Two

1 On November 25, 1985, Continental Steel declared bankruptcy. Much of the material in Chapters 1 and 2 comes from discussions with Kent Achors; Phil Kauble; Dave Breeden; Russ, the proprietor of Russ's Tavern; the management at the Steel Inn; Mayor Bob Sargent; Dick Ronk; and local news accounts — especially those printed in the *Kokomo Tribune*.

Chapter Three

1 Taken from discussions with Wil Danesi.

Chapter Four

1 Background for this chapter comes from Tom Peters, *Thriving on Chaos* (New York: Knopf, 1987) and Stanley Davis, *Future Perfect* (Reading, Mass.: Addison-Wesley, 1987), 10-40.

2 John Naisbitt and Patricia Aburdene, *Megatrends 2000* (New York: William Morrow, 1990), 137.

Chapter Five

1 Paul Hersey and Kenneth Blanchard, *Management of Organizational Behavior* (Englewood Cliffs, N.J.: Prentice-Hall, 1982), 157.

2 This defect rate is what Motorola calls six sigma quality.

3 Professor Robert Hall contributed three of these factors; they are described in Robert W. Hall, H. Thomas Johnson, and Peter B.B. Turney, *Measuring Up: Charting Pathways to Manufacturing Excellence* (Homewood, Ill.: Business One Irwin, 1991).

4 The four factors that Marcus identifies as most important to productivity improvement were derived from studying the following sources:

- Robert Hayes and Kim B. Clark, "Explaining Observed Productivity Differentials between Plants: Implications for Operations Research," *Interfaces* 15, no. 6 (November/December 1985): 3-14.
- Robert Hayes and Kim B. Clark, "Exploring the Sources of Productivity Differences at the Factory Level," in *The Uneasy Alliance: Managing the Productivity-Technology Dilemma*, ed. K.B. Clark, R.H. Hayes, and C. Lorenz (Boston: Harvard Business School Press, 1985), 151-194.
- Robert Hayes and Kim B. Clark, "Why Some Factories Are More Productive than Others," *Harvard Business Review* September/October 1986: 66-73.
- Roger W. Schmenner, "Behind Labor Productivity Gains in the Factory," *Journal of Manufacturing and Operations Management* 1, no. 4 (Winter 1988): 323-338.
- Roger W. Schmenner, "Comparative Factory Productivity" (report to the U.S. Department of Commerce, Economic

Development Administration, Research and Evaluation Division, July 1986).
- Roger W. Schmenner, "The Merit of Making Things Fast," _Sloan Management Review_ (Fall 1988).
- Roger W. Schmenner and Randall L. Cook, "Explaining Productivity Differences in North Carolina Factories," _Journal of Operations Management_ 5, no. 3 (May 1985): 273-289.
- Roger W. Schmenner and Boo Ho Rho, "An International Comparison of Factory Productivity," _International Journal of Operations and Production Management_ 10, no. 4 (1990): 16-31.

5   Wess Roberts, _Leadership Secrets of Attila the Hun_ (New York: Warner Books, 1987).

Chapter Six

1   Information about the Arsenal of Venice is compiled from Robert C. Davis, _Shipbuilders of the Venetian Arsenal_ (Baltimore: Johns Hopkins University Press, 1991), and Frederick Chapin Lake, _Venetian Ships and Shipbuilders of the Renaissance_ (Westport, CT: Glenwood Press, 1975).

2   See note 1.

3   _Pero Tafur, Travels and Adventures, 1435-1439,_ ed. Malcolm Lett (New York, Harper & Bros., 1926), quoted in Frederick Chapin Lake, _Venetian Ships and Shipbuilders of the Renaissance_ (Westport, CT: Glenwood Press, 1975).

4   Alvin and Heidi Toffler, _Power Shift_ (New York: Bantam Books, 1990).

5   Information about Thomas Tompion is from Jeremy Rifkin, _Time Wars_ (New York: Henry Holt, 1987).

6   The Eli Whitney story is adapted from an account in Roger Burlingame, _Whittling Boy_ (New York: Harcourt Brace & Co., 1941), ch. 23. For more on Eli Whitney, see Constance Green, _Eli Whitney and the Birth of Modern Technology_ (Boston: Little, Brown, 1956), and Jeanette Mirsky and Allen Nevins, _The World of Eli Whitney_ (New York: MacMillan, 1952).

7 Captain Wadsworth's letter was published in Roger Burlingame, *Whittling Boy* (New York: Harcourt Brace & Co., 1941), 327-329.

8 The Henry Wells story is told in more detail in Alden Hatch, *American Express* (Garden City, N.J.: Doubleday, 1950).

9 The Herman Hollerith story is adapted from Robert E. Breeden, *Those Inventive Americans* (Washington, D.C.: National Geographic Society, 1971).

Chapter Seven

1 Henry Ford's words are taken from the following sources:

- Henry Ford, *Today and Tomorrow,* special edition of Ford's 1926 classic (Cambridge, Mass.: Productivity Press, 1988).
- Ford Motor Company, *The Ford Industries* (Dearborn, Mich.: Ford Motor Co., 1925).
- Robert Lacey, *Ford: The Men and the Machine* (Boston: Little, Brown, 1986).

Chapter Eight

1 The principal source for information on the Big Bear Market and A&P was William Walsh's *The Rise and Decline of the Great Atlantic and Pacific Tea Company* (Secaucus: Lyle Stuart, 1986). The first supermarket was actually opened in 1930 in Jamaica, Queens by George Cullens, a former branch manager for Kroger Grocery and Bakery. Kroger thought the concept was crazy when Cullens proposed it to management.

2 Information about McDonald's was gathered from John F. Love, *McDonald's — Behind the Arches* (New York: Bantam, 1985) and Ray Kroc, *Grinding It Out* (New York: St. Martin's Press, 1990).

3 Information about Kemmons Wilson and Holiday Inn is from William B. Walton, *The New Bottom Line* (New York: Harper & Row, 1986), 4-5.

4 Information about Kiichiro and Eiji Toyoda is from James P. Womack, Daniel T. Jones, and Daniel Roos, *The Machine that Changed the World* (New York: Rawson Associates, 1990).

5 Taiichi Ohno's words are taken from Taiichi Ohno with Setsuo Mito, *Just in Time for Today and Tomorrow* (Cambridge: Productivity Press, 1986).

6 The context for Lou's flashbacks to Bataan: On July 9, 1942 the American Army on Bataan, sick and starving, surrendered. The Japanese captors forced their prisoners, many of whom were wounded, to march nearly 100 miles to Fort O'Donnell in northern Bataan. Due to inhumane treatment, thousands lost their lives on the march and thousands more died once they reached the camp at Fort O'Donnell. In early February of 1945, U.S troops, under MacArthur, began to retake the Philippines. As U.S. forces neared the islands, the Japanese evacuated thousands of POWs on "hell ships." Packed in the holds, thousands of men died before reaching Japan or Formosa. Lou's flashbacks are derived from accounts by Bataan survivors Sergeant Forrest Knox and Privates First Class Blair Robinett and Andrew Aquila, transcribed in Donald Knox's *Death March* (New York: Harcourt Brace Jovanovich, 1981).

7 Background on the Toyota supplier Yanmar can be found in James P. Womack, Daniel T. Jones, and Daniel Roos, *The Machine that Changed the World* (New York: Rawson Associates, 1990).

Chapter Ten

1 The information in Lou's report on Sam Walton comes from Vance H. Trimble's *Sam Walton* (New York: Dutton, 1990).

2 The supporting information on digital signal processing for Laura's report on fast-responding hunters can be found in Gene Bylinsky's "A U.S. Comeback in Electronics," *Fortune*, April 20, 1992: 77-86.

Chapter Eleven

1 Harold's Faig's comments are culled from the author's conversations with him in addition to material from Peter Nulty's "The Soul of an Old Machine," *Fortune*, May 21, 1990: 67.

2 Marcus's comments about the four factors of Japanese product development success are drawn from James P. Womack, Daniel T. Jones, and Daniel Roos, *The Machine that Changed the World* (New York: Rawson Associates, 1990), 112-117.

3 Information about the Ford Taurus project comes from Robert L. Shook, *Turnaround* (Englewood Cliffs, N.J.: Prentice-Hall, 1990), 150-163.

Chapter Thirteen

1   Peter Senge, *The Fifth Discipline* (New York: Doubleday, 1990), 89-92.

Chapter Fourteen

1   Some of the material in the Harley-Davidson story in this chapter is adapted from Peter Reid's *Well-Made in America* (New York: McGraw-Hill, 1990). Financial information regarding Harley-Davidson comes from *The Value Line Investment Survey*, edition 11, August 27, 1993.

Chapter Fifteen

1   The Douglas Aircraft story is culled from the author's conversation with John Wolf.

2   Carl Sewell, *Customers for Life* (New York: Doubleday Currency, 1990).

3   Peter Senge, *The Fifth Discipline* (New York: Doubleday, 1990).

Chapter Nineteen

1   The Kano Model was introduced in Noriaki Kano, Shinichi Tsuji, Nobuhiko Seraku, and Fumio Takahashi, "Attractive Quality and Must-be Quality (1), (2)," a presentation given at the Japanese Society for Quality Control annual meeting, October 1982; this presentation was published in *Quality, JSQC* 14, no.2 (Tokyo: Japanese Society for Quality Control, 1984).

2   Mary Walton, *The Deming Management Method* (New York: Perigree Books, 1986), 29.

3   Philip B. Crosby, *Quality without Tears* (New York: McGraw-Hill, 1984), 160.

4   For more on PIMS, see Robert D. Buzzell and Bradley T. Gale, *The PIMS Principles: Linking Stratey to Performance* (New York: Free Press, 1987).

5   Kaoru Ishikawa, *What Is Total Quality Control? The Japanese Way*, trans. David J. Lu (Englewood Cliffs, N.J.: Prentice-Hall, 1985), 45.

6   Quoted in Earnest C. Huge, ed., *Total Quality: An Executive's Guide to the 1990s*, APICS Series (Homewood, IL: Dow Jones-Irwin, 1990), 5.

7   For more on Deming's bead game, see Mary Walton, *The Deming Management Method*, 40-41.

8   Robert D. Buzzell and Bradley T. Gale, *The PIMS Principles*, 109-111.

Chapter Twenty

1   The errors-and-management-cycles chart in this chapter, as well as Marcus's comments on source inspection and *poka-yoke* devices, are derived from Shigeo Shingo's *Zero Quality Control: Source Inspection and the Poka-Yoke System* (Cambridge, Mass.: Productivity Press, 1986).

2   Carl Sewell, *Customers for Life* (New York: Doubleday Currency, 1990).

Chapter Twenty-Two

1   Much of the information about Western Electric and Joseph Juran comes from the author's conversations with Blanton Godfrey, director of the Juran Institute.

2   The passages about Walter Shewhart are taken from Shewhart's own book, *Economic Control of Quality of Manufactured Product* (New York: Van Nostrand, 1931).

Chapter Twenty-Three

1   Manager pipeline chart is reprinted courtesy of Ken Stork.

Chapter Twenty-Five

1   The story describing the beginning of *USA Today* is taken from Peter S. Pretchard's *The Making of McPaper* (New York: St. Martin's Press, 1987).

Chapter Twenty-Six

1 Principles 5, 10, and 14 are similar to those offered by Peter Senge in *The Fifth Discipline* (New York: Doubleday, 1990). The author offers thanks and apologies to Dr. Senge.

2 Patricia Myers, "Organizational Learning Process," in *Research Policy 1990*, 92-115 (Amsterdam: Elsevier Science Publishers, 1990), 458-59.

A Special Note

In my teaching and consulting engagements around this country, I have observed the heroic efforts of many people to turn their companies around. Many have demonstrated the energy, dedication, and leadership that is characteristic of the Guardians and Warriors in this book. Listing their names is my way of thanking them for all of us who depend on the success of American Business.

– Jim Swartz

Guardians

Dr. Ron Anjard
Frank Arambarri
Sheryl Smith-Bailey
Keki Bhote
Dr. Dan Bills
Kent Bluhm
Norm Bodek
Jim Brock
Alan Bossidy

Jim Cameron
Dick Campbell
Don Carr
Dave Claspell
Phil Conrad
Dan Crishon
Wil Danesi
Parviz Danesghari
George Duncan

Tom Endres

Paul Everett

Ron Forbes

Ron Gill

Dr. Robert Hall

Stephen Hopkins

Alex Hutchins

Erling Illokken

Jim Jones

Ann King

Cal Kirby

Jack Knuth

Ed Lai

Joe Lehman

Dan Lineham

Laura Louis

Mike Louis

Al Matallano

Charlie Mays

Len Meier

Leo Moore

Bill Mueller

John Nugent

Thomas Pavliscak

Bernie Pierce

Ron Pogue

Steve Polston

Emmett Poyner

Lee Sage

Dick Siever

John J. Sherwood

Barry Shulak

Ron Smith

Candace Somers

John Stanley

Tom Stephens

Ken Stork

Greg Swartz

Joe Swartz

Julie Thorpe

Alan Updike

Dan Wallace

Dudley Wass

Bob Wehner

Wayne White

Dave Young

Warriors

(Individuals are listed with their affiliations at the time the book was researched and written.)

AC Electronics – Fred Brinson

Allied Signal Kansas City – Bob Wehner, Jack Knuth, Ron Smith, Jim Robb, Rich Lavelock, Bob Dean, Don Prindle, Don Oswald, Harry Price

Allison Gas Turbine – Barry Chapman

Alpine Corporation – Bernie Pierce, Seizo Ishiguro

Anchor Corp. – Fran Olmstead, John Nugent, Jim Cameron, Stephen Hopkins, Alex Hutchins, Bill Cavalari, Jo Anne Broe, Fred Cox, Mike Ouellette, Dan Lutkus, Mary-Ann Burr, George Passabet, & Bobby

Anheuser-Busch – Larry Pierick

Bar-S – Tim Day, Ken Stinn

Batesville Casket – Mike Ertel, Gus Hillenbrand, Dan Hillenbrand, Denny Knigga, Jacky Arvin, Gary Henby, Jeff Seely, Garry Vosahlik, Mike Valz, Dick Meyer, Ralph Jolie, George Haufler, Rick Lovorn, Bart Bartling, Evan Pritz

Beacon Light – Laura Louis

Binney & Smith – Charles Dietterich, George Nagle

Buick Motor Co. – Mike Orris, Danny Manner, Don Niles, Gil Lamont

CASI – Sam Kendes

CPC, GM – Kurt Johnson

CalPlate – Tom Korzenecki, Dorothy Sheraga

Cardell Corp. – Larry Terryn

Cincinnati Milacron – Harold Faig

Cygnus Systems – Greg Swartz, Mona Adams, Kim Childers

Delco Electronics – Ron Gill, George Duncan, Jim Brock, Jack Chapin, Joe Hanna, Charlie Mays, Kathy Ligocki, George Johnson, Bob Schumacher, Jim Hall, Charley Rine, Ed Craig, Joe Rice, Byron Prahm, Ron Shimanek, Bill Gray, Gary Robertson, Mike Burns, Chiquita Meyers, Cindy Murphy, Dick Murphy, Bob Armstrong, Charlie Radliff, Don Almquist, Harry Olson, Walt McIndoo, Jim Cain, Bill Carr, Jim Schneider, Bob Cameron, John Holmes, Bill Hargraves, Pat O'Donnell, Dave Lemasters, Dave Snyder, Les Wilkinson, Tom Stansberry, Gus Riggs

Delco Remy – Dick Campbell, Ron Pogue, Joe Lehman, Dan Crishon, Chris Stark, Ron Davis, Dennis Strader, Dennie Emerson, Alan Bowley, Gerry Dembroski, Gary Skelding

Douglas Aircraft – John Wolf, David Braunstein, Hank Skibbe, Bob Hood

Dresser Industries – Larry Shefferly, Phil Schwab, Ed Larger, John Cash, Bill Sines, Martin Valentin

EDS – Pradeep Nijhawan, Jerry Pierce

EG&G – Robert Fischbein

Electron Dynamics – Erling Illokken, Dan Wallace, Leo Moore, Ron Forbes, Dave Young

Endevco – Phil Conrad, Len Meier, Jim Jones, Sheryl Smith-Bailey, Jim Chung, Margie Mattingly, Frank Lally, Irby Roostie, Evie Milliken, Chuck Brathwaitte, Marlene Brown, Jim McIntosh, Mark Serpa, Mike Will, Greg McCumber, Jim Metzler, Don Minton, Michael Gross

Ernst & Young – Lee Sage

Ford Motor – "Red" Poling, Dudley Wass

Fortifiber Corp. – Stuart Yount, Robert Thoms, Carl Thoms

Garrett Industries – Wil Danesi, Frank Geldert, Roy Ekrom, Alan Updike, Frank Doran, Mike Peddie, Rich Reynolds, Ron Schultz

General Electric – Ed Spurgeon

General Motors – Don Atwood, Robert Schultz, Dick Donnelly, Jack Smith

General Tire – Gil Neal, Delmar Dague, Jerry O'Neil, John Hendrickson

Golden State Foundry – Herb Christian, Keith Christian, Chuck Love, Herman Pawelka

Granville-Phillips – Dr. Dan Bills, William Ringer, Tammy Harland, Jerry Howard

Harley-Davidson – Vaughn Beals, Rich Teerlink, Willie Davidson, Dave Baldwin, Ken Schmidt

Hermetic Seal – Andy Goldfarb, Chris Bateman, Phil Efland, Dennis Moore

Hewlett-Packard (Boise Printer Div.) – Mike Louis, Vivian Wright, Jenard Jobes, Steve Simpson, Chuck Walter, Skip Creighton

Hiatt and Associates – Dale Hiatt

Hough Enterprises – Ken Hough

Hughes Research – Ron Finnila, Tim Magness, Wayne White, Pauline Pretz, Bonnie Epperson, Carrie Weatherwax, Nancy Bell, Dennis Strand

Hughes Industrial Products – Enid Polovick, Tom Zogorski

Hughes Aircraft – Ken Armstrong, Al Mataliano, Don Carr, Jeff Grant, Cal Kirby, Ed Lai, Bill Mueller, Frank Arambarri, Karen Jenkins, Georgia McQueen, Thomas Pavliscak, James Roberts

Indiana University – Dr. Robert Hall, Dr. Roger Schmenner

Industry Week – John Sheridan

Inter-Tel – Thomas Hanson

Intelligent Controls – David Nystrom

Juran Institute – Dr. Blanton Godfrey

Kelco Industries – Michael Kelly

Kemet – Bernd Scheumann, Tony Cappela, John Piper, Charles Culvertson, Jim McKlintock, Bruce White

Lansdale Semiconductor – Dennis Dill

Lectron Products – Richard Sorenson, Al Primavera, Ron Brzuch

Lennox Industries – Bruce Smythe

Lorentson Mfg. – Leonard Lorentson

Magnaquench – John Croat, Kent Bluhm, Dave Claspell

Martin Marietta Energy Systems – John Stanley, Steve Polston, Ann King, W.E. Thompson, Dan Lineham, Leon Couch, Ron Wells, Allen Moore, Margaret Morrow, Martha Polston, Wayne Carlton

Mason-Hanger – Emmett Poyner, J.D. Schulte, Mike Pascal

Mass Systems – Edward Acres, Charles May

Mylas Communications – Martin Mylas

Motorola – Ken Stork, Carlton Braun, Keki Bhote, Lee Craft, Bob Galvin, Jim Washburn, Lance Williams

PCM – Henry Goldman

Phillips Plastic – Jeff Thompso

Physio-Control – Terry Hofrichter

Powertrain Division, GM – Tom Endres, Tom Stephens, Parviz Danesghari, Jim Gumbleton, Jim Myers, Roger Dye

Pratt & Whitney – Norris Taylor

Presto Foods – Bruce Coffey, Richard Clark

Productivity, Inc. – Norm Bodek, Diane Asay, Frank Hammitt, Karen Jones

Purdue University – Suresh Chand

Quality Training and Technology – John Hendrickson

R.G. Smith – David Szink

RPL – Larry Milazzo, Henry Fishman

Santa Barbara Research Center – Dr. Fletcher Phillips, Don Merchant, Dick Siever, Bob Cinzori, Jim Mount, Kip Cramer, Bob Ledbetter, Ed Gould, Ray Calderon, Sam Ryan, Dave Burke

Saturn – Chuck Striddle

Sherwood & Associates – Jack Sherwood

Simpson Timber – Paul Everett, Lee Gillis, Dave Kratzert

Smiland Paint – John Long, Bob Smiland, Bronk Smiland, Paul McGrath, John Teats, Bob Zerbel, Ray Russel, Mary Ann Ross, Steve Entzel, Ron McVicar, Betty Weaver, Efrain Curiel

Sparling – John Adams, Bill

Syracuse University – Dr. Patricia Myers

Target Magazine – Dr. Robert Hall

Tektronix – Candace Somers, William Belgard

TTI – Mike Will, Greg McCumber, Gary Kaller, Paul Smith

United Auto Workers – Tony Long, Al Curella, Dick Thomas, Jeannie Rink

Unisys – Tom Gunn

Vickers International – Leveta Vickers

Wish Images – Ira Wish

Yorktown Tool & Die – J.S. Dunn

About the Author

During his 15 years in the engineering and program management area at Delco Electronics, James Swartz held positions of senior physicist, senior product engineer, engineering product manager, product assurance manager, and program manager. In his 10 years of manufacturing experience he served as production control manager and manufacturing plant manager. He has held university teaching positions at Indiana University, Purdue, Ball State, and Tuskegee Institute.

Selected to lead a research team to investigate competitive capabilities of international businesses, he has examined some of the best companies in the United States, Japan, and abroad.

In the past 10 years, Mr. Swartz has led or facilitated over 200 successful designs or redesigns of manufacturing, engineering and business systems at AC Electronics, Simpson Timber, Granville-Phillips, Hughes Aircraft, General Electric, Kelco Industries, Chemtronics, Motorola, Martin Marietta Energy Systems, Mason Hanger, Kemet, EG&G, Federal Express, Allied Signal, Garrett Processing, Sparling, Delco Electronics, Deltronicos, Powertrain Div. of GM, Cadillac Motor, Buick

Motor, Calplate Inc., Anchor Corp. Santa Barbara Research, Presto Foods, Endevco, TTI, York, Fortifiber, ITT Aerospace, and Albuquerque Microelectronics.

In addition, he has conducted workshops at APICS, Productivity conferences, USDOE, United Technologies, Bissel Co., Lectron Products, McDonnell-Douglas, Hewlett-Packard, Bar-S, Indiana University, Arthur Young, Dresser Industries, United Auto Workers, Saginaw Division of GM, Spectralab, Quartz Devices, Argotech, and Ideal Standard.

Mr. Swartz is the founder of Cygnus Systems Inc., a manufacturer and retailer, and is president of Competitive Action, Inc. As a GM fellow, he received an M.S. in physics from the University of Illinois.

Index

Other Books from Productivity Press

Productivity Press publishes and distributes materials on continuous improvement in productivity, quality, and the creative involvement of all employees. Many of our products are direct source materials from Japan that have been translated into English for the first time and are available exclusively from Productivity. Supplemental products and services include membership groups, conferences, seminars, in-house training and consulting, audio-visual training programs, and industrial study missions.

Call toll-free 1-800-394-6868 for our free catalog.

20 Keys to Workplace Improvement
Iwao Kobayashi

This easy-to-read introduction to the "20 keys" system presents an integrated approach to assessing and improving your company's competitive level. The book focuses on systematic improvement through five levels of achievement in such primary areas as industrial housekeeping, small group activities, quick changeover techniques, equipment maintenance, and computerization. A scoring guide is included, along with information to help plan a strategy for your company's world class improvement effort.
ISBN 0-915299-61-5 / 252 pages / $39.95 / Order 20KEYS-B135

The Battle to Stay Competitive: Changing the Traditional Workplace
The Delco Moraine NDH Story
Charles R. Birkholz and Jim Villella

This inspiring and quick-reading book recalls in vivid detail the changes undertaken by Delco Moraine NDH, General Motors' Brake Systems Division, that earned them a position as a world class supplier of automotive components. This case study documents the company's efforts to strengthen their competitiveness through synchronous manufacturing, the coordination of resources (man, machine, and materials) to eliminate waste.
ISBN 0-915299-96-8 / 110 pages / $12.00 paper / Order BATTLE-B135

Productivity Press, Inc. Dept. BK, P.O. Box 13390, Portland, OR 97213-0390
Telephone: 1-800-394-6868   Fax: 1-800-394-6286

Caught in the Middle
A Leadership Guide for Partnership in the Workplace
Rick Maurer

Managers today are caught between old skills and new expectations. You're expected not only to improve quality and services, but also to get staff more involved. This stimulating book provides the inspiration and know-how to achieve these goals as it brings to light the rewards of establishing a real partnership with your staff. Includes self-assessment questionnaires.
ISBN 1-56327-004-8 / 258 pages / $29.95 / Order CAUGHT-B135

Continuous Improvement in Operations
A Systematic Approach to Waste Reduction
Alan Robinson (ed.)

Here in one place is the world's most advanced thinking on Just-in-Time, Kaizen, Total Employee Involvement and Total Productive Maintenance. This handy book brings you a compendium of materials from our best-selling classics by world-famous manufacturing experts. The excerpts you'll read offer wisdom and experience that is unique to the developer of each approach. The authoritative introduction integrates the developments of these manufacturing gurus within a twofold theme, the elimination of invisible waste and the creation of a work environment that welcomes and implements employees' ideas.
ISBN 0-915299-51-8 / 406 pages / $34.95 / Order ROB2C-B135

Cycle Time Management
The Fast Track to Time-Based Productivity Improvement
Patrick Northey and Nigel Southway

As much as 90 percent of the operational activities in a traditional plant are nonessential or pure waste. This book presents a proven methodology for eliminating this waste within 24 to 30 months by measuring productivity in terms of time instead of revenue or people. CTM is a cohesive management strategy that integrates just-in-time (JIT) production, computer integrated manufacturing (CIM), and total quality control (TQC). From this succinct, highly-focused book, you'll learn what CTM is, how to implement it, and how to manage it.
ISBN 1-56327-015-3 / 200 pages / $29.95 / Order CYCLE-B135

Productivity Press, Inc. Dept. BK, P.O. Box 13390, Portland, OR 97213-0390
Telephone: 1-800-394-6868   Fax: 1-800-394-6286

Demass
Transforming the Dinosaur Corporation
M.M. Stuckey

This eye-opening book show how inside many of America's manufacturing giants sheer size — massiveness — has become an obstacle to staying competitive. Demassification, or "demass," is the structural remedy to the inflexibility and relatively slow time-to-market of these giant corporations. This book provides a model for radical decentralization and improved speed-to-market with a thorough description of the demass process.
ISBN 1-56327-042-0 / 283 pages / $24.95 / Order DEMASS-B135

Handbook for Productivity Measurement and Improvement
William F. Christopher and Carl G. Thor, eds.

An unparalleled resource! In over 100 chapters, nearly 80 front-runners in the quality movement reveal the evolving theory and specific practices of world-class organizations. Spanning a wide variety of industries and business sectors, they discuss quality and productivity in manufacturing, service industries, profit centers, administration, nonprofit and government institutions, health care and education. Contributors include Robert C. Camp, Peter F. Drucker, Jay W. Forrester, Joseph M. Juran, Robert S. Kaplan, John W. Kendrick, Yasuhiro Monden, and Lester C. Thurow. Comprehensive in scope and organized for easy reference, this compendium belongs in every company and academic institution concerned with business and industrial viability.
ISBN 1-56327-007-2 / 1344 pages / $90.00 / Order HPM-B135

The Improvement Book
Creating the Problem-free Workplace
Tomo Sugiyama

Learn how to set up a participatory problem-solving system in your workplace. Focusing on ways to eliminate the "Big 3" problems — irrationality, inconsistency, and waste — this book shows how to start a "problem-free engineering" program, and includes two chapters of examples to use in small group training activities, as well as a workbook for individual use (extra copies available).
ISBN 0-915299-47-X / 212 pages / $55.00 / Order IB-B135

Productivity Press, Inc. Dept. BK, P.O. Box 13390, Portland, OR 97213-0390
Telephone: 1-800-394-6868   Fax: 1-800-394-6286

Managerial Engineering
Techniques for Improving Quality and Productivity in the Workplace
Ryuji Fukuda

A proven path to managerial success, based on reliable methods developed by one of Japan's leading productivity experts and winner of the coveted Deming Prize for quality. Dr. W. Edwards Deming, world-famous consultant on quality, says that the book "provides an excellent and clear description of the devotion and methods of Japanese management to continual improvement of quality." (Training programs on CEDAC, the award-winning system outlined in this book, are also available from Productivity.)
ISBN 0-915299-09-7 / 208 pages / $44.95 / Order ME-B135

Measuring, Managing, and Maximizing Performance
Will Kaydos

You do not need to be an exceptionally skilled technician or inspirational leader to improve your company's quality and productivity. In non-technical, jargon-free, practical terms this book details the entire process of improving performance, from why and how the improvement process work to what must be done to begin and to sustain continuous improvement of performance. Special emphasis is given to the role that performance measurement plays in identifying problems and opportunities.
ISBN 0-915299-98-4 / 284 pages / $39.95 / Order MMMP-B135

A New American TQM
Four Practical Revolutions in Management
Shoji Shiba, Alan Graham, and David Walden

For TQM to succeed in America, you need to create an American-style "learning organization" with the full commitment and understanding of senior managers and executives. Written expressly for this audience, *A New American TQM* offers a comprehensive and detailed explanation of TQM and how to implement it, based on courses taught at MIT's Sloan School of Management and the Center for Quality Management, a consortium of American hi-tech companies. Full of case studies and amply illustrated, the book examines major quality tools and how they are being used by the most progressive American companies today.
ISBN 1-56327-032-3 / 606 pages / $49.95 / Order NATQM-B135

Productivity Press, Inc. Dept. BK, P.O. Box 13390, Portland, OR 97213-0390
Telephone: 1-800-394-6868   Fax: 1-800-394-6286

Performance Measurement for World Class Manufacturing
A Model for American Companies
Brian H. Maskell

If your company is adopting world class manufacturing techniques, you'll need new methods of performance measurement to control production variables. In practical terms, this book describes the new methods of performance measurement and how they are used in a changing environment. For manufacturing managers as well as cost accountants, it provides a theoretical foundation of these innovative methods supported by extensive practical examples. The book specifically addresses performance measures for delivery, process time, production flexibility, quality, and finance.
ISBN 0-915299-99-2 / 448 pages / $55.00 / Order PERFM-B135

The Sayings of Shigeo Shingo
Key Strategies for Plant Improvement
Shigeo Shingo

Quality Digest calls Shigeo Shingo "an unquestioned genius — the Thomas Edison of Japan." Shingo "offers new ways to discover the root causes of manufacturing problems. These discoveries can set in motion the chain of cause and effect, leading to greatly increased productivity." Hundreds of examples illustrate ways to identify, analyze and solve workplace problems.
ISBN 0-915299-15-1 / 207 pages / $44.95 / Order SAY-B135

The New Standardization
Keystone of Continuous Improvement in Manufacturing
Shigehiro Nakamura

In an era of continuous improvement and ISO 9000, quality is not an option but a requirement, and you can't set or meet criteria for quality without standardization. Standardization lets you share information about the best ways to do things so that they will be done that way consistently. This book shows how to make standardization a living system of just-in-time information that delivers exactly the information that's needed, exactly when it is needed, and exactly where it is needed. It's the only way to sustain the results of your improvement efforts in every area of your company.
ISBN 1-56327-039-0 / 286 pages / $75.00 / Order STAND-B135

Productivity Press, Inc. Dept. BK, P.O. Box 13390, Portland, OR 97213-0390
Telephone: 1-800-394-6868   Fax: 1-800-394-6286

Vision Management
Translating Strategy into Action
SANNO Management Development Research Center (ed.)

For over ten years, managers of Japan's top companies have gathered at SANNO University to brainstorm about innovative corporate management methods. This book is based on the proven methodology that evolved from their ideas. It describes how the intangible aspects of vision-based strategy can be integrated into a concrete implementation model and clarifies the relationship among vision, strategy, objectives, goals, and day-to-day activities. ISBN 0-915299-80-1 / 272 pages / $29.95 / Order VISM-B135

The Visual Factory
Building Participation Through Shared Information
Michel Greif

If you're aware of the tremendous improvements achieved in productivity and quality as a result of employee involvement, then you'll appreciate the great value of creating a visual factory. This book shows how visual management can make the factory a place where workers and supervisors freely communicate and take improvement action. It details how to develop meeting and communication areas, communicate work standards and instructions, use visual production controls such as kanban, and make goals and progress visible. Includes more than 200 diagrams and photos. ISBN 0-915299-67-4 / 305 pages / $55.00 / Order VFAC-B135

TO ORDER: Write, phone, or fax Productivity Press, Dept. BK, P.O. Box 13390, Portland, OR 97213, phone 1-800-394-6868, fax 1-800-394-6286. Send check or charge to your credit card (American Express, Visa, MasterCard accepted).

U.S. ORDERS: Add $5 shipping for first book, $2 each additional for UPS surface delivery. We offer attractive quantity discounts for bulk purchases of individual titles; call for more information.

INTERNATIONAL ORDERS: Write, phone, or fax for quote and indicate shipping method desired. For international callers, telephone number is 503-235-0600 and fax number is 503-235-0909. Prepayment in U.S. dollars must accompany your order (checks must be drawn on U.S. banks). When quote is returned with payment, your order will be shipped promptly by the method requested.

NOTE: Price are in U.S. dollars and are subject to change without notice.

Productivity Press, Inc., Dept. BK, P.O. Box 13390, Portland, OR 97213
Telephone: 1-800-394-6868 Fax: 1-800-394-6286

Productivity Press, Inc. Dept. BK, P.O. Box 13390, Portland, OR 97213-0390
Telephone: 1-800-394-6868   Fax: 1-800-394-6286